How to improve
Triumph
TR7
TR7-V8
TR8

Also from Veloce –

SpeedPro Series
4-Cylinder Engine – How to Blueprint & Build a Short Block for High Performance by Des Hammill
Alfa Romeo DOHC High-Performance Manual by Jim Kartalamakis
Alfa Romeo V6 Engine High-Perfomance Manual by Jim Kartalamakis
BMC 998cc A-Series Engine – How to Power Tune by Des Hammill
The 1275cc A-Series High Performance Manual by Des Hammill
Camshafts – How to Choose & Time them for Maximum Power by Des Hammill
Cylinder Heads – How to Build, Modify & Power Tune Updated & Revised Edition by Peter Burgess
Distributor-type Ignition Systems – How to Build & Power Tune by Des Hammill
Fast Road Car – How to Plan and Build Revised & Updated Colour New Edition by Daniel Stapleton
Ford SOHC 'Pinto' & Sierra Cosworth DOHC Engines – How to Power Tune Updated & Enlarged Edition by Des Hammill
Ford V8 – How to Power Tune Small Block Engines by Des Hammill
Harley-Davidson Evolution Engines – How to Build & Power Tune by Des Hammill
Holley Carburetors – How to Build & Power Tune Revised & Updated Edition by Des Hammill
Jaguar XK Engines – How to Power Tune Revised & Updated Colour Edition by Des Hammill
MG Midget & Austin-Healey Sprite – How to Power Tune Updated & Revised Edition by Daniel Stapleton
MGB 4-Cylinder Engine – How to Power Tune by Peter Burgess
MGB V8 Power – How to Give Your Third, Colour Edition by Roger Williams
MGB, MGC & MGB V8 – How to Improve by Roger Williams
Mini Engines – How to Power Tune on a Small Budget Colour Edition by Des Hammill
Motorsport – Getting Started in by S S Collins
Nitrous Oxide High-Performance Manual by Trevor Langfield
Rover V8 Engines – How to Power Tune by Des Hammill
Sportscar/Kitcar Suspension & Brakes – How to Build & Modify Enlarged & Updated 2nd Edition by Des Hammill
SU Carburettor High-Performance Manual by Des Hammill
Suzuki 4x4 – How to Modify for Serious Off-Road Action by John Richardson
Tiger Avon Sportscar – How to Build Your Own Updated & Revised 2nd Edition by Jim Dudley
TR2, 3 & TR4 – How to Improve by Roger Williams
TR5, 250 & TR6 – How to Improve by Roger Williams
TR7 & TR8, How to Improve by Roger Williams
V8 Engine – How to Build a Short Block for High Performance by Des Hammill
Volkswagen Beetle Suspension, Brakes & Chassis – How to Modify for High Performance by James Hale
Volkswagen Bus Suspension, Brakes & Chassis – How to Modify for High Performance by James Hale
Weber DCOE, & Dellorto DHLA Carburetors – How to Build & Power Tune 3rd Edition by Des Hammill

Those were the days ... Series
Alpine Trials & Rallies 1910-1973 by Martin Pfundner
Austerity Motoring by Malcolm Bobbitt
Brighton National Speed Trials by Tony Gardiner
British Police Cars by Nick Walker
Crystal Palace by S S Collins
Dune Buggy Phenomenon by James Hale
Dune Buggy Phenomenon Volume 2 by James Hale
Motor Racing at Brands Hatch in the Seventies by Chas Parker
Motor Racing at Goodwood in the Sixties by Tony Gardiner
Motor Racing at Oulton Park in the 60s by Peter McFadyen
Three Wheelers by Malcolm Bobbitt

Enthusiast's Restoration Manual Series
Citroën 2CV, How to Restore by Lindsay Porter
Classic Car Body Work, How to Restore by Martin Thaddeus
Reliant Regal, How to Restore by Elvis Payne
Triumph TR2/3/3A, How to Restore by Roger Williams
Triumph TR4/4A, How to Restore by Roger Williams
Triumph TR5/250 & 6, How to Restore by Roger Williams
Triumph TR7/8, How to Restore by Roger Williams
Volkswagen Beetle, How to Restore by Jim Tyler
Yamaha FS1-E, How to Restore by John Watts

Essential Buyer's Guide Series
Alfa GT by Keith Booker
Alfa Romeo Spider by Keith Booker
Citroën 2CV by Mark Paxton
Jaguar E-type 3.8 & 4.2 by Peter Crespin
Jaguar E-type V12 5.3 litre by Peter Crespin
Mercedes-Benz 280SL-560SL roadsters by Chris Bass
Mercedes-Benz 'Pagoda' 230SL, 250SL & 280SL roadsters & coupés by Chris Bass
MGB by Roger Williams
Morris Minor by Ray Newell
Porsche 928 by David Hemmings
Triumph TR6 by Roger Williams
VW Beetle by Ken Cservenka and Richard Copping
VW Bus by Ken Cservenka and Richard Copping

Auto-Graphics Series
Fiat & Abarth by Andrea & David Sparrow
Jaguar MkII by Andrea & David Sparrow
Lambretta LI by Andrea & David Sparrow

Rally Giants Series
Austin-Healey 100 by Graham Robson
Ford Escort MkI by Graham Robson
Lancia Stratos by Graham Robson
Peugeot 206 by Graham Robson
Subaru Impreza by Graham Robson

General
1½-litre GP Racing 1961-1965 by Mark Whitelock
AC Two-litre Saloons & Buckland Sportscars by Leo Archibald
Alfa Romeo Giulia Coupé GT & GTA by John Tipler
Alfa Tipo 33 by Ed McDonough and Peter Collins
Anatomy of the Works Minis by Brian Moylan
Armstrong-Siddeley by Bill Smith
Autodrome by S S Collins & Gavin Ireland
Automotive A-Z, Lane's Dictionary of Automotive Terms by Keith Lane
Automotive Mascots by David Kay & Lynda Springate
Bahamas Speed Weeks, The by Terry O'Neil
Bentley Continental, Corniche and Azure by Martin Bennett
BMC Competitions Department Secrets by Stuart Turner, Marcus Chambers & Peter Browning
BMW 5-Series by Marc Cranswick
BMW Z-Cars by James Taylor
British 250cc Racing Motorcycles by Chris Pereira
British Cars, The Complete Catalogue of, 1895-1975 by Culshaw & Horrobin
BRM – a mechanic's tale by Richard Salmon
BRM V16 by Karl Ludvigsen
Bugatti Type 40 by Barrie Price
Bugatti 46/50 Updated Edition by Barrie Price
Bugatti T44 & T49 by Barrie Price
Bugatti 57 2nd Edition by Barrie Price
Caravans, The Illustrated History 1919-1959 by Andrew Jenkinson
Caravans, The Illustrated History from 1960 by Andrew Jenkinson
Chrysler 300 – America's Most Powerful Car 2nd Edition by Robert Ackerson
Chrysler PT Cruiser by Robert Ackerson
Citroën DS by Malcolm Bobbitt
Classic Car Electrics by Martin Thaddeus
Classic Cars, How to Paint by Martin Thaddeus
Cobra - The Real Thing! by Trevor Legate
Cortina - Ford's Bestseller by Graham Robson
Coventry Climax Racing Engines by Des Hammill
Daimler SP250 'Dart' by Brian Long
Datsun Fairlady Roadster to 280ZX – The Z-car Story by Brian Long
Dino – The V6 Ferrari by Brian Long
Dodge Muscle Cars by Peter Grist
Ducati 750 Bible, The by Ian Falloon
Dune Buggy, Building a – The Essential Manual by Paul Shakespeare
Dune Buggy Files by James Hale
Dune Buggy Handbook by James Hale
Edward Turner: the man behind the motorcycles by Jeff Clew
Fiat & Abarth 124 Spider & Coupé by John Tipler
Fiat & Abarth 500 & 600 2nd edition by Malcolm Bobbitt
Fiats, Great Small by Phil Ward
Ford F100/F150 Pick-up 1948-1996 by Robert Ackerson
Ford F150 1997-2005 by Robert Ackerson
Ford GT – Then and Now by Adrian Streather
Ford GT40 by Trevor Legate
Ford in Miniature by Randall Olson
Ford Model Y by Sam Roberts
Ford Thunderbird from 1954, The book of the by Brian Long
Funky Mopeds by Richard Skelton
GT – The World's Best GT Cars 1953-73 by Sam Dawson
Hillclimbing & sprinting by Phil Short
Honda NSX by Brian Long
Jaguar, The Rise of by Barrie Price
Jaguar XJ-S by Brian Long
Jeep CJ by Robert Ackerson
Jeep Wrangler by Robert Ackerson
Karmann-Ghia Coupé & Convertible by Malcolm Bobbitt
Lambretta Bible, The by Pete Davies
Lancia Delta HF Integrale by Werner Blaettel
Land Rover, The Half-Ton Military by Mark Cook
Laverda Twins & Triples 1968-1986 Bible by Ian Falloon
Lea-Francis Story, The by Barrie Price
Lexus Story, The by Brian Long
Lola – The Illustrated History (1957-1977) by John Starkey
Lola – All The Sports Racing & Single-Seater Racing Cars 1978-1997 by John Starkey
Lola T70 – The Racing History & Individual Chassis Record 3rd Edition by John Starkey
Lotus 49 by Michael Oliver
MarketingMobiles, The Wonderful Wacky World of, by James Hale
Mazda MX-5/Miata 1.6 Enthusiast's Workshop Manual by Rod Grainger & Pete Shoemark
Mazda MX-5/Miata 1.8 Enthusiast's Workshop Manual by Rod Grainger & Pete Shoemark
Mazda MX-5 Miata: the book of the world's favourite sportscar by Brian Long
Mazda MX-5 Miata Roadster by Brian Long
MGA by John Price Williams
MGB & MGB GT – Expert Guide (Auto-Doc Series) by Roger Williams
MGB Electrical Systems by Rick Astley
Micro Caravans by Andrew Jenkinson
Microcars at large! by Adam Quellan
Mini Cooper – The Real Thing! by John Tipler
Mitsubishi Lancer Evo, the road car & WRC story by Brian Long
Montlhéry, the story of the Paris autodrome by William 'Bill' Boddy
Moto Cross – the golden era by Paul Stephens
Moto Guzzi Sporting Twins 1971-1993 by Ian Falloon
Motor Racing – Reflections of a Lost Era by Anthony Carter
Motorcycle road & racing chassis designs by Keith Noakes
Motorhomes, The Illustrated History by Andrew Jenkinson
Motorsport in colour, 1950s by Martyn Wainwright
MR2 – Toyota's mid-engined Sports Car by Brian Long
Nissan 300ZX & 350Z – The Z-Car Story by Brian Long
Pass the Theory and Practical Driving Tests by Clive Gibson & Gavin Hoole
Pontiac Firebird by Marc Cranswick
Porsche Boxster by Brian Long
Porsche 356 by Brian Long
Porsche 911 Carrera – The Last of the Evolution by Tony Corlett
Porsche 911R, RS & RSR, 4th Edition by John Starkey
Porsche 911 – The Definitive History 1963-1971 by Brian Long
Porsche 911 – The Definitive History 1971-1977 by Brian Long
Porsche 911 – The Definitive History 1977-1987 by Brian Long
Porsche 911 – The Definitive History 1987-1997 by Brian Long
Porsche 911 – The Definitive History 1997-2004 by Brian Long
Porsche 911SC 'Super Carrera' – The Essential Companion by Adrian Streather
Porsche 914 & 914-6: The Definitive History Of The Road & Competition Cars by Brian Long
Porsche 924 by Brian Long
Porsche 944 by Brian Long
Porsche 993 'King of Porsche' – The Essential Companion by Adrian Streather
Porsche Racing by Brian Long
Porsche Rally History by Laurence Meredith
Porsche: Three generations of genius by Laurence Meredith
RAC Rally Action by Tony Gardiner
Redman, Jim – 6 times world motorcycle champion by Jim Redman
Rolls-Royce Silver Shadow/Bentley T Series Corniche & Camargue Revised & Enlarged Edition by Malcolm Bobbitt
Rolls-Royce Silver Spirit, Silver Spur & Bentley Mulsanne 2nd Edition by Malcolm Bobbitt
Rolls-Royce Silver Wraith, Dawn & Cloud/Bentley MkVI, R & S Series by Martyn Nutland
RX-7 – Mazda's Rotary Engine Sportscar (updated & revised new edition) by Brian Long
Scooters & Microcars, The A-Z of by Mike Dann
Singer Story: Cars, Commercial Vehicles, Bicycles & Motorcycles by Kevin Atkinson
SM – Citroën's Maserati-engined Supercar by by Brian Long
Subaru Impreza: the road and WRC story by Brian Long
Taxi! The Story of the 'London' Taxicab by Malcolm Bobbitt
Toyota Celica & Supra by Brian Long
Triumph Motorcycles & the Meriden Factory by Hughie Hancox
Triumph Speed Twin & Thunderbird Bible by Harry Woolridge
Triumph Tiger Cub Bible by Mike Estall
Triumph Trophy Bible by Harry Woolridge
Triumph TR6 by William Kimberley
Unraced by S S Collins
Velocette Motorcycles - MSS to Thruxton Updated & Revised Edition by Rod Burris
Volkswagen Bus Book, The by Malcolm Bobbitt
Volkswagen Bus or Van to Camper, How to Convert by Lindsay Porter
Volkswagens of the World by Simon Glen
VW Beetle Cabriolet by Malcolm Bobbitt
VW Beetle – The Car of the 20th Century by Richard Copping
VW Bus – 40 years of Splitties, Bays & Wedges by Richard Copping
VW Bus, Camper, Van, Pickup by Malcolm Bobbitt
VW Campers by Richard Copping
VW Golf: five generations of fun by Richard Copping & Ken Cservenka
VW – The air-cooled era by Richard Copping
VW T5 Camper conversion manual by Lindsay Porter
Works Minis, The last by Bryan Purves
Works Rally Mechanic by Brian Moylan

First published in December 2006 by Veloce Publishing Limited, 33 Trinity Street, Dorchester DT1 1TT, England. Fax 01305 268864/e-mail info@veloce.co.uk/web www.veloce.co.uk or www.velocebooks.com
ISBN 13: 978-1-84584-045-7. ISBN 10: 1-84584-045-3. UPC 6-36847-04045-1.
© Roger Williams and Veloce Publishing 2006. All rights reserved. With the exception of quoting brief passages for the purpose of review, no part of this publication may be recorded, reproduced or transmitted by any means, including photocopying, without the written permission of Veloce Publishing Ltd. Throughout this book logos, model names and designations, etc, have been used for the purposes of identification, illustration and decoration. Such names are the property of the trademark holder as this is not an official publication.

Readers with ideas for automotive books, or books on other transport or related hobby subjects, are invited to write to the editorial director of Veloce Publishing at the above address.
British Library Cataloguing in Publication Data - A catalogue record for this book is available from the British Library. Typesetting, design and page make-up all by Veloce Publishing Ltd on Apple Mac.
Printed in India by Replika Press.

How to improve
Triumph TR7 TR7-V8 TR8

ROGER WILLIAMS

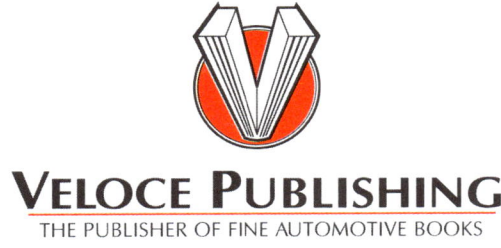

Contents

Acknowledgements	7
About the author	7
Foreword	8
Introduction	9
Using this book	10

1. Planning an upgrade/conversion .. 11
Purchasing considerations 12
Which engine? 12
Engine short-list summary 15
    Fast road cars 15
    Ultra-fast road cars 15
    Competitive cars 15
    Other component changes 15
Brakes, wheels and tyres 17
Bodyshell changes 18
Which transmission do you plan? 18

2. Upgrading the brakes 19
Safety first 19
What's important? 20
    Brake size 20
    Pad materials 21
        EBC Kevlar brake pads 21
        Hawk brake pads 21
    Cooling the brakes 21
Front calliper options 22
    Capri 2.8 injection callipers 23
    Rover SD1/Vitesse callipers 24
    Volvo brake conversions 24
    Princess four-pots 24
    Radial mounted callipers 25
    Hi Spec motorsport 26
    AP Racing callipers 26
    Wilwood 27
Front Disc/Rotors 27
    One-piece rotors 27
    Two-piece discs 27
Brake servos/boosters and master
  cylinders 28
    Servos 28
    Single master cylinders 29
    Twin/parallel master cylinders 30
The rear brakes 30
    Proportioning/bias/balance/
      pressure-reducing valves 31
    Converting the original PRV 31
    Residual pressure valves 32
    Rear disc brake conversions 32
Handbrakes 33

3. Wheels and tyres 34
Wheel diameter 35
Rim width 36
Road wheel offsets/spacers 36
Stud pattern 37
Wheel materials 38
Central wheel patterns 38
Wheel centring 39
Tyres 39
    Profiles 39
    Diameter calculations 39
    Tyre size calculators 40
    Speedometer accuracy 40
    Speed ratings 41
    Tyre tread patterns 41
    Directional tyres 42
    Caring for your tyres 42
Conclusion 42

4. Body trim, strengthening and
roll-cages 43
Aesthetic changes 43
    Front spoilers 43
    Wheelarch extensions 44
    Body re-styling kits 45
    Fitting fibreglass panels 46
    Colour coding 47
    Headlamp fairing 47
Trim improvements 47
    Upgraded hoods 47
    Dashboard trim 47
    Seat and trim upgrades 47
    Electric windows 48
Bodyshell strengthening 49
    Safety structures 50
    Rear roll-bars 51
    Roll-cages 51

5. Suspension, steering and axles ... 54
Front and rear suspensions 54
    Ultra–fast road and competition 57
Steering improvements 58
    Strut top bearings 58
    Steering rack ratios 60
    Power steering 60
Other front suspension improvements ... 61
    Uprated anti-roll (sway) bar 61
    Lower roll-centre 61
    Front hub bearings 61
The rear axle 62
    Stronger rear axles 62
    Rear axle ratios 63
Limited slip differentials (LSDs) 65
Rear suspension options 65
    Improve the control arms 65
    Strengthen the mounting points 66
    Remove the rear roll-bar 66
    Trailing arm location 66

6. 4-cylinder engine upgrades 68
Upgrading the original 8-valve engine . 68
    Standard 8-valve engine upgrades ... 68
    Subsequent 8-valve upgrades 69
Sprint (16-valve) engine upgrades 70
    Introduction to the 16-valve engine 70
    Fitting a 16-valve – method 1 71
    Fitting a 16-valve – method 2 72
    Fitting a 16-valve – method 3 72
    Sprint engine assembly 74
    4-cylinder hints 79

7. Gearbox, clutch and propshafts ... 80
5-speed conversions 80
V8 conversions 81
Ultra-fast and competition gearboxes .. 82
The T5 gearbox 82
Quaife R380 gearbox 84
The Toyota option 85
Aftermarket gearboxes 85
Automatic gearboxes 86
Bellhousings and clutches 87
Flexible clutch hose 87
Size rule of thumb 87
Clutch master cylinders 88
Clutch slave cylinders 88
Speedo cables 89
Gearlever/stick location 89
Gearbox rear cross-members 90
Propshafts and driveshafts 91

8. Acquiring and upgrading a Rover V8 .. 92
Engine options 92
    Fast road applications 93
    Engines suited to ultra-fast road cars .. 93
    Competition cars 93
Acquiring an engine 93
    Engine sources 94
Compression ratios (CR) & cylinder heads .. 94
    The ultimate cylinder head 97
Upgrading the early engines 98
    Oil pressure/flow 98
    Flywheels 98
Lubrication upgrades 99
    Oil coolers 99
    Oil pump variations 100
    Speedier oil return 100
    Priming the oil pump 101
    Sumps and gaskets 101

Other universal improvements 102
    Camshaft. 102
        Installing a camshaft.. 102
        Camshaft drive.. 103
    Transplanting EFI engines 103
    Starter motor. 103
    Crackcase breathers and filler 104
    Further reading. 104

9. Fitting out a V8 engine bay 105
The pre-assembly preparation 105
    The cross-member/K-frame. 105
    The bodyshell 106
    The gearbox.. 106
    The engine 106
Fitting the V8. 107
The manifolds 109
    The exhaust manifold and system . 109
    Range Rover exhausts. 111
    Acquiring a system 111
    Exhaust wraps 112
    Inlet manifolds.. 112
Alternator and radiator 113
Closing the bonnet/hood. 116
Concluding points 117

10. Cooling – all engines.. 118
Summary. 118
    The 4-cylinder.. 118
    V8 engines 119
Building cooling into the car.. 120
    Engine build quality 120
    Flush the waterways. 120
    Watching the temperature.. 120
    Modern fuel 121
    Battery/charging capacity. 121
    The radiator 121
Maximising flows. 122
    Air flow 122
    Coolant. 123
    Conventional water pumps 124
Fans 124
    Mechanical puller 124
    Electric fans 125
    Pusher fans 127
    Puller fans 127
    Electric water pumps 127
Coolant additives/alternatives/tips. 128
    Antifreeze 128
    Additives 128
    Alternative coolant ('For-Life'). 129
    Radiator cap 129
    Air-conditioning notes 129
    Cooling the oil 130

11. Improving the sparks. 131
The ignition system 131
Contact breaker improvements 131
    Retro-fitted breakerless systems.. 132

Distributor replacements 133
Ballast resistors 134
High-tension ignition components 135
    Distributor caps 135
    Sparkplugs.. 135
    The plug leads 137
Charging the ignition coil. 137
Engine management improvements.. 139

12. Carburettor induction 140
Carburettor design principles 140
Atomisation 140
The SU carburettor. 142
    Road tuning stage 1.. 143
    Road tuning stage 2.. 143
    Improved air cleaners 144
    Track day/competition tuning.. 144
    Other SU tips 144
V8 AFB induction. 145
    The Holley 145
    The Weber range 147
    Holley/Weber comparisons.. 147
    AFB inlet manifolds 149
    Installations 149
Related induction details. 150
    AFB air filters. 150
    Fuel pumps 151
Further reading. 151

13. Electronic fuel-injection & engine management.. 152
4-cylinder Bosch EFI. 153
8-Cylinder Bosch EFI 155
Programmable systems 158
    Edelbrock 159
    Haltech 159
    MoTeC 159
    Holley 159
    MegaSquirt 159
    Webcon Alpha.. 160
    Lumenition 161
Rover V8 engine management 161
Common features 161
    Fuel supply. 161
    Wiring harness 163
    Sensors 163
    Idle air control (IAC) 163
    Throttle position sensor (TPS) 163
    Coolant temperature
       sensor (CTS) 163
    Manifold absolute
       pressure (MAP) 163
    Oxygen (O_2) 164
    Diagnostic link (ALDL) 164
    Check engine light 164
    Ignition timing and control. 164
Throttle body-injection 164
    Mounting the throttle body 164
    Accelerator cable 165

Air intake 165
Port fuel-injection 165
    Fuel injectors. 166
    Accelerator cable 166
    Air intake.. 167
    Diagnostics and programming 167
Conclusion 167
Further reading. 167

14. Electrical and instrument improvements 168
Alternator upgrades 168
Battery related matters. 171
    Location 171
    Battery drain 172
    Battery/electrical isolators 172
    Alternator voltage control.. 172
    TR7 and TR8 switches. 173
    TR7-V8 engine bay wiring
       modifications 173
    Preparing your own harness 174
Starter motors and wiring 177
    High-performance starter motors. . 177
    Battery to starter cable 177
    Starter earth.. 177
Instrument upgrades 178
    General upgrades.. 178
    Oil pressure gauge 178
    V8 temperature gauges.. 179
    Speedo re-calibration 180
    V8 tachometer (RPM counter). . . . 180
    Instrument panel lighting 180
Electric windows and central locking 181
Improved lighting 181
    Courtesy lights. 181
    Direction light audible warning 181
    Extra direction flashers 181

15. Engine transplant projects 182
Steve Redway's Rover V8 conversion.. . . 182
Jay Foster's Ford 3800cc project 188

16. Weight watchers.. 194
Unsprung weight 195
Weight outside the wheel base 196
Weight located high in the car.. 196
The engine.. 197
Conclusion 198

Appendix.. 199
Principal TR7 and TR8 specialist clubs and
    suppliers 199
    Clubs. 199
    UK performance specialists
       (in alphabetical order) 199
Overseas performance specialists 201

Index.. 203

Veloce SpeedPro books -

  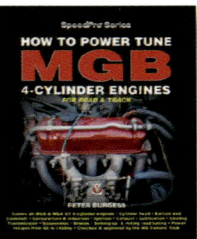  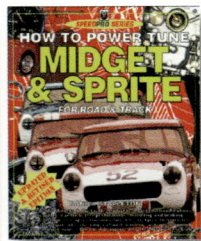 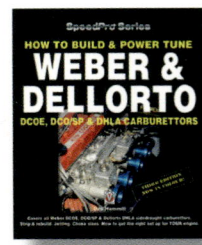

ISBN 1 903706 76 9   ISBN 1 903706 91 2   ISBN 1 903706 77 7   ISBN 1 903706 78 5   ISBN 1 901295 73 7   ISBN 1 903706 75 0

 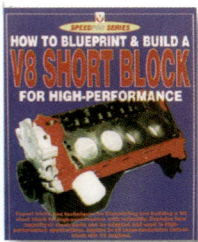  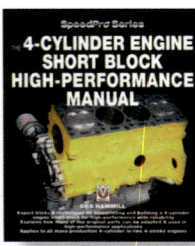 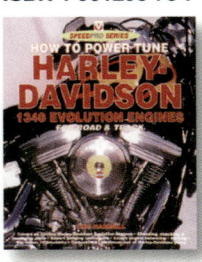 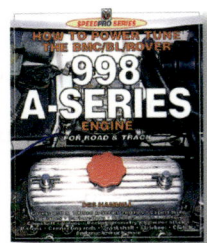

ISBN 1 904788 93 9   ISBN 1 874105 70 7   ISBN 1 84584 019 4   ISBN 1 903706 92 0   ISBN 1 903706 94 7   ISBN 1 901295 26 5

 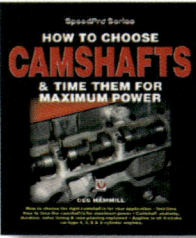  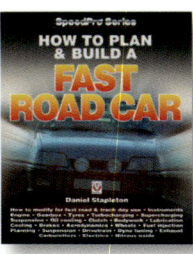 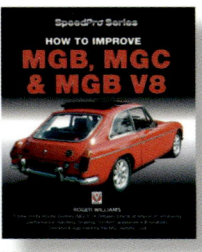 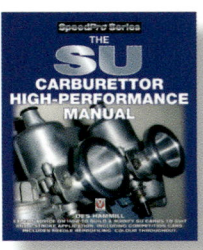

ISBN 1 84584 023 2   ISBN 1 903706 59 9   ISBN 1 903706 73 4   ISBN 1 904788 78 5   ISBN 1 901295 76 1   ISBN 1 84584 073 9

 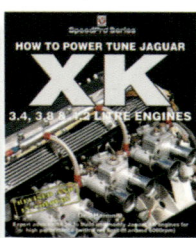 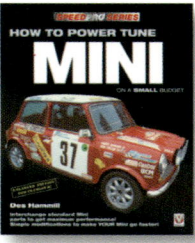  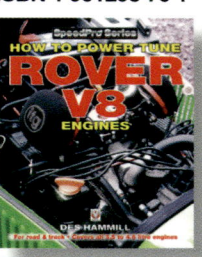 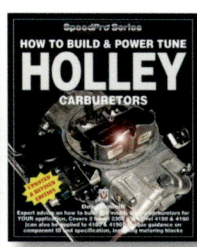

ISBN 1 903706 99 8   ISBN 1 84584 005 4   ISBN 1 904788 84 X   ISBN 1 904788 22 X   ISBN 1 903706 17 3   ISBN 1 84584 006 2

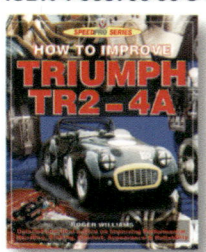  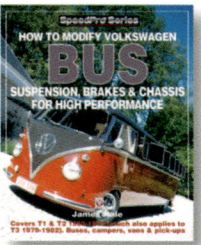 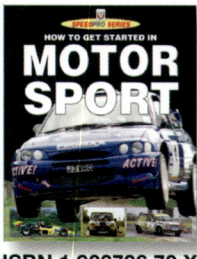 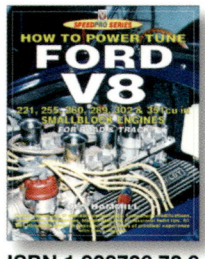 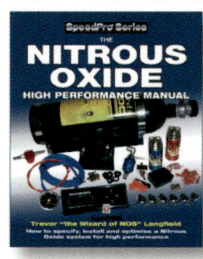

ISBN 1 903706 80 7   ISBN 1 903706 68 8   ISBN 1 903706 14 9   ISBN 1 903706 70 X   ISBN 1 903706 72 6   ISBN 1 904788 89-0

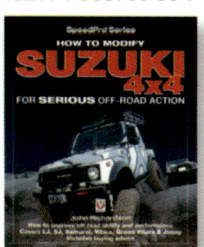  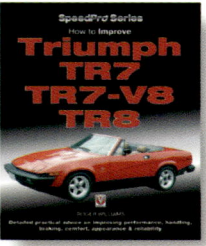

ISBN 1 904788-91-2   ISBN 1 84584 021 6   ISBN 1 84584 045 3

- more on the way!

Acknowledgements

This book never would have been written without the help of a great many enthusiasts. Help in the encouragement sense, but more particularly practical help through their unstinting supply of information, photographs and diagrams. Whilst I appreciate every contribution, the full list is too extensive to mention everyone, but I hope all will accept my grateful thanks.

I would, however, like to single out a number of crucial contributors without whom there really would have been no book. John Sykes of TR Bitz suggested this series, got me started with a huge initial contribution and provided much by way of technical help and introductions along the way. I had tremendous technical and/or photographic support from, in alphabetical order, Mike Collins and Garth Jupp of Rimmer Bros, Jay Foster, Rob and Simon Hebditch of Robsport International, William Parris, Steve Redway of the TR Register, Neil Sawyer, Steve Taylor, James TenCate, Peter Whitehorn, Steve Wilcox and Simon Carr at S+S Preparations, and last but not least, Triumph Rover Spares Pty Ltd of Australia. Also, Veloce's thanks go to the TR7 enthusiasts who kindly donated pictures of their cars to feature on this book's cover: front cover, Paul MacDonald; rear cover main and top left pictures, Paul MacDonald; top centre and inset left, Steve Taylor; top right, Remco van Voorhuizen; inset right, Barry Logan.

Special words of thanks go to Philip Johnstone of Triumph Sports Owners Association in Australia, and Brad Wilson of Wedgeparts (USA). Both contributed not only a great deal of information and illustrative material, but also spent hours of their time answering questions, reading the manuscript, making invaluable suggestions and wielding the blue pencil expertly in order to make this book publishable. All Wedge enthusiasts owe them a vote of thanks. Finally, thanks to Steve Redway for his final check of the manuscript, Brad Wilson for his meticulous last review, and Peter Cox of Moss-Europe for setting the scene in his foreword.

These books would not have got off the ground without the collective help of all these dedicated enthusiasts, to whom I am very grateful indeed, and I dedicate this book to them.

About the author

Roger Williams was born in 1940 in Cardiff, brought up in Guildford and attended Guildford Royal Grammar School.

Aircraft became his first love and he joined the de Havilland Aircraft Company in 1957 as a production engineering apprentice, and very quickly added motor cars to his list of prime interests. During the ensuing six years he not only completed his apprenticeship and studies, but built two Ford-based 'specials' and started a career in the manufacturing engineering industry as a production engineer. Works managerial and director posts followed, and these responsibilities, together with his family commitments, reduced his time for motoring matters to a minimum.

Roger's business interest progressed to company doctoring, which he enjoyed for some ten years, specialising in turning round ailing engineering businesses for public groups in the UK. In 1986 he started his own consultancy business which allowed him to renew his motoring interests. His company specialised in helping improve client profitability by interim management or consulting assignments, whilst his spare time was and continues to be devoted to motor cars and writing. Roger has owned numerous MGBs, all of which he rebuilt. He still has two of his favourites – the V8 powered variants – and has three MGB books in print. More recently he has become involved with the Triumph marque and has restored a TR6 and a Stag.

Roger and his wife have retired to France. He has two married daughters and is a Fellow of the Institute of Mechanical Engineers and a Fellow of the Institute of Production (now Electrical) Engineers.

Foreword

The 'new' Moss-Europe was established in 2000, and today the organisation and its new range of catalogues (using exploded drawings, part numbers, hints and information) are taken for granted. Although the new catalogues include model specific performance pages in the enhanced full colour accessory section, we recognise that a series of independent books focused on the whole TR-improvement market is of immense value to almost every owner, and thus to the friends of TR. Furthermore, such a book is particularly valuable for owners of the 'Wedge' TRs, where the number of specialist suppliers and tuning equipment are less numerous than that for earlier TRs. So, insofar as the book relates objectively what equipment, options and upgrades are available to the Wedge owner and evaluates the cost and effects such changes might bring about, we think it an invaluable aid for someone about to hand over their hard-earned cash. I think you'll agree that Roger Williams has now done his bit to help owners of not only the original TR7 and TR8, but the growing number of TR7-V8 conversion owners too.

It is around 30 years since the TR Register brought like-minded TR fans together. It's quite surprising that there have been so many comings and so few goings of suppliers to the marque in that time. Hardly any have left in disgrace, and I like to think that all friends of the marque have made their contribution, even if it was only to improve the breed and overall standard of service. The typical TR owner nowadays drives a modern car, yet still expects a 25-50 year old classic to demonstrate sports car performance. The good news is that with a little help from these friends and some realistic analysis from Roger, it probably can – though the costs will be regrettably 21st century, rather than the ones we fondly remember.

So, who are the friends and where does Roger come into it? The biggest friends for the Wedges are Moss Europe and Moss Motors, our US associates. In the UK, we have Rimmer Bros, Robsport International. and S+S Preparations. Across the pond are Wedgeparts, TSI Automotive and The Wedge Shop, whilst if you live in the southern hemisphere, Australia is home to Triumph-Rover-Spares. All these specialists contribute to the performance market in some way, and I feel Rogers's job has been to assess their products and techniques. This a pretty daunting task considering there are numerous suppliers and several models involved. *How to improve Triumph TR7, TR7-V8 & TR8* is a book dedicated to looking at the marketplace as it is today, by an unbiased TR enthusiast, and should guide the TR owner through the exciting products and upgrades that are available. Follow the author's thoughts and guidance and you will have a good chance of ending up with the dream TR you always hoped for rather, than the nightmare you dreaded.

Pete Cox
Director, Moss Europe

Introduction

Deciding which topics to include and the best order to present them within a book on TR7 improvements proved surprisingly difficult. Every reader will have a different agenda, but most, when they decided to buy this book, were probably thinking solely of improvements that make the car go faster. Nevertheless, there are other considerations, and I eventually concluded that the book must cover modifications that benefit the safety, reliability and maintainability of the cars as well as those that are straightforward performance-enhancing improvements.

Eventually I decided to sequence this book on the premise that most readers already own, have recently bought or are about to buy a very tidy but largely serviceable Wedge, and wish to explore what improvement options are available. Consequently, the improvements are generally discussed from the viewpoint of a rolling improvement programme, which in turn requires readers make changes in an order that has their safety in mind – the brake and road-holding improvements first, engine power increments next and, last but not least with the TR7, details related to electrics and body-shape. If, therefore, you think it strange that engine tuning comes further back in the book than you might expect, you will now appreciate the reasoning behind that decision.

There could be unhappy consequences if a reader implemented a series of unbalanced changes to their car, even if the order of change is correct. Although not an exact science, and with numerous areas of overlap, I have tried nevertheless to help you get the balance right by sub-dividing most of the modifications into three categories:

Fast road cars
Ultra-fast road cars
Competitive cars

I think the first category is self-explanatory, but a few words about the other two may be helpful. Ultra-fast road cars first. Not only do they fit the niche between "competition" and "fast road", but they also meet the ever growing interest and support for track days and club circuit-racing. Cars that are taken to track days by owners intent on serious fun will often be built to an ultra-fast road specification, and although these cars may not be raced in the usual sense of the word, they are still built to a very high spec indeed. Their cost will likely be significantly higher than the average fast road car, and while they will spend some time on the race-track, they will need to be sufficiently tractable to be driven on the road as well.

My category of competitive cars probably applies to a relatively small number of readers, but covers quite a broad spectrum of relevant events. Those that want to rally their TR will probably need to have it extensively improved, and most such cars fall within this category – though you may see that many of the improvements I have classed as "ultra-fast road" are also applicable to competitive rally cars. These days most of the rallies for classic cars, particularly those of extended duration, include one and sometimes several circuit days. Then there are sprint cars, cars focused on hillclimbing and, of course, straightforward race cars. In practice, the motor racing world is subdivided into numerous classes – neverthless, I trust this outline will offer some help and guidance!

Using this book

As stated in the author's introduction, the purpose of this book is to guide you through the upgrading of a number of TR sports car models – all those produced with the Wedge-shaped bodyshell between 1975 and 1981. The body shape and suspension hardly changed during this period, but the technical specification of the engines certainly did. The 4-cylinder engine was developed with a then technically advanced Sprint variant, and an 8-cylinder engine was introduced. Both factory developments have spawned a great number (possibly more than were originally produced by the factory!) of converted TR7's. The aim of this book is to give current and would-be owners of Wedges information on the improvement options open to them, and, where appropriate, how to shoehorn a larger engine into the bodyshell. Consequently, whatever car you own there will be chapters that do not apply to you, but that we hope you will still read and find interesting.

The book is not intended as a restoration, workshop, operations or spares manual, but is intended to supplement these sources of information. Nor is it a tuning manual, although several chapters cover modifications and equipment that improve an engine's performance. You would be well advised to purchase the manual(s) relevant to your particular model before embarking upon a significant repair, modification or upgrade. If you plan to simultaneously restore and improve your car, then you will also need *How to restore Triumph TR7 and TR8,* by Roger Williams. All of the components/service prices are approximately those prevailing in the UK at the time of publication. These prices will be subject to normal market forces and will, of course, tend to rise with economic inflation. You should allow for these factors when calculating your budget.

It is possible that the goods and services mentioned will become unavailable or altered with the passage of time.

Dimensions given in the illustrations are in millimetres, unless otherwise stated. Line illustrations are not to scale. References to right side and left side are from the point of view of standing behind the car.

Important! During work of any type on your car, your personal safety must always be your prime consideration. You must not undertake any of the work described in this book yourself unless you have sufficient experience, aptitude and a good enough workshop and equipment to ensure your personal safety.

The author, editors, publisher and retailer cannot accept any responsibility for personal injury, mechanical damage or financial loss, which results by errors or omission in the information given. If this disclaimer is not acceptable to you, please immediately return, unused, your pristine book and receipt to your retailer who will refund the purchase price paid.

Veloce Publishing Ltd

Chapter 1
Planning an upgrade/conversion

It really is worthwhile spending time planning your upgrade or conversion. Part of the planning and preparation process involves visiting some suppliers, talking to owners of converted cars at your local TR group/club and exploring relevant exhibitions. Evaluate the various options and the effect each has on your budget. Prepare yourself for the fact that the larger the engine upgrade you opt for, the larger the number and the greater the extent of the changes you'll be required to make – generating BIG expense if you choose the most powerful engine.

For the finished car to be safe and a pleasure to drive, the conversion MUST be a balanced one, i.e. ALL the constituent components must not only fit together but also be suited to each other. I'm sure you have already understood the point, but it is so important that I'd like to explore a couple of examples at the extremes of the engine-power band. If you go for an engine with modest power, say a 2000cc Sprint unit producing perhaps 140/150bhp, you will be able to use upgraded but correspondingly modest wheels, tyres and brakes. However, if you decide you are going to fit a 300bhp engine, not only must you give all the other parts of the car some thought, but the rear drive, wheels, tyres, hubs and brakes MUST be commensurate with the available power. Each will inevitably be bigger and thus more expensive than the Sprint upgrade. Although the available power from the second option is about twice that of the Sprint conversion, the expense of the wheels, tyres and brakes will more than likely make it four times the cost. Furthermore, this trend will apply throughout the car.

Your plan may also be influenced by the time you can devote to the project, by the skills and equipment available or by the car, engine or gearbox you have in the garage.

The car, specifically the condition of the bodyshell, must be a major consideration. It is foolhardy to think you can drop a very powerful engine into a tired, rusting bodyshell. If your bodyshell is in poor shape, then you should be thinking initially about a restoration project rather than an engine transplant or upgrade. Only if the shell is (really) sound should you contemplate increasing the power under the bonnet.

Some readers will have the skill and resources to carry out a simultaneous restoration and upgrade, but many others will need to plan and budget for the purchase of an ex-warm-climate bodyshell. Readers with a 4-speed car in their garage will need to carry out a 5-speed conversion and thus need a TR7 with 5-speed transmission and axle still in situ.

The number of options is endless, and depends entirely on where you are starting from and where you want to get. No two projects will be the same, and

SPEEDPRO SERIES

1-1-1 Double-bulged bonnets like this can be purchased as spares – you should not buy a second-class shell just because it has the requisite bonnet.

you need to assess your priorities and plan accordingly. Time planning is never wasted and I hope this first chapter will have already set you thinking.

PURCHASING CONSIDERATIONS

If you are in the happy position of buying a TR7, TR7-V8 or TR8 with the object of upgrading or improving it, you must be equally analytical about the donor car you buy. You are unlikely to be worried about the condition of the original engine, and have the luxury of seeking out non-runners provided they are appropriately priced. However you should, I suggest, only contemplate cars with sound bodyshells, and prioritise any that have undergone recent restoration and have evidence to back up the current owner's claims. If you are unsure about any aspect of the car's integrity, either look elsewhere or get the shell structurally checked by experts.

If you were planning a V8 conversion, a later 'double-bulge' bonnet seen at 1-1-1 would be an asset.

The paintwork on a donor car will be very expensive to change (pic 1-1-2) or refurbish and needs to be your next priority. Is the quality and colour of the donor car's paintwork acceptable? If you cannot stand the colour, find out the cost of a (good quality) re-spray before buying – you could be in for an unpleasant surprise.

Your next consideration should be whether the car offers 5-speed transmission. The gearbox is reasonably easy to change, and while the transmission should never be given preference over a sound bodyshell, the ideal donor will have a good quality 5-speed gearbox, propshaft and rear axle. Because the V8 engines produce their power at far lower revs than the 4-cylinder engine, a higher ratio differential (lower numerically) will be necessary for driving comfort and fuel economy. The 3.08 ratio differential was standard on the TR8.

The hood and/or trim on your would-be car are almost immaterial considerations, so long as you have a hood frame included in the deal. If you do not like the colour and/or the condition of either, by all means use these as bargaining points, but buy the car and build fitting a new hood or a change of trim into your plan.

During the course of the project you are likely to end up with some surplus parts. Depending upon the extent of the planned changes, you could, in the worst case, have the

1-1-2 This beautifully finished car would be snapped up by most. The non-standard colour may not be your first choice, but a well-painted sound body in a colour you can live with is important, and probably worth buying.

engine, gearbox, propshaft, radiator, exhaust and carburettors surplus to your needs quite early on. You are unlikely to want these spare parts hanging around your garage. A part-exchange deal with some of the Wedge specialists is one possible means of selling these. Indeed, several suppliers will take, say, 8-valve engines in part exchange for a refurbished 16-valve unit. However, you may get a better price if you were to advertise the parts on the internet or via the various TR clubs' 'spares for sale' columns.

The cost of converting a TR7 to a high-powered V8 car can be considerable, and will demand time and reasonable garage facilities. For some, particularly those more interested in the end result than the job, the best solution may be to buy a well-converted car. Use this book to familiarise yourself with the best way to convert the car before you go looking. Needless to say, there are differing standards of conversion, and it is important that you buy wisely. Some details of what to look for are included in *How to restore Triumph TR7 & 8*.

However, you may still be undecided as to what engine to fit – so let's explore some engine options.

WHICH ENGINE?

Without doubt, the easiest, quickest and cheapest performance upgrade is via a Sprint 16-valve engine conversion pictured at 1-2-1. You can, of course, tune the original 8-valve engine, but frankly the cost effectiveness of a 16-valve 4-cylinder conversion makes 8-valve tuning unattractive.

However, even better performance and more relaxed driving can be had from a low-cost V8 conversion. It does not have to be a tuned engine (pic 1-2-2) or even a refurbished one to transform the car into a genuine performance sports car far superior to the original TR7.

PLANNING AN UPGRADE/CONVERSION

1-2-1 A Sprint 16-valve engine is most noticeable from its different rocker cover, and requires no more than a straightforward engine change. Probably for this reason there are surprisingly few 8-valve tuning facilities available, although we will explore what is in a later chapter, together with fitting a 16-valve 4-cylinder upgrade.

1-2-2 A V8 conversion is more complicated than a Sprint upgrade, but a basic one using an engine like this need not be horrifyingly complicated or expensive if you plan it correctly.

1-2-3 A tuned high-performance Rover V8 like Neil Sawyers' rally car engine will unquestionably add to the complexity and cost, not only of the engine itself but of the knock-on changes that are required. The carburettors are Weber DCOE 45s.

1-2-4 This is a late 4600cc Rover engine, but all Buick/Rover engines require the oil-filter be repositioned and all Rover engines of the SD1, and post-SD1, era need the large front pulleys changing.

Yet many enthusiasts feel that if they are sticking a V8 in their TR7, it may as well be a high-performance one. Picture 1-2-3 shows a Rover option, but the alternatives are considerable, and some superb sports cars have been constructed using a wide variety of different engines. The Chevy 350, Buick 231 V6, GM60° V6 and the Mercedes-Benz – all aluminium V8s or V6s – have been very effectively used. Despite the numerous choices, the TR7 was designed from the start for the all-aluminium Buick/Rover V8.

The Rover V8s offer a very wide variety of capacity and power options within the one 'umbrella' – from 3500cc and 150bhp, up to 5000cc and well in excess of 300bhp! For this reason, 90 per cent of V8 conversions use a Buick/Rover engine of one capacity or another, so I make no apologies if this book leans towards the use of these. Not only will it be the easiest engine to fit, but the weight allows the resulting car's front/rear balance and predictable road-holding characteristics to be retained – subject to prudence when driving enthusiastically on wet roads. The aluminium construction is the key to this feature, but its size, many of the sumps, capacity and power options, tuning equipment and ready availability all convince me it's the engine of choice.

The Rover V8 engine is found in the USA in various capacities. In fact, the Rover 4.2-litre engine is surprisingly accessible and makes for almost the ideal TR7-V8 engine, second only to a late 4.0-litre Rover unit. Of course, the Buick/Oldsmobile/Pontiac and early Rover 3500cc/215in^3 engines are still around, and offer the same light weight as the later Rover units; consequently, they should be on any US enthusiast's short list of power-plants. Also available on both sides of the Atlantic are the later Rover engines seen at photograph 1-2-4, with their 4000cc/238in^3 and 4600cc/282in^3 capacity.

Our US cousins are spoilt for alternatives. They have a plentiful supply of Ford 302 (seen fully dressed at 1-2-5) and Chevy small-block engines to choose from. These engines are heavier but offer even larger capacity and the opportunity of very high power/torque outputs. They also have a huge array of aftermarket tuning equipment available, including aluminium cylinder heads on view at 1-2-6, which reduce the incremental weight to more manageable proportions.

Fitting most Ford 302 engines, with their front-mounted distributors, presents something of a challenge

SPEEDPRO SERIES

1-2-5 Possibly more powerful than some, this Ford 302 motor (destined for a TR6) came equipped with GT40 aluminium head, roller cam, Edelbrock inlet manifold and dual Edelbrock (500cfm) carburettors. You might have difficulty closing the TR7's bonnet/hood with those air filters but they will not take long to change for something slimmer.

1-2-6 Aluminium cylinder heads are essential to both Ford and Chevy engines destined for a TR7 engine bay. They are available as the aftermarket fitment seen here, but also with either brand of engine when purchased as a new/complete crate unit.

under the low slopping bonnet of the TR7. However, there was one Ford 302 used in the Thunderbird between 1991 and 1994 that will fit the TR7, as a result of being specially designed to fit in place of the V6. It doesn't have a front sump, and the brackets, front cover, distributor and water pump were shortened to make it a similar size to the later Ford V6, looked at in chapter 15.

Nevertheless, even when fitted with aluminium cylinder heads, all these popular iron-block engines are 125 to 200lb (60 to 90kg) heavier than the original TR7 engine. In view of this increased weight, I have not devoted too much time and space to them. Too heavy an engine up front adversely affects the original car's even weight distribution, and detracts from the predictable road-holding. The increased vehicle weight will necessitate the brakes be upgraded, even for a (relatively) light-engined fast car. A heavy fast car will require you to further upgrade the brakes to counter the additional inertia. Extra weight will also make it necessary to revise the front suspension.

However, there are other engine-fitting considerations, starting with the sump/oil pan and chassis clearance. The TR7's front suspension is mounted on a sub-frame, cross-member or, as our US cousins call it, a 'K-frame'. This means that any engine fitted to the car requires a sump/oil pan with minimal depth at the front, in order to provide clearance between sump/oil pan and cross-member. Most Ford 302s are thus eliminated.

The majority of Chevy sumps/oil pans are not a factor in deciding whether to use this engine. Furthermore, the distributor is at the rear of the engine where the TR7 has the majority of under-bonnet space, although you will need to do away with the fresh-air intake. In fact, Chevy 'small-blocks' have been used to replace the relatively small original engine – as pictures 1-2-7-1 and 1-2-7-2 demonstrate. However,

1-2-7-1 This lovely black TR7 has a Chevy 406 small block underneath the bonnet, although from here you would not think so – just some larger wheels and tyres. However ...

1-2-7-2 ... things take on a different perspective from this side of the bonnet. However, you still cannot see the rear sub-frame that was necessary along with traction bars, coil-overs and a re-worked rear suspension.

almost every part of the car requires changing too, and our example also required a rear sub-frame to feed the power safely into the chassis, an appropriately uprated gearbox and a commensurately stronger rear axle! Yet the weight of this engine and the complexity of the installation brings me to prefer the Rover.

The Rover SD1 sump/oil pan shape seen at picture 1-2-8 is ideal for fitting this engine into a TR7, as the first 8in is very shallow and the full depth of the sump does not come into effect until the rear two-thirds of the engine.

The pre-SD1 engines only require a change of sump. There is no need to

PLANNING AN UPGRADE/CONVERSION

1-2-8 The SD1 sump is the ideal shape, but not all Rover engines are so equipped. The early engines (as fitted to Rover P5B and P6 cars and the even earlier Buick/Pontiac/Olds) and the later Range Rover and Discovery engines all had a deeper front part to their sumps/oil pans. Consequently, if your engine is from the early or later production period, you will also need to buy and fit SD1 parts to provide clearance over the TR7 cross-member.

alter the oil pick-up point or pipe/sieve. Post SD1 Rover engines are a shade more complex since they still need a re-shaped sump but do not have a windage tray, and the oil pickup is located towards the middle of the sump. Consequently these engines require a complete SD1 sump, tray, pickup and fittings purely to provide the essential cross-member clearance.

ENGINE SHORT-LIST SUMMARY

With so many Rover engines and the very easily-fitted Sprint engine still available, I decided to explore the following short list of options. Bearing in mind the importance of balancing engine power with appropriate brakes, suspension, etc., I have divided these engine upgrades into the three performance categories:

Fast road cars

The original TR7 UK spec engine offers 105bhp that can be tuned to 115bhp. The US engines and those markets that necessitated a lower compression ratio engine start from a lower output figure.

A Sprint engine offers 130bhp as removed from its Dolomite donor, and we will explore how to effect that transfer. However, you can get an extra 40bhp from the 16 valve Sprint engine over the standard 8 valve TR7 engine, provided all the correct ancillary equipment is fitted. Thus the Sprint engine (see chapter 6) can give as much power as the original TR8, although it will never provide the V8's glorious torque.

The TR8 engine provides 130/140bhp, and we will look into fitting one in a TR7 in chapters 8 and 9.

Ultra-fast road cars

An ex-SD1 engine provides 155bhp, is easily tuneable to 175bhp and can provide up to 210bhp with minimal trouble. We will look at how in chapter 8. Early V8s from Buick, Rover P5B and Rover P6, as well as the SD1 engine, can be upgraded to 250bhp and beyond! This is also covered in chapter 8.

Range Rovers and other Rover-powered vehicles can donate my favourite V8s, the 3.9/4.0 litre versions. These have the additional attraction of bringing with them a reasonably modern fuel-injection system and offer a great deal of potential.

Competitive cars

A 4600cc Rover V8 engine can provide 300bhp plus, which when equipped like that seen in photograph 1-2-9 transforms the TR7-V8 and TR8 into very potent sports cars.

1-2-9 A 'full-works' Rover still fits into the engine bay in this beautifully prepared competition TR8. Four DCOEs are plain to see (I guess with 45mm venturi), but did you spot the coil fastened onto the front left radiator bracket?

Other component changes

It is vital that you do the full conversion and don't just drop a V8 (or, for that matter, a Sprint) engine into the car! The changes will take you to every part of your vehicle, from the radiator to the rear axle. The main component changes are to the engine, sub-frame, possibly the gearbox (if your car is a 4-speed model) exhaust system (as pictured at 1-3-1), propshaft, brakes, suspension and the rear axle ratio. If your car is fitted with a 4-speed axle it will be necessary to change the whole rear axle.

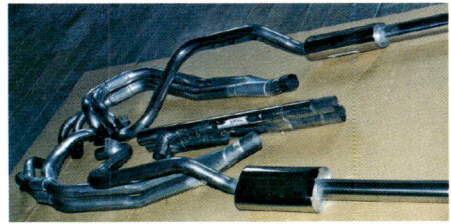

1-3-1 Once you get into a V8 conversion, several new component parts are required that are both unavoidable and expensive. The V8 manifold and exhaust systems are a case in point.

SPEEDPRO SERIES

1-3-2 This is the original TR8 low-profile EFI plenum. The Federal SD1 EFI system was very similar, but such original parts may not be available and, consequently, you will need to plan modifications for the parts that are to hand. Note the double-bulged bonnet.

The Sprint conversion can require relatively few and minor changes. This is not so with a V8 conversion, and you need to prepare carefully if you are thinking about this, even more so if you plan a particularly powerful one. Unlike fitting a Sprint engine, the bonnet will not close if you merely drop an ex-SD1 Rover V8 into the engine bay. British Leyland found it essential to fit a special lower-profile SD1-like inlet manifold and, of course, a second bulge in the bonnet. Even so, it still had to fit carburettors with stub tops to the TR8 carburettors, and the low-profile plenum chamber pictured at 1-3-2 to the fuel-injected variants.

Obviously there are decisions to make about the engine and associated ancillary parts, too. It is the numerous additional parts that we need to focus on first, because the question is: do you buy a kit of V8 conversion parts, or do you buy each part as and when you need it? Clearly cash-flow will play some part in your thinking, but it is more the 'proven-kit or self-selection' decision that needs attention. Each supplier's offering varies slightly, but on balance you will get the following in a typical V8 conversion kit:

• A cross-member/K-frame that forms the heart of all the V8 conversion kits. Shortly there is an important paragraph about engine height, which I urge you to digest.
• Engine mounting brackets (that bolt to the engine block) and the flexible (rubber) mounts. These are exactly as per the original TR8. A modified TR7 gearbox cross-member is included.
• A TR8 V8 specification water radiator, with top and bottom radiator mounting kits to ensure the radiator is properly located forward and below its TR7 position. A set of TR8 water hoses will also be included.
• An electric fan. An SD1 engine will come with a viscous fan on the water pump, which you could modify and re-locate to the crankshaft pulley as in the non-air-con TR8s. However, it will be ageing – you are better to fit a new electric fan and thermostatic control switch. The stat switch needs to be fitted on the front left side mounting panel, and the manual-override switch in a convenient place on the dashboard. The make of fan will depend on who is supplying your kit, but a wiring diagram is usually included.
• A stainless steel fabricated exhaust system including a pair of manifolds/headers and a full twin tail-pipe system, mounting brackets and hanging rubbers.
• Throttle and manual choke cables, electric fuel pump, K&N air filters, BAF SU carburettor needles, oil-pressure switch, uprated oil-pressure relief valve.
• Shorter propshaft with a sliding joint and a pair of universal joints.
• Wiring loom, 8-cylinder rev counter and wiring diagram.
• Basic vented brake kit.

Do note that a kit does not include the all-important engine, flywheel, gearbox, clutch parts, bell-housing, carburettors, engine ancillaries and higher-geared rear axle – all of which will need to be acquired and possibly refurbished. It is my impression that most kit supplies are aimed at converters wanting a fast road car, possibly those thinking in terms of taking a standard SD1 engine and dropping it into their TR7 engine bay. Nothing wrong with that plan whatsoever – some lovely TR7-V8s have been born using that formula. However, beyond that level of conversion you will be requesting so many additions/options to the basic kits, it might be better to start from a list of your needs and price them up individually.

Whichever route you follow you will also need the starter motor, and both the distributor and any external amplifier/ballast resistor associated with that distributor/coil. Note that there were about four different combinations of SD1 distributor/amplifier – unless you plan to replace the ignition system with a modern set-up, you must acquire both the distributor and its associated external ignition components. The distributors are becoming scarce and it is important that your engine, at the very least, includes a sound distributor body. With the body you can buy and fit a modern ignition system (perhaps a good idea in any event), but without it you will have to find an aftermarket solution (usually a Mallory distributor) – adding more cost to your project.

Before you buy a conversion kit or any components, you need to appreciate a little about the height of

PLANNING AN UPGRADE/CONVERSION

1-3-3. These very attractive wheels are 14in alloys. The reason behind increasing the 13in wheel diameter is mainly to allow the size of the front brake discs to be increased to a size commensurate with today's traffic speeds and density.

1-3-4 A typical front brake upgrade, utilising a pair of wide-mouthed iron callipers straddling a ventilated disc. As attractive as this sounds, it can – and for some powerful cars must – be improved upon by using alloy callipers spaced away from the centre of the hub to allow a larger diameter, and thus more effective, disc than this arrangement.

the TR8 engine in a TR8 engine bay. BL decided the car had to be supplied with a power steering rack, that obviously needs more space under the engine sump than a TR7's manual rack. Thus a conversion kit that includes a TR8 sub-frame can accept a power steering rack. However, if you buy a sub-frame with the very popular lowered engine-mounting brackets, you will certainly have an easier job fitting the engine under the bonnet but you will never be able to fit anything other than a TR7 un-powered steering rack.

TR8 power steering-racks are rarely available – nevertheless, I will include information on sources of PAS over the following pages.

The basic conversion kits are also aimed at SU/Stromberg carburettor conversions. I've included information on more powerful carburettor alternatives, as well as a chapter on electronic fuel-injection.

In short, you are best planning your conversion meticulously and sending out a list of the parts you want to suppliers of your choice. Ask for a quotation from each and an assurance that they will provide you with telephone technical back up if you get into difficulties during your conversion. Furthermore, I would speak to as many owners of TR7-V8 converted cars as you can, and ask not only about the quality of the parts but also the follow-up expertise provided. These attributes are just as important, maybe more so, than straight price.

BRAKES, WHEELS AND TYRES

After selecting the engine and power you want from your upgrade/conversion, the next most urgent considerations are the wheels and tyres. It is possible to fit some measure of brake upgrade beneath the standard 13in wheels, preserving the appearance of originality. However, in my opinion, and this may come as a surprise to many, ALL TR7's, even absolutely standard cars, need to have their wheels upgraded to at least the 14in diameter example seen in photograph 1-3-3. This is primarily to increase the brake capacity, although there is the secondary advantage of a greater range of tyres becoming available. There is more detail in chapter 3, but briefly here let me mention that the car was designed to cruise at 55mph and stop in light traffic density. Even so, the brakes were barely adequate and, with the increases in speeds and traffic density, a standard cars brakes need upgrading. Something similar to photograph 1-3-4 is a step in the right direction.

I do concede that 14in wheels provide adequate, if not brilliant, brakes for all standard and fast road cars. However, owners that envisage an ultra-fast road car need to be thinking of brake discs which need the capacity of 15in wheels – similarly, competitive cars will benefit from 16in wheels. In all cases alloy wheels are available, and provide the dual bonus of light weight and improved

SPEEDPRO SERIES

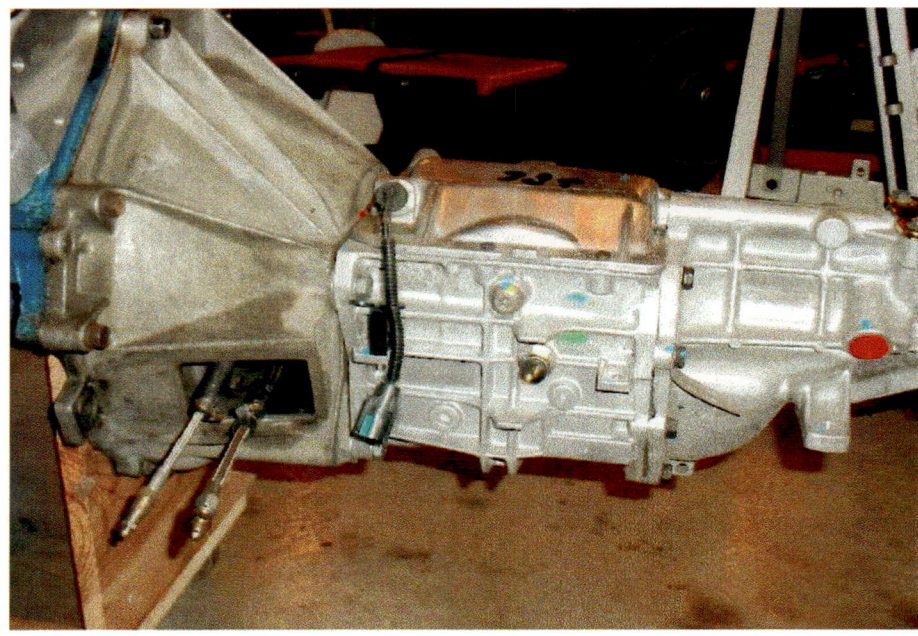

1-3-5 Another view of the T5 – a Ford version judging by the extra length of the bell-housing. Its all-aluminium construction is clear from this shot. The twin pipes exiting the clutch-lever opening are, in this case, for an HTOB (hydraulic throw-out bearing) which actuates this car's clutch.

BODYSHELL CHANGES

Because the car was originally designed to accept the Rover V8 engine, the conversion of a standard TR7 to a TR7 Rover V8 is relatively straightforward, and can be carried out by any competent DIY car enthusiast. There are no bodyshell modifications to carry out for fast road and ultra-fast road cars, although it is absolutely essential that your bodyshell is in first class order and capable of handling the extra stresses any of these more powerful engines impose upon all parts of the car.

Competitive cars will require some strengthening of the bodyshell, and you will find this outlined in chapter 4.

WHICH TRANSMISSION DO YOU PLAN?

The TR7 was fitted with two gearboxes during its life – initially the weak 4-speed unit, then the 5-speed LT77 Rover box. If you have a 4-speed gearbox in your car you need to change it for something stronger. The 4-speed was barely adequate for the standard engine in standard tune, so any form of engine tuning or upgrade will swiftly dispatch your 4-speed gearbox to the scrapyard. Hence the need for a plan that incorporates a stronger gearbox.

For all fast road and ultra-fast road cars the easiest gearbox to fit is a late LT77 5-speed TR7 unit. If you are staying with the 4-cylinder engine you will need a perfectly standard and readily available TR7 bell-housing and clutch operating mechanism. If you are fitting a V8 engine you will need a V8 bell-housing, which will be harder to find, as will a number of different clutch operating details. We will explore these in chapter 7.

For competitive level conversions, the LT77 box is unlikely to be adequate in the long-term. The easiest fitment would lead you to choose the LT77's successor – the newer, stronger R380 with the advantage of synchromesh on all gears. Both these gearboxes have the added attraction of requiring the least tunnel changes. Alternatively a Getrag (ex-most of the larger BMW saloons/sedans) and/or a suitable Borg-Warner (now Tremec) T5 gearbox, seen at 1-3-5, will handle the power but you will need a bespoke bell-housing and clutch mechanism. An ex-Toyota Supra gearbox is another gearbox worth considering provided your power is below 400bhp.

The rear axle will require upgrading. The ratio almost certainly needs to be changed in any event, but if you are thinking of power in excess of 250bhp then the strength of the axle warrants thought too. In the USA, Ford axles are plentiful, available in a variety of strengths, with or without 'posi-traction' (LSD) and with or without rear disc brakes (if they are on your shopping list). The axle will require modification – possibly shortening, but certainly with regards to the mounting methods. We explore these matters in chapter 5.

www.velocebooks.com/www.veloce.co.uk
All books in print • New books • Special offers • Gift Vouchers

Chapter 2
Upgrading the brakes

The TR7 brakes, frankly, were rubbish, and the TR8's only marginally better. The first time I drove a TR7-V8 it was a friend's car I had borrowed. I stopped the car after a couple of miles to open the bonnet/hood and check whether there was a servo/booster, that the fluid reservoir was full, and whether I could see anything that was making the brakes virtually non-existent! I was due to use the car for a week, but was so unnerved by the poor brakes that I stuck it in my garage and walked!

I was not the only one to notice the poor brakes. The story goes that the TR7 development engineers used to play a game of chicken with the TR7s and '8s they were working on. They would get the car up to an agreed speed of about 90mph down the back lane that ran along the inner boundary at Canley, and see who could leave braking until the last possible moment before taking the 90 degree bend at the end of the straight. It was not unusual that the bend was overshot, and the car descended down the bank on the far side! Apparently, the engineers knew that the brakes were useless, and it would be fascinating to hear why Triumph never improved them. I can only surmise they were just adequate for the USA's 55mph speed limits of the day.

In today's litigious society Triumph would have to attend to the brakes, but you will appreciate why this could be the most important chapter in this book and why brakes are the first component up! Furthermore, several other changes stem from brake modifications – notably the road-wheel type, size and diameter. We will study those details in chapter 3.

SAFETY FIRST

If you are upgrading the power from the engine you really MUST upgrade the brakes on a TR7 or TR8. For rolling improvement projects the brake improvement MUST be carried out BEFORE you effect the engine change.

The original TR7 and TR8 braking system used metric fittings and threads. However, when you are changing any brake (or indeed clutch) hydraulic part, be aware that thread forms, the depth of thread, and other factors relating to the integrity of the system can change from component to component. Two parts may look exactly the same, but one can employ imperial thread forms while the alternative could have metric thread forms and/or a different depth of thread. In the USA, some specialist equipment can have alternate thread forms, too. It is absolutely essential that you remain alert and ensure that every single union is correct, sound and will remain so for many years to come. A union should not fall into place nor should it be inexplicably tight. Manufacturers often used different diameters of unions to guard against front and rear pipework being accidentally swapped. Watch for and respect such conventions, because

SPEEDPRO SERIES

it may not be you working on this car for the rest of its life. If in any doubt whatsoever, consult professional brake experts – your life or that of an innocent third party may depend upon it.

If it's necessary to have any part of your braking system – calliper-mounting brackets, for example – fabricated or welded, you MUST have an experienced braking specialist carry out the work. Some of the forces involved are huge and the consequences of failure unthinkable. If you have any uncertainties about what you are doing, ask a specialist or use a proven kit of parts from one of the specialised suppliers.

As you assemble your new braking arrangement, it is VITAL to check that the disc/rotor you have fitted extends beyond the outer edge of the brake pads – a few millimetres is sufficient. If, on the other hand, your pad material extends out beyond the diameter of the disc, you are going to lose some of the pads braking effect straight away – obviously undesirable. Much more seriously, you could eventually find you have no front brakes at all, particularly if you are using relatively thin (say 1/2in) discs/rotors. The solution is to buy a larger diameter disc – if not, after a few thousand miles both halves of the pad material may meet, and the main part of the pad is prevented from making proper contact with the disc, whereupon the car loses its ability to stop!

If any of the ex-production car callipers you plan to use have to be split apart, do so very carefully, for there are pitfalls. The first mistake is to shot, and or bead-blast a split calliper. Don't – you will damage the inner faces and potentially create a mid-calliper leak.

The inter-face seals are (deliberately) hard to come by. Either get a professional to re-assemble your callipers with new seals and the correct, properly torqued high-tensile bolts, or at the very least buy your seals before splitting your callipers.

Several ex-production iron callipers are fed with two hydraulic lines, one to each half of the calliper(s). If you are fitting these callipers to a car of the TR7's era, some plumbing rearrangements will be required. This is often easily accomplished by a 'bridge' pipe, but there will be occasions when the calliper(s) need to be split apart and internally cross-drilled. For this you are best having a professional brake specialist carry out the conversion. Spot-facing and additional seals are required, and there are plenty of ways to get it wrong.

When you have completed your upgrade or changeover, do not forget to bleed your brakes. It surprises me how many enthusiasts fit their callipers upside down and then wonder why they cannot get a good solid feel to their pedal. The calliper bleed nipple MUST go at the top if you want the air in your system to bleed.

WHAT'S IMPORTANT?
Brake size

The front brake disc/rotor diameter is probably the most important contributor to the effectiveness of the brakes. 70 per cent of any car's braking effect comes from the front – they are doubly important as compared to the rear brakes. I don't believe all owners see that it is the diameter of the front brake disc/rotor that has the single most effect on braking efficiency. We'll look at other factors in a moment, but rest assured, you should always fit brake discs of the maximum diameter that your road wheels will allow.

For many years, Triumph fitted $10^{13}/_{16}$in (275mm) diameter discs to the front and 15in road wheels to the car. For the TR7 and TR8, the road wheels were reduced in diameter to 13in, and consequently the disc/rotor diameter to 9.7in (245mm), decreasing the effectiveness of a Wedge's brakes in two ways. Not only is the mechanical advantage (i.e. the distance from the centre of the pad to the centre of the hub) reduced, but the pads have to be reduced in width due to the limited space between the wheel hub and the outside edge of the brake disc/rotor. Consequently, TR7s were fitted with MG Midget brakes, and TR8s with only slightly bigger pads on the same diminutive diameter discs/rotors, though the thickness of the rotor was marginally increased to 14mm. However, the larger the disc, the greater the mass to absorb the heat, and the greater the surface area to radiate that heat post-braking.

The second most important consideration for upgrading your TR's front brakes is the squeezing capacity of the callipers. The surface area of the piston(s) is an effective comparison in this respect. For example: the original TR7 and TR8s have two-pot callipers (i.e. they have 2 pistons). The TR7 pistons are 51mm in diameter, while the TR8's are 54mm diameter. The TR7 pistons offer about 4085mm^2 area, while the TR8's larger and more powerful pistons have a combined surface area of about 4580mm^2 (2 x Pi x 27mm x 27mm). So if you are going to replace your TR7 callipers, the upgraded units need to have a piston surface area of at least 4500mm^2 just to bring them up to TR8 squeezing capacity.

There are several four pot callipers with about 41mm diameter pistons, offering 15 per cent extra squeezing capacity over the original TR8 callipers. However, there is a subsequent increase in pedal travel with the standard master cylinder, which many would find unacceptable. To improve the stopping power of our TR, we need to strike a

UPGRADING THE BRAKES

2-1-1 Although there is not a material increase in squeezing capacity, the Princess four-pots on the left clearly offer an opportunity to increase the area of pad in contact with the disc, compared to the calliper (which is very similar to that of a TR8) and pad on the right.

balance between some extra squeezing capacity and too much. The solution to the increased pedal travel is to fit a larger capacity master cylinder – and we'll look at that detail shortly.

The relative areas of the brake pads also play an important part in their effectiveness, and increasing the pad area will obviously improve the braking effect. In this context, the extra pad area offered by most four-pot callipers will improve the brakes proportionally to the increase in pad area. Therefore you will be interested in the brake pad areas for reference purposes. Standard TR7 pads are 2680mm^2 and a TR8 pad provides 3481mm^2 – on view at photograph 2-1-1.

Pad materials

The 'grab' or 'bite' offered by differing pad's friction materials and/or differing manufacturers is another important factor in brake effectiveness. A change of material/manufacturer is in fact the simplest method of bringing about some improvement in braking. There are numerous excellent pad manufacturers, but space dictates I touch on just two:

EBC Kevlar brake pads

Kevlar is very expensive but an excellent binding fibre; non metallic with low abrasive qualities and therefore cleaner and easier on discs/rotors. Friction levels of conventional pads vary from 0.25 up to 0.35 friction factor. EBC tells me that its 'Greenstuff' pads have 0.46 friction, and so expect most users will notice an immediate improvement in bite.

The alternative grades of Kevlar pads are Black, Red, Yellow, Blue and Green. Most feel Green is best for all road-going applications, and the trade will normally include Green pads in its upgrade kits unless an alternative is requested. Black Kevlar pads still offer an improved coefficient of friction over non-Kevlar materials, albeit slightly less than Green. If you expect to use the car mostly for fast road application with occasional track use, you will be served better by the next grade up – Red. If the car is to be used extensively on the track, Yellow will be the grade to specify, while endurance track work demands Blue grade Kevlar pads.

Hawk brake pads

Hawk Performance Inc utilises Ferro Carbon materials in its pads, which it has developed and manufactured for the racing community. Hawk says that all Ferro Carbon materials are non-fade, and offer lower wear rates and higher friction values than any other competitive materials available on the market today.

Hawk makes a wide range of compounds, and I've selected four relevant ones to evaluate in a little more detail. HP compound is designed for fast and ultra-fast road use and provides high friction, hot or cold. Hawk says it offers long disc/rotor/pad life, yet generates extremely low dust and is virtually noise free. HP Plus compound is for ultra-fast road and competitive use, and Hawk tells me that it can be used on the race-track and then driven home safely – provided you have checked that adequate pad thickness remains! It advises that the compound generates extremely high friction and is resistant to "elevated" temperatures, but expect increased disc/rotor/pad wear, noise and dust. It declares it suitable for club racing events. K compounds provide a medium frictional pad that operates virtually from cold at low cost. It is intended for light-duty road/racing applications. Blue 9012 is a medium-to-high torque brake compound, providing low pad and disc/rotor wear in ultra-fast road, rally and circuit use. Specifically recommended by Hawk for low-to-mid temperature effectiveness.

Cooling the brakes

The final factor to consider is the cooling afforded to the brakes – not just the discs/rotors, but the callipers too. The cooling is best looked at in different ways, starting with the discs/rotors. The mass of the brake discs/rotors themselves, and their cooling ability, are the factors that ensure the brakes do not fade during application and are ready for the next. The mass of the disc is a measure of its ability to absorb the heat generated by braking. Therefore, 22mm thick ventilated discs not only offer a higher mass and are thus better able to soak up heat, but are manufactured with internal ventilation, further increasing their ability to handle and dissipate the heat caused by pad-disc friction.

Cross-drilled holes in the disc/rotor can further add to the disc's effectiveness through slightly improved cooling, but more particularly they improve dust and gas clearance as the discs get (really) hot. Furthermore, the cross-holes (and any radial vanes, if incorporated) also speed the clearance of water from the disc/rotor in wet conditions. They are an additional benefit in many applications, but only delay the onset of fade to a very slight

SPEEDPRO SERIES

2-1-2 It will be the additional mass and improved internal ventilation from this vented disc that mainly delays the onset of fade, rather than the cross-drilled holes.

2-1-3 This rally-style front valance is ideal for ducting air towards the front brakes, and can be very effective.

degree. We can see a ventilated and cross-drilled disc/rotor in 2-1-2.

However, we need to be careful not to overdo the increased thickness/mass of the disc/rotor for there is a conflict of interests – increased thickness raises unsprung weight which adversely affects road-holding!

Disc/rotor cooling can be improved by fitting a pair of tubular ducts, directing air from the front of the car onto the disc/rotors and callipers. The ducts can be fitted below the front valance, on view at 2-1-3, or blended into it. The usual diameter of the ducts is 3in (75mm), and in days gone by I have used old heater corrugated pipe. However, these days Allstar makes specially designed brake-ducts and mating hoses. The hose is designed to direct air via front-mounted air ducts, and is flexible, non-kinking and made to withstand 525°C. It is available in 3in or 4in double ply silicon-coated fibreglass, with a coiled steel support and smooth interior for unrestricted air flow. Put some mesh over the intakes to prevent road debris, particularly small stones, being directed into the brakes.

We will look at the road-holding benefits of an additional front spoiler in the chapter focused on bodywork (chapter 4). The frontal spoiler is a major benefit generally, but one significant downside is that it reduces the flow of air to the front brakes, unless you at least incorporate a pair of brake cooling slots in the spoiler. However, the cooling effect will be increased greatly if the spoiler has a pair of Allstar ducts blended into the back face, and the gathered air is directed onto the brakes via strategically placed hoses on either side of the car.

While the location of each inlet duct is up to you, about 12in (30mm) inboard from the front corner of the car (i.e. just inboard of the front suspension strut) is usually the best compromise. Air-pressure increases as the inlets move toward the centre of the car but, while a central location helps the volume of air directed onto the disc/rotors, it also increases the duct length and causes securing and routing complications.

The dust shields mounted just inboard of the disc/rotor can affect brake-cooling, too. Modern day vehicles rarely employ a dust shield, as it inhibits air flow to the disc. I suggest eliminating your dust shields, particularly if you are employing ducted air to cool the brakes. You may have to remove it in any event to accommodate most enlarged calliper options! However, if totally eliminating the dust shield does not appeal, try copying the TR8's (seen at 2-1-4) to form an air scoop.

The last cooling factor is the calliper piston material you specify. Stainless steel is superior – and therefore preferred – in that it transmits less heat to the brake fluid than the cheaper, chromed mild-steel pistons. However, ceramic is even better. Wilwood markets some of its pistons under the name Thermlock, and says that these pistons reduce calliper temperatures by more than 30 per cent over stainless steel pistons, without the need for fluid re-circulation. Fluid temperatures are reduced, seal life extended and calliper life prolonged by reduced wear in the piston bores.

FRONT CALLIPER OPTIONS

We have already covered the additional mechanical advantage offered by increased diameter disc/rotors. Yet with the TR7 and 8, achieving this is rather more difficult than it appears. Apart from the restriction imposed by the car's standard wheel diameter, it is the calliper mounting lugs on the TR7's front

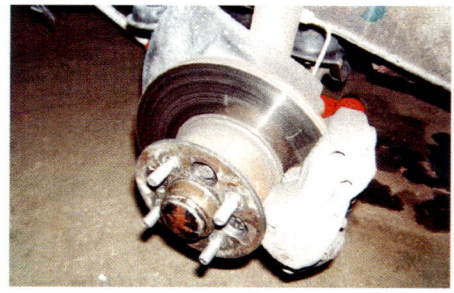

2-1-4 This is the TR8 brake setup, the dust shield shape (unique, to my knowledge) is intended to direct cooling air onto the disc – although I must admit to doubting its effectiveness without a pair of well-directed cooling ducts.

UPGRADING THE BRAKES

suspension legs (having being designed to be compatible with the 245mm diameter disc/rotors) that bring about the problem when conventional lug-mounted callipers are to be used. This difficulty can be seen in drawing 2-1. Since all the lug-mounted callipers I have encountered have a very similar mounting hole to outside disc/rotor dimension, the TR7's suspension leg mounting limits the extra disc/rotor diameter that you can accommodate. You may find a calliper with extraordinarily long mounting lugs that will increase the disc diameter capacity – if so, please write to me care of the publisher! However, few of the following options allow for the diameter of the disc to be increased to the 275, 285 or 295mm that I think a performance car warrants, and thus offer only marginal improvement

Capri 2.8 injection callipers

Kits based upon these callipers and discs are available from both Robsport International and S+S Preparations, and

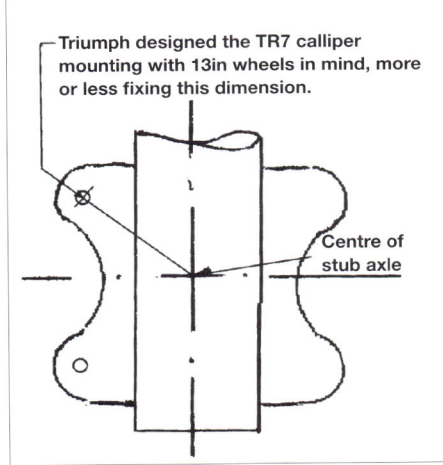

D2-1 The TR7 and TR8 calliper mounting plate – note how the distance to the calliper's mounting hole affects the distance the calliper is from the centre line of the strut.

2-2-1-1 The disc/rotor diameter on the Capri upgrade kits is only fractionally larger than standard, although the kit's disc is ventilated, which should delay the onset of brake fade.

2-2-1-2 The ventilated disc comes from a vehicle other than a Capri, as the calliper's internal spacer is in view here. Also in view is how the TR7's original calliper mounting restricts the disc diameter.

can be seen at 2-2-1-1 and 2-2-1-2. This arrangement does not necessitate an increase in wheel size, as the callipers will usually fit within the standard 13in alloy wheel. However, the clearances are very small, and occasionally you will need to fit a 6mm thick spacer between each front wheel and hub. In this event be sure that your wheel studs are long enough, and if in doubt fit 6mm longer studs, too. Check your road wheel offset to retain the original steering characteristics.

The Capri callipers require the spacer or donut seen at 2-2-1-3, fitted between disc/rotor and hub. The callipers are still two-pots with 54mm diameter pistons, so offer some added squeezing capacity over the TR7 units, but I would not expect them to be a major improvement on the TR8 brakes. Robsport tells me the Capri calliper was chosen because it is not too heavy – a problem that can manifest itself as wheel-shake under braking. The shaking is accentuated by wear in the

suspension components, particularly the bushes, but gets even worse as the weight of the callipers increase. Heavy callipers are also best avoided, as they increase the front suspensions unsprung weight, which increases the inertia and detracts from the car's road-holding.

The standard kits do not include the Greenstuff pad material I consider essential, nor are the disc/rotors cross-

2-2-1-3 This is the spacer required to adapt the Capri callipers to the TR7's hubs, and to provide for the correct offset for the disc/rotors included in this kit.

23

SPEEDPRO SERIES

drilled. This kit, properly installed, will improve the stopping power of a TR7, but I also understand that the Capri Owners Club promotes the four-pot Princess calliper (which we will explore shortly) as a braking upgrade!

Rover SD1/Vitesse callipers

Rover SD1 cars were fitted with two types of calliper. By far the majority was fitted with non-ventilated discs/rotors and the associated two-pot (57mm pistons) callipers seen at 2-2-2.

The Vitesse-specification SD1 Rovers offer ventilated discs/rotors, and thus wider-mouthed four-pot (4x41mm pistons) callipers. These same callipers were used on some Range Rovers, too. The callipers bolt straight onto the TR7 mounting lugs, and in standard/stock Rover form, the callipers straddle 10.2in (257mm) diameter discs/rotors. Rimmer Bros offers this arrangement as the basis of its brake-kit Three (on view at 2-2-3-1 and 2-2-3-2), which must be used with 14in or larger wheels.

Volvo brake conversions

There are some Volvo 240-based callipers which I would not recommend be fitted to a TR7 or TR8. In some respects, Volvo 240 callipers offer an excellent basis for an upgrade, and could really come into their own when used with an expansion bracket. They have four 38mm diameter pistons but, like the Rover units above, some versions were used over ½in thick solid discs/rotors. However, some 240 models were fitted with 22mm thick ventilated discs/rotors, which make their callipers seem ideal candidates, as picture 2-2-4 would appear to endorse.

The drawback is that the mounting lugs don't allow for a significant increase in disc diameter, nor do the holes match

2-2-2 These SD1 two-pots offer some increase in squeezing capacity over our earlier options, but the disc diameter and thickness is little better than that of the original TR, and the upgrade probably of minimal benefit

the TR7/8 suspension legs. Some users mill the mounting holes slightly wider to fit the TR legs – leaving figure-of-eight shaped holes. Therefore, the use of directly mounted Volvo callipers is, to my mind, unacceptable. The weakened mounting lugs may not cause problems initially, but in due course fatigue can set in. They would certainly fail any road worthiness test where the examiner could see the elongated holes.

Princess four-pots

The Austin Princess was not a car sold into the US, and consequently this is not an easy option for our Stateside cousins. In fact, ex-Princess four-pot callipers have been in great demand in recent years in the UK, and so are more-or-less unobtainable this side of the Atlantic too! The mounting lugs are compatible with the TR's hole centres and, in standard form, these four-pot iron callipers are ready to straddle ½in (12.7mm) discs/rotors. However, the 10mm spacers seen in photograph 2-2-5, positioned between each half of the calliper, widen them sufficiently to straddle 22mm thick vented discs/rotors – hence their popularity.

The original piston diameter is

2-2-3-1 Rimmer Bros brake kit Three uses a Vitesse calliper and disc with a unique hub adapter, which allows the disc to be used in a TR7 hub.

2-2-3-2 This shot is particularly interesting, showing the original 247 x 9.7mm brake disc, calliper and 2680mm^2 pad alongside a Vitesse 257 x 20mm disc, 4400mm^2 pad and calliper.

2-2-4 A pair of apparently ideal Volvo 240 callipers. Unfortunately, the mounting lugs do not fit the TR7 front strut.

38mm, so offers 4537mm^2 – better than a TR7 by about 10 per cent, but they offer no practical squeezing improvement over a TR8, though the

UPGRADING THE BRAKES

pad area will be about 15 per cent larger than the TR8's and the vented discs will delay fade. However, when bolted directly to the Triumph suspension leg, you will be limited to 250mm diameter discs/rotors – only marginally larger than standard. High-friction pads should bring about an improvement, even if the benefit is unspectacular.

In standard form they have three bleed nipples, are fed with two hydraulic pipes and can give new users problems bleeding the front brakes. The best solution is to have your original callipers reconditioned and internally cross-drilled to hydraulically link the two halves, thus reducing the number of feed pipes and active bleed nipples to one each. When callipers are available, Rimmer Bros offers them as the basis of its brake kit Two, which can be seen at 2-2-6.

You may think that I have devoted a lot of space to a basically unobtainable calliper – and you would be correct, were it not for the fact that replicas (shown in picture 2-2-7) are now available. In fact, the replicas are superior to the originals in several ways. The Hi Spec units are slightly more powerful than original Princess callipers, which makes them a very worthwhile upgrade for all Wedges. The disc diameter restriction still applies, although you might squeeze 260mm discs under a replica's bridge, until you start to consider radial mounting your callipers.

Radial mounted callipers

Having listed numerous callipers with mounting lugs, and explained how their use on the TR7's suspension legs effectively restricts the disc diameter, at this point I suggest, if you want really good brakes, finding some aluminium callipers with radial mountings. To explain

2-2-5 This is not an original Princess calliper; nevertheless, this Hi Spec four-pot illustrates the use of spacers perfectly.

these, I have prepared drawings D2-2 and D2-3 (overleaf). The latter shows our calliper in two parts, and where the flexibility of a radial mounted calliper comes from.

There are differing designs of intermediate bracket for radial mounted callipers. The appropriate brackets and bolts (often called mounting kits) need to be purchased with your callipers, and they need disc diameters and mounting-hole centres that are compatible with

2-2-6 Rimmer Bros brake kit Two includes Princess callipers, a special hub adapter/spacer and a vented disc. This illustration shows perfectly the fitting and the pipework required to install the plumbing for the Princess calliper. The calliper fits into the TR7 13in alloy wheel, but doesn't clear the TR7 13in steel wheel.

2-2-7 The Hi Spec Motorsport Princess replicas are made from aluminium and are lighter than the originals. The replicas have four pistons, each of 38.6mm (1.52in) diameter giving 4682mm^2 piston area.

2-2-8 A radial mounting bracket awaiting the (in this case) bolted calliper.

your car and intended disc. Some are specially machined blocks, some little more than the L-shaped bracket on view at 2-2-8, while others come with studs to secure bracket to calliper (although I believe AP Racing leaves you to resolve your own brackets). This two-piece method of fixing not only allows you to 'stretch' the calliper's mounting position, but also permits minor adjustments of the calliper's position using shims, so space within the road wheel becomes the only restriction you have to enlarging the brake discs to a worthwhile size.

25

SPEEDPRO SERIES

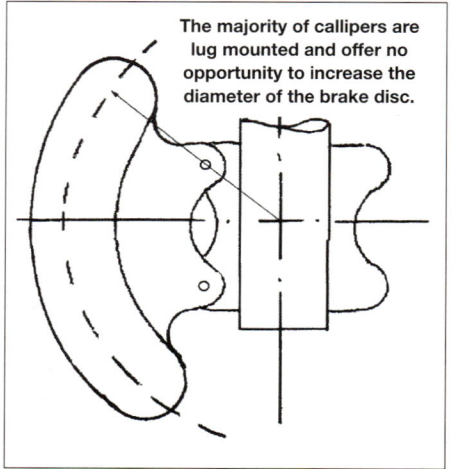

The majority of callipers are lug mounted and offer no opportunity to increase the diameter of the brake disc.

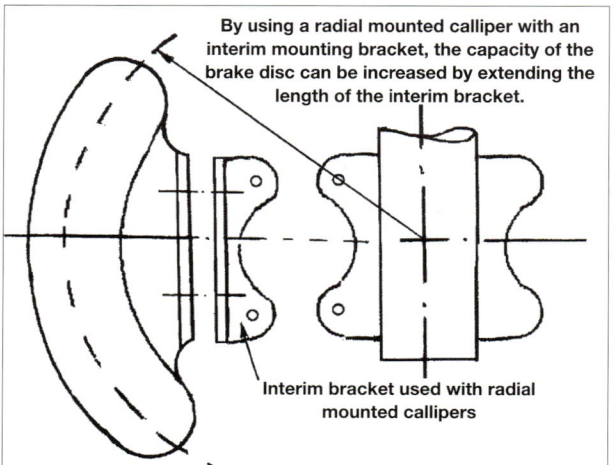

By using a radial mounted calliper with an interim mounting bracket, the capacity of the brake disc can be increased by extending the length of the interim bracket.

Interim bracket used with radial mounted callipers

D2-3. Our radial mounted calliper is now in two parts. The calliper's original mounting lugs have disappeared and been replaced by a plain flat plate. The lugs securing this intermediate bracket to the suspension leg are still there, but now with a faceplate that marries with the base of the radial calliper.

D2-2 Our sketch, now with calliper in place and the inflexibility this offers.

Here is a summary of the disc diameter and the required road wheel size:
275mm diameter discs/rotors require 14in diameter road wheels.
285mm discs/rotors require 15in road wheels.
295mm discs/rotors require 16in road wheels.
Many companies make aluminium callipers with radial mounting options:

Hi Spec Motorsport
Its billet, radial mounted calliper kits for the TR7 and TR8 are shown in 2-2-9. Hi Spec makes two-, four- and six-pot callipers which enables it to select the most suitable calliper for each application. However, it is the four-pots that are most relevant to the vast majority of TR7 and 8 applications. These are available in three versions:
Four pistons, each of 1.52in (38.6mm) diameter, giving 4682mm^2 piston area.
Four pistons, two of 1.625in (41mm) and two of 1.5in (38mm) diameter, giving 4908mm^2 piston area.
Four pistons, each of 1.625in (41mm) diameter, giving 5280mm^2 piston area.

The mid-option callipers are called differential callipers. They are 'handed', and thus always need to be mounted with the smaller piston at the disc's entrance to the calliper. Bearing in mind that the standard TR7 callipers have a piston area of 4085mm^2 and the TR8 of 4580mm^2, it seems clear that the first option will not increase the squeezing capacity over much, although the brakes will improve via larger discs and increased 'grab' from your pads.

AP Racing callipers
There are advantages and disadvantages to following the AP Racing route, regardless of the diameter disc/rotors you plan. The most significant advantage is that the callipers are very rigid indeed – brought about by very substantial fastening, the use of unusually thick steel plates behind the pads, and the absence of spacers. Also, the slim design of the bridge part allows for the largest possible disc diameter. Four- and six-piston callipers are available. The CP7040 and CP5570 models provide for radial mounts and six differential pistons, while the CP6600 and CP5200 models

2-2-9 Hi Spec's TR7 kit includes 285mm ventilated discs, radial brackets and, of course, the callipers of choice. The callipers come fully sealed against grit and water.

use radial mounts and four differential pistons, two of 38.1mm and two of 41.25mm diameter.

The cost of AP callipers (and their rotors) is the main disadvantage. The callipers are two, three and four times the cost of competitive products (depending on your comparison), and you will need to get the radial mounting brackets machined by a specialist. I include these callipers only on the basis that they are appropriate to a minority of (probably) competitively-minded readers – particularly those required to retain 13in diameter road wheels with the subsequent limitations this imposes on disc/rotor size.

UPGRADING THE BRAKES

Wilwood

Most auto enthusiasts have heard of the American-made aluminium Wilwood callipers. It made a low-cost range called Dynalite, seen at 2-2-10-1 and 2-2-10-2, but the Superlite range is probably most enthusiasts' preferred choice, particularly as there is now an improved version called Superlite II. The billet NDLR was the nearest radial mounted I could find at the time of writing. It is made in a variety of versions, but the model for 298mm diameter x 20.6mm thick discs with four 44.5mm pistons was the smallest, and thus the nearest suited to a TR7 that I could find.

Wilwood makes a range of expansion plates, and you may find some suited to the TR7 that allow you to use the Superlite II design with mounting lugs. These four-pot callipers are available with 35mm (3849mm^2) or 44.5mm (6222mm^2) diameter pistons, and incorporate the piston seals that I consider essential to the longevity of road-going cars. The callipers are spaced to suit 21mm or 28mm thick discs/rotors. Diameter options range from 260mm to 335mm.

Wilwood also makes the six-pot radial mounted calliper, seen at photo 2-2-11, for the very fastest of competition cars.

FRONT DISC/ROTORS

A few words on discs/rotors are appropriate at this juncture. Most discs up to 285mm are single piece castings, with a raised centre to provide the offset required by most applications. Once you get to about 295mm diameter discs/rotors, you'll find that most discs come as two-part assemblies. The actual braking surface is still made from a cast iron disc, but the central mounting part of the disc is made from a separately turned piece of duraluminium billet.

One-piece rotors

Most readers' cars will require one-piece steel disc/rotors. These are the norm – at least for discs of about 295mm (a little over 11.5in) diameter. Thereafter, all manufacturers employ a two-piece bolted construction made up of an inner bell/hat and an outer, cast steel disc/rotor braking surface, the latter in all such cases being flat (i.e. without offset).

Your brake specialist supplier will have access to various manufacturer's catalogues, and be able to select the correct thickness/offset and diameter to suit your application. Don't forget that the outside diameter of a disc can easily be turned down. The central holes are easily re-drilled (in different locations, of course) if their standard PCD does not suit your hub fixings. The quality of the material is important – I recommend you use a reputable make. The cheap alternatives could warp and need replacing or, possibly, skimming.

Two-piece discs

Once the disc diameter reaches 295mm, you will have to buy your discs in two-piece format. In fact, some disc manufacturers, for example AP Racing, only supply discs in two parts regardless of disc diameter, as seen in picture 2-3-1-1 (overleaf). Picture 2-3-1-2 (overleaf) also shows the separate bell available from many manufacturers in three materials – cast iron, spun steel and billet aluminium.

Allstar supplies bells/hats in all three materials, but other manufacturers specialise in a range of mountings in one material. Wilwood bells/hats are precision machined from a high strength aluminium alloy, but come in a wide range of offsets and wheel stud patterns. You can order part-machined options to accommodate special/custom stud patterns. Most

2-2-10-1 These are MGB with lug mounted Wilwood Dynalite callipers. Nevertheless, the braking surfaces are flat, ventilated ...

2-2-10-2 ... 300mm (12in) x 22mm (⅞in) and carrying part number AM5863. The cross-drilling on the braking surface, the separate alloy bell, and the fastening of bell to braking surface are all in clear view.

2-2-11 An example of Wilwood's Superlite callipers – in this case, a six-pot one.

braking specialists will turn up a suitable bell/hat, with an appropriate offset to position the braking surface in the centre of your calliper. Naturally, they will have to be mindful of the braking surface mounting diameter and hole

SPEEDPRO SERIES

positions, not to mention the mounting holes for the hub. In this event, the chances are that the material used will be aluminium. Photograph 2-3-2 shows a 295mm disc from Hi Spec.

AP Racing makes the best braking surfaces. They can be five or six times competitors' prices, and remember you still need to have the bells made. Its rotors are lightweight, durable, and feature either 28 or 36 long, curved vanes. They come fully heat-treated, ground and balanced for optimum reliability and performance. Other disc thicknesses are available, but its 21mm option will be most reader's choice.

Colin Pendle told me that after several cheaper options on his competition car, he finally converted to AP Racing callipers and discs. Once fitted, the pad material range was vast. Carbon metallic seemed the best bet, and they proved to be excellent straight from the box – no bedding required unlike the DS11 of old – but were quite brutal to the disc. Two or three races wore the pads out, and two sets of pads destroyed the discs, so a full season used six sets of pads and two, possibly three, pairs of discs – which proved expensive. Then Ferodo DS3000 pads arrived. These provide for three or four races from a set of pads, and the disc-life is extended to two seasons. Costs for either pad are very similar, so overall the Ferodo pads offer much better value for money.

Colin concludes that the most critical aspect about stopping a race car is the pad material. Consequently, before choosing a manufacturer of callipers or discs, read the specification sheets about the pad qualities available. Establish whether the totally different pads for summer cruising, fast road, or track days are available, and ask around to find out whether they really work.

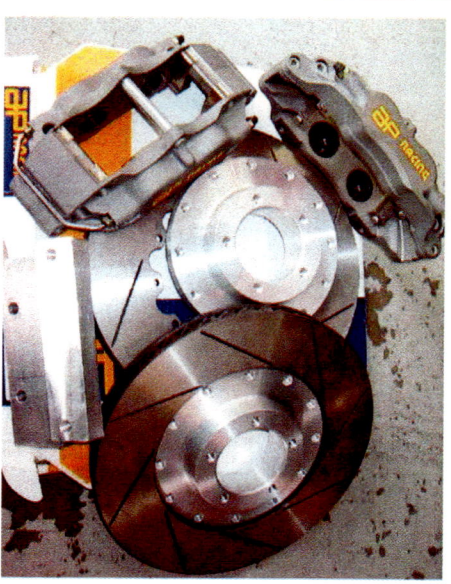

2-3-1-1 AP Racing's excellent kit as supplied by TRS in Australia. The braking surfaces for most two-piece discs are usually 'handed', particularly those with vanes seen here.

2-3-1-2 This Hi Spec photo demonstrates why two-piece disc construction is more expensive than single-piece, showing the fastening of the separate central bell, or hat as it is called Stateside, to the braking surface.

BRAKE SERVOS/ BOOSTERS AND MASTER CYLINDERS

One possibly interesting and helpful master cylinder upgrade is the early Rover SD1 plastic reservoir, which will fit the

2-3-2 This TR7-V8 uses Hi Spec's 295mm diameter, ventilated two-piece discs.

TR7 and TR8 brake master cylinder. This may not only help from a spares point of view, but it also offers a standard 45mm reservoir cap (which is easier to attach bleeding equipment to), and incorporates a fluid level sensor, too.

Servos

It may come as a surprise to learn that, more often than not, competition cars run without a brake servo/booster in order to increase the driver's 'feel' (information relayed back from the car). When driving 'on the ragged edge', brake servos/boosters can mask what is happening between tyre and road, and tend not to be progressive enough for the fast boys. Furthermore, brake servos, contrary to popular belief, do not actually increase a car's braking performance. They are helpful in reducing the pedal pressure required to brake, but competitive drivers are not looking for such aids and would prefer the feedback they get from an unassisted pedal.

In contrast, modern drivers of everyday cars generally enjoy the light pedal one gets with servo/booster assisted brakes, and I guess that few new cars are produced without a brake servo fitted as standard. So, when upgrading your TR7 and 8 brakes, there is little value in fitting an uprated servo/booster unless you are simultaneously uprating the callipers, discs/rotors and master cylinder. In these circumstances a servo/

UPGRADING THE BRAKES

master cylinder upgrade will be a very worthwhile improvement. The question is, what to fit and from where?

While the TR7 and 8 used the same master cylinder (more in a moment), they did NOT use the same servo. The TR7 servo has a case diameter of 205mm, whereas the TR8's is more like 225mm diameter, providing slightly more than 20 per cent additional (area of diaphragm) assistance when braking.

However, Rover's SD1 and Sherpa van assemblies both offer a double benefit. Not only is the servo/booster larger than the TR8 servo, reducing pedal effort, but the respective master cylinder (that MUST be fitted with the Servo) also has a larger bore. As you increase the bore of your brake master cylinder, you move more brake fluid for any given stroke of the pedal. However, this increases the (unaided) pressure required when applying the brakes! Nevertheless, the overall effect of the Rover SD1/Sherpa assembly is widely recognised as very beneficial, and is a standard improvement for fast road and ultra-fast road cars. Sadly, the Sherpa was never sold in the USA, but new units can be purchased from UK specialists.

The Rover/Sherpa servo/master cylinder assembly is not, however, a direct replacement for the Wedge units, and requires some modifications. The bolt holes through the bulkhead/firewall are the same, but the bigger diameter of the Rover servo/booster is likely to foul on the bulkhead/firewall – it may need slight bulkhead 'dressing', and/or a thin spacer between servo and bulkhead to replace part number CRC250. For some servos/boosters you may need to increase the PCD (pitch circle diameter) of the four mounting holes in the bulkhead, and MOST IMPORTANTLY fit substantially thick and large diameter washers to each mounting stud, before securing the servo with new nyloc nuts.

There are real benefits from this upgrade, but a couple of other problems to overcome, too. Before you get to the final securing operation you need to increase the length of the Rover servo's input shaft, so that the clevis fork reaches your brake pedals. It may be easier to talk to the various specialist Wedge suppliers; certainly S+S can supply a brand new SD1 servo, master cylinder and fitting kit for circa £200. However, check that the brake pipes exit the master cylinder to your satisfaction. The Rover SD1 pipes exit the master cylinder on the right, whereas the TR7/8 are on the left for both LHD and RHD variants. However, it appears that a Jaguar XJ6 (Series III) master will also fit the later SD1 booster, and the pipe exits on the Jag master cylinder vary between LHD and RHD, so you can choose your exit pattern.

Single master cylinders

It is easy to presume that all twin hydraulic braking systems are fed by a single master cylinder, fitted with tandem pistons and two take-off ports. The single tandem cylinder is certainly the most convenient arrangement for road-going cars, but as we'll see shortly, competition (and some ultra-fast road) cars are frequently fitted with two parallel-mounted individual master cylinders and, as we've already established, no servo assistance. However, before we get onto that rather special case it is worth devoting a few lines to the more normal tandem brake master cylinders, and the effect of bore diameter on your brakes, so that you can adjust yours if and when necessary.

The bore of a master cylinder becomes important if you fit callipers with increased piston area. They squeeze the disc/rotor harder because of the larger surface area but, by virtue of this larger dimension, will require more fluid to move them forward than would have been the case with the original smaller pistons. So larger calliper pistons are basically good, but will result in your having to push the brake pedal further than was originally the case, to dispel the additional brake fluid required by the pistons.

Some drivers may not be unduly concerned by some additional pedal travel but many, including yours truly, find it (very) unnerving! If the pedal travel was long to start with, it may be the consequence of poorly-adjusted rear brakes. We will look into a solution under the heading "Residual pressure valves", within the main heading "Rear brakes". However, if you already suffer a

2-4-1 This master cylinder and servo are Rimmer Bros part number RB7656, which I suspect to be an ex-Sherpa, reconditioned and modified for TR7 assembly.

2-4-2 An early SD1, or possibly a genuine TR8, Lockheed brake servo finished in gold. Later SD1 Girling units are black. Note there is just enough room in the TR7 for it to fit without the outer flange fouling on something. As removed from its donor, the push-rod that connects to the brake pedal is about 1in (25mm) too long for the TR7. The brake master cylinder is possibly from the same car or an early SD1, but the reservoir is from a different car, because late SD1s have a large filler cap incorporating a fluid level sensor.

fair amount of pedal travel and then add larger calliper pistons, the travel is likely to be enormous and unacceptable to virtually all drivers, not to mention their annual test stations! The solution? A larger bore master cylinder to move more fluid each time you press the pedal.

An increase in master cylinder diameter needs to be thought about. As you increase it, so the effort required to move the pedal rises proportionally – if you overdo it you could get a much heavier pedal than expected, but that is why some of the bigger master cylinders are coupled to a large diameter servo.

It may help if I quickly summarise the main master cylinder bores and their piston areas:
- TR7 and 8 – both use the same master cylinder with a bore diameter of 20.6mm (0.811in), giving 343mm^2 as our starting reference. However, SD1 used a 22.2mm diameter master cylinder, providing 387mm^2 (TR7 plus 11.4 per cent).
- Sherpa 400 – some models were fitted with a 23.8mm master cylinder and T65 servo. The master cylinder provides for 445mm^2 (TR7 plus 29.7 per cent).
- Sherpa – 285, 310 and 350 series 1982-1989. Many specs used 25.4mm master cylinder (with T65 Lockheed servo). Master cylinder area is 507mm^2 (TR7 plus 48.8 per cent).

As removed from donor vehicles, the push-rod to the TR7 brake pedal is likely to be a shade too long. There are three options:
- Pack the servo away from the bulkhead with box-section steel, then bolt the servo to the box and the box through the bulkhead. It sounds worse than it looks, because the box section 'spacer' is largely hidden by the scuttle's overhang.
- Cut the excess length from the middle of the push-rod that goes between the servo and pedal, and weld the two ends back together. High-quality welding is essential.
- Cut the excess length from the middle of the rod and run a left-hand die up one end and a right-hand die up the other. Turn and tap a turnbuckle sleeve to match. The advantage of this is that after adjustment you get the distance spot-on, with (if you choose), no free brake pedal travel. However, the thread forms and sleeve must be faultless, as the loading on the shaft is very large indeed whenever you brake hard.

Twin/parallel master cylinders

As 2-4-4 shows, it's possible to alter the front to rear balance and allow for its adjustment from time to time, as conditions require. In this Racetorations example, the normal close-coupled master cylinder is replaced by two separate master cylinders actuated by a balance bar – giving you the advantage of a servo with any combination (within reason) of front/rear balance. However, while the majority of competitive cars run with this master cylinder arrangement, most do so without a servo. Tilton makes the cylinders, though Wilwood also offers a very similar range. Both are available from Pitstop or Summit in the USA, or Demon Tweaks in the UK.

Tilton's 75 series of master cylinders are made from aluminium, and anodised to minimise wear and corrosion. You can specify a small reservoir (4oz/126cc) for space saving, or the normal reservoir taking 10.7oz/316cc. Some examples can be seen at 2-4-5. Anti-spill filters and residual pressure valves are included in both types of reservoir. The cylinders are available in $5/8$in, $7/16$in, $3/4$in, $13/16$in, $7/8$in, $15/16$in, 1in, and $1 1/8$in bore sizes, but I would start with a pair of about $7/8$in diameter (21.6mm) and move up to 1in (25.4mm) or down to $3/4$in (19.1mm), as experience dictates. They MUST be coupled with an adjustable balance bar – also available from the same manufacturers and retailers. Without the servo/booster, you will need to fit a SUBSTANTIAL plate over the hole in the bulkhead/firewall, and re-cut two 1.25in (32mm) holes at about 2.25in (57mm) centres – or whatever suits your precise equipment.

I feel it important that the front cylinder is routed straight to the front callipers, but that an adjustable proportioning valve (more soon) is fitted in the line to the rear cylinders. Seek and follow the advice of your retailer.

THE REAR BRAKES

In my view, the braking capacity of the 5-speed axle's drum brakes should be more than adequate for standard, fast road and ultra-fast road cars. In fact, many competition cars find them generally suitable. The car's tendency to lock up at the rear, and the subsequent presence of a rear limiting/proportioning/balance valve, confirms that the underlying rear brake capacity is satisfactory. However, control of that

2-4-4 This is a TR6 installation, which nevertheless illustrates the fitting of twin brake master cylinders.

UPGRADING THE BRAKES

capacity may warrant attention and, in particular, the ease with which front/rear brake balance can be adjusted.

The (UK) experts are divided over the value of this next change, but a number of conversions – V8s in particular – have increased the power of the rear brakes by increasing the diameter of the rear slave cylinders. This is achieved by replacing the original, 5-speed, 17.5mm bore wheel cylinders with the 19mm diameter cylinders from a 4-speed axle, which increases the pressure on the brake shoes. Factory practice on original TR8s was to fit the larger 4-speed cylinders. The theoretical improvement in rear braking effect is 18 per cent, but I suspect that in practice, the overall difference in braking is minimal. To my mind, this change would exacerbate the car's tendency to lock up the rear brakes, so it needs very careful thought. I might consider it were I fitting harder (thus less 'bite') rear shoes, but only if I had an adjustable pressure-reducing valve fitted (more shortly). However, the clinching detail is that increasing the wheel cylinder diameters is certain to increase pedal travel, but, unlike the front brakes, to no good effect. Therefore, I cannot see the benefit of an increase in wheel cylinder diameter, and it is not a trivial swap because the roll pins that locate the cylinder require changing.

If you want to increase the rear braking effect, you can 'play tunes' with the frictional grab of the rear shoe lining material – but I would guess that only competitive cars would be interested in this practice. The range of options is huge, but typical materials would be Mintex M20 (the usual first stop – pun intended!). Many competition cars are still very happy with M20 linings, but for competitors requiring some durability from their rear brakes, collate-metallic material is an option. This is a more

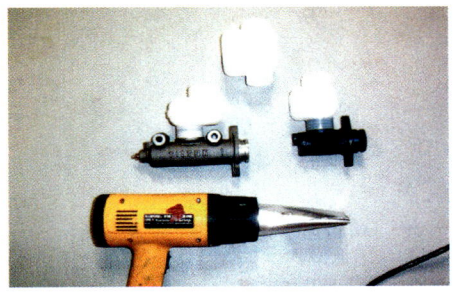

2-4-5 This picture is included to illustrate Tilton's master cylinders and also how, with great care, you can use a heat gun to alter the reservoirs to suit your particular application.

expensive compound, but offers the highest friction coefficient of any brake shoe material, and is a major step forward in terms of stopping power. It requires a rigid 'bedding-in' routine.

The rear brakes on a 5-speed axle are more than adequate for the vast majority of cars, and any front/rear balance changes necessary can be obtained by fitting an adjustable rear limiting/proportioning/balance valve. There are several ways of achieving this.

Proportioning/bias/balance/pressure-reducing valves

These units seem to enjoy a variety of names – I will call them PRVs (pressure-reducing valves). From a safety point of view, the standard PRV on a TR7 and TR8 is very important, but it is factory set and not adjustable. It is a major advantage to be able to adjust the front to rear brake balance quickly and easily, particularly after you have effected a change within the braking system (e.g. a different grade of pads or shoes). If you are not absolutely sure whether the front or rear brakes are locking up first, a video usually offers a swift answer.

Proprietary adjustable PRVs are available from Demon Tweaks in the UK, and Pitstop or Summit in the USA. A Tilton unit is available for about £75/$100, and fits in place of the car's existing PRV on the driver's turret. There are other makes available and naturally, when it comes to brakes, AP and Wilwood offer excellent alternatives. The Tilton range includes a lever-operated model, providing a swift visual reference to which of the seven reduction positions you have set. When located within the cockpit it allows a rally co-driver en route adjustment of the brake force to the brake line in question.

Another method of varying the front/rear balance might be particularly relevant once large front brakes are fitted. You can remove the original PRV completely, and connect the front brake lines directly to the front brakes. It's then possible to install a proprietary PRV into the rear line, and adjust it for maximum braking without rear lock up.

Converting the original PRV

You can modify the existing valve in two ways. If you want to increase the pressure on the rear shoes, but vary that increase from time to time, you can do that by following this procedure but leaving the original spring length unchanged. There may be a few instances where a reduction in rear brake pressure is required from Triumph's original setting. In this case, you need to follow these suggestions but shorten the internal spring by about 1½ turns (and grind the shortened end flat) before re-assembly. Note, however, that if your car is not locking the rear wheels, you should not need to modify the tensioning spring.

In either instance you need to get the valve off the car, and gently remove the pressed end-cap from the body of the valve. This is actually the most difficult, important part of the job, for you will need to remove the cap with the very minimum

SPEEDPRO SERIES

of damage, such that it can be re-used. The alternative necessitates your turning a replica cap.

You will need something pointed, with a hardened end that you can slip into the groove turned into the body at the end of the cap. Slide your lifting 'hook' under the swage, and rock the hook gently to lift each swage as little as possible, such that the cap can be eased off the main body and over an 'O'-ring in the second groove. You do not want to damage the 'O'-ring or you face finding a replacement.

Check the inside lip of the cap carefully for burrs that need to be removed, to prevent damage to the 'O'-ring seal upon re-assembly. Check too that there is no brake fluid inside the cap. Ideally it should be dry, so if there's more than a drop you need to replace the whole valve. If all is well, pictures 2-5-1-1 to 2-5-1-4 should help you convert the cap to make the valve adjustable.

To re-attach the cap to the body of the valve, you will need to take the new adjusting screw out of the cap and use a G-clamp to hold the cap home in its original position on the valve. Only when you are sure you have it completely home (i.e. past the 'O'-ring) should you use a centre-punch to tap the swages back into the groove round the body, thus attaching the cap. Check it's completely secure.

If you have re-used the spring at its original length, you will not need to wind the adjuster/screw far beyond taking up initial slack to increase the rear brake pressure. If you have reduced the length of the spring, then you will need to start completely from scratch, experimentally. Remember that once the adjusting screw has taken up the slack on a shortened spring, you will need to wind the screw in perhaps a couple of turns (depending how much length you removed) to get back to something like the original rear brake pressure. Always

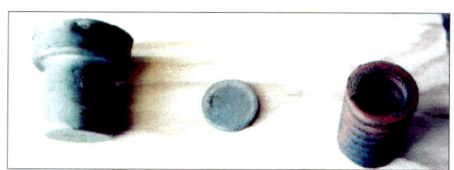

2-5-1-1 As removed from the body of the valve – the spring, cap, and disc.

2-5-1-2 A $5/16$in (8mm) screw about $7/8$in (20mm) long and two nuts will be required, as will the clearance hole seen here in the cap. The end clearance on LHD cars is limited, so choose your adjusting screw mindful of this. The cap end and one nut will need prepping for brazing/tig welding.

2-5-1-3 Centre the nut to be welded to the cap end with a temporary internal nut, and weld it. It is a very good idea to anneal the open lip of the cap to facilitate re-crimping.

2-5-1-4 Grind the end of the bolt flat where it will push against the disc. Clean the modified cap, re-paint and allow the paint to harden before starting re-assembly.

remember to 'lock off' the locking nut, even if you are just going out for a quick test spin.

Residual pressure valves

If you suffer from excessive first-stroke pedal travel, it's likely that your rear brake (auto) adjusters are allowing too much clearance between drum and shoe. Consequently, your first dab on the brake pedal is likely to be longer than you would want. The obvious first remedial stops are the rear drums, shoes and adjusters – but my experience is that a solution is easier planned than executed! The answer? A valve positioned in the rear brake line, which allows brake fluid to travel towards the slave cylinders without hindrance, but slows the return travel. This has the short-term effect of closing up the clearance between shoe and drum, and reducing the pedal travel of subsequent applications.

These are of little benefit on roads when the application of the brakes is infrequent, but an excellent aid otherwise, particularly in off-road/competitive situations. They are available but, I think, unnecessary for callipers. Off-road cars will find a RPV helpful if fitted to the line feeding the drum brakes.

Note that there are two types of RPVs – those intended for callipers (working with a back pressure of 2psi), and those made for drum brakes that require 10psi to allow fluid to pass through them. Wilwood RPVs are made from billet aluminium, and the rear ones are colour-coded red for easy identification. It is vital that you use the correct one for your application.

Rear disc brake conversions

The contribution the rear brakes make to the braking effect of most cars is 30 per cent – less when the front is diving and the centre of gravity is transferring forward. Only competitive cars are likely to fully utilise rear disc brakes. S+S Preparations has developed a very nice disc-brake conversion kit for the rear axle

UPGRADING THE BRAKES

2-5-2-1 This rear disc conversion requires the simultaneous fitting of S+S's uprated servo/master cylinder, and an adjustable PRV (not supplied with the kit for some reason) for maximum benefit.

2-5-2-2 The integrity of the welding on the two calliper-mounting brackets is paramount. S+S recommends you have it carried out professionally if your own welding is anything less than first-class.

2-5-2-3 An additional bonus of this change is that the TR7 (and TR8) handbrake, which S+S regards as poor in standard form, becomes outstanding with S+S disc brakes fitted to the rear. If your TR7 handbrake is ineffective, drawing D2-4 may help.

which it says, if fitted in conjunction with an adjustable bias valve, increases the rear braking effect to 40 per cent. Pictures 2-5-2-1 to 2-5-2-3 show what is involved.

There are two ways to get this upgrade on your car. You can have S+S overhaul your rear axle (including changing the ratio, if required), weld the disc mounting brackets to the hubs and fit the new single-pot callipers and hubs. This route may well appeal to those carrying out the ultimate V8 conversion, as the whole change over is done for you at a cost of about £1000, which I feel represents good value for money. However, if that route does not appeal, or you live too far away to be shipping axles around the world, you can buy the complete kit, do your own mounting bracket welding and assemble the brakes for £600. These rear discs are 235mm in diameter – which is not significantly less than the front brake disc diameters on a standard car.

HANDBRAKES

I have heard more than one suggestion that the TR7 handbrake is ineffective. If yours falls into that category, consider drawing D2-4; it shows how a completely reversible modification can be done to increase the mechanical advantage of your handbrake. The drawing shows an extension from 70 to 100mm to the handbrake levers on the rear of the backplate, but if the result is still not to your satisfaction you can, within reason, change the length of the extension pieces.

Before you contemplate the modification, it really would be wise to ensure none of the contributory problems I outlined in the earlier *How to restore Triumph TR7 and 8* book apply to your car. If everything is indeed in tip-top order, consider extending the handbrake levers on the rear back-plates illustrated by pictures 2-5-3-1 and 2-5-3-2.

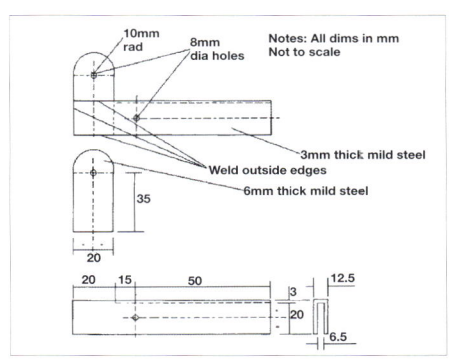

D2-4 Removable handbrake lever extensions.

2-5-3-1 If you are dissatisfied with your handbrake's effectiveness, these extension pieces can be fitted to the end of your handbrake levers ...

2-5-3-2 ... like this. The picture is of my TR6, but serves to illustrate the suggestion.

Chapter 3
Wheels and tyres

The wheels and tyres are so important to a successful upgrade that I felt they deserved early attention. The diameter relies on the brakes you have selected, and can in turn dictate what rear axle ratio you fit. The width of the wheels allows the use of wider tyres, which benefits both handling and ride. More rubber on the road will also improve stopping ability, because the brakes stop the tyres and the tyres stop the car. The wheels and tyres are instrumental to the car's road-holding, steering and stability. They can also necessitate several bodyshell alterations, and may even require changing the suspension spring ratings.

As you will have gathered from chapter 2, I think, controversially perhaps, that in today's world even a standard TR7 needs 14in diameter wheels. The original 13in wheels are just too small to allow a currently adequate diameter of front brake disc/rotor. Clearly, the designers of the TR7 were working with completely different road conditions to those of today. Small wheels were the trend back in the 1970s, possibly one consequence of BL's Mini car. Now the trend – at least in Europe – is for bigger and bigger wheels and lower and lower profile tyres. I doubt Triumph's designers could have envisaged the move towards wide wheels and the range and extent of low-profile tyres now available. Thus, as we plan our conversion, we need to bear in mind the close links not only between wheels/tyres and brakes, but the suspension too. Consequently, I thought we'd best resolve the wheel/tyre issue sooner rather than later.

As you get towards the end of the chapter you may wonder if I forgot wire wheels or 'knock-on' alloys. The answer is no. The correct wire wheels could be fitted to a standard car and maybe to a fast road car – but only for aesthetic reasons. Today's alloy wheels are far more effective at keeping an enthusiastically driven car on the road than 'wires', and thus I have not included them on the grounds of performance. Furthermore, I believe neither wires nor knock-ons have a place on an ultra-fast road or, of course, competitive car where 200-300+ ft/lb of torque are involved! In fact, once you get into the range of engine torques fitted to ultra-fast road cars, you really need to be thinking whether the five-stud wheel fixing seen at 3-1 is not essential! So wires are

3-1 The five-stud fixing is obvious, but you may be interested to hear that the holes are usually put into a 'blank' wheel by the retailer.

WHEELS AND TYRES

not even on my list of options, but we will touch on five-stud wheel fixings again when we look at front and rear suspensions in chapter 5.

The improvements modern wheels and tyres make to a TR7, TR7-V8 or a TR8 can be dramatic. I believe that the biggest single improvement you can make to your TR's handling and braking can be achieved by using modern wheel and tyre technology. Increasing the width of the tyre that comes into contact with the road can extend the road-holding benefits. This is done by increasing the size of the wheel and decreasing the aspect ratio of the tyre, as seen in picture 3-2.

You must be comfortable, of course, with the aesthetic qualities of your selected wheels. Beauty is a completely personal matter, and a subject that I am not going to discuss other than to show a few (of the dozens) of wheel options available starting with the impressive and aesthetically-pleasing cars seen in pictures 3-3 and 3-4.

Your wheel selection must be chosen with gear ratios, tyre size, bodywork, brakes and unsprung weight very much in mind. We do need to explore these details – it's hard to know where to begin. However, since stopping is fairly important, and since we have already examined the brake issue, let's start with selecting road wheel diameters.

3-3 This TR7-V8 is looking good on 15 x 7J front Minilites, fitted with 195 x 50 R15 Goodyear Eagle F1 tyres. The rears are 15 x 8J wheels with 225 x 50 R15 Eagle F1 tyres ...

3-4 ... while this TR7 Sprint looks equally good on its MGF 16 x 7J wheels, introduced during the 2000 model year. The MG VVC model uses the same wheels. These are fitted with 195 x 50 R16 tyres. Note the Rimmer Bros body kit.

3-2 These tyres have the same outside diameter, but it is clear the wheels are of different diameters. The left side Minilite is actually an early (before they changed to 16in) MGF 15 x 6J wheel, with a 195 x 50 R15 tyre. On the right is a 13in TR7 alloy with the conventional TR7 tyre.

WHEEL DIAMETER

There can be few readers who do not know that the standard TR7 and TR8 wheel diameter was a minuscule 13in. As outlined in the previous chapter, the size of the front brakes generally (and the disc diameter in particular) has a major impact upon the size of the wheel you can fit.

I believe most standard and certainly all fast road cars need 14in wheels, an example of which is seen

3-5 A 14in x 5.5J alloy with a central pattern called 'Hockenheim'. They were popular with MGB owners as a result of their open centre and a pattern that would grace any car. This wheel is fitted with a 185 x 70 R14 tyre.

in photo 3-5. This diameter allows the fitting of 273mm diameter discs/rotors. This is really quite a modest disc/rotor size – no larger than was fitted to the MGB. A 14in wheel allows for a lower profile tyre than, say, the standard 185 x 70 used on the 5-speed cars, and permits a little more rubber on the road. A 195 x 60 R14 will change the overall gearing of the vehicle by an insignificant amount. Tyre availability changes too, and if – as I believe to be the case in the US – 185 x 70 R13 tyres become less available, you help yourself in several ways with a change of wheel size.

Even if you are planning a fast road car, you may still prefer to fit 15 inch wheels. These allow for 195 x 60 R15 tyres, thus increasing the footprint from standard while not materially affecting the overall diameter of the tyre, and allowing for greater brake capacity.

Ultra-fast road upgrades need at least 15in diameter wheels, to allow for both increases in brake disc size to 285mm, and the road-holding that such an engine deserves. Of course, there is nothing to stop you using 16in wheels, but for the majority of ultra-fast road-going conversions, 15in diameter wheels will be adequate.

SPEEDPRO SERIES

3-6 This is another MG wheel – a 17in version of the RV8 pattern, specially manufactured for Clive Wheatley Conversions. The usual diameter of RV8 wheels, with the same lattice pattern, is 15in.

Competition V8s, particularly if they are heavy cars, do need the brake capacity provided by a 16in or 17in diameter road wheel pictured in 3-6, and of course the grip provided by a compatible rim/tyre width. Remember, however, that you cannot go on increasing the rim/tyre width without eventually getting into trouble with tyre contact. Bodywork is the obvious problem, though front anti-roll bars shouldn't be entirely forgotten.

RIM WIDTH

Rim width should be the improver's next consideration. Factory rim widths were 5.5J (or 5.5in) wide and, while engine capacity and available power must be factors, the intended tyre width will be the most influential in deciding your wheel rim width. Tyre widths must only be married to compatible rim widths, although there is some relationship with wheel diameter because you will find that for a given rim width you will, within reason, be able to fit a wider section tyre to that same rim as the wheel diameter increases. In short, a 6J rim on a 16in wheel with take a slightly wider section tyre that a 6J rim on a 14in wheel. Take professional advice, however, for an incorrect marriage of rim and tyre could be lethal.

For standard and fast-road cars a 6J (6in) wide rim is ideal, and should not present any wheelarch interference problems. A 6.5J rim can necessitate adjustment to the rear arch and often results in interference on the floor seam at the rear of the front wheel well.

With today's competition engines in mind, 225 section tyres on 7in (even 8in!) rims are becoming more and more commonplace. However, you will not get a 7in (177mm) rim under a standard TR7 wheelarch, and will certainly need significant wheelarch extensions for the 8J rim. Consequently, our wheel and tyre selection also affects body shape and style!

You may need to change the offset of the wheels and/or flare wheelarches to allow for wider wheels and tyres. Picture 3-7 shows a 7J wheel, and the next section explores offsets.

ROAD WHEEL OFFSETS/ SPACERS

The offset of a road wheel is the distance between the centre of its rim width and the back, or mounting face, of the wheel boss. The offset is (usually but not absolutely always) said to be positive when the wheel 'sits-out' from the

3-7 This Minilite looks huge from this angle, but is only a 7J rim on a 15in wheel.

centre-line of the wheel, and negative when the rim moves closer to the centre of the car. Offset is always measured in millimetres, regardless of the rim being measured in inches! Drawing D3-1 is drawn with positive offset and may help you picture the critical nature of road wheel offsets. I have heard the amount of space required from rear rim to mounting face referred to as 'backspacing' – this diagram records what backspacing means, and specifies several other terms commonly used when talking about road wheel sizes.

The offset is sometimes cast into the wheel as 'ET', and in the case of standard TR7/8 wheels it is 25mm. Wheels with a smaller offset will often fit. One popular upgrade is to fit 15in diameter MGF wheels, although they have offset of 20mm.

If you have a problem with the inside of a wheel/tyre fouling the wheelarch or suspension, and are tempted to fit a set of spacers, don't – or at least think twice! Picture 3-8 shows a typical proprietary spacer.

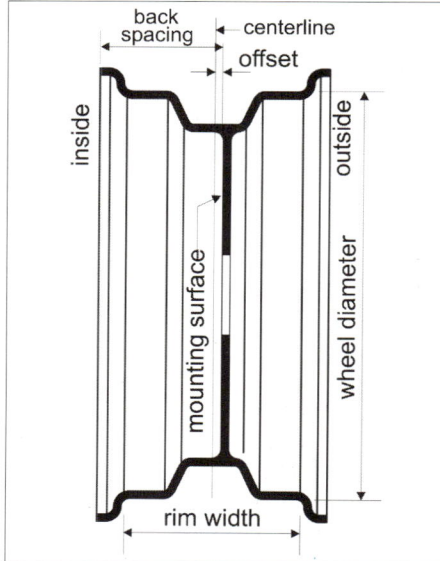

D3-1 Road wheel offsets and terminology.

WHEELS AND TYRES

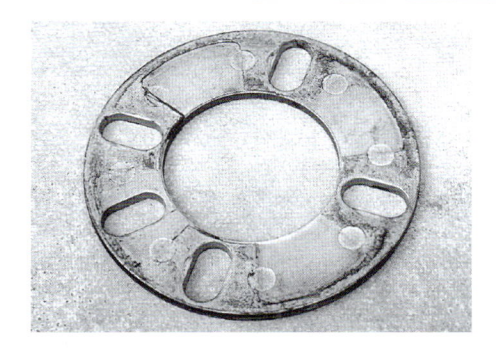

3-8 Proprietary wheel spacers come in a variety of thicknesses, but all need to be used with care.

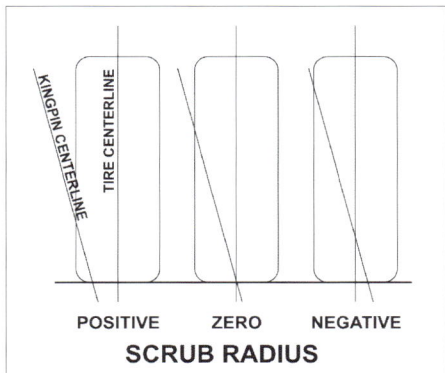

D3-2 Scrub radii details.

3-9 This nice looking Compomotive wheel with low-profile tyres is interesting for an additional reason – we can see the shape of the centre pattern provides excellent clearance for the SD1 four-pot callipers.

3-10 I'm not convinced this is ex-SD1, but it is an example of a five-stud mounted 14in wheel on a Grinnall-converted car.

The central bore size of the wheel centre is (or should be) a load carrying component, and consequently should be a reasonably tight fit on the 'boss' machined onto the centre of each hub. This is another reason for not using wheel spacers, as the dissipation of loads through this central boss becomes lost, and its contribution has to be carried by the wheel studs instead! (I will return to the importance of this central boss shortly.) You are better buying a set of wheels with a different offset to correct the problem, as spacers put additional loads on the wheel studs. Furthermore, most improvers fail to extend the length of the studs to compensate for the 'lost' wheel-nut threads!

If you are still contemplating spacers (albeit with lengthened studs!), consider the effect that spacers have on tyre scrub radii. Drawing D3-2 examines positive, negative and zero scrub radii. Short of changing front suspension struts, you have no control over the angle of the kingpin – but the width and diameter of the tyre, the offset (or backspacing) of the road-wheel and any spacers you fit can and will alter the scrub radius. You need to maintain a positive scrub radius, but don't want to overdo it! You are unlikely to approach negative scrub radius (unless you fit very large tyres indeed!), but you will affect the steering if you extend the offset and/or fit spacers, so you need to approach this part of your conversion with caution. Rather like several other conversion details, there is much to be said for using the same combination of wheels and tyres (without spacers!) as a previous successful conversion, thus taking advice from an experienced specialist.

You cannot assume your selected wheel size will automatically provide adequate offset for front brake calliper clearance. Different makes and different styles of wheel offer varying calliper clearances, as picture 3-9 shows. Consequently, before buying a full set of alloy wheels, I strongly recommend that you borrow a friend's or buy one wheel on a returnable basis, and try them on your preferred front brake setup before settling on a particular design – certainly before having tyres fitted to them.

STUD PATTERN

The fixing-stud pattern need cause you no concern if you have a standard TR7 or are considering an upgrade to a fast road car. You will continue to use the standard four-stud fastening pattern on a pitch circle diameter (PCD) of exactly 3.75in. Competition cars are equally clear-cut – the power they enjoy and the stresses they place on the wheels and studs necessitate five-stud pattern wheels and, of course, compatible hubs (usually ex-Rover SD1).

As an aside, Mark Grinnall fitted Rover SD1 struts to some of his cars, which entailed major complications with the damper inserts. They were specials made by Spax to fit to TR7 turrets, but enabled the cars to use SD1 callipers and SD1 14in five-stud wheels, pictured at 3-10. I asked Mark Grinnall for more information about his modified cars, but sadly none was forthcoming. Nevertheless, to my mind this was a

37

SPEEDPRO SERIES

clever modification, although it meant cutting the axle flange from the SD1 rear axle and welding it to the TR7 axle, to provide for uniform five-stud wheels front and rear.

Between these clear-cut extremes are the ultra-fast road cars. This is a grey area, and I think the selection of the number of wheel studs depends to some degree on the extent of engine tuning, how frequently the car will be subjected to track days, and the owner's preference. I've used a 210bhp Rover V8 engine in an MGB for 15 years but never take the car on track days, and consequently feel comfortable with the standard MGB four-stud wheel/hub pattern. Were I to tune the engine further, enlarge its capacity, or start to track day the car, I think I would want to seriously consider five-stud wheels and hubs. In short, consider five-stud wheels if your engine is producing in excess of 250bhp.

WHEEL MATERIALS

The change in wheel technology since I started writing automotive books has been amazing. The growth of alloy wheels, with the attendant reduction in unsprung weight, has effectively made steel wheels obsolete. Today it is just a question of which alloy wheel suits your needs best.

There are complications when it comes to selecting materials – while the majority of wheels are made from aluminium, there are those that are made from magnesium alloys. Magnesium wheels are primarily intended for racing, and are more expensive and lighter without losing strength. Aluminium wheels are absolutely excellent – I run all my cars on "ally" wheels.

Take care when buying wheels. If yours is a road car, specify the road-going version of any selected pattern, as some aluminium patterns are also available in a thinner racing version, which I wouldn't advise in a big-engined V8 conversion.

CENTRAL WHEEL PATTERNS

The main purpose of this section is to help you look past the shape of the wheel to its centre boss, and the brake-cooling considerations associated with the pattern. Remember the central boss of the wheel should be a tight fit over the boss of the hub. After that, you could be forgiven for thinking that the only things that matter about the central part of a wheel are its bolt pattern and whether or not it appeals to the eye. In fact, wheel design (and therefore air flow) might have a major impact on your car's braking characteristics. Alloy wheel patterns that use a thin spoke design allow high volumes of air to pass through them, providing a significant cooling effect on the disc/rotor and, to a lesser extent, the calliper. Do not underestimate the value of this cooling air flow and the contribution it makes to efficient braking.

If you doubt this, let me recount an example of a friend's MGB V8 that was initially fitted with 5.5 x 14 72-spoke wire wheels, standard MGB V8 callipers and half-inch thick V8 discs. In this form, the car's brakes were spectacularly good, even with the 220bhp V8 engine pushing it forward. However, in very wet weather the brakes proved to be too exposed, and would show a momentary dead response period until the water had been cleared from the discs.

The owner thought he was over-stressing the wire wheels and hubs, and that a change to the 6 x 14 alloy Minilite wheels was prudent. Surprisingly, this dramatically changed the car's braking characteristics, even though the original tyres were transferred and the rest of the brake system remained unaltered. The brakes became only marginally adequate in the dry, and brake fade was very easily induced. Conversely, in even the heaviest of downpours the brakes responded immediately.

3-11 Two of Robsport's wheel/tyre offerings: on the left, a 15 x 6J fitted with 195 x 50 R15, and on the right, an MGF wheel on the same size and tyre spec. Needless to say, like all the wheels we have been looking at, these have the same 3.75in stud PCD, dating back to the early Triumph days.

WHEELS AND TYRES

Obviously the Minilite wheel pattern was not allowing as much air to the brake discs and was not cooling the brakes adequately, although the wheels were keeping them dry. The solution here was a pair of air ducts made from two or three inch diameter flexible air hose to cool the discs, but it is the effect on the brakes caused by the change of wheel-pattern that I am emphasizing.

A friend's recommendation is the best way to select a central wheel pattern. I've added photograph 3-11 with a couple of very acceptable suggestions, but there are a lot more central patterns out there.

WHEEL CENTRING

I mentioned the importance of the central boss a few lines ago, and how it both centered the road wheel on the axle hub and dissipated some of the stresses. There are other wheel-centring factors to think about when buying new road wheels. Wheel nuts with tapered/beveled faces are probably the most common method, but a (possibly growing) number of alloy wheels use a plain (parallel) shank to the wheel nut as it passes through a (sometimes very) tight and precisely bored hole in the wheel centre. Alloy wheels are obviously made from softer material than steel and this allows the tapered nuts used on steel wheels to loosen over time, hence the choice of plain shank fastenings for alloy wheels. These methods, particularly if the central boss engages on the hub, will give safe wheel location and centering – provided of course, that they are properly fitted and maintained.

However, note that the diameter of the centre hole in any replacement wheels you contemplate is important. Some wheel manufacturers use an adapter to allow them to standardise their centre hole size, yet enable the wheel to fit a wide variety of hubs.

There is danger for the unwary. If you inadvertently fit the incorrect wheel nuts with too small a shank, there will be excessive clearance between wheel and nut – demonstrated by drawing D3-3 – and you will lose not only the initial centering register but also the retention capability of the system. If there is play between the shank of the wheel/lug nuts and the mounting holes, you will be relying on friction to locate the wheels. No matter how tight you get the wheel/lug nuts, the wheels WILL move around as you drive, which will wear the nuts and/or the wheel surface, and loosen them. Consequently, it is imperative that you buy and fit new wheel/lug nuts simultaneously with your new alloys, in order to ensure you have the absolute minimum clearance required.

TYRES
Profiles

A short note on radial tyre profiles is appropriate at this point. The profile is governed by the aspect ratio of the tyre. All tyres have an aspect ratio of at least 80 per cent, which is to say the wall height is only 80 per cent of the declared tread width. If you have a '175' radial tyre on your TR with no additional aspect ratio figure shown, then you may assume the wall height is 0.8 x 175, or 140mm (5.5in).

If your tyre is marked (on the wall) as, say, 185/70 or 185 x 70, you will gather that this tyre has a 70 per cent aspect ratio and a wall height of 129.5mm (5.1 inches).

For the TR7 and 8 try a car fitted with 50 profile tyres. The responsiveness will be greatly improved but the harshness of the ride will increase, due to the fact that there is much less flexibility in the side walls. It is this reduction that improves the responsiveness! 195 x 50 R15s, 195 x 55 R15s or 205 x 50 R15s are all excellent from the road-holding point of view but try a friend's car first. I think you will be amazed.

Diameter calculations

It may help you to know how to calculate the overall diameter of any tyre size

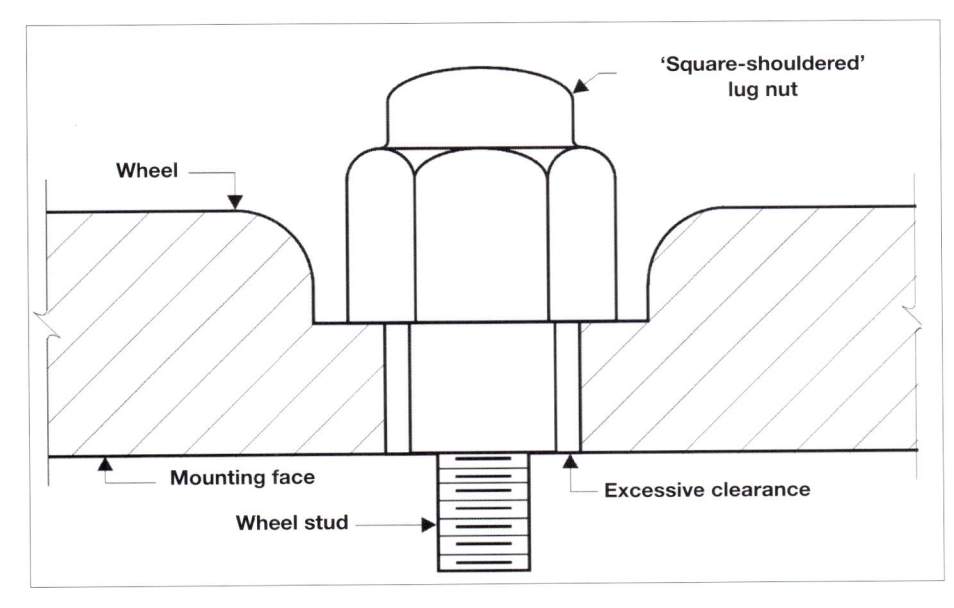

D3-3 Plain shank wheel nuts.

SPEEDPRO SERIES

you are contemplating. Not only is this relevant to the gear ratios on your car, you may find it helpful to estimate the accuracy of your speedometer after a tyre size change. The overall diameter of a tyre is 'wheel diameter + twice the tyre wall height'.

We calculated the tyre wall height earlier using its aspect ratio, so as an example let's calculate the overall diameter of a 15in wheel fitted with a 195 x 60 tyre:

15 + (2 x 195 x 0.6mm)
or 15 + (2 x 117mm)
or 15 + 9.2 inches
or 24.2 inches (diameter)

You can use the diameter to work out your approximate road speed per 1000rpm in fourth gear (note in fourth, not fifth gear!). Multiply the tyre diameter by 2.975 and then divide by your rear axle ratio. For the above tyre, with say an axle ratio of 3.5, you would get 20.5mph/1000rpm, or about 72mph/3500rpm. Keep in mind that tyre size data is only approximate and varies slightly between manufacturers and, of course, as the tyre wears! Nevertheless, this may help you decide not only whether your speedo needs re-calibrating, but whether you have the right combination of rear axle ratio and tyre size. We will look at rear axle ratios in chapter 5.

Tyre size calculators

There are a number of tyre size calculators that can be found on the internet. Simply enter the current size and they automatically return alternatives that maintain overall gearing. A couple to check are:
www.dsm.org/tools/tiresize.htm
www.rochfordtyres.co.uk/TyreCalc.asp

Note that one uses the US spelling (tire) and one the UK, and sizes that are available in the UK may not be so readily available Stateside.

Furthermore, these calculators generate all the mathematically possible combinations, some of which may not be real-world tyres!

Speedometer accuracy

A change in tyre size may slightly upset the speedometer's accuracy, but a change of rear axle ratio will certainly necessitate corrective action. Conversions using the Rover 5-speed gearbox may be able to compensate for the changes by altering the speedo gear unit that drives the LT77's speedometer cable. Conversions using non-Rover gearboxes may need to correct inaccuracies by having the speedometer head itself recalibrated, following the directions listed later in the section.

The Rover LT77 gearbox has two gears that affect the revolutions of the speedo cables. The first, a worm gear, is fitted to the output shaft on the gearbox. You will need to remove the rear cover to access, view and possibly change it. The standard TR7 (3.9 ratio axle) worm is white with 7 teeth, and carries a part number TKC 1273. The TR8 (3.08 axle) worm is black with 8 teeth. Should you need to buy one, it has a part number of TKC 1274.

The mating pinion gear on the end of the speedo drive cable came with a variety of teeth. The most frequent were the TR7s with 23 teeth, and the TR8 with 22 teeth, but the full list can be seen below.

If you have changed the rear axle ratio and wish to get your speedometers calibration back to something that more closely resembles the original, the obvious first step is to select the most suitable combination of original worm and driven gears. If thereafter you feel you need to fine-tune, here are some alternatives:

3.45 rear axle – output worm: White (7) with Green (21) pinion

3.45 rear axle – output worm: Black (8) with Blue (24) pinion

3.08 rear axle – output worm: White (7) with Orange (20) pinion

3.9 rear axle – output worm: Black (8) with White (25) pinion

If you can't get the speedometer calibrated to your satisfaction with the range of gears available, or if you are

Gear teeth	Gear colour		Rear axle ratio	Vehicle	Pinion gear part no.
20	Orange	TR8	2.85		219001
21	Green	TR7	3.45	Late TR7 and autos	219002
22	Red		3.08	Original TR8	219003
23	Black	TR7	3.9	Original TR7	219004
24	Blue		3.45		219005
25	White		3.45		219006

Speedo drive cable – pinion gear teeth details.

WHEELS AND TYRES

using a non-Rover box, you will have to recalibrate the speedo head itself. In this case, you will need to have the correct wheels and tyres on the more or less finished car (to get the weight about normal), and the tyre pressures at their correct level. Measure the rolling radius of your rear wheels – i.e. the distance from the centre of the rear wheel to the ground.

Mark the speedometer cable at the dashboard end with sticky tape, and put another piece of tape on a rear wheel. Get some friends to push you forward six revolutions of the road wheel. You can drive the car forward if it's easier with a friend counting the road wheel turns, but in either event you need to be counting the revolutions of the speedo cable. Six and one-quarter would be a typical speedo cable result.

Send the rolling radius and cable revolutions information, together with the speedo, to any recalibration shop (there are a couple of suggestions in the appendix) for a refurbished and recalibrated speedometer.

Speed ratings

A cautionary word on the speed rating your tyres must comply with to satisfy the law and insurance regulations, never mind your own safety considerations. Here is an abridged list of the speed rating letter codes and the respective maximum speed capability. You must ensure the rating on your tyres is adequate for the maximum speed capability of your car, whether or not you use it.

In the UK the following are the principal ratings of interest:

- T   118mph
- U   125mph
- H   130mph
- VR   over 130mph
- V   150mph
- ZR   over 150mph

As an of example, an original standard 3500cc TR8 should sport absolutely no less than "H" rated tyres.

In the USA the abridged list is as follows:

- T   118mph
- U   124mph
- H   130mph
- VV   150mph
- Z   over 150mph

It would be prudent to increase the speed rating of your tyres as your engine power increases the speed potential.

Tyre tread patterns

The make of tyre and the tread pattern are very individual choices. I doubt there are any poor tyres made today – the competition would ensure that such a manufacturer would not stay in business long. However, the car, its driver, intended use and owner's preferences make suggesting tyres very difficult. Also, tyre technology advances at an amazing pace, so any suggestion I make here today will likely be out of date by the time you read the book!

Nevertheless, the tyres are so important to the car's performance that you are probably best talking not only to friends with similar cars, but also to retailers in your area. Your tyres need to be considered in parallel with your suspension spring rating. A low-profile tyre (say 50 per cent aspect ratio) will have much less give in its wall than a tyre with a 70 per cent aspect ratio. Consequently, a slightly softer spring may be appropriate for the 50, or similar low-profile tyres.

You need to bear in mind the hardness of the compound, for this affects wear-rate and grip dramatically. This line of thought takes you onto the use that the car is to be put to. A soft compound will generate wonderful grip, but everyday use of the car may necessitate a harder compound, and thus a different tyre to what you might select if you were just thinking of a blast on dry Sundays. If you are lining up a few track days each year, you may need to think again about make, compound and tread pattern, and even budget for a second set of wheels and tyres – and a means of getting them to the track!

Tyre technology has leapt forward in the 25 years since TR7s were born. Today, the Avon ZZ 70 per cent profile tyre in particular provides huge cornering capabilities for the early cars, and is used extensively in historic racing and road rallies. However, they are likely to wear out alarmingly fast in road use! I was not successful when asking Avon for more details of its products, but I believe many of the ZZs are available in two compounds and that the harder one proves to be a very enjoyable tyre for fast road use.

Whether on road or track, the appearance needs to be right on our TRs, and the Avon's 70 per cent profile does indeed look good. TR7 and 8s will generally use a lower-profiled tyre such as Yokohama 032. I asked Yokohama for details of the applicable tyres currently available in the UK. I am indebted to it for the following summary:

Fast road and ultra-fast road options – A539 road tyre. Sizes used are 195 x 60 R15, H-rated or 205 x 60 R15, V-rated

Yokohama does a high-performance road tyre called the AVS Sport. If not available in your required size, consider the A539 V-rated tyre as the next most suitable.

Your choice of rally tyres entirely depends upon the road surface, but Yokohama tells me you would probably use A035 gravel tyres available in sizes 185 x 65 R15 or 195 x 65 R15. Compounds available are soft or super soft, selection depending on the length

SPEEDPRO SERIES

of the stages. Again, variables such as air/road temperature and length of stage would dictate the compound.

Directional tyres

Watch out for directional tyres – a consequence of advancing tyre technology. These have their inside, outside, and direction of rotation stipulated, and these instructions MUST be adhered to.

Caring for your tyres

Whatever the make/compound/pattern of tyre, you are best to buy your tyres at the last possible moment. Neither engines nor tyres appreciate being stood around for months or years while a car is modified/converted/restored. Tyres actually harden with age, so a tyre bought yesterday will perform better than exactly the same tyre bought a year ago. They also need to be stored upright and ideally in the dark – do not leave your intended road tyres on a car undergoing an extensive upgrade or conversion outside. Nor should you leave them on a static car in storage, as this creates flat spots which may not come out with use. In both cases fit a set of slaves. Your retailers may be pleased to give you an old/bald set of the chosen size, against your agreement to buy the road-going set when the car is nearly finished.

Tyres are an expensive and a safety-critical component, and it is in your interests to look after them carefully. If the majority of us store tyres we will lay them horizontally one on top of the other, i.e. wall laying on wall. This is not good for the tyre and it is no accident that every tyre-fitting company you visit stores its stock vertically. Keep all tyres away from sunlight as far as possible, and certainly do not store them in a high temperature location, such as the loft.

3-12 Maestro 15 x 5.5J wheels – compare the rim width with that visible in a ...

All tyres, but particularly competition tyres, need to be fitted with the bead seated perfectly onto the rim. Alloy and steel wheels with rim corrosion need to be particularly carefully fitted, especially if to a competition car. The corrosion usually prevents the tyre making an airtight seal with the rim. In many cases a professional alloy wheel restorer can dramatically improve the seal by skimming a sliver of material off the inside face (although some countries declare it illegal to use wheels "weakened" in this way) and then power-coating the whole of the wheel.

Check and adjust your tyre pressures, as far as practical, when cold. You can dramatically shorten the life of even the best tyres by inflating them incorrectly. Tyre pressure is a very unpredictable and individual variable, as some of the professional racing applications prove. Cars can come into the pits in order to get an extra pound of pressure in, say, the rears – which is enough to change the handling characteristics of the car! OK, so we are not quite in that class, but you should never over- or under-inflate as this may

3-13 ... Montego's 15 x 6J wheels.

cause severe damage to tyres and/or rims, particularly when accelerating, braking or cornering. There needs to be some flexibility too, for the best pressure will change from circuit to circuit as road surface conditions vary. Under-inflation causes excessive heat, reduces load carrying capacity, and increases tread wear that results in a loss of performance, whilst over inflation brings about irregular wear rates, rapid wear in the centre of the tyre, light steering characteristics, and an uncomfortable ride.

CONCLUSION

If you are planning a fast road car, you may be interested in a couple of low cost wheel options. Ex-MG Maestro alloy wheels are 15in diameter (with 5.5J rims – more next – pic 3-12) and will fit any of the Wedge cars, offering a low-cost method of upgrading to a larger wheel diameter. However, even more desirable are ex-MG Montego 15in alloy wheels, because they have a 6J (6in wide) rim seen at 3-13. Both wheels will take a 195 x 55 R15 tyre, but the 195-tyre width will sit better on a 6in-wide rim. I have heard of no wheelarch fouling problems, and that the four-stud pattern matches the standard TR7/8 centres perfectly. When buying the wheels ensure you get the Montego wheel nuts, too.

Chapter 4
Body trim, strengthening and roll-cages

Leaving aside restoration, there are various reasons for upgrading the trim and/or attacking the bodywork on your TR7 or TR8 – the changes necessitated by wider wheels or suspension, the strengthening needed by a roll-cage and/or competitive use, and straightforward aesthetic improvements. If it is bodyshell restoration you are planning, you will need to look at the earlier title (also available from Veloce), *How to restore Triumph TR7 and 8*.

Bodyshell strengthening around the rear suspension mountings becomes more important as the available power/torque increases. A Sprint or 150bhp V8 road-going conversion should involve little rear-end shell strengthening, provided the original material is in good condition – but this situation can change, as the power from the V8s these days can go beyond 300bhp. Those going racing or rallying will need to improve their safety by not only fitting a roll-cage, but also by strengthening the rear suspension mounting points. We will look at these issues a little later, and start the chapter with a review of the more frequently required aesthetic and wheelarch upgrades.

AESTHETIC CHANGES
Front spoilers

They say that beauty is in the eye of the beholder, but there are few beholders who like the original, blow-moulded plastic spoiler fitted as standard/stock to the original TR7 and TR8. Not only were they aesthetically unloved by many, but any spoiler is vulnerable and the material very hard to repair, therefore many have been damaged or knocked off and remained so. They are available new, but most owners would like any replacement to be a visual improvement on the original. Furthermore, it would help if the replacement was more easily repaired (i.e. made from fibreglass), and even better if it is of benefit in a practical sense by improving stability as well as engine and brake cooling.

Front spoilers can be purchased as part of a body kit or individually, and a couple of examples can be seen at 4-1-1-1 and 4-1-1-2. There is also a fibreglass replica of the BL Motorsport rally car spoiler (available individually) – to my eyes, it offers the most pleasing look. Apart from its appearance (see 4-1-2), it reduces air pressure underneath the car at speed, adds to front-end stability, and ducts air to both the radiator and brakes.

4-1-1-1 Robsports rally spoiler/scoop while ...

43

SPEEDPRO SERIES

4-1-1-2 ... sadly, this Viper body kit is no longer available as the mould tool is broken. However, note how the front bumper is included in the one-piece front moulding, which, to my mind, makes for a very attractive and practical front end. Perhaps the mould will be repaired before long.

4-1-2 A very neat rally spoiler installation.

It is almost inevitable that a spoiler will get clobbered a few times in its life. Although the instructions and the moulding may suggest that self-tapping screws are all that is necessary to secure it, I would not recommend relying solely on self-tappers. There is a good chance it will move, so at the very least you need to run a generous bead of silicone around the mating faces. However, if you should hit a kerbstone, even fibreglass spoilers will split around the screws. The best solution is to screw and (fibreglass) bond the spoiler to the car, as detailed on page 46.

Wheelarch extensions

As I mentioned in the previous chapter, a TR7 will run with up to 15in x 7in wheels with 205 x 50 x 15 tyres, provided you reduce the internal lip on the rear wheelarches. You can reduce this lip by two means. The best route is to hammer and squeeze the lip up and out, so that it lays (reasonably) flat against the inside face of the wing/fender. The lip is (or should be) two skins of material spot-welded together, and so will be very reluctant to change shape. Considerable force will be necessary, and a lot of external reshaping, filling and spraying of the wing/fender once you've achieved your primary objective. Do not forget to make good the under-wing rust proofing.

The alternative method is to grind the lip away in the areas affected by the wider tyres – about half the length of the wheelarch arc, concentrated in the centre. The more material you grind away, the more you reduce the strength of the wheelarch, and the easier it becomes for water to ingress between the two pieces of metal. Both these disadvantages are accented once you start to remove spot-welds. Consequently, it is necessary to run certainly one and, where the metal removal has been rather enthusiastic, probably two beads of weld right round the affected lip. One bead should seal the now-open 'mouth' of the lip, and it may be essential to weld-clamp the two halves together while this operation is carried out. The second bead is to restore some strength into the weakened lip. You may also find that the front tyre, when turning on full lock, can foul the seam in the front floor pan where it joins the bulkhead/firewall – particularly when reversing over uneven surfaces.

The majority of readers will have to extend the wheelarches of the car to provide full bodywork coverage (a legal requirement in the UK) of even wider tyres. There are two alternative methods here, too. Probably the most common method at the rear was pioneered by Mark Grinnall's conversions, and involves welding front arches. It can be seen at photographs 4-1-3-1 and 4-1-3-2.

Alternatively, fibreglass extension mouldings are available from Rimmer Bros and Robsport to accommodate 8J rims/220mm tyres (or wider!) – but you need to consider the consequence of full-suspension upward travel, and whether there is any likelihood of the tyre fouling the wheelarch. If this looks likely, corrective action is essential.

4-1-3-1 A Grinnall conversion always looked very smart. Copying the wheelarch extensions involves you in a fair amount of body and welding skills but ...

4-1-3-2 ... certainly looks very well balanced and gives no impression whatsoever of a modified car.

BODY TRIM, STRENGTHENING AND ROLL-CAGES

If you do need to increase the clearance by removing material from the top of the wheelarch, you will lose the strength of the lip and need to add metal and weld to compensate. I would add to both the strength of the wing and the waterproofing of the change by laying fibreglass mat/cloth over the extension pieces, and wrapping it generously under the lip of the wheelarch.

You may need to increase the height of the wheelarch before fitting the extension pieces. This would be particularly relevant to cars where the ride height has, or is about to be, lowered. It is possible that a revised bump stop will be sufficient to stop the wheel fouling the arch when the rear suspension spring-rate has been significantly uprated.

Body re-styling kits

Body re-styling kits are very much a matter of preference. They will certainly change the appearance of your TR7, although they will hardly make it a unique example. Be aware of the perception that many have been fitted to cover up a tatty/corroded body. If you are seeking to buy a TR7 and plan to view one fitted with a full body kit, examine the car with particular care. If you have a sound TR and are contemplating fitting a body kit, take account of the general perception already mentioned, and the fact that you could reduce the number of potential buyers interested in a re-styled TR7.

The fit of some body styling kits is poor by genuine enthusiasts' standards, and will necessitate significant trimming and modification to get it to fit well. Most panels are made from fibreglass, and are reasonably easy to alter and will indeed cover the rusting/tiring areas of a TR7 bodyshell if that is your objective. The fitting work involved is outlined on the next page, and is no 5-minute task

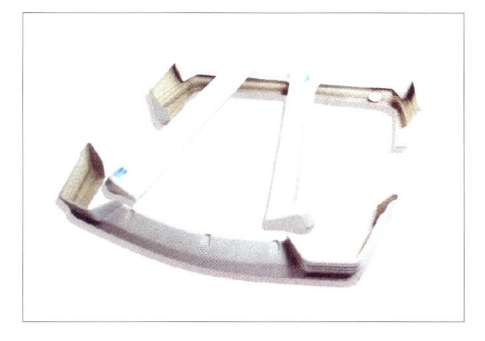

4-1-4-1 This is Rimmer Bros' MkII body kit as delivered to you. You will likely need a set of wheelarch extensions, too.

4-1-4-2 I guess it is logical to start at the front and work round the car.

4-1-4-3 This is the front wheelarch in place and ...

4-1-4-4 ... the sill/rocker ...

4-1-4-5 ... and the rear arch.

4-1-4-6 Finally, there is no alternative but to spray the car.

going right around the car. Furthermore, a good quality re-spray will be required. You may find the sequence of pictures 4-1-4-1 to 4-1-4-6 helpful.

I would discourage owners of original TR8s from considering a re-styling kit, although I would be comfortable with a rally spoiler being fitted – but not every enthusiast would agree with even that change.

Unfortunately, I have not found a styling kit that includes a rally-style spoiler. However, a re-styling kit is

SPEEDPRO SERIES

4-1-5-1 The Rimmer Bros MkII kit certainly sets the car apart ...

4-1-6-2 ... the back.

4-1-5-2 ... in any colour you like.

4-1-6-1 Rimmer Bros' MkIII kit is perhaps a little more subtle from both the front and ...

available from S+S Preparations. Two are available from Rimmer Bros in the UK, and pictures of these are found at 4-1-5-1 to 4-1-6-2. There also used to be the TR40 kit, which transformed the TR7 (or TR7-V8, of course) into a similar shape to a Ferrari F40, but that kit is no longer available.

In the USA, Lanocha Racing Systems LLC created its body kit based on SCCA Trans Am and IMSA GTO class rules. The kit, seen at 4-1-7, widens both front and rear wings/fenders, and incorporates a unique frontal panel. Their basic kit comprises front-left and right wings/fenders, rear-left and right wings/fenders, and a front air dam/spoiler, but further optional extra panels (rear spoiler, doors, bonnet/hood and boot/trunk lids) are also available if required.

Fitting fibreglass panels

There is usually an excess of material in one or two places on most fibreglass panels, and this needs to be removed. Hold the panel temporarily in place with duct tape while you assess things. Remove material slowly, possibly trimming off only half what you think is necessary, before holding the panel up again and, probably, again. When it fits to your satisfaction, drill the securing holes in both panel and car.

You can fit the panel to the car next, but it is generally agreed that prepping the panels off the car is easier. Look and feel for bubbles in the external gel-coat. These are soft spots that need to be broken open, cleaned out and filled. Rub the panel down and prime-paint it.

Offer the panel up again, but this time mark around the periphery of the panel with a soft pencil, to show the limits of where you want it bonded to the car. Clean this area back to bare metal and degrease it.

Fibreglass resin cures via heat generated by the chemical reaction between the resin and the hardener you add. If you are experienced in fibreglassing, you should be able to make up a resin/hardener mix that gives you half-an-hour before going off. If you are not very experienced it might be worth making a couple of small test mixes, because you'll need all the time you can get. Don't do the bonding on a hot day, as this accelerates the speed of setting. Whatever your mixing skills, you'll be prudent to pre-cut the bond matting needed. Cut something like six 2in (50mm) squares (two for each screw hole), and about ten strips of approximately 6in by 2in (150 x 50mm) to bond each panel to its cleaned body work. Soak the matting pieces in resin and put them in place. One goes on the car inside the pencilled lines and one on the panel. Swiftly offer the panel to the car, align the screw holes and quickly fasten the screws.

Let this thoroughly set before applying body filler to the appropriate places, whereupon, of course, you need to spray the panel and the surrounding area in body colour.

4-1-7 The front moulding forms an air dam using the silhouette of the standard/stock front bumper, and provides not only cooling air for the water radiator, but brake duct openings, too.

BODY TRIM, STRENGTHENING AND ROLL-CAGES

Colour coding
Colour coding the sills and/or the bumpers are popular changes. Colour coding the sills in particular can improve the car aesthetically, adding to the sleekness by painting the sills body colour in place of the standard black. This change is particularly effective with light/bright colours such as yellow, white or Persian Aqua, and together with a front spoiler could transform your TR7's appearance without the need to resort to a body kit.

Headlamp fairing
Mike Willis' works rally development car was used as a test bed for various ideas, including weight reduction tests. Only one car was modified in this manner but some interesting headlamp changes were tried. These can be seen at 4-1-8.

TRIM IMPROVEMENTS
Upgraded hoods
We explored fitting a new hood in *How to restore Triumph TR7 and 8* (Veloce), and consequently I do not propose to do more than touch on the subject here. However, I did feel I should draw your attention to the pros and cons of a mohair hood upgrade. They are heavier, bulkier, and attract more dirt than a hood made from vinyl material. However, they are stronger, flexible in all temperatures and do deaden wind-noise – so take a look at some when next you need to replace your hood. You will see a picture of one at 4-2-1.

Two grades of hood are available for the TR7 and TR8 from most of the UK suppliers – a black vinyl one made by the original suppliers, and the usual alternative a mohair hood made by the same very experienced supplier, and costing about 75 per cent more than the vinyl hood. S+S also supplies a bespoke addition to the normal choice, with a handmade mohair hood option. They are all made to order, and so are available in any colour you like with piping colour of your choice, but they cost in the order of 2½ times the vinyl hood. Hood fitting, at least by experts, takes about 3 to 4 hours.

Dashboard trim
Changing the trim is a very individualistic thing, and one man's upgrade can be someone else's downgrade. However, there are two changes that most owners agree enhance the appearance of most cars, starting with dashboard trim. Most of the UK specialists can provide a very nice wooden fascia. S+S Preparations, perhaps moving into the 21st century, specialise in a carbon-fibre dashboard kit. You must make up your own mind whether you prefer the original, a vinyl over-painted original, a wood-veneer or a carbon-fibre finish – but at least you have a choice! Some specialists offer a wooden insert to replace the vinyl trim around the gearshift, and also matching wooden gear knobs and inserts for the switch panel.

4-1-8 One weight reduction trial involved making and fitting these fairings, along with Vauxhall Chevette units, to replace the heavy and complex TR7 standard arrangement.

4-2-1 When new, you cannot beat the appearance of a well-fitted Mohair hood.

Seat and trim upgrades
The traditional luxury upgrade to internal trim is leather, particularly on the seats. Leather seat covers and, if required, leather door trim can also be supplied for the TR7 and 8. Excellent examples can be seen at 4-2-2 and 4-2-3.

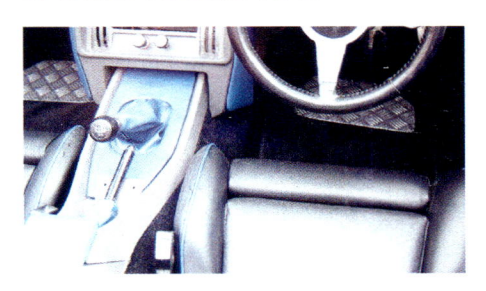

4-2-2 Leather is a very popular luxury upgrade, and here we see two upgrades for the price of one – Toyota MR2 leather seats.

4-2-3 Leather trim again – this time a superb S+S Preparations door panel.

47

SPEEDPRO SERIES

I know I am in the minority, but I find leather seats either initially too hot or too cold – particularly in an open car – and, over a long summer's journey, they're inclined to make me uncomfortably damp. Furthermore, you need to be careful with your apparel when leather seat covers are fitted, as the studs on the rear pockets of many jeans will scratch the leather in no time. As such, leather covers are not my personal preference, and I much prefer seat covers in a good cloth material.

Some aftermarket seats incorporate loudspeakers in the top section or headrest. These are a great idea for the roadster, where the door-mounted speakers are inadequate and extra speakers fitted to the rear deck are muffled when the hood is down. A cheaper alternative is to fit the cloth Miata/MX5 seats seen at 4-2-4 – which I find are excellent from a comfort point of view, and indeed have headrest speakers, too.

Aftermarket bucket seats are available. One example can be seen at picture 4-2-5, or if you are thinking of serious competition, at 4-2-6. That said, the TR7 seats generate a feeling of security, and most road-going drivers find them very comfortable. Consequently, the best solution for the majority is to have your existing TR seats re-covered. When the seats are stripped the hinge area must be checked for the usual fatigue cracks, and strengthening gussets are best welded in as a matter of routine. Any cushions that are tiring need replacing, as discussed in *How to restore Triumph TR7 and 8* (Veloce).

Tall drivers may find that the front section of the seat base is more comfortable if raised, providing increased support for the thighs. The potential benefit can be assessed by trying 1 to 1½in (30-40mm) of foam under the thighs for a week or so. If you think the seats are more supportive,

4-2-6 Malcolm Paris kindly sent this shot of his hillclimb-prepared TR7-V8 fixed head. These Corbeau bucket seats were won in a competition by the previous owner, and fitted using seat mountings from Sparco. A three-point harness is also fitted.

then have the foam incorporated into the seat refurbishment.

Carpet sets are available in a wide variety of colours and qualities. Although carpets seem more a restoration than an improving issue, it's worthwhile mentioning that closely woven wool carpets are the best route to a well-trimmed car. The cheaper 'open' weaves, as the name suggests, open up when bent over the sills in particular and give a far less satisfactory finish. S+S can also provide the very nice carpeted boot trim you see in photo 4-2-7. It adds a touch of class well above the standard card trim panels, and is highly recommended if you are looking to improve your TR7's appearance.

Electric windows

I guess we have become spoilt by the proliferation of electrically-operated windows in modern cars. In any event, I received several suggestions that this book should include some information about fitting electric window controls. The first problem to check for is whether the Wedge's window-winder mechanism is strong enough. Due to inadequate thickness of the toothed sector plate,

4-2-4 They are seen here in my TR6, and while Miata-MX5 or Mazda 323 seats are great, they're getting hard to find in the UK.

4-2-5 If you are going to do some track days and spirited driving, then a bucket seat with better support may be necessary. This example is available from Restorations Ltd.

BODY TRIM, STRENGTHENING AND ROLL-CAGES

4-2-7 There is no doubt that a boot carpet adds a touch of class to a road-going car.

they wear badly. The most practical solution – whether you are retaining manual winders or switching to an electric lift motor that drives this mechanism – is to simply reverse the sector plates by transferring the assemblies from left to right and right to left.

It is necessary to wedge each window glass almost to its highest point, and remove the four bolts holding the assembly to the door. Push the winder-handle shaft in and backwards to release the two rear pivot wheels, then forwards to remove the other pair. Remove the assembly through the bottom hole in the doorframe and mark it appropriately 'left' or 'right'. The main difference between each assembly will be the location of the spring and the limit stop on each sector plate. The springs need to be reversed, while new limit stops formed by bending the second and third teeth over in each assembly.

For those electrifying their window lifts, you have two solutions. The easy one may be to buy a brand new pair of units for about £125 (including UK delivery) from BTU International Car Parts Group, which told me that it does indeed do a conversion kit for TR7s, but failed to send any further details.

There is much more work – but maybe much more satisfaction, too – in adapting a pair of ex-SD1 electric window lift mechanisms. The trick is to marry the SD1 motor to the TR7 scissor-mechanism, and then drill some new holes in the doorframe to mount the SD1 motor unit. If you are stripping the SD1 yourself try to acquire the door wiring harnesses, the relays, the overload protection and, of course, the switches. Most cars have their electric window switches mounted either side of the central console. The TR7 gearlever seems to leave very little room here, though I understand that the last TR7/8s had the position of these extra switches marked on the back of the console that straddles the transmission tunnel – just below the heater levers. So it could be possible to mount them there, or unobtrusively in the row of switches central to the fascia – particularly if yours is a three-switch car. Your alternative switch might be from a mid-80s XR3i, or other Ford Escort Ghia model.

BODYSHELL STRENGTHENING

The front mounting points of the rear suspension arms and radius rods are prone to break away from the bodyshell, particularly when extra stiff bushes are fitted and/or the suspension is subjected to extremes in movement, such as on rough roads or rallying. Even for cars put to normal use you are advised to check this area carefully for cracks and to re-weld and strengthen as necessary. However, when significant additional power is to be fed into the shell, it is also imperative that you strengthen all suspension mounting points with additional material, gussets and seam welding. In extreme cases you may find pictures 4-3-1-1 to 4-3-1-3 helpful,

4-3-1-1 This is the how the works originally strengthened the shell, to provide a secure mounting for the rear suspension's trailing link top arm. The square vertical member transfers the load onto the heel board and floor, while the horizontal tube not only strengthens the suspension mountings, but also ties together the roll-cage, suspension, tunnel, floor, and both sills.

4-3-1-2 This is TR Enterprises' modern rally car. You will note that Steve Hall has added an additional cross-tube, and further local reinforcing where each tube meets the shell.

4-3-1-3 From the other side of the heel board: Mike Willis' works rally car's rear suspension top arm, and its body attachment point.

SPEEDPRO SERIES

4-3-2 The TR Enterprises shell has been further tied together, and the front suspension turrets strengthened by running the roll-cage forward to the turrets, as arrowed here. Can you spot the door bars, too?

particularly if you are going rallying with parallel link rear suspension in a high-powered car.

Being a monocoque design, and prone to rusting, the body definitely needs some help protecting the driver in a competitive situation. A roll-cage adds stiffness to the shell – even if the cage is never put to the ultimate test in an accident, it will increase the stiffness of the body and allow the suspension and tyres to do their work, while giving the driver a much better feel for the car.

The method of fitting a roll-cage varies from manufacturer to manufacturer, but in any event they must be installed as near the inner panels as possible. You need to weld link attachments to screen uprights close to the top of the dashboard, to the roof front and rear – in fact, just about anywhere the cage is close to the inner panels. Make sure the design you are going to use has forward bars through the bulkhead to the suspension turrets, as seen in photograph 4-3-2. These are imperative if you are to reduce weight by fitting fibreglass front wings. You should ideally have a cross brace under the dashboard to the two front cage uprights, and another welded as low as possible, across the rear bulkhead behind the seats. Fitting a cross brace under the bonnet is also very worthwhile, and can be seen in picture 4-3-3.

Seam welding as many body panels as possible is another route to increasing the rigidity of the shell for the serious competitor.

Safety structures

As you may have gathered from the previous summary, anyone contemplating a competitive car needs to focus on the type, design and manufacture of safety or roll-cages very early in the planning stage. Apart from the bodyshell itself, it could be said that the safety structure needs to be the next item purchased. There are two reasons for this comment. Firstly, the mounting points for the roll-cage need to be securely welded to the chassis and, usually, the safety cage needs to be selected such that it can be fitted into and through parts of the shell. Motorsport is regulated in the UK by the MSA (Motor Sports Association). It issues its regulating information annually in its *Competitors' Yearbook*, which is universally known as 'the blue book'. The relevant sections within it are J (racing), K (rallying) and Q (safety), with the acceptable bar and cage designs sketched within section Q.

The requirements differ between types of competition, and you need to study the relevant ones carefully. For example, if I am understanding the regulations correctly, you will find that you can race a 1991cc TR with minimal protection (just a roll-over bar shown in drawing Q1), but you need a full cage (drawings Q5 or 6) for the same car to go stage rallying! I hear that the stage rally requirement was upgraded a few years ago, when it was realised that some of the 'historics' were going faster than some of the modern cars. Probably a very wise move, and one that historic race cars will possibly follow in due course.

All material is specified within the Q section as high quality, cold

4-3-3 The turrets are strengthened in the other direction by these cross-braces. A fuel-injected V8 engine may need the brace to be V-shaped, and linked to the rear bulkhead near the bonnet catch.

BODY TRIM, STRENGTHENING AND ROLL-CAGES

drawn seamless tube. In the UK, you used to have a choice of two material specifications and respective wall thicknesses – cold drawn seamless carbon steel to a minimum yield strength of 350N/mm, and lightweight aircraft T45, the latter being preferable given that it has a tensile strength of approximately twice that of the standard cold drawn seamless tube (CDS). However, the T45 option was withdrawn by the MSA in 2005.

The welding used right through the structure needs to be of the very highest quality, and while there does appear to be an option, I am pretty certain that only a full-penetration, gas-shielded weld will be regarded as satisfactory. Great care needs to be exercised when welding heat-treated steel in order not to decrease the strength or ductility of the material, which again points to this being a job for the professionals.

Rear roll-bars

The basic roll-bar is defined by drawing Q1 in the blue book, and consists of a hoop with rear support. It bolts to the back of the floor and the inner rear wings, and adds absolutely nothing to the rigidity of the car. Rally specification bars have no diagonal braces, while race-spec bars (pic 4-3-4) are made from the same material, but have welded or removable diagonal braces. I have to wonder how protective this would be in the event of a real shunt, and cannot help but think such roll-bars would deform if the car rolled while travelling forward, when the windscreen would certainly collapse.

Roll-cages

The real improvement to protection and stiffening is obtained from a full roll-cage, built as per drawing Q5. There are two types of roll-cage – those that bolt together, a feature which is almost mandatory for the fixed head TR7s and '8s, which can be seen in photo 4-3-5. However, without the constraints of a roof, DHC/Roadsters can use a pre-welded structure.

The strength of the TR7's chassis is adequate for fast road applications, without the need for stiffening. However, any competition car will require a roll-cage for safety reasons alone, but they have the added advantage of further stiffening the chassis and thus improving the car's handling. In fact, the handling under competition conditions is vastly improved, and this must have been a big step forward in the development of the TR7 for stage rallying. Logically, it must also benefit those thinking of ultra-fast road cars.

Mounting points are on the floor at the front and rear of the doors, and the inner wings. The official mounting

4-3-4 A roll-bar in the course of manufacture. Most bars come in a choice of two widths. In both cases, the rear hoop's main legs extend to the floor. The narrower bars fit between the wheelarches to allow the hood to be erected, while the wider option fits on the wheelarches and protects the driver more, but does not allow the hood to be raised. The back-stays for this arrangement mount to the top of the wheelarch, thus minimising cockpit intrusion.

4-3-5 Safety Devices' full cages are, like the majority of its competitors' offerings, designed to substantially stiffen the whole structure of the car, and to protect the driver simultaneously. This bolted construction cage is going into a FHC car, but will transform a DHC/Roadster's rigidity beyond belief, making it almost as rigid as a saloon car.

SPEEDPRO SERIES

4-3-6 The shell's mountings for the cage are vital – note how this rear mounting point has been pre-prepared by Safety Devices, and integrated into the surrounding parts of the shell's structure.

4-3-7 The right side rear hoop is attached to the bottom of the B-post, while the rear diagonal is attached to the rear deck next to the (reinforced) damper mounting. Note also that the area below the rear window is sealed from the passenger area to protect the crew from oil, battery acid and fuel leakage that may occur in the boot following a crash.

4-3-8-1 This is the works rally car's integral approach, demonstrated by this junction of the tube that runs over the windscreen, the left A-post support and the top longitudinal. The top of the quarter light is just visible as a reference point. The roof and windscreen sections are cut, opened up and reformed around the roll-cage tube, before being welded to the tube throughout its length.

4-3-8-2 Modern safety cages are not 'let into' the shell in quite the same way, and you can see that the fore-aft tube over this door is close to but not integral with the roof structure.

details are specified in section Q of the MSA book. However, to help in what is a difficult installation, Safety Devices puts small strong feet, pictured at 4-3-6, on the floor of the car to fix the cage to, whether it is a welded or partially bolted structure.

However, even with a first class, professionally stressed, fully developed and beautifully made product to hand, the chassis mounting points are all important, so substantial plates welded to the side of the chassis rails and well-gusseted are an essential foundation for these critical safety additions. An example can be viewed at 4-3-7. Again, the MSA Yearbook incorporates several pages of requirements – both with respect to the mounting point design as well as material thickness, areas and fastenings.

The best roll-bars and cages are only as effective as the mounting of the cage to, or within, the structure of the car. Examples of both techniques can be seen at photographs 4-3-8-1 and 4-3-8-2. The cage is normally bolted to the chassis – albeit after the additional feet have been welded to the chassis to spread the stress points. Therefore, the proper installation of a substantial and effective roll-cage starts before any fittings or trim can be contemplated.

Door bars are not shown in drawings Q5 and 6, but are required for competition. Most designs fit them low (almost at floor level) at the front, slanting upwards to the rear-top of the door. Consequently, they offer minimal impedance to entry and exit and provide a good leg support, but restrict the size of seat that can be fitted. Some cages allow for these to be unbolted, but whether welded or the assembled type, they should be specifically designed not to make getting in and out of the car any more difficult. If indeed detachable sidebars make little difference to entry and exit difficulties, you are probably better with the reduced weight, fewer protrusions, increased strength and simplicity of the welded/fixed sidebars! Removable members are permitted, but understandably the assembled joints must comply with approved designs. The removable members must not be part of the main roll-bars and all fastenings must be of adequate size and material specification. Picture 4-3-9 shows a door bar.

I guess most would-be competitors will buy a proven, ready-made, professional product when it comes to something where, literally, life and death rely on it doing the job it was designed to. It is imprudent, to say the least, to try and develop these components as you go along! All UK cages should be manufactured to MSA Certification standards. Naturally, other countries have similar standards (e.g. CAMS being the Confederation of Australian

BODY TRIM, STRENGTHENING AND ROLL-CAGES

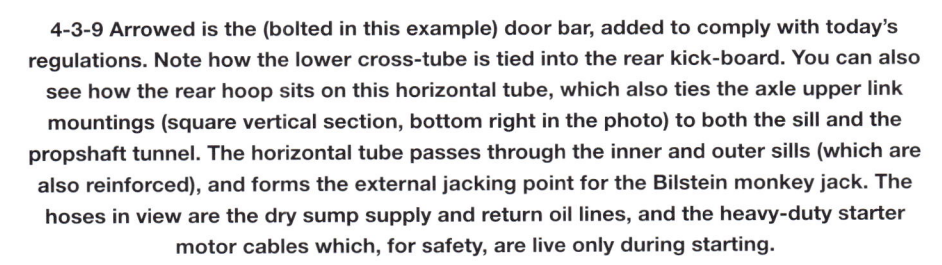

4-3-9 Arrowed is the (bolted in this example) door bar, added to comply with today's regulations. Note how the lower cross-tube is tied into the rear kick-board. You can also see how the rear hoop sits on this horizontal tube, which also ties the axle upper link mountings (square vertical section, bottom right in the photo) to both the sill and the propshaft tunnel. The horizontal tube passes through the inner and outer sills (which are also reinforced), and forms the external jacking point for the Bilstein monkey jack. The hoses in view are the dry sump supply and return oil lines, and the heavy-duty starter motor cables which, for safety, are live only during starting.

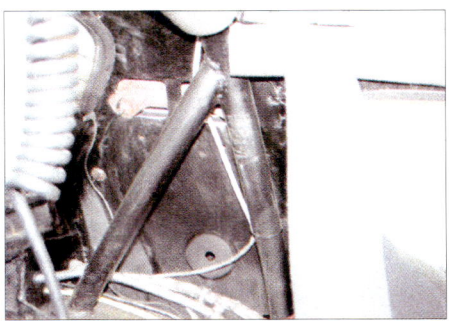

4-3-10 This shot by Neil Sawyer shows the top of the left rear hoop in close-up. The diagonal member at the top of the picture strengthens the rear deck mounting, while the grey closed-cell foam on the right is padding to protect the navigators helmet in the event of a crash. The hanging spiral is the intercom cable, while you can see the braided fuel-hose and fire-extinguisher plumbing at the very bottom of the picture.

Motor Sport) and you must get the appropriate quality assurance for your location before parting with your cash. You could well find someone who can supply a very professional-looking but uncertified product, but most such cage builders are not conversant with the latest developments and subtleties, and are best avoided.

Generally, your cage will be a compromise between cost, weight and complexity. A very comprehensive cage that is light in weight may be relatively costly, particularly if made from the best material. It is worth finding a specialist who can achieve a balance, rather than choosing one who can build a lightweight but basic cage that offers little protection in the event of a hefty 'moment'. Four manufacturers will be found in the MSA Yearbook, including the experienced specialist that contributed to this section – Safety Devices. Its contact details can be found in the appendix, and I am indebted to it for several of the excellent pictures that accompany this summary.

Padding is also covered in section Q, and must be fire retardant. Moulded polyurethane will be most competitors choice, although high-impact Confor foam can be used too, and is seen in picture 4-3-10. Nonetheless, water pipe insulation is popular as a result of it being 10 per cent of the cost! However, you are best spending the extra cash on the real thing, because roll-cages are really hard and you hit them on every worthwhile bump!

www.velocebooks.com/www.veloce.co.uk
All books in print • New books • Special offers • Gift Vouchers

Chapter 5
Suspension, steering and axles

I found it difficult to frame this chapter in light of the relationship between the suspension, wheels, tyres, and steering. Something as simple as your choice of tyres can influence the suspension's ride and the steering's weight and sensitivity – you certainly need to read this with wheels and tyres at the forefront of your mind.

FRONT AND REAR SUSPENSION

The most important aspect of the suspension on standard and fast road cars is that it is in good order. Everything on a TR7 or TR8's suspension wears, and quite rapidly, even on a conservatively driven standard/stock car. Owners of untuned cars will be better off with a standard suspension setup that is in good order, rather than a worn/shot arrangement of any sort. If you want a car with the TR7 and TR8's soft suspension (compared to almost every other sports car), then replace any worn suspension bushes with original rubber ones.

These days the vast majority of owners wish to firm up the ride and sharpen the handling from what Triumph originally planned. For these owners there is a well proven formula, consisting of fitting harder road springs, harder shock absorbers, harder (i.e. polyurethane) bushes and an anti-dive kit. The last item may require a short explanation, aided by illustration 5-1-1. The kit consists of a pair of spacers usually about 1in (25mm) thick, fixed between the front anti-roll/sway bar mountings and the sub-frame. This alters the geometry of the front suspension (by adjusting the strut location) sufficiently to reduce the car's original tendency to nose dive under heavy braking. This kit is very simple to fit, effective, and should be fitted to every car regardless of what suspension or other upgrades are contemplated. You can even make your own anti-dive

5-1-1 One half of a simple but effective anti-dive kit. This one was shot at Robsport.

spacers, provided you fit appropriate high-tensile bolts.

A full, balanced suspension upgrade requires a four-part package, ideally ordered as one kit and fitted in one session. The first part of the package involves stronger road springs all round. The original springs were soft by design (94lb/in front and 165lb/in rear), while an upgrade package will

SUSPENSION, STEERING AND AXLES

5-1-2-1 You can see the uprated version of these Robsport springs is clearly shorter ...

5-1-2-2 ... and this shot of TSI springs clearly depicts the shorter uprated spring, with its thicker material and closer wound coils (obviously on the left). TSI springs are available from Wedgeparts, and ...

5-1-2-3 ... you can see the difference on the front strut, too.

include a 200lb rating for most fast road applications. These springs are shorter than standard, some by 2in (50mm) (as illustrated in pictures 5-1-2-1 to 5-1-2-3), which lowers the ride-height by 1in (25mm). The resulting lower centre of gravity will reduce body-roll when cornering, and combined with the firmer ride provided by the stronger springs, will give a more positive feel to the steering, cornering and road-holding. However, note that with shorter springs there is a possibility that one can become dislodged from its correct location in the spring pan, so it is necessary to fit shorter travel dampers.

Robsport points out that it has variations from the standard kit to suit individual applications. Harder or softer road springs, with or without further reductions in ride height, are all available on request. TS Imported Auto in the US also sells special TR7/8 road springs, and guarantees they will not set or sag. Its springs are fully compressed during manufacture, until all coils are touching. If the spring returns to the original length when released from this process, it subsequently cannot be damaged by normal use. It recommends installing them simultaneously as a car set, because they lower the car by 1in (25mm) from its original designed ride height.

The next item in your suspension upgrade kit will be a set of uprated telescopic dampers. Robsport tends to stick with Spax as they provide reliability at a reasonable price, but it agrees that other tubular dampers perform well – such as the Konis seen in picture 5-1-3. On the front, damper inserts are required for the struts. There are varying views on adjustable dampers. Robsport suggests non-adjustable Spax on the front are perfectly adequate for road use, although adjustable front inserts are available and can be supplied,

5-1-3 The Koni damper is Spax's main competitor; the front 'inserts' are shown here.

albeit at twice the cost. They are easily adjusted on the car, but in the majority of road-going applications the owners find no need to adjust them, and most will have spent cash unnecessarily. The non-adjustable Spax are very effective, and will be completely suitable for road and occasional track days.

S+S Preparations follows the same line of thought, except it recommends Japanese telescopic units by KAYABA (usually branded KYB) because they are self-adjusting. The self-adjustment is achieved via an internal bleed arrangement. S+S points out that this helps their average client, who is not usually experienced at suspension tuning and might be unable to manually adjust dampers advantageously. For this reason, S+S chose and tested these KYB state-of-the-art dampers and found they offered superb road-holding, which automatically changes with the road conditions and how you are driving, and all without the need to tinker with the settings. Furthermore, their reliability has proved to be absolutely first class. Wedgeparts agrees and uses the slightly softer USA KYB part numbers 363015 on the front and KG5550s on the rear.

There is one detail to watch for when buying front damper inserts. Quality parts such as those from KYB, Koni and Spax will have the undercut feature (shown in photograph 5-1-4, overleaf) on their TR7/8 designated dampers. You need to look carefully

55

SPEEDPRO SERIES

5-1-4 This machine undercutting (arrowed) is important, and the mark of a quality TR7/8 damper.

at any unbranded product you are offered before parting with your cash, for without this undercut you will likely damage the centre of your top mounting dish.

At the rear (without the complication of a strut to insert the damper into, and provided the dampers you fit can be adjusted on the car), adjustable units are usually the best option. Spax require a clockwise turn of the adjuster screw – seen in photograph 5-1-5 – to stiffen, and anticlockwise to soften.

I have one thought on dampers, particularly for those contemplating frequent track days – the extra expense of adjustable dampers front and rear is almost certain to prove worthwhile.

There is universal agreement that a polyurethane bush kit is essential to augment the springs and dampers. Polyurethane bushes stiffen all the suspension pivots, and eliminate the very undesirable movement/flexing of suspension components and rear-end steering. Robsport recommends and supplies Superflex's Everflex grade of polyurethane bushes. They are a high quality and very suitable bush made in Australia, and fitted with internal stainless steel sleeves/tubes as standard. The sleeves are an important detail of Superflex bushes, as they not only strengthen the inside of each

5-1-5 A replacement set of Spax gas shocks/dampers for, in this case, the rear. The arrowed adjusting screw is located at the bottom of the damper when installed.

bush to minimise distortion, but also ensure that all subsequent work on the suspension is not frustrated by the bolts rusting into the bushes. Furthermore, Superflex bushes are easy to fit – helped by the design allowing you to fit the un-sleeved bush before slipping the sleeve in. The resultant suspension will be harsher, and the car will transmit more road noise than was originally the case, but the Superflex bushes only require a big vice/vise to install. In fact, they are much easier to fit than replacement rubber bushes. If you are still nervous or get into difficulties, Robsport does an exchange/bush-fitting service for the rear suspension arms.

S+S Preparations recommends Polybush because it can supply the bush kit in three degrees of harness. Its hardest bushes are coloured red, and are for race applications only. The most popular bush is medium hardness and orange, and is sold to 90 per cent of owners seeking a fast road suspension setup. For clients seeking the advantages of polyurethane that more or less replicates the original rubber bushes, a blue soft grade is available and seen at 5-1-6-1. These offer easier fitting than rubber, less noise through the vehicle, and more controlled movement without a noticeable increase in ride harshness.

You may prefer a more individual assessment of each bush rather than the 'one size fits all' approach used by the polyurethane bush kits, in which case the following suggestions may help:
- Front inner track control bush – a hard bush should not cause harshness, and will firm up the handling without significantly affecting the ride.
- Front anti-roll-bar end bushes – hard bushes can be fitted without any adverse effects.
- Front anti-roll-bar centre bushes – again, hard bushes can be fitted without any adverse effects, apart from slight extra road noise (photo 5-1-6-2).
- Sub-frame bushes – fit soft polyurethane; hard are too harsh.
- Rear suspension, large/front – fit hard solid bushes at the front
- Rear suspension, small/rear – use

5-1-6-1 A sample set of blue (soft) polyurethane bushes. Note the important stainless central tube protruding for this shot.

SUSPENSION, STEERING AND AXLES

5-1-6-2 We see both anti-roll/sway bar bushes here, and, as a bonus, the front-left, K-frame polyurethane bush is in view, too.

standard rubber bushes in the rear of the arm to reduce vertical bump harshness and axle noise.

Rimmer Bros devotes two pages of its latest catalogue to suspension upgrades, and in particular gives you a choice of standard, hard rubber and polyurethane bushes. On those same pages you will see illustrated the anti-dive kit we explored earlier.

The UK specialist also caters for racing TR7s. Its respective suspension kits have the hardest of the polyurethane bushes available but, in the case of S+S Preparations, could also include height-adjustable front suspension legs. Such kits can and do incorporate even higher spring ratings, but the front ones also include front turret strengthening plates, which need to be fitted on top of the turret to reduce the likelihood of belling.

A further option for racing applications is to reduce the rear ride height (and thus the roll-centre) by fitting an S+S dropped rear link. This raises the axle instead of dropping the spring.

A reminder – if you use with uprated/shorter springs be sure to use the uprated shorter bump stops, too.

Ultra-fast road and competition

There are many suspension options and opinions for competitive cars, but a generally accepted rule of thumb is that the stiffer the dampers and springs the more rigid the car will feel, and the more important the tyre compound becomes. However, go too far with stronger springs and the car may handle well, but will be uncomfortable to drive for any significant distance.

Some competition cars use coil-over spring/dampers, so that the ride heights can be varied in order to adjust corner weights. This is quite a critical point, as the balance of the car is determined by weight transfer whilst cornering, and traction during acceleration or braking. Most enthusiasts recognise that a 50/50 front to rear balance is ideal but not possible with a TR7. The best that most achieve is about 54 front/46 rear. To compensate you need to make sure the body sits about 1in (25mm) lower at the rear. This gives the car less chance of locking rear brakes under heavy use, and aids traction. When you see a standard/stock TR7 they always appear to sit very high at the rear. This may emphasise the wedge look, but does not enhance the balance.

Dampers vary in their adjustability. Some adjust for bump and rebound, some are adjustable for bump with damped rebound, while top of the range offerings are gas filled with remote adjustments, and can cost over a £1000 per corner. I guess you need to be a very serious competitor, and know what to adjust and when, to put these most expensive dampers on your shopping list.

Spring rates must vary according to the tyre you are required to use or choose. In the UK many race categories necessitate retaining a 13in wheel, but the choice of rim-width is more flexible. With 7J rims and Yokohama 1B 60 profile A048R tyres, competitive spring rates of 525lb/in at the front and 185lb/in at the rear win races. Most race cars work on the basic principal of a 3:1 front-rear spring ratio as giving the best balance and grip. Another rule of thumb in this context is the more grip available (i.e. if you were allowed to fit slicks), the harder the springs required. It is not unheard of for 1000lb/in front and 400lb/in rear spring rates to be fitted – although how the driver feels after a while on a rough track is another question.

I thought you would be interested to see some shots of the front and rear suspension on Neil Sawyer's Group 4 TR7-V8 Rally car. Many of the details are referred to in this chapter and illustrated by the frontal pictures at 5-1-7-1 to

5-1-7-1 The front homologated suspension comprises TR7 stub axles and Bilstein adjustable uprights, seen off and ...

57

SPEEDPRO SERIES

5-1-7-2 ... on the car. The uprights are attached to Ford ball-race top mounts, as were almost all the group 4 cars at the time, i.e. Escort RS2000, Vauxhall Chevette HS, Talbot Lotus Sunbeam.

5-1-7-3. The rear detail can be seen in 5-1-8-1 and 5-1-8-2.

STEERING IMPROVEMENTS

All owners recognise the desirability of increasing the size of the footprint their tyres make on the road, but also must accept that the downside is heavier slow-speed steering. There is bound to be a body of opinion that believes the answer lies with power steering, and while I agree that this is a solution, it is also an expensive one. Reducing the friction within the original manual rack and pinion arrangement is going to make a considerable difference and may, in the majority of cases, prove to be all that is necessary to alleviate the problem – certainly at a fraction of the cost. So if your upgraded car is tough to park, before you put your mind to fitting power steering, do try an anti-friction bearing at the top of each front suspension strut.

5-1-7-3 The height adjustment is carried out via a threaded section of the front strut. This is a modern S+S Preparations version, manufactured for competitive cars.

The problem is twofold. Even in the best of circumstances, the thrust rotation that occurs between washer UKC9395 and the thrust bearing UKC329 is a problem. The material that the rotating faces are made from and the lubrication (or lack of it) are bound to contribute, and maybe Delrin material and molybdenum disulphide grease would offer a marginal improvement.

However, there is a second longer-term problem in play. As the thrust bearing UKC329 wears down, the rubber dust seal UKC2043 gets trapped and rolls up slightly to bind between part number UKC9395 and the spring pan UKC5042. This causes the heavy steering and stuttering as the strut turns. A change of material and added lubrication will undoubtedly help postpone this problem, but with the present design, the potential for steering problems remains.

The short and long-term solution lies in replacing the present high-friction top swivel arrangement with a proper bearing, reducing the frictional drag when the suspension leg turns.

Strut top bearings

Probably the most important design change any owner can make to the steering is to fit an anti-friction thrust

5-1-8-1 The rear-left Bilstein shock absorber. Did you spot that the top suspension arm runs fore and aft, rather than being angled inwards as on a standard TR7?

5-1-8-2 Neil Sawyer kindly removed the left spring to give us a clear view of the Watts linkage, rosejointed axle location. The left chassis tower and brace to the right-side chassis rail are visible. Also visible coming towards the camera is the axle bracing tube, from the Panhard rod mounting to the axle casing. The right chassis rail has to be cut out and reinforced to clear this axle brace on full articulation. Routing the exhaust over such a large axle and the Panhard rod attachments presents a considerable challenge! Both upper parallel trailing arms are visible, too.

SUSPENSION, STEERING AND AXLES

5-2-1-1 The concentric TAS top ball will be most readers' preference, while ...

5-2-1-2 ... the adjustable/eccentric model is more suited to the competition fraternity, and some 50 per cent more expensive than the concentric version, but it also offers the facility for adjustable camber on each front wheel.

bearing to the top of each suspension strut, in order to update the pathetic original swivel bushing. Every other MacPherson strut car I have heard of uses some form of this at the top of its suspension struts – except the TR7 and TR8! This improvement is applicable whether you want to fit power steering or stay with the original TR7 manual rack.

There are several ways it can be achieved. The simplest is to fit a spherical bearing (mono-ball) and housing, seen at 5-2-1-1 and 5-2-1-2, to the underside of the strut tower on the inner wing/fender. Supplied worldwide by Trans Auto Sport (TAS), these products come with two basic designs of housing – concentric or an adjustable/eccentric version. Whichever style you choose, the housings will have been machined from billet aluminium in two parts, sandwiching a spherical bearing between them. The bearing precisely locates the top of the strut and damper.

Then there are K-Mac camber and caster kits (contact details for this Australian company are in the appendix). These use either a teflon-coated or a (replaceable) urethane spherical bearing. They are reputed to be very easily and quickly adjusted under load (i.e. no jacking necessary), and K-Mac says they are "essential" if lowering the suspension or fitting wide/low-profile tyres. I would certainly expect them to allow you some negative camber, and/or to increase the caster angle to improve the responsiveness of the steering and high-speed directional stability.

An alternative is to fit a roller-bearing as a replacement for UKC329. A popular bearing is used on the top of the UK Ford Escort or Sierra (in the US the Sierra is known as the Mercury Merkur) struts, which lightens the steering commendably. However, there is a major disadvantage. The standard rubber dust seal will not fit, and its omission will almost certainly lead to a deterioration of the new bearing as road dust and spray enters. Therefore, you need to fit additional dust sealing rings around the bearing. These will certainly lighten the steering, but also sit the car about ½in higher at the front – which most owners find undesirable. Consequently, these top mounts are usually fitted with lowering front road-springs. An important detail when fitting this sort of top bearing is to ensure the rubber cap is replaced in the top of the suspension tower, to ensure no water or dirt has direct access to the thrust bearing.

Finally, pictures 5-2-2-1 to 5-2-2-6 show TS Imported's very thin needle roller-bearing kit, and how to fit it. It is available from Wedgeparts in the USA, while in the UK Rimmer Bros sells what I believe is a very similar kit.

5-2-2 1 Start fitting a needle roller kit by removing the original large washer to expose the old plastic bushing, and ...

5-2-2-2 ... fitting the Delrin bush and lower bearing washer from the kit.

5-2-2-3 Next, you position the needle bearing and ...

SPEEDPRO SERIES

5-2-2-4 ... the upper bearing washer.

5-2-2-5 It is important to pull up the damper rod to fully engage the Delrin bush. Incidentally, the parts seen in the bottom-left of this photo are discarded.

5-2-2-6 Position the cone before fitting the upper strut mount to it and tightening a new main nut – ideally using a pneumatic wrench, which is almost essential. Note the twin spring compressors, which are also essential for this task.

Steering rack ratios

We have already explored one route to reducing the friction within a TR7 and TR8 steering – although I doubt changing the top strut bearing will compensate completely for the additional resistance that wide-section tyres incur at slow speed. However, did you know that TR7 manual steering racks have two different lock-to-lock ratios? The gearing within the rack alters, in order to change the amount of road-wheel turn for a given amount of steering-wheel movement. As the ratio decreases, the steering gets heavier but more responsive, particularly at high speed. The vast majority of TR7s (i.e. those built up to 1980) were fitted with a rack that required $3\frac{3}{4}$ turns of the steering wheel to move the road wheels from full lock to full opposite lock. However, a $4\frac{1}{2}$ turn rack was fitted as standard to cars built after this date. You can identify the later racks with picture 5-2-3 and the 'ribbed' castings employed at each end of the rack. This lightens the feel of the steering as compared to the $3\frac{3}{4}$ rack, but makes it less responsive to movement of the steering wheel. Better for parking, not so good for fast driving, many would say – but in fact, if you have fitted wider tyres and are finding the car difficult to park, a $4\frac{1}{2}$ rack may be the ideal compromise. The two racks are completely interchangeable, and when buying a service exchange manual steering rack S+S will even provide you with the ratio of your choice, regardless of which rack you are trading in.

Those with racing or numerous track days in mind will be more interested in improving the directness or responsiveness of the steering, and the solution lies in reducing the number of turns using an S+S Quick-Rack. These offer $3\frac{1}{5}$ turns lock-to-lock, and are available on an exchange basis, or S+S can supply the pinion on its own (i.e. no exchange but self-fitting).

Power steering

As you increase the width of your tyres the steering gets heavier, particularly at

5-2-3 This is the later, higher ratio steering rack casting, with its 'ribbed' castings employed at each end of the rack.

5-2-4 A genuine TR8 power steering rack – LHD, of course. There are very few about these days, and RHD TR8 power racks are even harder to find. At one point Rimmer Bros was able to supply a power rack for TR7/TR7-V8 conversions, but these too are no longer available.

parking speed. Not everyone is happy to wrestle with heavy steering, which is why the TR8 was fitted with a hydraulically-assisted power steering rack (seen at 5-2-4), driven from a pump hung on the front of the engine. There used to be a hydraulic power steering rack upgrade available for TR7 and TR7-V8s. I'm not sure why it is no longer available, but perhaps because the supply of the SD1 and Stag power racks it was based on is now too small to make ongoing production viable. Such kits certainly reduce the effort required to manoeuvre the car at slow speed, but they also make the steering very light at higher

SUSPENSION, STEERING AND AXLES

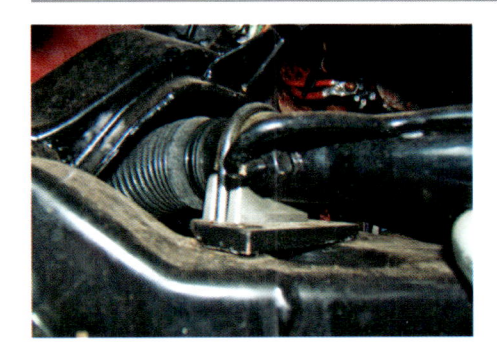

5-2-5-1 This shows Wedgepart's Maval Unisteer rack installed in the TR8 height sub-frame. It is essential to install the rack before the engine, or else the engine will have to be suspended and the sub-frame removed. Furthermore, ...

5-2-5-2 ... the close proximity of the rack inlet/outlet ports to the sub-frame and sump necessitated the use of banjo fittings, seen here.

speeds too, generating significant oversteer in a short wheelbase car like the TR7 – which can be disconcerting, to say the least.

Genuine TR8 power steering racks are extremely rare, and expensive if you do find one. Wedgeparts in the USA has developed a LHD and RHD (the latter on special order only) substitute power steering rack for TR7-V8 conversions. The lower steering shaft is a hybrid of the TR7's and a Sweet Manufacturing racing u-joint. The rack is designed to utilise the pump fitted to most late-model Range Rover V8 engines and thus, if you are acquiring a Rover V8 to fit in your TR7 and have a desire for power steering, do ensure that the pulleys, pump, mountings and drive belts come with the engine.

The Wedgeparts rack is a tight fit in the TR8 sub-frame, but bolts directly to the sub-frame in the original manner. It can be seen in photos 5-2-5-1 and 5-2-5-2.

OTHER FRONT SUSPENSION IMPROVEMENTS
Uprated anti-roll (sway) bar

There are heavier anti-roll bars available for both the front and the rear of the Wedges. The front one, which I regard as the primary method of controlling body roll, is increased in diameter from 19mm to 22mm, and consequently increases the resistance to roll by 30 per cent. I use a 22mm bar on my MGB V8s, and can assure you I get very little roll! Much depends on the use that you put your car to, but I guess that only the competitive owners will need to also uprate their rear anti-roll-bar, in addition to making all the changes to the suspension discussed earlier. In the USA, TSI supplies a competition-proven stiffer replacement bar. It is a bolt-on direct replacement, and available from TSI or Wedgeparts.

You will increase the effectiveness of your anti-roll-bar, be it uprated or standard, by fitting the central mountings and the outer attachment

5-2-6 Lower the roll-centre of a McPherson strut car by fitting extra steel spacing bushes between all four frame mountings and the chassis. One such point is arrowed here.

points with VERY hard polyurethane bushes. The competitive cars will actually be fitted with rosejoints that may rattle slightly, but allow no give whatsoever and so transmit all the resistance to roll from one side of the car to the other. It would be my suggestion that you uprate the front bar using moderately hard bushes. If that proves insufficient for your needs, experiment with harder front bushes before resorting to an uprated rear bar.

Lower roll-centre
Most owners will only fit increased depth spacers between the chassis and front sub ('K') frame to accommodate a V8 engine. However, these spacers (picture 5-2-6) lower the front roll-centre slightly without raising the car, so are a marginal road-holding improvement. The suspension is a MacPherson strut – by putting in say ½in (12mm) spacers, you lower the inner-track control arm mount by 10mm.

Front hub bearings
The front outer wheel-bearing on a standard/stock TR7/TR8 is very small in relation to the size and cornering weight of the car. This places undue stress on the bearing, resulting in distortion in the

SPEEDPRO SERIES

5-2-7-1 The standard outer bearing is shown in a TSI modified hub. Note the extra space around the bearing.

5-2-7-2 The same modified hub, now with the much larger bearing and central shim sleeve that is required. The shim needs to be secured to the spindle using bearing loctite.

outer wheel-bearing and race housing. Ted Schumacher experienced problems when racing his TR8 and solved the problem by machining material from the hub, allowing it to accept a much larger outer bearing. Modified hub kits are only available on an exchange basis, but TSI kit comes with the re-machined hubs seen in 5-2-7-1 and 5-2-7-2, new bearings and a rear seal.

THE REAR AXLE

The Triumph 4-speed axle is not suited for any improved TR7. The racing fraternity will always opt for a 5-speed rear axle, and owners contemplating fast road driving should do so, too. In fact, even the 5-speed rear axle can come apart under extreme use – the axle tubes are only a press-fit in the differential casing with a couple of dowels to secure them, and they can separate! These tubes need welding to the casing if you wish to avoid rear-wheel steering in the middle of a competition.

That said, in normal fast road and ultra-fast road use, the TR7 rear axle gears are tough and resilient and should handle 250bhp all day – possibly up to 300bhp most of the time if in good order, and provided they are not abused. There will be a minority of readers who wish to put more than 300bhp on the road, and are wondering how this can be achieved. A different axle is the solution, and we will look at that before studying rear axle ratios.

Stronger rear axles

In the USA, converters are spoilt for choice. For reference, the TR7 axle weighs about 165lb. You may be surprised to hear that you can not only upgrade the strength of the rear axle but, in some cases, reduce the weight of it, too! A short list of stronger US axles might be Chevy S10 (160lb/73kg), Ford 9in (186lb/85kg), Ford 8in (149lb/68kg) and the Dana 44 (195lb/89kg). The light weight and the legendary strength of the Ford 8in (seen at 5-3-1) would seem to make it the axle of choice, but if we are seeking a 300bhp capability the 9in crown wheel (ring gear) units are the ones to go for. Gear sets for these differentials are readily available – with ratios ranging from 2.47 to 4.10 to 1 – and relatively inexpensive. In fact, lower ratios are available too, but unlikely to interest V8 converters! Current prices are about $170 from suppliers such as Summit Racing Equipment and other

5-3-1 The Ford 8in (referring to its ring gear) rear axles are plentiful, and their strength legendary. This axle has just undergone conversion at D+D Fabrications, and simultaneously fitted with Wilwood rear discs.

mail order companies. Furthermore, Ford produced quite a number of axles with Posi-Traction (limited slip) differentials, and these are available from almost any salvage yard. The few extra dollars for a limited slip unit will be well worth the expense, as they vastly improve traction. You may consider it an additional advantage that many Fords will come with disc brakes. Failing that, discs can easily be procured at a salvage yard or from aftermarket sources.

The Ford units must be narrowed to fit under the TR7's wheelarches, but in truth most owners will widen the wheelarches instead. Nevertheless, most US towns have at least one automotive machine shop that can narrow rear ends as a matter of course, and the procedure is neither terribly complicated nor expensive. Currie Enterprises will help if you are in any difficulty.

In the UK, the choice of axles stronger than an SD1 or TR7 5-speed, and workshops with axle-narrowing experience, is not quite so wide. A Sherpa, Transit or some other rear-wheel drive van might be one starting point for the basic axle; after all, the

SUSPENSION, STEERING AND AXLES

5-3-2 The 5-speed TR7 axle also used on all TR8s. Note the various suspension attachment points.

MG RV8 Salisbury axle stems from a van's, albeit with a different rear ratio and an LSD. I think a much better, albeit a more expensive, option is to use the same axle as the TR7 works rally cars to cope with their extra power – the Salisbury 4HA model. Whether you want to narrow an existing axle, fit a different axle ratio (or both), incorporate a limited slip differential (more shortly) or buy a 4HA, the UK solution lies in Salisbury Transmissions.

Before you subcontract the narrowing work, you need to have planned not only the width (brake drum to brake drum) you want, but also the wheel-studs, brakes (thus the drums and back-plates), handbrake cable fixing, hydraulic hose mounting and all-important suspension mountings. There's no point in having standard TR7 suspension brackets welded if you are going to use one of the (even more) positive methods of locating the rear axle, which we will explore shortly.

The Rover SD1 axle is no stronger than the TR7 5-speed, but is 5in wider and has a 5-stud wheel fixing. Specialists carrying out top of the range conversions with high-output V8s use the SD1 axle (and front suspension) to increase the track width. This might be your opportunity to handle all these changes simultaneously.

Rear axle ratios
There are four axle ratios used in the Rover SD1/TR7 5-speed axles. All are interchangeable, but the external appearance is as per 5-3-2 in all cases.

3.9:1 – TR7 standard fitment with 5-speed gearbox and the SD1 2000.

3.45:1 – used on all TR7 autos, US TR7s from 1980 and SD1 2600 manual and 2300 manual/auto models.

3.08:1 – used in all 3500 manual/autos and 2600 automatics, and of course TR8s.

2.84:1 – SD1 Vitesse and Vanden Plas EFi only, and very rare.

The 3.9 standard/stock TR7 ratio should be retained for cars that have not appreciably increased their power, low-cost Sprint conversions, and hillclimb/sprint competitive cars where the standing start is the main concern.

The 3.45 ratio is probably good for road-going Sprint conversions where engine tuning has taken place, and for most race and rally cars. It gives the best overall acceleration, and at most circuits the engine should be at peak revs in fourth gear at the braking area of the fastest parts – which is just about ideal. The advantage of fourth gear in competition is that it is the 1:1 ratio that goes straight through the box, and therefore offers the least drag/mechanical loss within the transmission. V8 conversions using this axle will have an acceleration advantage, but at the expense of high-speed cruise economy.

The 3.08 ratio is much more suitable for moderate to high-powered V8 conversions, since it makes for relaxed and economical cruising and utilizes the V8's wonderful torque.

The 2.84 ratio, if you can find one, would only suit large capacity/high bhp output, V8-engined cars. V8 conversions using the original Borg Warner auto slush-box may find this a good compromise. Acceleration will be poor, but economy and relaxed cruising should be practical.

V8 converters in the US will probably find Rover rear axles with the alternative gear ratios less readily available. However, Towery Foreign Cars or TSI will be happy to oblige with the necessary parts.

The vast majority of readers will not need to do more than change the ratio of their original TR7 rear axle. But make no mistake, you definitely need to raise the axle ratio for all V8 conversions, and as I have intimated above, some Sprint conversions will benefit from this, too. You need to start by acquiring a Rover SD1 axle with the appropriate ratio. The safest and most straightforward way to get your TR7 axle ratio changed is to then give both of them to your nearest gearbox/axle specialist. You may reduce costs if you (carefully) strip the diff assembly, pinion, shims and bearings from the SD1 axle.

The extension piece (picture 5-3-3-1) comes off the SD1 axle easily enough, but thereafter you will need some special tools (starting with that

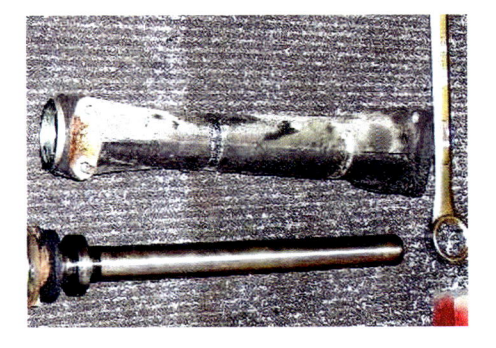

5-3-3-1 The SD1's front extension tube assembly. Note the bar bolted to the front flange. Alternatively, this internal tube could be cut in half and a substantial cross-shaft welded to the internally-splined end.

SPEEDPRO SERIES

5-3-3-2 This is the sort of aid that's essential to restrain the differential pinion, whilst dealing with the retaining nut. The four fastening studs are, of course, for attaching to the pinion. There appears to be a slight 'set' in the arm, which is not an illusion, but does demonstrate the force often required to move the retaining nut.

5-3-3-3 The (ring) spanner (left) is attacking the pinion nut, while the one-time extension piece keeps the pinion from turning.

5-3-3-4 Success brings this reward – from left to right, along the bottom: the (collapsed) spacer, the front bearing, the pinion nut, and the SD1 oil seal in its alloy housing. On the TR7 the seal and housing bolt to the nose of the axle, but with an SD1 it sits in the extension housing and should be discarded.

seen in 5-3-3-2) to help you remove the drive-flange nut. Removing the oil seal from the front of the diff casing should not prove a problem, but you are then faced with the main pinion nut. A ring spanner and long extension are essential to loosen this nut, but the main problem is to simultaneously keep the pinion shaft from turning. The SD1's discarded propshaft extension may prove the solution. Its internal spline will slip over the external one on the pinion, but you need to secure a large, thick crossbar to the extension, as seen in photograph 5-3-3-3. The pinion nut will not be parted easily, but you'll eventually be able to remove the pinion through the back of the diff and enjoy a view similar to that shown in 5-3-3-4.

Rebuilding a back axle is a unique task, which is why most entrust the work to an expert. If you have any thoughts of swapping the axle ratios yourself, read the relevant section of the official BL SD1 manual to decide if you have sufficient tools and understand the setting up of shim packs, etc. It's also well worth talking to someone who has rebuilt a back axle, as there are several details you need to get absolutely correct. For example, there are markings on the end of the pinion which need to be used in conjunction with your own measurements for calculating shim pack thickness, and it is highly likely that you will need to have at least one, possibly several, shims' surfaces ground to the requisite thickness.

It is essential that you understand terms such as end float, pre-load and backlash, and how to measure them. End float is measured with a dial test indicator, while pre-load on the pinion bearing is frequently misunderstood, and must be set between 12-14lb force per inch. This is usually abbreviated to in/lb, which could be thought of as inch-pounds, or a 1lb (0.45kg) weight on the end of a 12in (300mm) bar. Backlash in the crown wheel and pinion (ring gear) will require the use of engineers blue to ascertain the position of the pinion's contact on the crown wheel teeth, and whether a change of spacers is needed.

The next potential stumbling block is the infamous collapsible spacer, which sits astride the pinion shaft and is squeezed up when you apply the pre-loading to the pinion bearings. It's basically a tube with an internal groove around its bore, meaning it 'collapses' when the pinion nut is re-tightened. It is only intended to be used once and replaced, if it is ever necessary to service the pinion. Part of the complexity of changing the ratio of your TR7 axle is that, today, you have to re-use an old collapsible spacer, as new ones are no longer available.

There are two solutions to this problem. The first is to find and fit a shim washer in series with the best of your collapsed spacers. Alternatively, since the spacers only ever collapse a few thousands of an inch, measure both used spacers, i.e. one from the SD1 and one from the TR7 axle. Slide them one at a time over a tight fitting piece of round bar, and progressively tap around the circumference of their ridges. Measure the expanded length of both spacers in about 6 places, and when you reconstruct the pinion assembly, use the one with the most uniform increase.

Setting the pinion pre-load is the most difficult task. You will require a bar about 6ft (1.8 metres) long to wind the nut up with. It is easy to forget that you are setting the torque required to turn the pinion assembly, not the tightness of the pinion nut. Consequently, this is a patience-testing process of tightening the pinion bearing nut slightly, then

SUSPENSION, STEERING AND AXLES

fitting the drive-flange and measuring the torque required to turn the whole pinion using the flange retaining nut. However, the pre-load tolerance is very small indeed compared to the significant pressure required to tighten the nut against its single-use collapsible spacer. Go past the top limit (14in/lb) pre-load tension, and it becomes essential to disassemble the pinion, take out the spacer, put a different one in, re-assemble and start the tensioning all over again.

Once you've set the pinion, only then do you offer up the crown wheel, and the bluing and spacing process mentioned earlier can start.

LIMITED SLIP DIFFERENTIALS (LSDs)

These deserve a mention if only because of the improvement in adhesion and traction they bring about for all cars. A very powerful car can be almost un-driveable until LSD is fitted, and LSD is an absolute must for any competition or very quick car.

LSDs work in one of two ways – automatic torque biasing or clutch/slipper controls. The former is much cheaper, and is a non-adjustable mechanical gear that allows more even power-distribution to both sides of the rear axle. For road-going use, Roadster owners with high power outputs should give serious thought to this option, as it has safety connotations, too. Quaife Power Systems provides an excellent automatic torque biasing LSD which became a standard feature on the MG RV8. It can be viewed at 5-3-4, and would be the route to follow for fast road TR7s and 8s.

However, the auto torque biasing would not transmit power evenly if one wheel were to lift from the ground – as may be the case were you to do some spirited driving on track days. If track

5-3-4 This is an LSD installation in an SD1 or TR8: you can see the difference to a normal differential and the absence of planet and sun gears.

days are likely to be part of your regular activity, or you have an ultra-fast road car, you may wish to explore the 50 per cent more expensive – but adjustable – Belleville washer tensioning clutch-plate LSD.

Salisbury plate-type LSDs were the originals, but as there was only a relatively small production run for the Triumph/Rover axles, second-hand ones have become fairly hard to find. Powerlok or Gripper systems work in much the same way, in that they all transmit as much power as possible to the road/track even if one wheel is in the air, and can be adjusted to suit your driving style! Note that clutch-plate LSDs can cause understeer, and will certainly affect cornering. When the clutch operates, both wheels are locked into turning at the same speed. Therefore, the car is more reluctant to turn corners because, when cornering, the outside wheel normally needs to turn faster than the inside wheel. The good news is that Gripper has modified another model of plate differential to fit Rover axle casings. It is highly recommended, spares are available, and it would be the one to go for if you are thinking of competition.

REAR SUSPENSION OPTIONS
Improve the control arms

As manufactured, the two lower/outer control arms are pressed into a top hat or channel section. They are already more than adequately strong for the standard TR7 and low-powered TR8, but if you are increasing the stresses on them by significantly increasing the power they are required to handle, then it makes sense to use their shape to your advantage by welding a plate down their length. This 'boxes' them in. Ensure you are not creating a water/rust box by drilling a couple of tiny drain holes first, and be sure to clean the faces of the 'hat' before seam-welding a rectangular piece of steel of a similar thickness to the original arm. The strengthening can be viewed at 5-3-5-1 to 5-3-5-3.

On ultra-fast road and competitive cars, all radius/trailing arm links are best re-fabricated and fitted with rosejoints. This allows for fine adjustment of axle/wheel alignment, and takes out of the pivot points all the compressive flex that would occur – even with the hardest bushes – under the extreme stresses imposed by high-performance cars.

5-3-5-1 The first stage when boxing rear suspension arms is to clean the bottom lips of the 'top hat' sections and paint the channel, only after which ...

SPEEDPRO SERIES

5-3-5-2 ... do you weld the strengthening or boxing plate in situ and ...

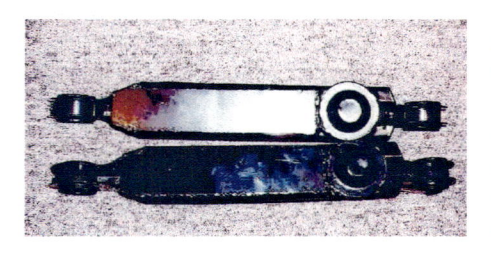

5-3-5-3 ... paint the exterior.

5-3-6 The axle mounting for the top arms needs to be re-fabricated to realign and strengthen it, and possibly to alter the ride height.

Strengthen the mounting points

There is much to be said for lowering both the rear suspension body mounting points and the attachment brackets where the trailing arms attach to the axle, in order to keep the suspension geometry unchanged. You should also strengthen all mountings on both chassis and axle (picture 5-3-6), using thicker material and extra gussets and bracing.

Remove the rear roll-bar

Racing car drivers can, of course, experiment in reasonable safety, and make their own minds up as to what suits their particular driving style and racing aspirations. There are race cars running very well for their owner with the rear anti-roll bars removed. Do not try this experiment on the road, but in racing circumstances the rear suspension links move as they wish and are not constrained by the rear anti-roll-bar, generating more rear-end traction.

Trailing arm location

Ultra-fast road and competitive cars often (probably unknowingly) copy early Aston Martins by fitting a pair of parallel trailing arms at each end of the rear axle, in order to dramatically improve the axle's fore and aft location. This arrangement is what the works rally cars used. In many cases, trailing arm location is augmented by one of two lateral restraints to prevent the axle from sideways movement.

The trailing arms would normally be fabricated from four equal length tubes, fitted with either polyurethane bushes or, in the case of very high-powered competitive cars, a pair of rosejoints at either end of each arm.

The lower chassis mounting points need to be significantly strengthened – and the area surrounding them reinforced – to dissipate the stresses. However, as the rear suspension is lowered, axle tramp can be induced. The further the suspension is lowered, the more the trailing arms slope upwards at the axle end. When power is applied to the rear wheels, these already angled

5-3-7 Thanks to Mike Willis, we can see here the chassis fixings for both the top and bottom trailing link suspension mounts. Note the access holes for the fastenings.

arms encourage the body to drop, which increases the angle and induces axle tramp. Consequently, as the rear suspension is lowered, it's advisable to raise the forward pivot point of the trailing arms. Competition vehicles should take this opportunity to have a couple of suitably-reinforced extra holes fitted above the standard position, making the forward arm pivot point adjustable. We looked at reinforcing the rear end in chapter 4, but I ask you to note that the stress of a very powerful engine, and the strain imposed by rally-like driving, caused the works rally cars to crack the suspension mounting points. The top points need to be repositioned to accommodate a fore-aft arm in place of the original angled link (picture 5-3-7).

Many will need to budget for and fit a pair of coil-over dampers with this modification, if only because the bottom spring platform will disappear with

SUSPENSION, STEERING AND AXLES

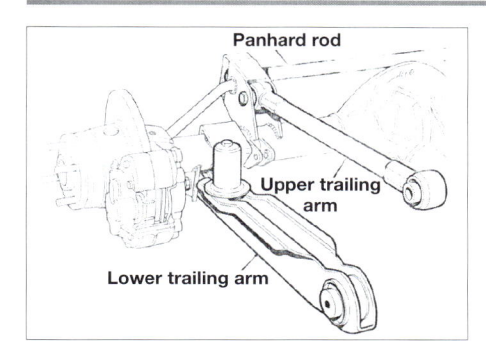

D5-1 Trailing link rear suspension.

the lower control arm. However, this change allows for the spring/damper to be repositioned directly over the axle and closer to the wheel, increasing the effectiveness of the suspension units. You will also need to recalculate your spring rates as the effective angle and length has changed.

A drawing of the trailing link arrangement appears at D5-1 and a photo at 5-3-8 (both thanks to Neil Sawyer), but you will already appreciate that the axle requires that two (each) top and bottom link mountings be fabricated/strengthened. Wolfit Racing advertises 4-link rear suspension made from tube, and fitted with a pair (one left-hand, one right-hand) of what it describes as ½in x ½in rod-end bearings. Although made for MGB cars, you might also take a look at Frontline-Costello's trailing link kit, if only to consider the sub-frame it uses to locate both trailing arms and the coil-over dampers each side of the car.

Whatever trailing link idea or kit you use, the axle's lateral location can be achieved by either running a panhard rod across the full width of the car (as seen in photograph 5-3-9), or through my personal preference, a Watts-linkage arrangement shown in 5-1-8-2. The panhard rod requires an adjustable rosejoint at each end – preferably one with a left-hand and one with a right-

5-3-8 These are the trailing links on Neil Sawyer's rally car, (just) showing the right-side upper spring mounting (spring removed), and the lower spring location trumpet that has been, in his case, retained on the lower location arm. The pivots for the trailing arms are rosejoints.

5-3-10 If you are going to use a panhard rod you will need to fabricate and brace one of these towers, while a Watts linkage actually needs two such chassis mounting towers.

hand thread, so that the rear axle location can be adjusted using the rod as a turnbuckle. One end of the rod attaches to the chassis via a small tower shown in photo 5-3-10, ensuring the rod lays across the back of the axle in as flat an orientation as possible.

The TR7 rear axle allows easy installation of a Watts linkage. The SD1 axle was located by a Watts linkage, and

5-3-9 The works rally cars used a stronger axle, called a 4HA, to cope with the extra power. It was borrowed from Jaguars (possibly the XK120) and Reliant Scimitars of the day. It was also used on some dump trucks, apparently! The other interesting feature in this shot is the Panhard rod which had rosejoints at each end. The axle attachment point is visible on the right.

5-3-11 This pivot is cast into the SD1's substantial axle cover plate and affords the opportunity to pivot your Watts linkage from here.

thus used a cast alloy plate behind the differential, with a pivot pin cast into it. This can be viewed at 5-3-11. Therefore, an SD1 pair of lateral arms and the central vertical pivot link are the ideal starting point. The lateral arms need shortening and mounting points will need to be welded to the TR's chassis, but the difficult part of most installations is completed – in a TR7's case – merely by swapping rear axle back-plates.

A Watts linkage restrains the axle well and dissipates the stresses across two chassis mounts. It lowers the rear roll-centre, yet is neutral in terms of not affecting the roll centre regardless of the suspension position.

Chapter 6
4-cylinder engine upgrades

UPGRADING THE ORIGINAL 8-VALVE ENGINE

There are relatively few tuning upgrades for the original TR7 engine. Certainly there are examples of gas-flowed cylinder heads, high-lift camshafts and twin Weber carburation on a standard 8-valve engine, shown in photograph 6-1-1, but those who are serious about a worthwhile increase in performance feel that the Sprint engine is a much better starting point. The fact there are relatively few 8-valve tuning parts available perhaps tells us something about its potential. Nevertheless, we should explore what is available to those wishing to retain their standard powerplant.

Standard 8-valve engine upgrades

Any engine tuner can add power to almost any engine, but inevitably the car will lose tractability and/or driveability;

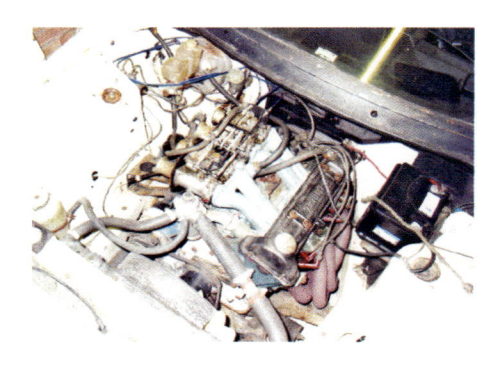

6-1-1 This great shot of a 'hot' 8-valve engine displays the pair of Weber DCOE 40 carburettors and free-flowing tubular exhaust perfectly. Note the intake trumpets on the Webers, the early expansion bottle, and the original mechanical fan.

thus engine tuning without any increase in capacity is always a compromise. Tuners have to be particularly careful with the TR7 engine, as it is fairly lumpy to start with and anything too drastic will make the car very unpleasant to drive. This is probably the reason behind the

6-1-2-1 A close-up of a different tubular exhaust manifold in situ, with an impressive balanced 4 into 2 into 1 arrangement ...

TR7 having fewer tuning accessories on the market than many other models.
Consequently, the most common upgrades for the standard 4-cylinder 8-valve engine are a few fairly modest 'bolt-on' parts. These usually focus on improved breathing via a stainless steel, free-flowing tubular replacement (seen at 6-1-2-1 and 6-1-2-2) for the original cast iron exhaust manifold and slightly restrictive exhaust system. The

4-CYLINDER ENGINE UPGRADES

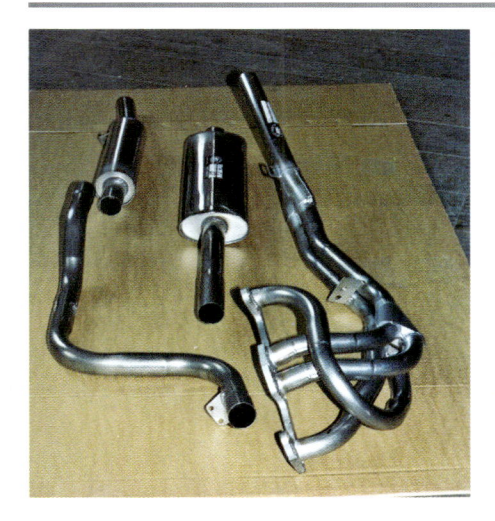

6-1-2-2 ... seen here in this S+S Preparations system.

6-1-3 The popular K+N air filters are used on 8- and 16-valve engines.

carburettor breathing is also attended to using a pair of K+N air filters (picture 6-1-3), and the essential richer needles for the carburettors – BAL size being the ones usually fitted as part of this upgrade. The manufacturers of these various bolt-on goodies claim that they each add about 5bhp to the engine's output. This should increase the power available from 105bhp (from an original engine in good condition and a reasonable state of tune) to 115bhp. These engines should also rev a little easier than the original power-plants.

Hardly an upgrade in the normal sense of the word, but one of the most frequent solutions for bad-running/missing TR7 engines is the plugs. NGK BP5ES are the best grade for a TR7 – and can transform most engines in a few minutes.

A 'spin-on' oil filter may not increase the engine's short-term performance, but makes for much easier and cleaner oil-changes. If you fit the larger type of spin-on filter it will increase the filtration area available, thus aiding longevity. The original oil filter has a throwaway felt or paper element held inside the cylindrical case. The 'spin-on' arrangement utilises a modern canister type of filter, where you unscrew and replace the whole filter and its outer case when it comes time to change it.

This upgrade is achieved by fitting an adapter to the engine pictured at 6-1-4-1, and using modern filters shown at 6-1-4-2. Thereafter, the adapter remains in situ, allowing the actual filters to be screwed (and subsequently unscrewed) from this adapter. You will need a 26mm socket to fit it, so check you have one before starting this job. Watch you get all the original lip-seal from its recess before you fit your adapter.

Electronic ignition is a further recommended upgrade. Piranha/Newtronic systems are particularly recommended, partly due to their excellent performance. Furthermore, its system currently replaces the whole base-plate within the distributor, leaving you with the option of keeping the old base-plate, contact breakers and condenser as an emergency stand-by. Note that a number of distributors were used on the TR7, the Delco Remy, the Lucas with centrifugal advance and vacuum retard and the Lucas with centrifugal advance only. Similarly, there are different static and dynamic timings, so take advice if selecting an alternative distributor (picture 6-1-5).

6-1-4-1 Robsport's spin-on oil filter kit can be used with ...

6-1-4-2 ... a wide range of filters. These are Ford Escort EFL500 and EFL 600. The longer version may only be suited to LHD, cars as the steering shaft on RHD cars may prove a problem.

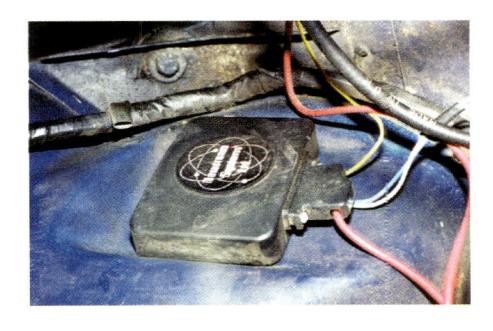

6-1-5 There are numerous other manufacturers of excellent ignition upgrades, but Newtronic seen here is highly regarded.

Subsequent 8-valve upgrades

S+S Preparations feels it can provide two further stages of tuning for a standard TR7 engine. Needless to say, the bottom end of the engine needs to be in correspondingly good condition.

SPEEDPRO SERIES

Owners with tired engines should remember that any improvements at the top of the engine adds stress to the bottom, and that any significant wear at the bottom will be revealed quite swiftly by bearing failures. That said, an engine in good shape will handle 130bhp – consequently, S+S offers its top of the range tuning kits as follows:

Its 'Supertune stage 2' kit comprises the basic upgrade described above, plus an exchange 8-valve cylinder head with unleaded valves/seats and ported and polished inlet and exhaust tracts. This further increases the revs available and boosts the power to 120bhp (pic 6-1-6).

S+S also offers its Supertune stage 3 kit, comprised of the basic first stage plus a fast road cam. The cylinder head is (still) ported and polished, but also fitted with enlarged valves, stronger valve springs, and modifications to increase the compression ratio. S+S claims that the engine is a little more lumpy, but still very drivable if the driver is prepared to make good use of the gearbox and release the engine's full potential of 130bhp.

However, unless you are into 'originality', to my mind there seems no point in spending money on refurbishing or upgrading an 8-valve unit, when the far superior 16-valve alternative is easy to acquire and fit.

SPRINT (16-VALVE) ENGINE UPGRADES
Introduction to the 16-valve engine

The 16-valve twin carburettor Sprint engine was introduced to the Triumph Dolomite in the early 1970s. Like several contemporary BL designs (e.g. the Mini), it was well ahead of its time, primarily in this case by utilising the breathing advantages of four valves per cylinder. Today this is something we take very much for granted, but in the early 1970s it was groundbreaking thinking in a volume engine.

The TR7 Sprint's uniquely-designed cylinder head can be seen at picture 6-2-1. It allows for easy maintenance and was adapted by BL from the slanted, 4-cylinder Dolomite engine. The block was also bored out to that of the TR7, and fitted with high compression pistons that gave the Dolomite 2 litres and enhanced power. Thus an excellent engine was born. The only things that subsequent operation has taught enthusiasts to be aware of are the high water pump, lubrication of the jack-shaft and radiator weaknesses. So be alert for signs of overheating, which can lead to head warping if not corrected quickly.

Unsurprisingly, early TR7 production plans included offering the 16-valve engine option seen at 6-2-2. The option was to be called TR7 Sprint, in line with the Dolomite Sprint's name. Opinions vary slightly as to how many pre-production units were made, 40 being about the average mentioned, but it is virtually unanimous that all were fixed head coupés released in 1977. Although otherwise identical to the Dolomite Sprint, the manifold exits at approximately 45 degrees, necessitating a new TR7 Sprint manifold similar to that shown in 6-2-3 before the engine will power a TR7.

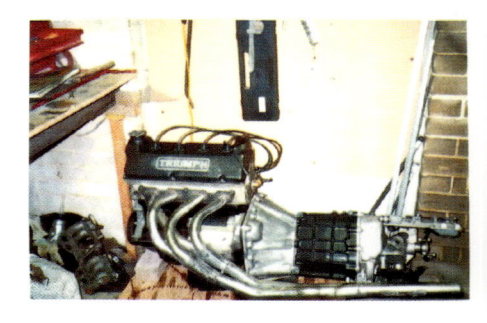

The Sprint version of this Triumph cylinder block generates 127bhp in the 'Dolly-Sprint', as it is affectionately

6-1-6 This S+S Preparations gas-flowed cylinder head will make an important contribution to better performance.

6-2-1 The Sprint's cylinder head with its 4 valves per cylinder, single camshaft and separate rocker shaft was ahead of its time. The inlet valves are opened directly via cam buckets while the exhaust valves use rockers to open them.

6-2-2 The original Sprint can be identified by the unique cam cover on view here and the cast iron exhaust manifold with twin vertical down-pipes – which is not in shot.

6-2-3 The unavoidable purchase when transferring a Dolomite Sprint engine to the TR7 is a new Sprint exhaust manifold.

4-CYLINDER ENGINE UPGRADES

6-2-4 Remove the 8-valve engine and gearbox in one – note the fan was removed before lifting began.

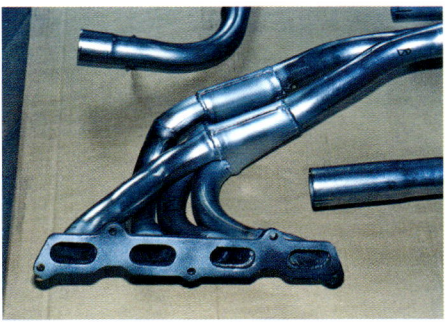

6-2-5 The TR7 Sprint's stainless manifold is readily available from most TR7 specialists. This one was photographed at S+S Preparations.

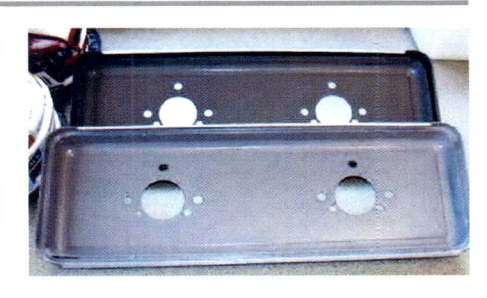

6-2-6-1 Part of an original TR7 Sprint air filter best replaced by ...

6-2-6-2 ... a pair of modern, low resistance filters, such as these K+Ns.

known. This increases to about 135bhp upon transfer to a TR7, courtesy of an improved exhaust manifold. Another contributor to this increase in horsepower is an electric fan – few Sprint conversions take place using the original Sprint viscous fan. The final contributor would be to incorporate electronic ignition as part of the upgrade, more for the reliability benefits than anything else.

Just to encourage you further, consider that the original Dolomite Sprints were listed as providing 135bhp, and consequently badged as Dolomite 135s. This power rating was reduced, however, reportedly because BL could not maintain the tight manufacturing procedures required to ensure every car met its specification. Nevertheless, it would not be unreasonable to assume that some Dolly Sprints pushed out 135bhp when new, and that with careful rebuilding almost any engine in standard tune should be able to provide that figure at the flywheel.

Most of us welcome the idea of extra power, so what is involved in the changeover?

This is basically an engine change, involving pulling the engine shown at 6-2-4. So if your 8-valve TR7 engine is tired, this is definitely one solution you should seriously consider. Note that this upgrade brings you into the same power band as an original TR8, but for a fraction of the cost, effort and time. Please note – you must upgrade the brakes before embarking on this increase in power.

There are three routes to the upgrade – we'll look at each in turn, but if you still have a 4-speed gearbox, upgrade to the sturdier 5-speed unit as you need one in place first.

Fitting a 16-valve – method 1

Your quickest and cheapest method is to buy a complete, rusted, Triumph Dolomite Sprint, and remove the full engine including distributor, manifolds, carbs, etc. The engine is available for about £150 in the UK, but if a Dolly Sprint engine is hard to find it's worth looking at some rusted or scrapped TR7s – you may just find one fitted with a Sprint engine. However, the more usual starting point is a rusted Dolly Sprint, so keep in mind that the Dolly's fan-unit is different and you either need to leave it behind or remove it once the engine is out of the car. The Dolly's fan assembly should be either replaced with your original TR7 viscous fan-unit or, better yet, replaced with a new electric fan. The only other additional part that is required by the Sprint TR7 that cannot be sourced from a Dolomite Sprint is the TR's exhaust manifold, seen at 6-2-5.

It would be prudent to change the clutch components with the engine separated from your gearbox. The majority of aftermarket clutches use one replacement unit for both 4- and 5-speed clutches, with the result that often the clutch bites right at the bottom of the pedal travel. Consequently, first and reverse gears are difficult to engage, so if you are offered a common clutch set this is probably best avoided. Borg and Beck are widely regarded as the best clutches for a TR7 – although it is important to stress which gearbox (i.e. 4 or 5-speed) you are using so that the correct spring rate is provided.

Few enthusiasts will go to all this trouble without wanting to make the most of their new engine's performance – in which case replacing the standard air filter (pictured at 6-2-6-1) with a pair

SPEEDPRO SERIES

of K+N air filters pictured at 6-2-6-2 and new, richer, BBT needles is the way to go. Note that these needles are only appropriate for a 16-valve engine with a free-flowing tubular exhaust manifold and K+N air filters.

A few more tips:
- Discard the Dolly's engine mountings and use your original TR7 engine mountings.
- Probably the most difficult part of the conversion is connecting the Sprint's cooling hoses into the TR7's heater. The 8-valve engine has a spigot on the plate at the back of the cylinder head, but the Dolly Sprint has a plain plate and an 'H' coupling within the rear pipe routes. You are probably best buying a new TR7 Sprint water transfer housing (which is available), and fitting it to the rear of the head before you put the engine in the car. However, it is possible to adapt the Sprint's ½in diameter pipe to the 7's ⅝in pipe using a 'step-up' adapter.
- You will have to re-use the TR7's original thermostat cover, identified in 6-2-7.
- The front pulley and timing plate from the TR7 and Dolly Sprint appear the same but have slightly different offsets, and the pairs must not be mixed. This comes about because the Sprint fan assembly is shorter than the 8-valve's. Either pair will actually fit a TR7 Sprint, but the TR7 8-valve pulley and plate are more readily available and are best re-used.

6-2-7 This fairly close view of the Sprint engine shows the top hose arrangement and thermostat housing.

- Unfortunately, the normal UK spec TR7 distributor will not fit under the Dolly Sprint's inlet manifold, so you have to fit the Dolly's Lucas 44D4 distributor, even though the most basic spares are hard to find.
- The Sprint's gearbox has an overdrive/fifth gear. It is heavier and more complex than the TR7's 5-speed box, and thus will hold few attractions for you.
- You will re-use your TR7 flywheel but this is surely the moment to have it refaced and, possibly, lightened by a kilo/2lb.
- Overheating is not unheard of with a Sprint engine, but all should be well if your original TR7 cooling system is in good condition and the Sprint tuning is correctly set. If either is questionable, resolve the problem. You are well advised to fit the most powerful (in cfm terms) 12in (300mm) diameter electric fan you can find.

Fitting a 16-valve – method 2

Most of the UK's TR7 specialists can supply a reconditioned Sprint engine using your ex-TR7 engine as the trade-in or core unit.

S+S can also provide what it describes as a full conversion kit for a TR7. It is about £2500, but is comprehensive in that it not only includes a fully reconditioned 16-valve 'unleaded' engine, but also a rebuilt Sprint distributor, fabricated exhaust manifold, stainless steel sports exhaust system, a (second-hand) inlet manifold, carburettors, K+N air filters, and a vented disc brake kit. You are only required to return your ex-TR7 8-valve engine and carburettors. Its 'unleaded' conversion includes phosphor-bronze internal sleeving for the valve guides. S+S believes it preferable to bore and sleeve the existing valve guides in situ, rather than risk taking a sliver off the aluminium head by pressing the worn guides out and putting new ones in their place. The new guide has an oil-retaining spiral for superior lubrication.

S+S Preparations also offers a part-exchange deal with two upgrade options:

Stage one comprises the above engine but with a ported and polished cylinder head, generating 150bhp and adding £400 + VAT to your bill.

Stage two still includes the ported head, but increases the output to about 160bhp with the addition of a performance camshaft and appropriate valve springs. This level of tune adds about £500 to the cost of your engine.

However, as I understand it, www.rimmerbros.co.uk can supply a brand new engine without the need for a core/trade-in, which I would have thought attractive to Sprint enthusiasts all over the world. You do then have to find a number of second-hand Sprint parts – many of which will be detailed in method 3, which follows.

Fitting a 16-valve – method 3

If you are thinking of fitting an overhauled or even warmed-up engine, this might be your preferred route because you can buy just the differing parts to convert your old TR7 engine to Sprint specification. These can be purchased as a kit from Rimmer Bros, S+S Preparations, and possibly other TR7 Sprint specialists like Brian Kitley Triumphs. Such kits contain mostly new parts, but you can probably save a useful sum by buying many of the parts second-hand and individually. Dolomite-orientated motoring clubs or auto-jumbles/swap-meets may present the best opportunities. However, before you rush to put either option into practice, let's explore the new and used parts you will need, and the specific 'Sprint'

4-CYLINDER ENGINE UPGRADES

preparation you need to take when rebuilding your original TR7 engine. I would also recommend you appraise the cost of each option, for you could find methods 1 or 2 more financially appealing – although this route may offer the most potential fun!

You will note that upgrading the engine is not just a case of bolting a 16-valve Sprint cylinder head onto the TR7 block, and that your shopping list will extend depending on the tuning you have in mind. However, as opposed to the 8-valve engine, the tuning potential of the Sprint is exciting because the engine can yield about 185/190bhp at the flywheel (around 140/145bhp at the wheels) – but you are not going to achieve these figures by transposing a used Dolly-Sprint engine! Nevertheless, it is quite feasible using a fully and carefully rebuilt/tuned engine, uprated camshaft, effective exhaust and inlet manifolds and a couple of Weber (or Dellorto) 45 carburettors.

If you do elect to basically rebuild your own TR7 engine with Sprint pistons, cylinder head and timing gear, do bear in mind that this is only practical if the 'bottom end' (crankshaft, bearings, etc) of your engine is in absolutely first-class condition. You will miss out on the cross-drilling (seen in photo 6-3-1) that a genuine Sprint crankshaft enjoys. Do not contemplate this route unless you are completely confident that your crank and bearings have been properly refurbished and fitted very recently. Most enthusiasts will have heard stories about tired engines (of any make or size) having their 'top-ends' attended to, only to 'knock out' the bearings shortly afterwards. This is a fairly common occurrence from which the Sprint engine cannot be excluded. The extra demands made by the high-compression pistons will not take long to 'finish off' a tired crankshaft and bearings. If you follow this self-conversion route, you will need the following second-hand Dolomite Sprint parts:

- A complete 16-valve head assembly including valves, springs, rocker shaft and rocker assembly, some of which can be seen at 6-3-2.
- A timing cover shown at 6-3-3.
- Duplex sprockets, chain, chain guides and tensioner shown at 6-3-4.
- An inlet manifold and possibly the ex-Sprint's carburettors (new needles may be required), carb-linkages and air box, photographed at 6-3-5.

6-3-1 The 16-valve cranks were cross-drilled as we see here, and are preferred, although you could have your 8-valve crank cross-drilled before having it refurbished.

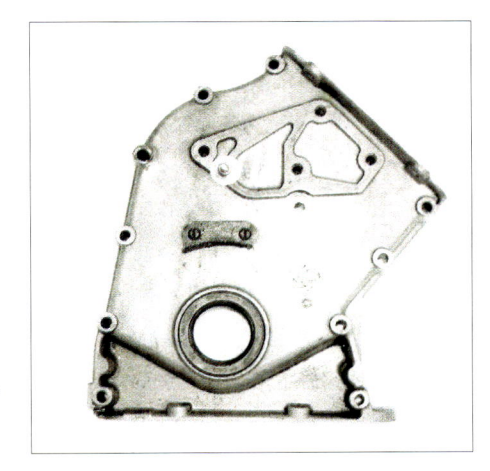

6-3-3 The 16-valve timing cover ...

6-3-2 A nearly complete 16-valve head but missing the cam and rocker shaft assemblies you will need.

6-3-4 ... and the timing components.

6-3-5 The 16-valve inlet manifold and twin SUs, normally HS6s. In this case these are HS8s (2in/50mm) carbs from Steve Small's rather special TR7 Sprint race car.

SPEEDPRO SERIES

6-3-6 This is the 16-valve cam cover with the sparkplug tubes clearly omitted. New original tubes are no longer available, but fortunately reproductions can be obtained from Sprintparts.

6-3-7 A genuine 16-valve piston. You can machine the twin inlet valve clearances in standard 8-valve pistons, but higher compression reproductions are available from Sprintparts and/or Rimmer Bros.

6-3-8 Another view of the HS8s we saw earlier, this time fitted with an ITG foam filter from the 'JC' series.

- A cam cover complete with the oil filler cap seen in photograph 6-3-6.
- A rear transfer housing.
- A distributor, rotor arm, distributor-cap.

Additionally you will need to buy the following new parts:
- New head bolts and studs.
- New main and big end bolts.
- Ideally a set of Sprint pistons – although you may have to use high compression TR7 pistons, machined as per photo 6-3-7.
- Cylinder head gasket.
- Spark plugs and HT leads.
- Points/contacts and condenser or a Newtronic electronic ignition kit.
- Exhaust manifold and sports system exhaust.
- A camshaft, probably a fast road spec and cam buckets.
- A set of uprated valve springs.
- An electric fan.
- Clutch assembly.
- TR7-Sprint water transfer housing.
- Carburettors to choice, along with free-flowing air filters similar to those pictured at 6-3-8.

In addition to the obvious crank, bore and other component preparation, you will need to carry out the following exceptional engine work:
- Lighten the TR7's original flywheel.
- Balance rotating parts.
- Dowel the cam to its sprocket.
- Braze the Sprint carburettor link-bar to TR7 bar.
- Modify Sprint airbox to take hot air sensor and TR7 outer cover and its air flap.

Sprint engine assembly

Assembling the 8-valve engine was explored in some detail in *How to restore Triumph TR7 & 8*. However, the 16-valve cylinder head is a shade different and warranted an explanation here. I have used pictures 6-4-1 to 6-4-31, kindly arranged by the team at Rimmer Bros and taken by Garth Jupp, to whom we are indebted.

6-4-1 Clean head thoroughly before starting the assembly.

6-4-2 The bottom half is almost ready for the head, so fit the Woodruff key and the Duplex crankshaft sprocket. The sprocket only fits in one position so there are no marks to align, but the crank and camshaft must be aligned later in the assembly sequence.

6-4-3 Ensure all four pistons have their valve clearance recesses (arrowed) in the correct position, and that all the components you are about to fit are thoroughly cleaned of their protective coatings and oiled before fitting.

4-CYLINDER ENGINE UPGRADES

6-4-4 Use two nuts locked together to allow you to fit the head studs. The Sprint engine is not so prone to seized head studs and bolts as are the 8-valve engines. Nevertheless, these studs and the bolts you will fit a little later are best lightly smeared with a copper-based high temperature compound such as Copper-Ease.

6-4-5 Drop all 16 valves in place – here, the 8 exhaust valves are just held off their seats by the workbench.

6-4-6 It is easier to fit the 16 valve spring seats with the head standing vertically. Then the ...

6-4-8 ... followed by springs, caps and the retaining collets that are being fitted here.

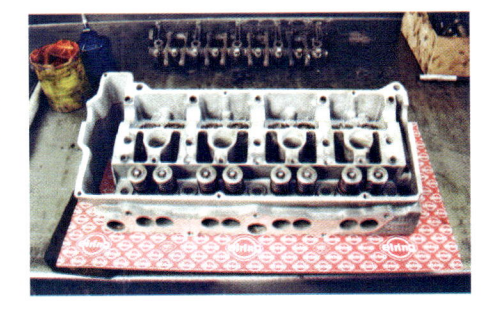

6-4-9 You need a valve spring compressor, (not shown here) and to compress each spring assembly in turn to get to this point where all 16 valves are in the head.

6-4-7 ... stem oil seals ...

75

SPEEDPRO SERIES

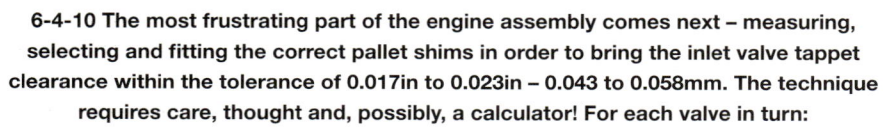

6-4-10 The most frustrating part of the engine assembly comes next – measuring, selecting and fitting the correct pallet shims in order to bring the inlet valve tappet clearance within the tolerance of 0.017in to 0.023in – 0.043 to 0.058mm. The technique requires care, thought and, possibly, a calculator! For each valve in turn:
1. Check the clearance between cam bucket and cam once the lobe of the cam has been cranked round to its fully-open position for that valve.
2. Using a set of feeler-gauges, measure the valve-clearance and calculate the change required to bring it within tolerance. I suggest you write down the answer!
3. Measure the thickness of the existing pallet shim and (adding or subtracting as necessary) calculate the thickness of the new pallet shim that will be required to replace the existing shim to effect the correct valve clearance.
Only then do you finally get to assemble the inlet valve shims as seen here and ...

6-4-13 With the camshaft secure and spun over to ensure there is no tightness evident, the rocker assembly can then be positioned ...

6-4-14 ... secured with nuts and washers and tightened down to ...

6-4-11 ... pop the inlet valve buckets in place ...

6-4-12 ... before oiling cam journals and laying the camshaft in place. You will then need to fit the five cam bearing caps in accordance with the number etched when they were originally line-bored. Tighten the caps down evenly and finally torque the caps down to the prescribed figure.

6-4-15 ... finish the pre-assembly of the cylinder head.

4-CYLINDER ENGINE UPGRADES

6-4-16 Before refitting the head, the mating faces need to be scrupulously clean. The head should have been lightly skimmed by a machine shop, but the block needs to be checked and cleaned as necessary. Use a scraper, followed by a Scotchbrite pad, then degrease with thinners before fitting the gasket.

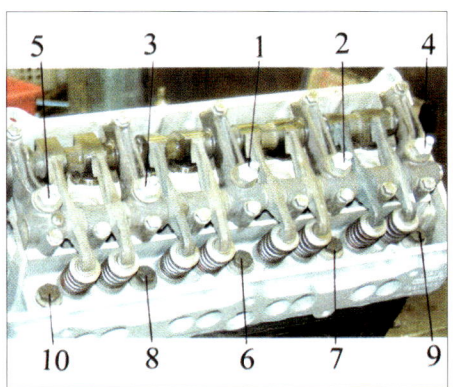

6-4-17 Fit the five head bolts and affix five nuts and washers to the studs, before pulling all ten down evenly and progressively to avoid distortion of the head. The sequence is shown here.

6-4-18 I always go round the same sequence several times starting at, in this case, about 40lb/ft. Then I go round with a torque-wrench setting of about 50-52lb/ft, and on the final occasion, after leaving things overnight, the final torque of 55lb/ft.

6-4-19 Seat the timing chain sprocket on the camshaft dowels, before fitting one of the high-tensile bolts. Clench the tab-washer securely. Turn the cam, fit the second high-tensile bolt and tab-washer and secure the latter. Re-turn the cam to align the timing line on the camshaft spigot with those on the front camshaft-bearing cap. Take great care not to disturb this setting until the final timing chain fitting and tensioning operations are complete. The duplex cam chain is fitted to the sprockets only after you have checked the crankshaft is still in the correct position.

6-4-20 Camshaft sprocket fixed to camshaft – note the tab washers have yet to be tapped over.

6-4-21 Loosely bolt the adjustable chain-guides in place. It is quite a good idea to fit the distributor at this point and check that the rotor arm points to the head of the last/rear inlet manifold bolt.

6-4-22 Fit the camshaft sprocket bracket then ...

77

SPEEDPRO SERIES

6-4-23 ... check that your new tensioner has a plastic spacer pre-fitted, before loosely bolting the tensioner in place. Tighten the various fastenings and remove the tensioner's spacer. Insert a 0.100in (2.54mm) feeler gauge between the slipper and body. Press down on the adjustable chain guide until the feeler gauge is just held, and tighten the adjustable guide bolt followed by the two remaining bolts. Remove the feeler gauge.

6-4-24 Fit the crank oil-thrower and use a little blue Hylomar to hold the front cover gasket in place. Wipe any surplus from the inside of the gasket to prevent it coming loose and clogging oil ways.

6-4-25 Press your new front oil seal into the front cover, grease the seal and position the cover on the front of the engine before ...

6-4-26 ... fitting and torqueing the cover bolts.

6-4-27 Turn the engine over and fit the oil pick-up/strainer. Using a very thin coating to hold the gasket in place, secure the sump gasket to the block before ...

6-4-28 ... fitting most of the sump bolts, although ...

6-4-29 ... two sump locations require nuts as fastenings.

6-4-30 Drift two core plugs into the exhaust side of the head and ...

6-4-31 ... into the block.

78

4-CYLINDER ENGINE UPGRADES

4-cylinder hints

Here are a few miscellaneous but hopefully helpful hints on four-pot engines:

- Camshafts – a summary of Piper camshafts is found in the following table:

Engine	Use	Duration	Valve lift (mm)	Rev range
4-cylinder 8 valve	Fast road	280	10	2000 to 6500
	Rally	292	10.3	2500 to 7000
4-cylinder 16 valve	Fast road	280	10	2000 to 6500
	Rally	290	10.3	2500 to 7000
	Competition	292	10.4	3000 to 7500

- TR7 cylinder head warping – Triumph provided very little extra material on the cylinder-head face to allow skimming in the event of head warping – usually caused by overheating. I mentioned this in the companion book (*How to restore Triumph TR7 & 8*) and that there are thick gaskets available for this eventuality. However, skimming the mating-face of the head will not cure the inevitable misalignment of the cam bores. The latter can be remedied by line-boring the cam bearing seats, but clearly it is better if the majority of the warp can be removed first. There is now a technique called heat straightening where the head is clamped over a central shim to a thick steel plate, and soaked in an oven to help straighten the head. Any subsequent machining is thus minimized.

Timing chain facts – the TR7 timing chain and related parts are the same as those used on the left bank of the Triumph Stag. The timing chains in a Stag are one of the aspects of the engine that you have to learn to live with. Granted, there are two on a Stag but some of my lessons may be helpful for TR7 owners – be they of the original or Sprint persuasion. First, you need to keep the chains very well lubricated – it is definitely worthwhile changing the engine oil and filter every 3000 miles. Secondly, I use a synthetic engine oil to maximise the lubrication of the chains – but be careful, use one without a load of detergents such as Castrol Magnatech for conventional engines (i.e. do NOT use Magnatech for modern engines). Thirdly, you will need to change the chains every 25/30000 miles or as soon as they start to rattle.

Rather like the clutch parts mentioned earlier in this chapter, some manufacturers have rationalised the variety of timing chains they produce. Consequently, like the clutch, you should definitely only fit the best you can buy and then only when the box has the manufacturers name on it. Before you leave the store or as soon as a new chain is delivered, take a close look at it and return any chain that has a removable link in it.

It is better to fit new chain guides, but if you are desperate the existing rubber covered guides can be re-used, provided the chain has not grooved them. However, the tensioner for an 8-valve engine is a major problem now that Reynolds OEM tensioners are no longer available. Those that are available partially block the oil-way, but I believe the best solution is to use a Rolon CT605 tensioner. This part is actually intended for the Dolomite Sprint engine so will be fine for any Sprint conversions, but will be too wide for an 8-valve engine. However, it does have the correct oil-way and is much the best solution. But it is essential that 8-valve owners (who have a narrower timing chain than 16-valve engines) cut off the extra width on one of the slipper pads (to match the 8-valve slipper pad width) in order to avoid the tensioner fouling the 8-valve cover. Whichever route you follow, do buy a branded product as it has been found that unbranded clone tensioners can lose their pads.

You MUST install the body that comes in the CT605 tensioner box. Do NOT re-use the original body as the ratchet mechanism is incompatible. However, the retaining bracket (that keeps the tensioner-piston from being ejected from the body in the event of a grossly slack chain) will be re-used. New tensioners don't come with the retaining bracket.

Exhaust systems and manifolds (headers) are not the sort of thing you want to be flying back and forth across the Atlantic, so I was interested to read that a US ANSA manifold/header and exhaust system are well thought of. Not only were they easy to install but, maybe more importantly, they brought about a big improvement to the engine's flexibility and power. Furthermore, they apparently sounded wonderfully mellow yet throaty. I am told that ANSA systems are still available for the TR7 and TR8.

Chapter 7
Gearbox, clutch and propshafts

5-SPEED CONVERSIONS

The whole basis of upgrading a TR7 is the 5-speed gearbox. Although there are relatively few 4-speed boxes, since the vast majority of owners agree that the 5-speed box is superior to its predecessor, we had best start by summarising the changeover.

The power generated by the cars for which the 4-speed box was designed was far less than the TR7's power; so the failure rate of the gearbox in a TR7 was quite dramatic. Consequently, most owners prefer the sturdier 5-speed box, particularly in view of its overdrive fifth gear, and the advantage this offers in high-speed cruising.

For the record, Sprint-engined cars use the same 5-speed gearbox, clutch propshaft, bellhousing and clutch actuation mechanism as the 8-valve TR7. If you're starting with a TR7 with an 8-valve engine and 4-speed gearbox, and seeking a Sprint upgrade, use the 5-speed gearbox conversion plan outlined here.

If it is your intention to do little more than upgrade your TR7 to 5-speed specification, buying another cheap TR7 is possibly the best way of obtaining the gearbox and necessary parts. In the UK you need to search for one made after October 1977, when the 5-speed box was standardised on all cars.

The LT77 (as BL called the 5-speed used in its TR7, TR8 and SD1 vehicles) gearbox can be seen at 7-1-1, and if in good order should prove to be very reliable for all Wedges up to about 250bhp. The bellhousing and clutch mechanisms changed from model to model, but the gearbox itself was largely the same, and so named because of the 77mm distance between the main and lay-shafts. Fourth gear was a direct 1:1 through-drive, but fifth gear provided a 0.83 ratio (0.79 VIN 402027 on) overdrive, i.e. 17 or 21 per cent.

The full changeover involves more than a straight substitution of gearboxes. The two models of car

7-1-1 The tough LT77 5-speed box handles the power from Rover's 4600cc engine, so should be strong enough for most TR7 applications. The bell-housing seen here is from a 4-cylinder engine. A different bell-housing is required for the TR8.

employed different ratio and style rear axles, the rear brakes were larger on the 5-speed, and the propshaft was different. Some interior trim varies, too, because the 4-speed's gearlever exits the tunnel nearer the back of the car than the 5-speed, hence the differences

GEARBOX, CLUTCH AND PROPSHAFTS

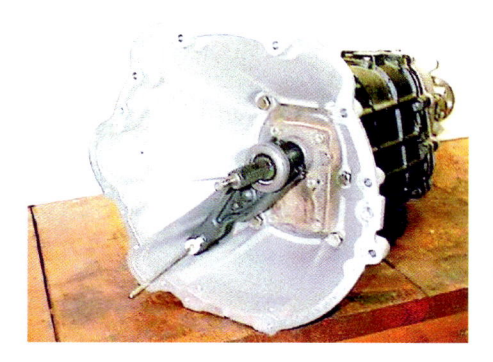

7-1-2 The 5-speed LT77 gearbox with its V8 bell-housing and conventional clutch release mechanism.

in the gearlever gaiter, mounting board and their numerous fixings. The clutches are different, but fortunately the flywheel accepts both – although using a 4-speed clutch with a 5-speed set-up can lead to problems. So, to change a TR7 car from 4- to 5-speed, you need the following:

● A 5-speed three-piece clutch set (new is recommended).
● A 5-speed box with bellhousing, thrust bearing carrier, lever fork, lower mounting including rubber, cross-shaft, mounting bolt and spacer.
● The gearbox's upper remote extension and gearstick, the stamped steel tunnel covers, five-speed gearstick gaiter and mounting trim-board and fastenings.
● A 5-speed propshaft complete with mounting nuts.
● A 5-speed rear axle complete with drums, and all the internals.
● The trailing arms are different between the 4- and 5-speed cars, but the 5-speed axle fits the 4-speed upper links.
● The 5-speed handbrake cable with the mounting ends.

Incidentally, do check the condition of the various components before fitting them to your car. I recommend checking the gearbox oil and its pump (the appearance of the old oil was covered in *How to restore Triumph TR7 & TR8)*. However, if the gearbox has been used with EP80 or EP90 oil (particularly in very cold weather), the pump may have been damaged and will need replacing.

Check the speedo drive gear on the main shaft and the pinion, and make any necessary changes (see chapter 3) to minimise speedometer inaccuracies. Check the front and rear seals for oil leaks and the reverse light switch operation, before filling it with fresh oil and fitting it in the car.

V8 CONVERSIONS

If your intention is to convert the engine to a Rover V8 power-plant, and the gearbox to 5-speed, you are probably better off finding a Rover SD1 V8 fitted with a 5-speed manual box. This will provide you with not only the gearbox, but also the engine, bellhousing and V8 clutch mechanism (the gearbox and clutch are seen at picture 7-1-2). You will need to purchase the TR7 rear axle separately, but you should get the essential 3.08 high-ratio axle crown wheel and pinion from the Rover's axle.

If carrying out a V8 conversion of less than 250bhp (we will explore higher-powered conversions a little later) to your 5-speed TR7, you may not need the gearbox, but you will certainly require the bellhousing and clutch-release mechanism. These days, you will be very lucky to find a V8 engine with a Rover V8 bellhousing and manual gearbox attached, unless you purchase an SD1. You will more than likely have to buy an engine with an automatic gearbox torque-converter fitted to the back of the crankshaft. In this event, you need to assemble a supplementary gearbox conversion kit to marry your TR7's 5-speed gearbox to the Rover V8 engine.

● The original clutch arm/fork and slave cylinder can be re-used, but you need to ensure that the pivot seat in the arm/fork is in good order and not about to wear through. If worn, either replace it or weld a patch to the rear.
● Used bellhousings are scarce, but new ones are now available from Clive Wheatley V8 Spares and RPI. If a used one is located, check the clutch slave cylinder fixing threads – the M8 threads are often stripped.
● Used V8 flywheels are also scarce, but new originals can be purchased from the same sources – although you may wish to buy a lightened aftermarket version. If you find an original, you can reduce the weight for road-going cars from 30lb to about 23lb by having a specialist turn material from the periphery of the flywheel – but take care and advice if specifying a new flywheel below approximately 23lb. If your engine came from an automatic you will also need to buy a pilot bush for the end of the crankshaft – part number 614263.
● You will have no difficulty in buying a new Rover V8 three-piece clutch assembly, but the Rover V8 clutch release bearing carriers are longer than the TR7 carrier. Robsport will weld and machine two TR7 carriers together for you, but will require your current one in exchange. However, I understand that there is also a combined plastic V8 carrier and thrust bearing available on the market, made by Borg and Beck. I can't be precise, but feel that all the later Rover V8 applications like RV8 used this, so try for part number GRB90258.
● Finally, you will need a shorter V8 pivot post to replace the very similar looking but overly long TR7's. They are inexpensive, available new, and can be identified from D7-1 (overleaf).
● The pressed V8 manual bellhousing dust cover is absent from the SD1 and, to the best of my knowledge, TR7-V8

SPEEDPRO SERIES

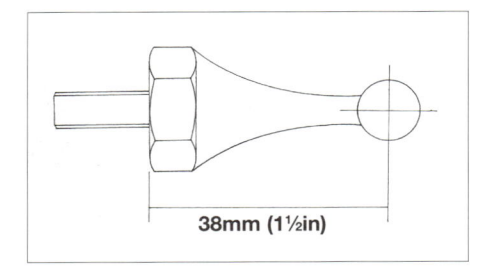

D7-1 Identification of V8 clutch arm pivot post.

catalogues. It might still be available from Triumph specialists under its TR8 part number, FRC 142. Used ones are sometimes available from specialists or the internet, or you might consider modifying the auto version. Wedgeparts tells me it needs a small batch to manufacture the part economically, but it might be another source to consider.

ULTRA-FAST AND COMPETITION GEARBOXES

The Rover LT77 will probably handle 300ft/lb of torque, but it could be short lived, particularly if the car is driven enthusiastically. Strapping it to a more modest engine generating 250ft/lb will offer some longevity. My Rover V8 generates about 200ft/lb, and I seem to get through LT77s every 20/25000 miles on the road. So, there will come a point when you need to plan fitting a stronger gearbox. The engine torque will be one consideration, but the use that the car is put to will also play a significant part – therefore we'd best look at alternative gearboxes before exploring clutch options. Within reason, any gearbox can be married to any engine, but obviously there will be problems if you fit an inadequate gearbox. Over-specifying has its drawbacks too – usually incurring space, weight and cost penalties. Selecting a gearbox with the right power/torque handling capabilities must be the first priority – thereafter ease of fitting becomes our principal interest.

The width of the bellhousing will need to be accommodated within the footwells and firewall/bulkhead of the TR, and the height of your intended gearbox will need to be accommodated within the gearbox/prop-tunnel. In certain cases, some modifications to the original sheet-metal panels need research, and the work involved in these changes increases the larger the gearbox becomes – hence my focus on 5-speed boxes.

THE T5 GEARBOX

Although there is nothing to stop UK enthusiasts fitting the T5 gearbox, its availability in the USA makes the T5 first choice for US readers. One version can be seen pictured at 7-2-1. Initially made by Borg Warner and latterly by Tremec, this 5-speed gearbox has proved very popular indeed. Many were fitted to Camaro, Firebird and Mustang cars and many of the boxes available in breakers' yards will come from these cars. Currently, the T5 is being fitted to Ford Mustang, TVR Cerbera and Tuscan, Chevy Blazer and S-10 Pickup, and the Ssangyong Musso and Korando models – many examples will be strong enough to use in all power/torque categories of TR7-V8 conversions or TR8 upgrades.

They are available new, so you can select the right capacity and fit for your purpose. They are also readily available second-hand in the USA. However, while it is probably true that all T5 boxes will handle the power from our fast road category of V8 conversions, I would avoid all pre-1985, pre-'World Class', used T5 boxes.

The later, better units are readily available in most areas, and are the result of the manufacturer re-engineering the transmission to increase torque capability and the

7-2-1 An ex-Camaro T5.

7-2-2 Another shot – this time the GM-style T5 is on the right (note the gearlever's length and angle), and can readily be compared to the Rover LT77/SD1 box.

smoothness of gear-changing/shifting. This took place in the mid-eighties, and included tapered bearings on main and countershafts to reduce noise and improve durability. Needle bearings under first through fourth gears improve high speed performance and reduce gear-changing effort. There is also a reverse synchromesh option (allowing immediate access to reverse), 3-piece non-metallic cluster synchro/blocker rings, and automatic transmission fluid (ATF), rather than gear oil, for lubrication. These uprated gearboxes are designated World Class to distinguish them from earlier models.

That said, it is generally accepted that a T5's longevity is more a result

GEARBOX, CLUTCH AND PROPSHAFTS

of mileage than the torque it has been subjected to. A high mileage, ex-high-performance T5 will probably shift poorly and die much sooner than an early T5 from a low-mileage car! Nevertheless, target the World Class units if you can.

The T5 weighs 30lb (14kg) less than the Rover SD1 gearbox since it has an aluminium case, and consequently will become more popular in the UK – particularly as the Rover box and clutch fittings get harder to find. Furthermore, the T5 avoids the complication of an oil pump and thus has less that can go wrong than a Rover box.

The T5s all have the same gear-case dimensions, but the gear-change extension housings vary, according to the gearshift position required by the original application. The parentage of your gearbox can also have a huge effect upon the ease of the marriage to your selected engine. Better to minimise the cost and problems where you can, and select a gearbox/bellhousing/clutch combination that is already compatible with your engine. The T5s were made for a variety of cars, and there are any number of ex-Ford T5s about, but if you are about to fit an engine from the Buick/Rover family you need to find a GM T5.

The GM version of this gearbox can be seen at 7-2-2. It's possible to use the GM T5 with a 215 type 3-speed bellhousing, or indeed a Rover bellhousing, but these require an aluminium adapter plate. An adapter plate – available from D+D Fabrications – might also be helpful when marrying a T5 to a Rover engine. You are likely to find the Rover crank and T5 first-motion shaft prevent the bellhousing closing to the back of the engine by some 0.375in (9mm). My preferred solution is a spacer (preferably aluminium) between engine and bellhousing. However, if you are

7-2-3-1 This is the original Rover 4.0-litre crankshaft tail with the dowel being removed while ...

still rebuilding the engine, you could consider closing the gap by altering the tail of the Rover crankshaft. Some additional information will be found at 7-2-3-1 and 7-2-3-2.

The GM T5 gearbox is built with an 18 degree twist to one side. This twist does not affect it being bolted to the bellhousing, although the rear gearbox mounting-bracket must accommodate the twist, and the shift lever will exit the tunnel at this angle unless reset accordingly.

The first four gears in all GM T5s are identical (2.95:1 first and 1:1 gear ratio in fourth). The fifth gear ratio can vary between a 0.73:1 or 0.63:1 overdrive gear. For very high speed cruising, the 0.63:1 gears seem favourite, but might be a little too high if using a 3.00 or 3.08:1 rear axle ratio. One solution would be to use a TR7 rear axle with a 3.45 ratio, providing good acceleration and low-revs fifth gear cruising. Maybe the 0.73 ratio is the best compromise, allowing use of a high ratio rear axle (thus a useful first gear) and a practical top gear (i.e. overdrive).

To select a used T5 most suited to your engine, first check the casting numbers on the gear-case. The GM model number for the T5 is 1352, and is included in the number cast into the

7-2-3-2 ... this is the end result. Note that in addition to the missing dowel, the end spigot is now 10mm shorter and the housing for the T5's spigot bearing enlarged. It was necessary to fit a temporary plug in the spigot bearing housing, to allow the lathe's tail stock to steady the crank while the spigot's length was reduced.

case. Next, weed out the T5 gearboxes which were not installed behind V8s. The V8 gearbox has 26 splines on the input shaft and 27 on the output shaft. On your short-listed gearboxes, look for the metal identification tag – it should be attached to one of the lower gear-case extension housing bolts. The tag will carry four lines of numbers and letters, respectively the Borg Warner part number, GM part number, gearbox serial number, and build date. The only numbers we should concern ourselves with are the Borg Warner and GM part numbers. Those gearboxes with a 0.73:1 fifth gear carry Borg Warner part number 1352-212 and GM part number 1019-2297. The 0.63:1 fifth gear gearbox carries Borg Warner part number 1353-213 and GM part number 1019-2298.

If you have access to the internet, for a more complete source of T5 identification and torque ratings take a look at: www.moderndriveline.com/Technical_Bits/transmission_spec.htm

I think you'll find the best used-T5 is that from a 1993-95 Cobra, and

SPEEDPRO SERIES

is rated at 310ft/lb. A tapered roller-bearing assembly replaced several roller-bearings and greatly improves durability. Strangely, non-Cobra T5s of that era retained the roller-bearings, and are consequently less desirable for very powerful conversions.

However, further T5 options became available following the 1995 sale of Borg Warner's gearbox interests to Tremec, with its changed marketing policy offering new Tremec products via aftermarket speed shops. Right through the range, these gearboxes can be purchased for Ford or GM applications, and consequently you need to specify your preference when ordering any of the new gearboxes available!

QUAIFE R380 GEARBOX

In the UK there is an updated and uprated Rover 5-speed gearbox that came on the scene about a year into MG RV8 production. Up to car number 643, MG RV8s used the Rover LT77 5-speed gearbox, but later cars switched to this R380 gearbox. Both weigh 110lb (50kg), but the R380 (seen in picture 7-2-3) has superior torque capacity.

Torque-rating is set based on two factors – engine torque and vehicle weight. The R380 was developed mainly for Discovery and Range Rover vehicles, which weigh approximately 4500lb. The rating is set so that the maximum loading and maximum torque input should not exceed the rating for the gearbox.

Apply this to the R380, when fitted in a vehicle of potentially half the weight of what it was designed to be used in, and the load on the transmission drops dramatically. Therefore the engines input torque can be correspondingly increased, yet still be within an accepted tolerance. This means that the R380 will easily live with above 300ft/lb, and I would expect it to be comfortable at 350ft/lb as long as vehicle weights are kept below, say, 2750lb/1250kg.

Remember that you can apply the same principles to any part of the transmission, including the clutch. Therefore, a Range Rover clutch designed to control up to 280ft/lb of

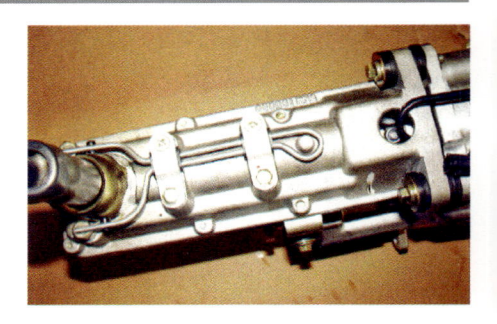

7-2-4-1 A quick glance leaves you thinking that this R380 gear-change extension is identical to the LT77's ...

7-2-4-2 ... but when viewed from the underside it becomes clear that the R380 is different, in that the reverse gear lock-out mechanism seems to be missing.

torque in a 2.5 tonne 4WD off-roader will be comparatively on holiday when fitted in a 350ft/lb, 1.25 tonne sports car, which will spin out any excess torque more easily even with the stickiest of tyres. So if you seek a suitable clutch for the R380 box, the related clutch set would be a good choice.

The gear-change pattern, gearlever and remote casting assembly warrant a few sentences. The R380 has a different pattern to the LT77, with reverse gear located in line with fifth, so a different reverse-gear lock-out arrangement is necessary. Consequently, the R380 has its own extension that looks identical to the LT77 extension from the top (picture 7-2-4-1). However, from below (picture 7-2-4-2) it becomes clear that there is

7-2-3 The R380, seen here with a V8 bell-housing, has the following ratios – 1st=3.321, 2nd=2.132, 3rd=1.397, 4th=1.0, 5th=0.77. This gearbox provides synchromesh on reverse gear, as well as on all five forward gears and is capable of handling 280ft/lb of torque.

GEARBOX, CLUTCH AND PROPSHAFTS

7-2-4-3 A check with an LT77 extension confirms that the reverse gear safety protection arrangements are indeed different. The LT77 is here at the back left of the extension while ...

7-2-4-4 ... the R380 is on the front and right side. Nevertheless, if essential, it is possible to fit an R380 lock-out mechanism to an LT77 extension (with some ingenuity).

a different reverse lock-out mechanism (pic 7-2-4-3). If you find it difficult to acquire a specific R380 gearlever extension, it is possible to fit the LT77's – but without modifications there is nothing to prevent you inadvertently slipping into reverse when exiting fifth. Therefore, most people modify the LT77 extension. Photograph 7-2-4-4 may help with this.

The R380 extension is no longer than the LT77's, but the alloy rear section of the R380 is about 1in (25mm) longer. Thus the back of the extension will almost certainly foul the rear opening in the TR7 tunnel, necessitating the reduction explained later in the chapter.

At the time of writing, the new boxes are still available from Clive Wheatley V8 Conversions and RPI Engineering, including the V8 bellhousing. In the US you may lean towards the Tremec box, but if you can find an R380 gearbox it will be easier to fit. The clutch, bellhousing, speedo drive, overall length, prop flange, and gear-change remote assembly and lever are common to the SD1/TR7 gearboxes.

THE TOYOTA OPTION

It is possible to use one of Toyota's excellent 5-speed gearboxes behind a wide variety of engines, including the Rover we are focusing on here. Additional Toyota gearbox options are available, but the gearbox of choice for most road-going applications must be the Supra alloy case (seen at 7-2-5), with its light weight (77lb/35kg) and strength.

If you are ordering a Toyota gearbox with your bellhousing and clutch, you have some choice over gear ratios. The W58 looks ideal for TR7-V8 conversions, but is available only occasionally. The W55 is usually in stock and possibly the one to go for.

AFTERMARKET GEARBOXES

The T5 is available in numerous guises, each with its own ratio and/or torque rating, and you'd do well to visit Summit to view the wide range of aftermarket options. There are a few things to consider regarding first-gear ratios before you buy an aftermarket box. The lower ratio of 3.35:1 may be attractive because the car will take off quicker than a higher-geared 2.95 ratio gearbox. However, the higher ratio gearboxes are about 10 per cent stronger than a comparable 3.35 unit, as the result of input to countershaft gear ratio. For serious track day use or competitive applications the 2.95 first gear is the way

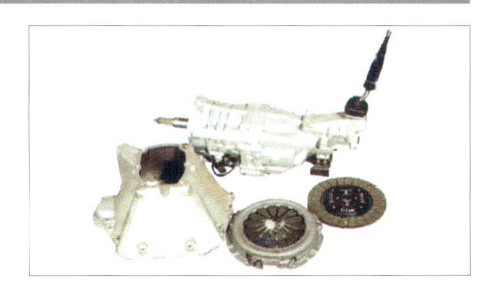

7-2-5 The alloy-cased Toyota Supra box will not quite handle the power/torque of the steel-cased versions that are good for up to 400bhp, but the internals are strong enough to be used by some of the competition cars when race regulations restrict drivers to using an original TR7 casing. Fitting kits are available from Triumph Rover Spares and/or Dellow Automotive.

to go, offering 305ft/lb torque capacity. That said, Cobra aftermarket units have been rated at 330ft/lb since 1993.

Tremec's 3550 handles 350ft/lb – but weighs in at 100lb, about 23lb more than a T5. The increase stems from its larger gear and shaft mass, which in turn allows the higher capacity – although some high-powered applications have still managed to break a few of the early units. Hence the introduction of the Tremec TKO with its changed input shaft – increased from $1\frac{1}{16}$ inches and 10 splines to $1\frac{1}{8}$ inches and 26 splines, while the output shaft went from 28 splines to 31.

D+D Fabrications recommends that Tremec gearboxes are given at least a 500 mile running/break-in light-duty before hard driving use, as a consequence of their brass synchro/blocker rings. These same brass rings mean aftermarket Tremec's should always be filled with GM synchromesh fluid, and not the Dextron used by the T5 and T56. The brass rings require the extra viscosity of the synchromesh fluid, whereas the carbon fibre rings in the

SPEEDPRO SERIES

7-2-6 The T56's six forward speeds must be every converter's dream (after a powerful engine!) – but ...

7-2-7 ... check out its size before you jump in. The (much) smaller comparison is a T5.

Borg Warner units work best with the lighter Dextron.

The T56 six forward-speed gearbox (picture 7-2-6) may be the ultimate gearbox/transmission option for high-powered road use, in view of its 440ft/lb capacity. It also enjoys an enviable reputation for strength and quality, but expect it to set you back over $2000. Its strength is partly derived from the 85mm distance between the mainshaft and countershaft, which controls the size of the gears. As this distance increases, torque capacity goes up by the square of the increase. By comparison, the T5's centre distance is 77mm as is the Rover LT77's. However, take a look at picture 7-2-7 before you plump for the T56.

Approach buying a T56 with care, since the bellhousing is integral with the gear-casing so you must get one that marries to your selected engine. Also be aware that the box weighs 115lb, that the bellhousing is bigger, and the box slightly taller too – so significant tunnel modifications will be required to install it in a TR7.

AUTOMATIC GEARBOXES

Although most people in the UK do not regard an automatic gearbox as suited to a sports car, in the USA the roads, driving habits and traffic conditions are different, which assures the continued popularity of the automatic gearbox in sports cars. However, getting the right gearbox makes all the difference. The TR7 3-speed Borg Warner type 65/66 won few friends, but the power of a Rover V8 engine puts a different complexion on auto boxes, so a few words on this conversion are relevant.

D+D Fabrications makes a variety of kits to couple manual and auto boxes to the Rover V8. The V6-style GM 700R4 is particularly well suited to the Rover V8 engine, particularly those fitted with the GM fuel-injection system described later in the book. Some fairly small, local, prop-tunnel enlargements will be required – photograph 7-2-8-1 may give you a feel for those changes, assisted by 7-2-8-2, which shows the 10in torque converter. If you are seeking out a used box, these were made from 1982 to 1992, but the boxes produced from 1987 are a slightly better version. They will be found in V6 Camaros, Firebirds and S10 GM trucks with 2.8- and 3.1-litre engines. The box, as purchased from D+D, will handle up to 400bhp and thus pose no power limitations. Post-1992 boxes employ computer control and are not useful in this application.

Whichever automatic gearbox you use, you will require a fluid cooler at the front of the car. The original TR7 auto coolers are still available from Rimmer

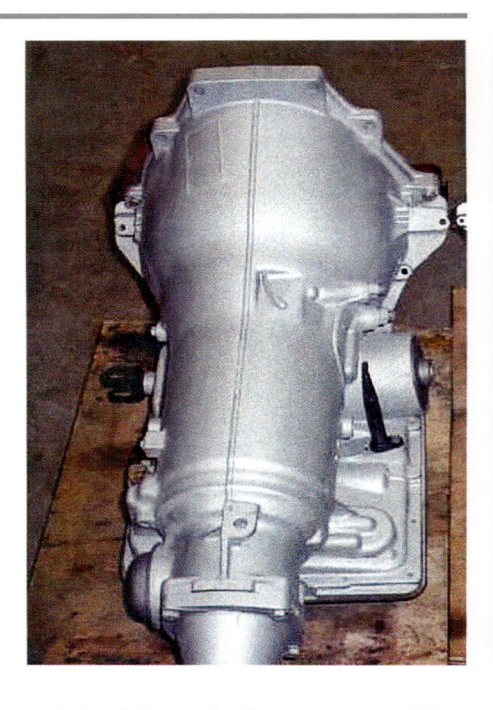

7-2-8-1 This is the V6-style (not the V8 version) of General Motors' 700R4 Auto gearbox. It is a 4-speed unit with a 0.7 (i.e. overdrive) top gear ratio. You can buy the whole package ready to bolt to your Rover engine from D+D Fabrications.

7-2-8-2 The 10in torque converter, seen here without its adapter plate, has a lock-up clutch facility for higher stall speeds. Furthermore, this relatively small converter allows for a smaller case size, at least at the front of the box.

Bros, but D+D includes a suitable cooler in its kit. The mounting holes are already provided in the TR7 body. If, however,

GEARBOX, CLUTCH AND PROPSHAFTS

7-3-1 This is a later stock Buick/Olds 215 bellhousing, drilled for both 3- and 4-speed transmissions. When the 215 first came out it was offered with a 3-speed gearbox, although a 4-speed was soon added as an option. The 4-speed needed a different bell-housing with larger bolt pattern so, in early 1962, the factory started drilling the bell-housing for both 3- and 4- speed transmissions: the 3-speed took the four inboard holes and the 4-speed took the four outer holes.

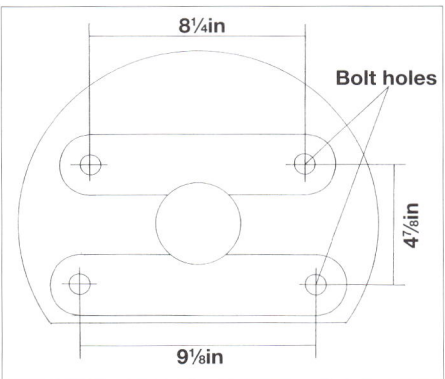

D7-2 General Motors' 215 4-speed bell-housing rear bolt pattern.

7-3-2. This is a Sprint engine, but the important detail is that the bell-housing for all TR7 4-cylinder engines married to 5-speed gearboxes is identical, and looks like this.

you are opting for a bespoke water radiator, it may be better to have the transmission fluid cooler incorporated into it (usually on the side).

Shifter assemblies (but not the knobs) are still available from Rimmer Bros, but the plastic trim that surrounded them on factory cars is extremely scarce, even used, and will require your ingenuity to adapt something similar.

BELLHOUSINGS AND CLUTCHES

When marrying a LT77 or R380 box to a Buick or Rover V8 engine, the ideal bellhousing is that from a Rover V8 SD1 or TR8. However, the Buick 215 4-speed or dual pattern bellhousing can be used, and can be identified by the bolt pattern shown in photo 7-3-1, and by drawing D7-2. Both gearboxes will also marry to the TR7 4-cylinder engines, providing you use the TR7 4-cylinder 5-speed bellhousing seen at 7-3-2.

Do not skimp when buying a clutch, particularly for V8 engines. Road-going V8-engined cars require reputable units, which have a brown spot marked on the clutch cover and green on the drive-plates. These may cost a bit more, but as these items are for fitting to LDV vans and Land Rovers, their quality is somewhat higher and will give much longer life with fewer problems than the plentiful cheaper options out there.

In competition terms, a paddle plate with 7in cover on a lightweight flywheel will improve engine pick-up considerably, both on acceleration and deceleration, with the added bonus of being far less weight to drag round the track!

FLEXIBLE CLUTCH HOSE

Take the opportunity of an empty prop-tunnel to fit a stainless braided (Aeroquip or Goodrich) flexible clutch hose to the clutch line. This is recommended for all Wedges, but particularly for V8 conversions because, with two exhaust pipes, there is no place to put the original clutch hose to stop it warming up, softening and losing its effectiveness. Some original plastic hoses have even been known to melt!

SIZE RULE OF THUMB

For moderately-powered road cars, a 9½in clutch will be adequate, while it might be prudent to use a 10in clutch for medium-powered engines. However, when you move up to high-powered applications, 10½in is where you probably need to be thinking. Bear the weight of the car in mind, for a marginal clutch in a 2000kg (4400lb) monster will be perfectly adequate in your 1250kg/2750lb TR7. The lower weight not only means less stress and wind-up in the transmission, but that tyre grip is lost earlier and the wheels can spin away the excess torque, although tyre grip makes only a small difference to the overall effect.

One interesting (and to the best of my knowledge unique) 'half-way' clutch is made by CenterForce, and pictured at 7-3-3 (overleaf). These clutches have centrifugal weights built into them that increase the clamping pressure as rpm builds up. The theory is that engines develop little torque at low speeds so only a weak clutch action is needed, but more clamping force is needed as speed and torque increase. This design gives a soft clutch pedal with no sacrifice in performance.

87

SPEEDPRO SERIES

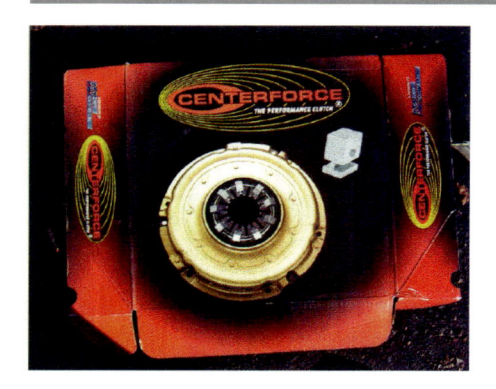

7-3-3 All Centerforce clutches have the (expanding) weights visible here, but are about twice as expensive as a conventional clutch. The 'weakest' (Centerforce I) was $156 for the pressure plate and about $85 for the friction plate at the time of writing. For more information visit www.centerforce.com.

However, much depends on what you intend to use the car for. Sprinting, drag racing or frequent 'hot starts' at track days may necessitate a heavy-duty clutch such as those supplied by McCleod. Be aware that these can require very heavy pedal pressures to disengage and, in a predominately road-oriented car, such clutches can be very uncomfortable to drive in traffic. Alternatively, an uprated AP (Automotive Products) clutch – probably just the drive-plate to start with – could be of use to sharpen the grip of the clutch. Take advice regarding your engine, gearbox and the clutch most suited to your application, and on the hydraulic cylinder sizes you intend to use. You could use a remote Lockheed brake servo to give servo assistance to your clutch pedal, but this is a complication best avoided.

While most UK readers will opt for a Rover SD1 (9½in) clutch set, in the USA Buick/Rovers use an aftermarket Chevy clutch with an HTOB (hydraulic throw-out bearing – more shortly). In the UK the clutch is moderately heavy, and I hear this is not much different in the US. I would guess about twice the pedal pressure required in an original TR7 is needed, and the full travel of the pedal, just to barely disengage the clutch.

CLUTCH MASTER CYLINDERS

The TR7 clutch master cylinder is ⅝in (15.9mm) in diameter. A ¾in (19mm) bore master cylinder moves about 40 per cent more fluid for the same stroke than the original master, but with a corresponding increase in pedal-pressure. In the UK Demon-Tweeks sells a range of AP master cylinders with 'remote' reservoirs. These compact master cylinders are suitable for all brake and clutch applications, are flange mounted, and have bore options from 0.55in (14mm) diameter through to 1in (25.4mm). There are various push-rod options for both the thread and length, and they can be fitted with a screw-in reservoir adapter that accepts a push-on hose of ⁵⁄₁₆in (7.9mm) inside diameter.

In the US, the ¾in bore Tilton master cylinder comes in four versions: regular, short, with a remote reservoir, and without one. The TR certainly has enough room to use the short (series 75) Tilton cylinder with reservoir for the clutch actuation. The Tilton cylinders come in 8 bore sizes, from ⅝in to 1⅛in, so if you need to make some adjustments you can vary the master cylinder bore accordingly.

The Tilton cylinder bolts in the standard/stock position, and allows you to refit the banjo, special bolt and clutch line. You will need to increase the size of the central hole in the pedal box to clear the OD of the Tilton cylinder, and transfer the TR7's original push-rod/clevis fork assembly to the Tilton or buy a replacement if yours is worn.

Don't forget, for a given size of slave cylinder – the bigger the bore of the master cylinder, the greater the amount of fluid displaced, thus the stroke of the slave cylinder is greater, but the clutch pedal feels heavier. In general, the clutch should engage about ⅓ of the way off the floor. If yours engages a lot nearer the top of the pedal's travel, you could find it worthwhile trying a smaller bore master cylinder, since this should reduce pedal pressure and help the clutch 'bite' closer to the floor.

CLUTCH SLAVE CYLINDERS

Most gearboxes will have an external slave cylinder bolted to the side of the box to operate the clutch. There are exceptions, and in cases where you are without a suitable means of operating the clutch, two solutions are available to you:
1) Fit a throw-out/clutch-release bearing to the nose of the box.
2) Fabricate a new bracket and use the existing mounting holes in the T5 gearbox to mount an external slave cylinder.

The hydraulic throw-out bearing (HTOB) is an annular ring slave cylinder mounted inside the bellhousing, as we see from photographs 7-3-4-1 and 7-3-4-2. It probably provides for the simplest installation, but in the event of a problem they have the major disadvantage of requiring the gearbox be removed to perform even the most minor repair. Such throw-out bearings eliminate the possibility of clearance difficulties in the area of the starter motor/external clutch slave cylinder and the chassis. Versions are readily available for virtually any gearbox/clutch combination from Tilton Engineering, McLeod Industries or Weber Performance Products. A couple of comparisons can be seen at 7-3-4-3.

The aftermarket external clutch

GEARBOX, CLUTCH AND PROPSHAFTS

7-3-4-1 HTOBs mount to the front of the gearbox inside the bell-housing like this. The annular hydraulic cylinder sits nearest the gearbox and advances the thrust bearing we see at the front of this example into the 'fingers' of the clutch pressure-plate, in order to release the clutch. HTOBs are more complex than a straightforward piston-like hydraulic cylinder. The lack of accessibility makes a remote bleed nipple essential, and the top line (protected with plastic wrapping) leads to the nipple situated outside the bell-housing.

7-3-4-2 This shot shows a T5 with HTOB actually inside the bell-housing. Note that both lines are protected from chafing by rubber hose sleeves.

7-3-4-3 Various types of HTOBs are available from a variety of manufacturers. Buy the correct one for application from a manufacturer with a reputation for quality and reliability.

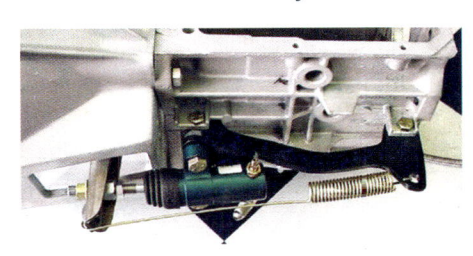

7-3-4-4 Autoworks International's T5 slave cylinder and bespoke mounting bracket. You can just see the hydraulic line connection point below the cylinder.

7-3-5 The simplest way to shorten the gearlever is to cut the required length off the top and extend the threaded section downwards. The retaining pressing tends to fatigue and it is likely that you will simultaneously need to fit a new one.

cylinder photographed at 7-3-4-4 is available from Autoworks International, and is made specifically for Ford T5 gearboxes that are normally cable-operated.

SPEEDO CABLES

The speedo drive from some gearboxes mentioned can be electronic, but most TR7-V8 conversions will continue to use a conventional inner/outer cable assembly. The length will probably differ from the original cable, but you can at least use that as a guide to the length needed in your converted car. If you intend to retain the original speedo instrument, the original cable will also provide a guide to the size of coupling needed at the dashboard-end of the cable. The gearbox will dictate the lower-end coupling arrangement.

Speedy Cables (in the UK) or your local V8 conversion specialists resolve any supply difficulties as far as the Rover box is concerned. I note that Lokar also offers a variety of speedo cables and accessories, and its catalogue may be worth exploring. If you are fitting a T5 gearbox to your conversion then a different set of speedo-drive solutions are called for. D+D Fabrications will have the answers and parts you need.

GEARLEVER/STICK LOCATION

Supra boxes have four gearlever/stick positions from the front of the box/rear of the bellhousing – 18in, 19in, 20½in and 21in. The 19in version looks preferable for TR7-V8 conversions, but I believe the 18 to be the most prevalent.

The T5 lever/stick distance from the rear bellhousing face depends on the version you are thinking about – the GM/Camaro is 21in, the S-Truck 12¼in, while the Ford is an almost ideal (for TR7-V8 conversions) 19½in.

The Rover's gearlever/stick might be a little taller than its 4-speed predecessor, but this can be resolved by shortening the 5-speed lever as per picture 7-3-5. However, the gearlever might also be slightly too far back in the propshaft tunnel for comfort. You can solve both problems simultaneously by carrying out the

89

SPEEDPRO SERIES

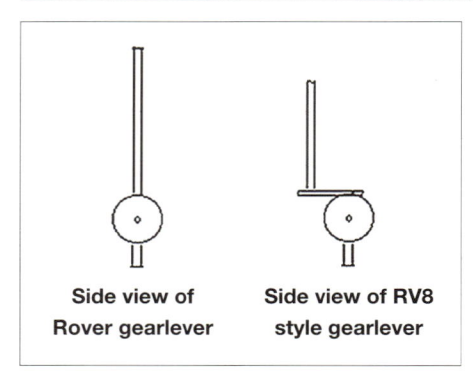

D7-3 V8 Diagramatic view of gearlever modification.

(Side view of Rover gearlever / Side view of RV8 style gearlever)

modifications to the gearlever shown in drawing D7-3. This requires you to cut the gearlever off the ball and chop whatever length you wish from the plain bottom of the gearlever. Before re-welding the gearlever back together, make up a flat intermediate plate which allows you to reposition the centre of the gearlever/stick an inch (25mm) or so further forward than originally.

There is a third possibility – the gearlever extension casting may foul the TR7's bodyshell. This is possible (but less likely) with an LT77 gearbox and extension, but almost certain with the R380 gearbox. You cannot simply enlarge the aperture in the tunnel as there is a very substantial stiffener pressing immediately behind the existing opening, so it is necessary to shorten the housing. There are two ways you can approach this. The simpler solution is shown in picture 7-3-6-1, but by this route it is possible that the bias spring itself and/or its front fixing may also require changing. The alternative, shown at 7-3-6-2, requires a much more complex cut, but avoids any subsequent bias spring complications.

After either of these casting changes, the gearlever length and/or its

7-3-6-1 You cannot cut more than about 1in (25mm) from the extension casting between the rod bearings without reducing the effectiveness of the bias spring and its mounting. This is the end result after two vertical cuts where the arrow is pointing.

position may still not be to your liking, in which case you will need to carry out the above alterations on the gearlever itself.

GEARBOX REAR CROSS-MEMBERS

The removable cross-member that supported the rear of the original TR7 gearbox seen in photograph 7-3-7 generally can be modified and used to support the new gearbox. The fine modification detail will depend on the gearbox in question, its position within the chassis and the actual flexible mounts to be used. If fitting a Rover gearbox, I recommend fitting TR8 rubber flexible gearbox pads. They are more expensive than the apparently identical

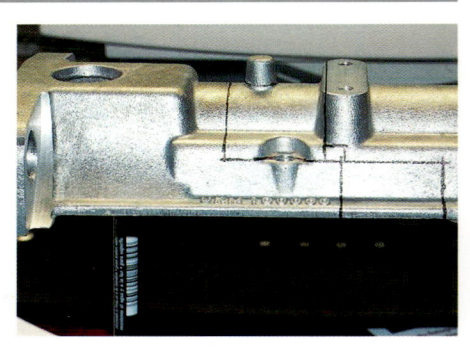

7-3-6-2 The cutting places are clearly marked with this alternative suggestion, and may be best done by first milling out the top and bottom sections of the extension casting before attempting the short horizontal cut. Alternatively, the horizontal cut could be avoided altogether if the rear of the top half-cut was aligned with the front of the bottom half-cut.

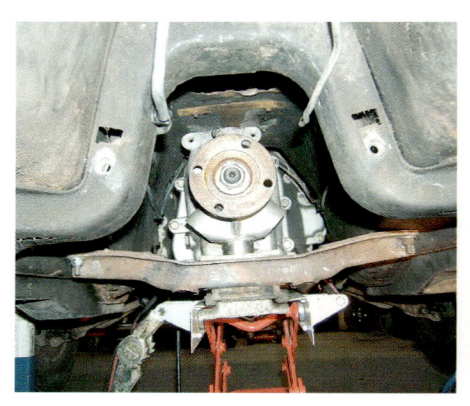

7-3-7 In cases where a 5-speed Rover box is retained, as here, the existing gearbox support will only need moving backwards with new securing holes drilled in the car's floor. However, if alternative boxes are to be fitted some (usually) modest modification and fore/aft relocation is all that is necessary.

Rover mounts, but in fact the TR8's are harder and less flexible.

The T5 uses a single rubber mount, and it is useful to fit a 'cape' of PVC sheet about 400 x 400mm over it, so

GEARBOX, CLUTCH AND PROPSHAFTS

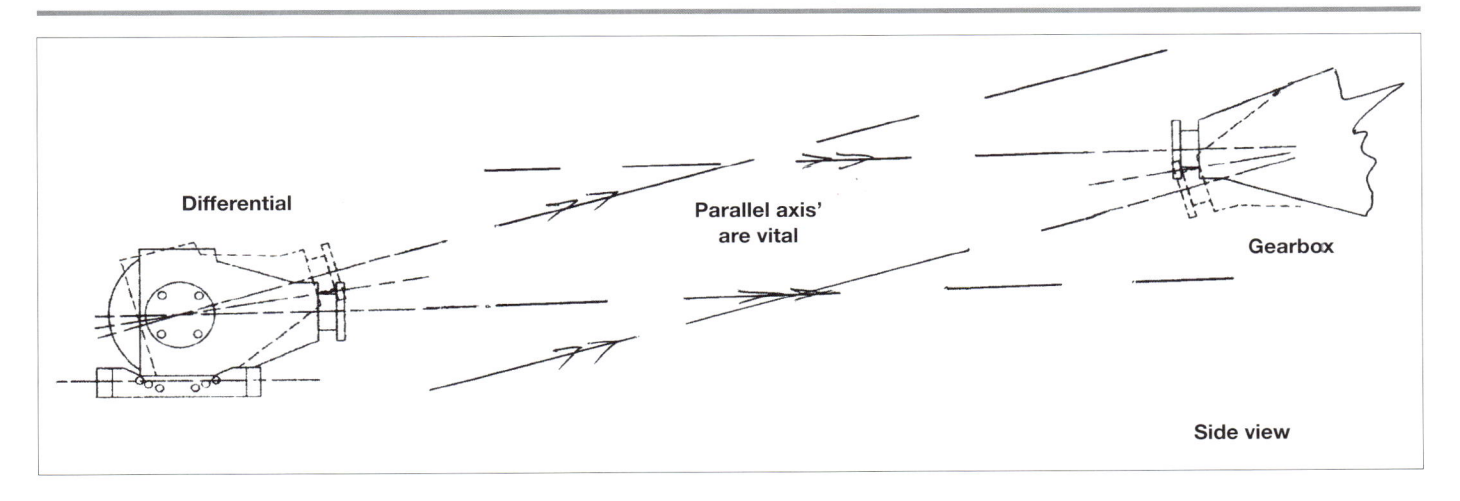

D7-4 Symmetrically and parallel-aligned axis for rear axle and gearbox flanges.

that any oil from the rear of the gearbox does not soak into the mount.

PROPSHAFTS AND DRIVESHAFTS

It goes without saying that most conversions will need a new propshaft. Four details require some thought.

- The length of the shaft will vary from that originally fitted to the car – the extent of the variation differing with the engine and gearbox fitted, and the position of the engine. Therefore, measure the 'at rest' length once all the main components are finally fitted. It does not take the specialists long to make a prop/driveshaft, so leave measuring and ordering it until you are sure there are no final positioning tweaks required. Photograph and caption 7-4 may give you some ideas.
- The flange sizes and PCD of both the gearbox and rear axle drive-flange require careful measurement. Some flanges are square, most are round, but you need to offer the right information to the propshaft manufacturer. If you are using a slightly unusual (e.g. a Toyota gearbox or Commodore rear axle) component, you may even need to send the respective flanges to the manufacturer.
- The diameter of the shaft is very important, and dictated by the torque of the engine and the end flanges.
- With increased power it is wise to change to a u-jointed prop/driveshaft. The standard/stock CV joints will not stand up to significant increases in power or torque. To some degree, the size of the UJ is dictated by the diameter of the main driveshaft. However, get the largest possible and best quality UJ fitted, and specify a UJ with grease nipples (many come without grease nipples under the guise of being maintenance-free).

In the UK, GKN Drivelines (for many years known as Hardy Spicer) makes propshafts to any specification you require, and is able to advise on the specification. There are numerous other specialists in both the UK and US, too. You can get prop/driveshafts ready-made at TSI imports in the USA. I used a TVR Tuscan propshaft in my conversions, had them cut to length and balanced, and over tens of thousands of miles they have proved faultless.

7-4 Make a virtue out of necessity by upgrading your propshaft when a replacement is called for. Those with sliding splines and twin universal joints are much more effective than the original Triumph TR7 offering.

You need to check the alignment of the gearbox with the nosepiece of the rear axle, so that the UJs on your propeller shaft are symmetrically aligned. Drawing D7-4 may help you appreciate what I am driving at. Any propshaft using two sets of the simple Hooke-type UJ out of phase will cause a jerky drive, as the front and rear UJs transmit the engine's revolutions in 'pulses'. In this context BL advised that the 4-speed propeller shaft should be retro-fitted with the CV joint at the rear (where the axis of drive has the greater angle) to minimise pulsing.

Chapter 8
Acquiring and upgrading a Rover V8

The Buick, Oldsmobile, Pontiac and Rover engines all stem from the same General Motors 1960s '215in^3' (3528cc) stock seen at 8-1-1. Although there have been many subsequent developments (pic 8-1-2) and numerous increases in capacity, they remain the engine of choice for the majority of TR7-V8 conversions. Any of these engines will give your conversion exciting performance, but needless to say that performance will vary with the engine specification you select. My intent here is not to give immense detail on tuning each of the many variants, because there are several excellent books that focus solely on that. However, I thought a basic outline of what is available and how it fits into our fast road/ultra-fast road/competition divisions would be beneficial.

For simplification, I will generally refer to the original trio of aluminium engines as 'Buick' – if only because of the Buick's original numerical superiority. Although the choice of capacities and state of tune varies dramatically these days, these Buick/Rover aluminium engines are undisputedly the easiest V8s to install in the TR7.

8-1-1 The heart of a huge number of Buick/Rover V8s is this 3500cc/215in^3 block. Later engines had differing ancillary fittings (the front timing cover in particular) but this casting remained virtually unchanged until the increased bore sizes generated more torque, necessitating increased rigidity.

8-1-2 This 3500cc ex-Rover Defender engine uses an identical block to that seen in picture 8-1-1, but the front cover, water pump, crankshaft pulley and position of the alternator have altered as developments have been incorporated.

ENGINE OPTIONS

The list of potential donor vehicles for this aluminium V8 engine is amazingly long, but many engines, indeed the majority, will have been fitted with an automatic gearbox/transmission. However, this need not present much of a subsequent flywheel/clutch gearbox problem.

ACQUIRING AND UPGRADING A ROVER V8

Fast road applications

The normally-aspirated versions of the Buick (Special and Skylark models), Oldsmobile (F-85, Cutlass and Jetfire models) and the Pontiac Tempest through 1961, 1962 and 1963 gave between 155 and 200bhp. The engines were 3500cc/215in^3, generated by eight 3.5in (89mm) bores and 2.8in (71.1mm) stroke.

1967-1975 Rover P5B/P6 3500cc units – initially with a 10.5:1 compression ratio – were a slight improvement over their US predecessors, in particular from 1973 when the rear crank oil seal was improved and the compression ratio dropped. A typical block from this era can be seen at 8-1-1. These units employed a narrow front pulley arrangement which makes slipping the engine into a TR7 even easier, but the oil pump capacity, crankshaft oil seal design and cylinder head efficiency for pre-SD1 engines is poor.

1976-1993 Rover SD1, Discovery, Defender, Sherpa models used a 3500cc/215in^3 engine which had better breathing (improved cylinder head/valve arrangement) and increased oil flow (longer oil pump gears). It can be seen in picture 8-1-2.

The 1988 US Range Rover was fitted with a 3947cc variant with 94mm bores, as a response to ever-tightening emission requirements. This engine capacity was standardized in the UK and other markets in 1989, and in 1993 for the Discovery. The MG RV8 used a fuel-injection 3947cc unit. A 4227cc engine using a long throw crank with the 94mm bores was also available in the USA – though in somewhat limited numbers in the UK.

Engines suited to ultra-fast road cars

From 1995 to date, Rover 4000cc and 4600cc/282in^3 engines are probably the best base for a TR7-V8 conversion, as

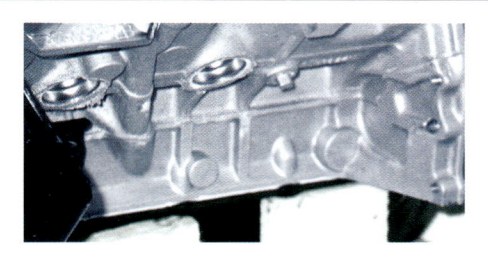

8-1-3 As a comparison to the photograph which follows, this picture shows a '4000' V8 block. In this case you will note the cross bolts are conspicuous by their absence (as is the case with all 3947cc engines).

they employ a stiffened block compared to the earlier engines with an identical capacity. My favourite would be the smoother 4000cc engine. Although designated '4000' to differentiate it from its elder sister, this generation of engines still uses the same 94mm bore as the previous generation, and the smaller engine is still of 3947cc capacity.

Competition cars

The 4600cc unit has the same 94mm bore, but achieves its enlarged capacity with a longer throw crankshaft. Like its '4000' sister, the 4600 unit has the advantage of a more stiffly cast block which, in the case of the 4600cc version, is further stiffened by five cross-bolted main bearing caps. The engine offers innumerable tuning opportunities that we will briefly explore later in this chapter, but in standard/stock tune this engine can be the heart of an ultra-fast road car.

Be aware, however, that the original front timing cover has no provision for a distributor, so if you want one you may also need to acquire an earlier front cover for this engine. They are available second-hand or new, but if you are buying a complete 'crate' engine you could specify that one be pre-fitted. Although the engines identified by

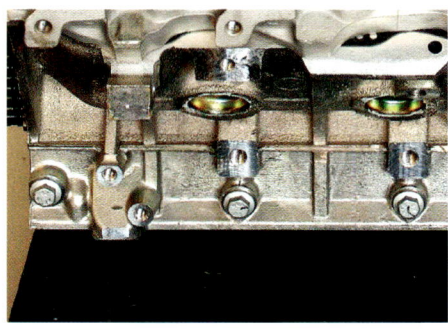

8-1-4 The 4600cc cylinder blocks have five pairs of cross bolts that go through the blocks into the side of the main bearing caps. This picture shows three in close-up.

photographs 8-1-3 and 8-1-4 are now out of mainstream production by Rover, surprisingly they are still available new today, for as long as component stocks last.

ACQUIRING AN ENGINE

The ease with which you can acquire a used (or a new) engine depends to some extent upon your location. There are a number of US specialists who stock a wide range of later, used Rover engines and there are still a number of the earlier Buick engines to be found in numerous breakers yards and at swap meets. I mentioned in chapter 1 that there is a reasonably plentiful supply of 4200cc short-engines in the USA. However, in spite of the availability of 4200cc parts being good news for US V8 enthusiasts, there is no doubt in my mind that the UK has the advantage when it comes to acquiring a used Rover engine.

The most frequent and easily available engine in the UK used to be the 3500cc ex-SD1. This may be changing as the 3.9 (not, note, the later and better 4.0) has been available since the very early 1990s and engines and spares are now readily available too. Nevertheless, either of these engines, although not at the top of the

SPEEDPRO SERIES

capacity or power available lists, offer an opportunity for a most cost-effective doubling of the power available to your TR7. They allow you to make your TR7-V8 superior to one using a basically stock 3500cc Buick engine, not only with respect to power but reliability too. The front oil seals are far superior and the daily benefit of their improved cylinder heads and oil volume should not be discounted. The original TR8 engine produced 137bhp with twin Stromberg carburation and cast exhaust manifolds. The standard SD1 engine is rated at 155bhp (the 3.9 marginally higher), but this is easily increased to 175-180bhp by the tubular exhaust manifolds and AFB carburation. No particularly special tuning is required, therefore, to make your converted TR7-V8 30 per cent more powerful than the original using a bottom-end standard SD1 V8 engine, and you can easily go to 200bhp with only relatively mild tuning if you wish.

Today the choice of V8 engines is very wide indeed, and it might help if I summarized the standard Buick/Rover engine capacities available to you:
3.5-litre/215in^3 – 88.9mm/3.5in bore + 71.1mm/2.8in stroke. Where it all started at 3528cc!
3.9-litre/243in^3 – 94.04mm/3.7in bore + 71.1mm/2.8in stroke. A 3.5-litre crank with new larger liners providing 3950cc.
4.0-litre/243in^3 – 94.04mm/3.7in bore + 71.1 mm/2.8in stroke. Same cc, but stiffer block, cross-bolted mains, bigger bearings.
4.2-litre/258in^3 – 94.04mm/3.7in bore + 77.0mm/3.03in stroke. A stroked 3.9-litre engine giving 4278cc.
4.6-litre/283in^3 – 94.04mm/3.7in bore + 82.0mm/3.22in stroke. Standard engine gives circa 200bhp and 300ft/lb torque.

There is also a 4.4-litre Australian 'square' engine. Few readers will encounter this unique unit but for those that are curious it used the original (88.9mm) bore with an 88.9mm stroke crankshaft, and provided 4414cc. The long stroke necessitated a unique taller block.

Engine sources

Rover P5B, P6, SD1 and Land/Range Rover vehicles were exported to the USA, so, whichever side of the Atlantic you are on, your local breaker may be able to provide a used engine for your V8 conversion. Naturally, Buick '215' engines are still available in the US and second-hand and/or rebuilt Rover and Buick V8 engines can be found at TS Imported Automotive, Towery Foreign Cars, D+D Fabrications, and Wedgeparts. Engines from wrecked Range Rovers (model years 1987-1992 are the favourite) can be found on eBay for $500-$1500, and can be advantageous if the EFI system is still fitted and included in the deal.

To keep costs under control, ensure the crank pulley, water-pump and pulley, alternator and mounting cradle, together with the COMPLETE fuel-injection system (if applicable) are included in any purchase you negotiate.

In the UK, your local breaker again will be the most likely source for engines, but there are several specialist Rover breakers listed in most classic car magazines. RPI is probably the biggest source of used and reconditioned V8 engines. At the time of writing, the cost of bare reconditioned engines are as follows:

Short engines – £1450 (3500cc), £1750 (3900cc)

Long engines – £1950 (3500cc), £2350 (3900cc)

They can be bought without exchanging a core unit for a modest extra charge, and are exported all over the world.

You can buy brand new 4000cc and 4600cc Rover 'crate' engines – either as bare short or bare full engines, or as a ready to run turn-key engine. These cross-bolted main bearing engines include new block, crank, rods, pistons, rings, timing gear and camshaft – fully assembled. All are hand-built and dynamically balanced and employ the latest, stronger block casting, a bigger journal crankshaft, fully enclosed main bearing caps, stronger rods and rod stud fixings. The short bare engine costs £1695 ex-works, while a full bare engine including fitted heads and rocker assemblies is currently available for £2695.

New 4000 and 4600cc fully assembled turn-key engines come complete, fully fitted out and ready to run. Also from RPI, they are fitted with a starter, wiring, alternator, 'serpentine' pulley belt system, fuel-injection system, clutch, flywheel, rocker covers, breathers, filters, timing cover etc. They too are hand-built and balanced, and come with a 'lifetime care warranty'. Complete engines of either capacity cost £4895 ex-works, but this excludes the ECU and Air Mass meter. Furthermore, stage 1 and 3 upgrades are available on all completely rebuilt engines.

COMPRESSION RATIOS (CR) AND CYLINDER HEADS

If you are offered a V8 engine without information as to its original specification, look on the left side of the engine (below the dipstick, on the horizontal surface where the head meets the block). It should have '9.35' stamped at the top if the engine is from a standard SD1 Rover. This can vary from 10.5 for the P5B Rover engines, to little more than 8:1 if the engine has come from numerous Range or Land Rover vehicles, a TR8 or MGB GT V8.

ACQUIRING AND UPGRADING A ROVER V8

8-2-1 The Rover pistons are lightly stressed and can usually be reused. Wear a pair of stout gloves for the cleaning operation and use this picture to help you reassemble the new rings in the correct order, starting from the bottom.

8-2-2 Whatever the make of inlet manifold you use (this example is a dual port Offenhauser), these faces must sit far enough into the engine's 'valley' to allow the inlet tracts to properly align. The use of either thick 'composite' head and/or valley gaskets could prevent proper tract alignment, and thus necessitates careful checking during assembly.

8-2-3 The, to my mind, preferable steel shim gasket ...

8-2-4 ... fitted without any sealer. Note the pistons are being reused and that their crowns have been cleaned before reassembly.

This number signifies the compression ratio, and is the result of a combination of components – principally (assuming the cylinder head is standard/stock) the pistons and the material the cylinder head gasket is made from.

This is a conversion book, so I am leaving tuning to the specialists, but I have to remind you that you must not machine the cylinder heads in an effort to increase the CR – you will destroy the relationship with the inlet manifold. Using different pistons is the route to changing the engine's compression ratio. If the engine you have acquired is in good shape and has a CR of 9.35:1, it is unlikely you will have to fit new pistons. You can have the engine bored and fit new pistons of course, but this is rarely essential. The engine is lightly stressed, and if you are on a budget just clean everything very carefully (particularly the ring-grooves seen in picture 8-2-1) and fit new rings. It's even worth looking for another second-hand engine if it transpires your first does need new pistons. If you are re-using the original pistons, ensure your reconditioning machinist hones your bores to break the bore glaze before you re-assemble the pistons/rings.

However, with so many engines these days having low compression ratios you could find yours has a CR of below 9.35 – in which case you will probably wish to increase the CR, and consequently need to buy a new set of pistons. In that event select 9.75:1 (Vitesse) pistons, for with today's fuels you are unwise to try to increase your CR beyond 9.75:1.

Composite and steel shim gaskets affect both the engine's CR and the register of the inlet manifold to the cylinder heads (picture 8-2-2). The standard head gaskets, up until 1996, are the thin all-metal shims seen in pictures 8-2-3 and 8-2-4. Rover, no doubt mindful of the engine's tendency for head gasket leaks, then introduced (as standard) a composite and relatively thick gasket that is reputed to be much more reliable. Simultaneously, Rover also reduced the number of cylinder head securing bolts from 14 to 10 – which we discuss shortly – but the composite gaskets do provide excellent sealing properties.

"OK, I'll use composites", I hear you say. The trouble is, they reduce your compression ratio by about 0.7 to 1. So, for example, if you have 9.35 to 1 pistons in your engine and change from shim to composite head gaskets, you will lower the compression ratio to 8.65 and lose a corresponding degree of performance. It is not so bad if you have 10.5 pistons fitted to start with, but for lower compressions I would recommend you stay with the original steel shim gaskets. I suggest you pre-coat them with an excellent sealant called Wellseal

SPEEDPRO SERIES

8-2-5 This photograph shows a post-1996 V8 block with an earlier cylinder head, and is included to illustrate the omission of the bottom row of cylinder head bolts (they were not tapped into the cylinder blocks!).

8-2-6 This photograph shows a late block with a late cylinder head which now also omits the holes for the bottom row of bolts! Note: the cross bolts at the bottom of the picture show this to be a 4600cc engine.

to improve the gasket's reliability and reduce the number of head fastenings you fit.

As already stated, the later blocks (4000cc and 4600cc) will not have provision for the lowest row of (four each side) cylinder head bolts, so even if you are marrying a pre-1996-cylinder head to a 4000cc or 4600cc block, you will have to omit these two lines of bolts. If you are fortunate enough to have a post-1996 head, you will find it does not have the bottom row of four bolt holes seen in photographs 8-2-5 and 8-2-6, forcing you to omit these bolts. In fact, current thinking is that you should omit these bolts from your head-to-block assembly even if it has provision for them. The ten main bolts per head provide for a 'ring' of 4-cylinder bolts around each cylinder. Experts feel that the extra bottom row of bolts do little more than distort the head slightly and reduce the pressure on the head gasket at the top of the head/block interface – where the majority of head gasket leaks occur. If in doubt, seek advice from your preferred V8 engine specialist, Burgess Automotive Performance (UK) or RPI. My advice would be to lightly slip the bottom row of four bolts into the head just to keep the dirt out. Do not tighten them down beyond finger-tight.

The cylinder heads on the Buick and early Rover engines deserve our attention, because the engines' asthmatic performance was mostly as a result of their cylinder head and valve design. The valves were too small and, along with the combustion chambers, were improved when the SD1 models were introduced. You can, of course, gain much by having your early cylinder heads reworked and gas-flowed. RPI in the UK and D+D Fabrications in the USA will be happy to help, but the most cost-effective improvement is to fit ex-SD1 cylinder heads to your early block.

Better yet, of course, get the ex-SD1 heads reworked and gas-flowed before you fit them!

Even SD1 heads with 1.57in inlet and 1.35in exhaust valves are really only suitable for engines up to 3500cc. The valves are not on the centre-line of the bore, which limits the scope to increase their size. In any event, as you increase the size of the valves over a 3500cc/215in^3 engine, you will find that the cylinder wall shrouds both of them, limiting the value of any incremental diameter. The close proximity of the cylinder wall to the valve lip can be seen in drawing D8-1, where you will note the reduction in shrouding that occurs when you increase the bore size to the 3.7in of post-3500cc engines. This is one reason why a 3.9/4.0/4.2 or 4.6 block is much the better bet. However, getting back to the cylinder head itself, the ports are too small also and the thin walls prevent your increasing the ports sufficiently. In the USA, D+D Fabrications can supply Buick 300 cylinder heads, which are an improvement over the Rover SD1 heads but are really not adequate as the capacity of the engine and the gas flow rate increases. The very latest Rover heads are a shade better and if you can find and use a pair of these you are

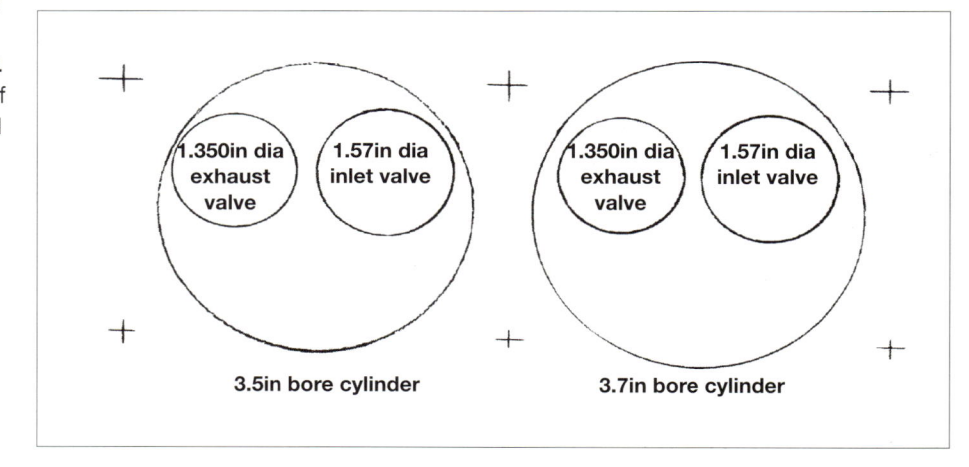

D8-1 Rover cylinder heads valve disposition.

96

ACQUIRING AND UPGRADING A ROVER V8

starting with (almost) the best available.

However, let's spend a moment looking at the 1964 Buick 300in³ aluminium cylinder heads. The 1964 aluminium heads weigh only 18.5lb each, complete with valves, springs and retainers, so from that point of view they are ideal – but they were fitted with better, yet still restrictive valves at 1.625in intake and 1.313in exhaust. Thus the standard/stock 300 heads will not breathe sufficient air and fuel to keep up with the demands of the larger engines, but they can be fitted with enlarged valves to increase their performance. The intake valve is replaced with a 1.720in diameter piece from the 1988-92 Pontiac 'Iron Duke' 151in³ 4-cylinder engine (Federal Mogul part number V2530). The 300 head's exhaust is opened up using Manley P/N 11667-4 Volkswagen 38mm (1.496in) stainless steel intake valves. The larger valves will require new seats, such as Precision PC 1500-31 (exhaust) and PC 1750-39 (intake), which any competent machine shop can easily install. The new valves and seats need a three-angle grind to help the gases follow the contour of the seats more readily, while the valve-stem lengths will need reducing.

Whatever your cylinder head, I strongly recommend you have them professionally gas-flowed (ported in the US). This might cost you £750 or so – but it will be money well spent. If yours is a budget conversion, while you may not achieve the full effectiveness of professional gas-flowed heads, there are improvements you can effect at home.

You will need to buy some relatively low-cost special but simple tools which, in the UK, Peter Burgess can supply. Working slowly and very carefully using a hand grinder, initially open both the inlet and exhaust port pockets to match the valve seat diameters. The face of the boss supporting the valve guide needs to be smoothed and shaped to minimize air flow restrictions. If you are fortunate enough to have found a pair of Buick 300 heads, there is usually a pronounced lip immediately behind the valve seat insert. This acts as a restriction that needs to be smoothed out. Remember that the head is relatively soft aluminium, and it is easy to remove too much material. You want to just match the edges of the insert and the port, but take care not to enlarge the port itself because this will slow down the charge velocity.

The next area of attention is the aluminium boss holding the valve guide. The step from the boss to the smaller diameter guide adversely affects a smooth flow so, with a long shank on the grinder, taper the boss gently down to the guide, being careful not to touch the guide itself.

Examine the walls of the ports behind the valves because these are sometimes excessively rough. You should not need the grinder, but carefully lap sand the walls, smoothing them and certainly removing any flashing but not actually enlarging the ports. Many think polished walls improve gas-flow, but a smooth finish is all that is required – you could spend hours bringing them up to a polished standard to no good effect. In fact there is a school of thought that argues a certain degree of port wall roughness is needed to keep the mixture in suspension.

The ultimate cylinder head

There is a better – if more expensive – cylinder head solution: Wildcat Engineering's bespoke casting can be seen in photographs 8-2-7 and 8-2-8.

I haven't explored them here as the information is widely available

8-2-7 For comparison with the following picture, this is a standard 3500cc SD1 head while ...

8-2-8 ... this is the ultimate Wildcat head. The valves, particularly the inlets, are noticeably bigger.

elsewhere, but there are now steel cranks, forged steel con-rods and forged aluminium pistons available at reasonable cost to strengthen the bottom end, but the main obstacle to extra power remains the cylinder heads. Wildcat Engineering has developed a new head casting for the Rover engine that bolts straight on and uses the same push-rod arrangement. The best fully worked Rover race-head manages to flow about 105 cubic feet per minute, but in its most basic form the Wildcat heads will flow 130ft³/m of gas as a result of their 1.85in diameter inlet valves, 1.55in exhaust, enlarged inlet port (2.1in²) and a 1.7in² exhaust port. The Stage 2 Wildcat Cylinder Head for race cars has flowed over 150ft³/m,

SPEEDPRO SERIES

8-3-1 Opening out the two primary oil-passages in the early blocks can be done by hand but you risk scrapping the block so, for the cost involved, it is best to leave it to professionals with the correct equipment seen here.

and helps a 5-litre Rover V8 to just under 450bhp.

UPGRADING THE EARLY ENGINES

The American GM 215s and the Rover P5B and P6 engines would benefit from the following upgrades:

Oil pressure/flow

These engines had both low oil flow volume and pressure, and consequently upgrading the oil system becomes a serious consideration, particularly in the USA with higher ambient temperatures.

Beginning with oil flow improvements, most US V8 converters drill out the 215's two main oil galleys to a ½in diameter. You'll see this in progress at 8-3-1. Naturally, the benefit will be reduced unless you also replace the standard 0.43in diameter oil pickup tube with a ½in diameter unit from a 1979-86 Buick V6. Some converters maximize the improvement by enlarging the oil pump pickup pipe to 0.62in diameter (15mm).

The vast majority increase the volume pumped by their oil pump. The Rover SD1 achieves higher volume by using longer oil pump gears in a deeper housing than early engines, and kits are available from Kenne-Bell and others that increase the oil flow by about 40 per cent. The details depend upon the engine and kit in question, but typically, a spacer plate is inserted between the base and the oil pump housing. This increases the depth of the oil pump housing, while longer (ex-SD1) pump gears are used to match the deeper housing.

Oil pressure increases are purely a question of a stronger pressure relief valve spring. The springs come in a variety of strengths, from 35 to 60psi, and are available from numerous specialists, including Kenne-Bell in the USA and several Rover V8 specialists (e.g. Real Steel, RPI, etc.) in the UK.

Flywheels

Chronologically, we need to discuss the US Buick and Oldsmobile flywheels first before briefly looking at the Rover V8 flywheel. There were Pontiac 215 flywheels made in the 1960s too, but they were different and relatively infrequent so we will disregard them.

All flywheels were manufactured from cast iron and individually balanced before fitting to their respective crankshafts and balanced again. GM employed two styles of manual gearbox flywheels, a light and heavy version. The light version seen in photo 8-3-2 weighs in at only 23lb, is flat faced on the clutch side (pictured at 8-3-3) and would be the ideal unit for an TR7-V8 conversion. The 'heavy' version flywheel incorporated an integral cast inertia ring around its circumference, which boosted the weight to 32lb. It is possible to machine the width (and therefore some of the weight) off this inertia ring.

There was only one version of the Rover V8 flywheel, although it does look very similar to its 2.3- and 2.6-litre sister-engine versions. The Rover V8 manual flywheel weighs 35lb in standard

8-3-2 The front of an Oldsmobile light flywheel. This flywheel not only offers increased acceleration but is balanced more carefully than the Buick versions via ...

8-3-3 ... an additional balancing hole drilled top left in this shot.

trim and, like the US 215 units, you are unlikely to regret having a specialist take yours down to 27lb, possibly even a pound or two lighter. But take care not to take too much off, and ensure you use a specialist who knows to takes the material off in the right places.

A mildly-lightened 25-27lb flywheel is for road use when you still need the engine to behave in traffic and to idle at, say, 900-1000rpm. For

98

ACQUIRING AND UPGRADING A ROVER V8

8-3-4 The Range Rover oil cooler take-off and return.

competition, go for a lighter flywheel and lightweight competition clutch (Tilton, Quartermaster and of course, AP) to speed the engine acceleration/pick-up – but expect idle to be lumpy, the clutch VERY heavy, and the car progressively un-drivable as the weight of the flywheel and clutch reduces. An alternative and certainly cheaper competition flywheel would use an auto car's flex-plate (without the torque converter, of course). The flex-plate is little more than a flat plate with a starter-ring gear shrunk on, and is much lighter than a conventional flywheel. You will then need to talk to the competition clutch experts to find a small competition clutch to fit.

Most specialists can supply billet-turned light flywheels in aluminium, aluminium with steel facing or, my preferred solution, a thin steel flywheel.

Take advice once your engine exceeds 200bhp, for additional bolts fastening the flywheel to crank may be required depending upon the flywheel (particularly the flywheel material) the power of the engine and the use the car is put to.

LUBRICATION UPGRADES

Regardless of the year of your Rover engine, consider incorporating the following improvements as you rebuild or fit your Buick/Rover unit:

Oil coolers

The SD1/TR8 oil filter location is not usually a problem when it comes to fitting a TR7 with a Rover or Buick V8 engine, but you may want to re-think the filter arrangement if you decide an oil cooler is advantageous.

In the case of a Range Rover engine, the take-off for the cooler is as simple as fitting the spacer we see at 8-3-4 between the filter and the oil pump base which the lines attach to.

Buick and Rover P6, SD1, etc. engines are fairly simple to change as far as engine take-off is concerned – fit a different oil pump base with cooler take-off and return connections in place. However, this will displace the usual filter mounting and necessitate fitting a different one. There are two basic solutions:

1) US converters can procure an oil pump base from a Buick 231 V6, with the word "METRIC' cast into the bottom of the base and seen in photographs 8-3-5-1 and 8-3-5-2. The metric base bolts directly to the Buick/Olds/Rover oil pump, and points the oil filter mounting horizontally. A remote oil filter kit with a 13/16-16 thread, such as Transdapt's (part number 1420 90), spins onto the metric pump base and has NPT female threaded ports for the inlet and outlet hoses to a remote oil filter and cooler.

2) In the UK, most V8 converters seeking an oil cooler fitting will use a replica MGB GT V8 oil pump base seen at 8-3-6. Like the US arrangement, it bolts straight onto the bottom of the oil pump and provides ports for an outlet pipe and a return pipe. The former goes to one side of the oil cooler, and from the other side of the cooler to a remote filter. A separate pipe then links the other side of the filter to the return port on the pump base.

The usual V8 remote oil filter

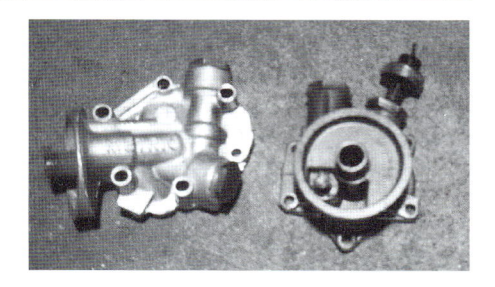

8-3-5-1 Buick V6 metric pump base, viewed from the bottom.

8-3-5-2 A rotatable oil filter shown on a Buick oil pump base.

8-3-6 This is a replica MGB GT V8 oil pump base. The cooler/filter take-offs are obvious, but you might be interested to know that the small angle bottom connection is for a pressure gauge.

99

SPEEDPRO SERIES

8-3-7 This is a chromed version of an oil filter cover/protector. It's sold primarily for aesthetic purposes from numerous outlets but works well in a protective capacity when you fit your oil filter under the front wing/fender.

location is normally as far forward on the right side of the engine bay as is practical. However, remember this engine is prone to sludge build-up probably because of its relatively low oil flow, and consequently if longevity is of any interest, you need to change oil and filter every 3000 miles or so. An alternative location for a remote oil filter is under the wing/fender behind the right-side headlamp. This location keeps the engine bay uncluttered and probably makes oil changes easier, although a sheet metal guard or the cover in picture 8-3-7 is required to protect the filter from stones thrown up by the wheel.

Oil pump variations

The 3500cc SD1, Defender et al and 3.9 Discovery engines use a camshaft-gear driven oil pump, with the sort of oil pick-up arrangement seen in photo 8-3-8. The oil is transferred via passages in the block and a pipe/strainer in the middle of the engine, seen in 8-3-9. The later engines used the best oil pump system of all the aluminium V8s – driven off the front of the crankshaft. Unfortunately, not only do these later engines have a different crankshaft, but also the oil pick-up arrangements

8-3-8 The typical early oil pick-up arrangement where the oil is drawn to the pump through the block via ...

differ. So, you basically need the whole bottom end of a 4.0/4.2/4.6 engine to benefit from the improvement. They collect their oil via a pipe from the sump, direct to the pump still located in the front cover but driven off the crank. There was a consequent change in sump design seen in photographs 8-3-10 and 8-3-11.

Note: not only do the oil pump arrangements change, but so do the water pumps. The Range Rover/Defender water pump is different in detail and mounted higher up on the front cover than, say, an SD1. However, provided you change the whole cover/water pump assembly, they will fit (8-3-12-1 and 8-3-12-2).

Speedier oil return

You will increase the volume of oil over the timing chain (enhancing longevity),

8-3-9 ... this strainer. Note the windage tray.

8-3-10 From inside the engine, the two types of sump. Top in this picture is the later sump with windage tray which is fitted to engines with crank-drive oil pumps while ...

8-3-11 ... externally there are differences too, with (bottom) the earlier design of sump fitted to camshaft driven oil pumps. Note the gearbox support plate to the left of the earlier sump is omitted from the later sump.

100

ACQUIRING AND UPGRADING A ROVER V8

and reduce the amount of oil in the top-end of the engine by getting it back to the sump quicker, if you drill two holes in the front of the block down into the timing chest (as shown in picture 8-3-13).

Priming the oil pump
Follow the workshop manual's instructions regarding filling your new oil pump with Vaseline (petroleum jelly), pictured at 8-3-14-1 and 8-3-14-2, before you bolt the new base to the oil pump housing. Without the petroleum jelly, your oil pump will not prime and you'll be without oil pressure. Do not use any form of grease, as only petroleum jelly melts. Grease could clog the oilways generally, and the pressure gauge take-off in particular.

The following tip may help in the event of zero oil pressure, assuming you have not blocked the oil pressure gauge take-off with grease! The standard start-up procedure with any new engine is to remove the spark plugs and turn the engine over on the starter until oil pressure is established. The V8 is no exception, although there is an additional option. In fact, you may want to follow this route anyway to ensure your lovely, newly-reconditioned engine gets oil from the first turn of the starter motor. Remove the oil pipe going from the front of the oil filter base to the cooler and, using a funnel, prime the pump by filling this pipe with engine oil. Reconnect the pipe. Remove the distributor. Cut a 3mm wide slot in a piece of 10mm diameter steel rod, and fit to your electric drill. Turn the oil pump drive tang with the slotted end of your rod and electric drill until oil pressure is established, remove drill, refit distributor and start the car.

Sumps and gaskets
Use a competition thickness sump gasket, as the standard Rover gasket

8-3-12-1 This is an example of a front cover from a serpentine drive-belted engine.

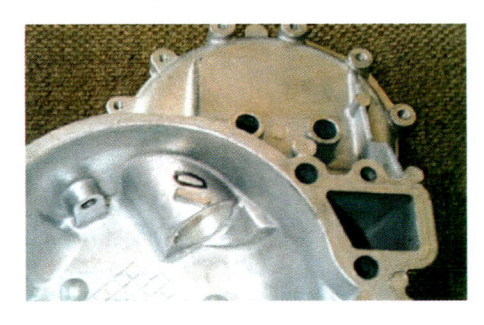

8-3-12-2 Here is another example that, with its provision for a dizzy, at first sight looks very promising. However, you may find the pulley arrangement difficult unless the engine came complete with all the front fittings.

8-3-13 Once you have found the best front cover for your conversion, drill these holes to allow extra lubricating oil to drain into the timing chain compartment.

is too thin and oil leaks will probably result between sump and block. The considerably thicker competition gasket

8-3-14-1 At the top of this shot you can see the original oil pump base. This is the UK replacement base with the essential petroleum jelly needed to pack the oil pump gears ...

8-3-14-2 ... tight, like this.

is available from JE Motor Engineering in Coventry, and seen at 8-3-15 (overleaf). An alternative is to apply lots of silicone gasket sealant – but take great care to ensure no surplus globules get inside the engine.

If your Rover sump is badly distorted around the mounting bolts, place it upside down on a flat surface and tap out the worst of the imperfections.

SPEEDPRO SERIES

8-3-15 Not very obvious from this view but care in fitting the sump/oil pan is worthwhile and the thicker gasket shown here is very helpful in preventing leaks. Above all, do not over-tighten the numerous sump fastenings.

8-3-16 This is a Buick 215 sump. Its low frontal section might have been designed with TR7 conversions in mind. If you have a Buick/Rover with a deeper front section the problem is easily resolved by fitting one of these slim-fronted sumps/oil pans.

The vast majority of Buick/Rover sumps/oil pans have a wonderfully low frontal section to their profile, as seen from picture 8-3-16. This provides for plenty of cross-member/K-frame clearance. However, ex-Rover P5B, P6 and most Range Rover sumps have a deeper frontal section for some reason, which can cause interference problems with this cross-member. You can modify the front of these sumps to allow adequate clearance over the cross-member and steering rack, but the best solution is to pick up an SD1 sump from a breakers' yard for £15 or so. This is the most cost-effective remedy, but be sure to get the SD1 oil pick-up, windage tray and spacers, as they too will be required if you have a Range Rover engine (picture 8-3-17).

OTHER UNIVERSAL IMPROVEMENTS
Camshaft

I believe the standard SD1 camshaft is the ideal camshaft for UK applications, and will give up to 200bhp without loss of torque or driveability. However, the standard 3947cc camshaft (available from RPI) is reputed to be even smoother, and good for an extra 10bhp even in 3500cc engines. The engine tends to knock the lobes off camshafts, and a cam change every 50000 miles is normal with Rover camshafts. Change the cam followers when fitting a new camshaft, and maybe consider a non-Rover unit at the same time.

A range of aftermarket alternatives is available, in addition to replacement original GM camshafts, for the US V8 converter. The shortlist for V8 uses might be the Crower 50232 for manual transmissions, or the Kenne-Bell KB Mark 2A. Another Kenne-Bell option is its KB 1XA with a slightly earlier power/torque curve (1000-5500 rpm). Kenne-Bell particularly recommends the 1XA with a Carter carburettor, but points out that the 2A does give superior mid- to top-end performance.

Crane is an alternative and very respected manufacturer in the UK, and it makes an excellent range of V8 hydraulic performance camshafts, offering sensible, uprated alternatives to that of the standard profile:

H180 (mild road) – high torque, offering slightly improved performance from otherwise standard engines, including those with an automatic gearbox. Power band is 1000 to 4500rpm.

H214 (fast road) – ideal for AFB carburettors and manual gearboxes. Power band is 1500 to 5000rpm.

H224 (road/rally) – also suited to AFB carburettors, but requires 'stage 2' cylinder heads to get the most from its 2000 to 5500rpm power band.

8-3-17 These are the SD1 oil pick-up, windage tray and spacers you will need.

Installing a camshaft

Whatever camshaft you choose, it requires care when fitting, starting and initially running it. Note that the Rover V8 engine and its derivatives are heavy on camshaft lobes, and consequently these camshaft installations require particular care. However, most premature camshaft failures, regardless of the engine involved, can be traced back to their first few moments of operation. This in turn is usually the result of incorrect installation, lubrication and/or running.

Always fit new cam followers with a new camshaft. In fact, wherever possible, buy and fit a complete cam-kit from your chosen manufacturer, since the associated parts are then correctly matched. Every new engine component, particularly every camshaft, that I have seen has had a wax-like protective coating which must be removed just before installation (wash it in paraffin/kerosene). Apply LOTS of cam lube

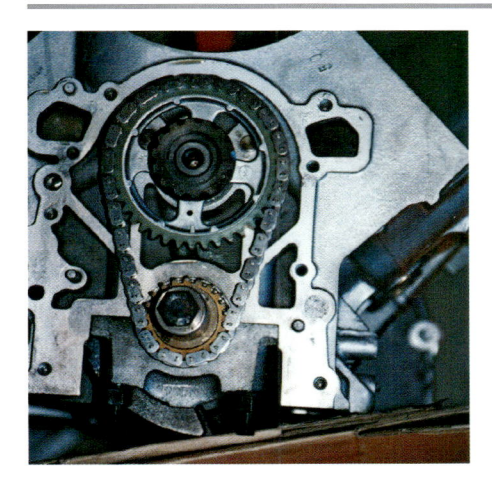

ACQUIRING AND UPGRADING A ROVER V8

8-4-1 The larger sprocket drives the camshaft and, on the Rover engines, is made from plastic, so is consequently susceptible to wear.

8-4-2 This JP Performance Products timing gear set is one of several worthwhile upgrades providing a duplex chain and hardened steel sprockets. This is a universal set; the multi-position crank sprocket needs care and some thought in order to get its position correct for the Rover engines, but …

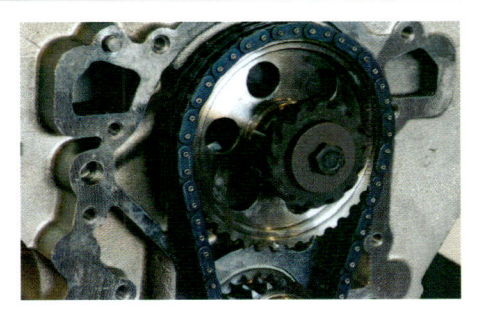

8-4-3 … once in place will provide years of hard service.

on the cam bearing and lobes (and followers), straight after washing the wax protection off.

On installation, it is also important to check the entire valve train to ensure that no interference is occurring, particularly with respect to valve spring binding. Ensure there is 0.030in clearance between the centre coils.

Clearly valve-to-piston contact must also be avoided and, as another rule of thumb, aim for a minimum of 0.060in clearance.

Always prime the lubrication system and get some oil-pressure up before starting the engine. Also, in order to avoid an initial long 'grind' on the starter, do everything you can to help the engine start quickly, e.g. prime the fuel system. Once running, do not allow the oil pressure or oil throw from the crank to drop by running the engine too slowly. 2500 to 3000rpm is ideal, and this needs to be maintained for perhaps the first 30 minutes to allow the camshaft to be run/broken in. Thus, take care not to tick over/idle the engine during this initial, camshaft-critical period.

Camshaft drive
While on the subject of camshaft upgrades, it seems appropriate to say that the plastic camshaft driving/timing gear seen at 8-4-1 should also be upgraded to something more substantial. You may lose out slightly in respect to noise levels, but more importantly your timing will be much more reliable and your timing chain less likely to stretch. In fact, this improvement is uniform across the range of GM and Rover V8 engines (including most of the later units) and involves fitting hardened steel gears and a double-row roller chain. Edelbrock or JP Performance Products (part number 5984), seen in photos 8-4-2 and 8-4-3, are available from RPI and either will do the business. TSI in the USA also sells a steel sprocket/chain kit.

Transplanting EFI engines
The majority of second-hand 3947cc units will come from Range Rovers (and probably be fitted with a Hot Wire injection system). Be aware that such a system's ECU has a speed limiter built in at 110-112mph to cope with the vehicle's S speed rated tyres. You can have a specialist eliminate the problem by re-chipping the ECU (RPI or numerous EFI specialists would be able to carry out this work quite cheaply). If you want a new 3947cc short engine, these are available from RPI.

Starter motor
The normal SD1 Lucas 3M100PE unit is all that fast road conversions need. Ultra-fast and competitive cars may, however, be better advised to fit a modern 'gear-reduction' high-torque starter motor. These dual-geared motors use less power to develop more torque than the conventional starter motor – and they are much more compact, too. If buying a used Range Rover engine a modern starter should be included in the deal. If you have to hand one of the several older starter motors that were fitted to the Buick and early Rover blocks, they will have either interference and/or torque-generating limitations when fitted to an increased capacity engine – particularly a high-compression one. These modern

SPEEDPRO SERIES

8-4-4-1 As you can see, a block-hugger exhaust manifold passes very close to the starter motor and, consequently, some thermal protection is essential. I fabricated this steel shield and put fibreglass insulation inside it before …

starters are very compact and have the solenoid tucked well out of the way.

Whichever starter motor you fit you need to consider providing it with some thermal protection, because the fabricated tubular manifolds/headers are close by and radiate a lot of heat. If your manifold/header is made from good quality stainless steel then exhaust wrap tape in the area of the starter motor will do the job. If you are using mild steel manifolds/headers then wrapping the manifold/header may not be such a good idea - in which case a heat shield between the starter motor and the exhaust is prudent. You can make your own using photo 8-4-4-1 as a pattern, but the MOULDED insulating ones seen at 8-4-4-2 are available from Clive Wheatley. Note too that the wiring to the solenoid suffers from the heat and is consequently prone to cracking. This could be dangerous if/when some insulation falls away, so slip some fibreglass sleeves over the wires.

Crackcase breathers and filler

In most cases the breather that fits atop the rocker cover will not cause bonnet/hood interference problems. The gauze filled units come in two heights – roughly

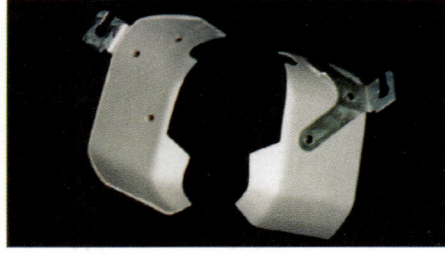

8-4-4-2 … Clive Wheatley started having these neat moulded shields made.

1in (25mm) and 2in (50mm) tall – and while you can cut the taller ones down it is easier to buy a shorter one in case you get into bother. Pictures 8-4-5-1 and 8-4-5-2 may help.

EFI plastic stubs are another alternative, available from your local Rover dealer. Check out part number ERR 3473A for your breather and ERC 247A for the filler adapter. Items screwing to the rocker covers require an O-ring/seal, but even when fitted, watch for and correct anything that extends through the cover and thus poses a danger of fouling the rocker gear below.

FURTHER READING

How to power tune Rover V8 engines by Des Hammill. Published by Veloce Publishing Ltd and available by post direct from the publisher. ISBN 13: 978-1-903706-17-6. Covers tuning all 3.5 to 4.6 engines for road and track.

Tuning Rover V8 engines by David Hardcastle.

Increasing the displacement of Buick-Olds 215 and Rover aluminium V8s (nine informative pages within D+D Fabrications' catalogue).

March 1985 issue of *Hot Rod* magazine. A six-page summary of the numerous combinations of components that have been used to extend the stroke and therefore the capacity of the basic 215in^3/3500cc engine to (amongst others) 245, 262, 289, 298 and 305in^3!

The latter is as near 5000cc as to make no difference. To obtain a reprint, send a $5.00 cheque to *Hot Rod* magazine, Peterson Publishing Co., 8490 Sunset Blvd, Los Angeles, CA 90069 USA (tel: 213-782-2000), asking for a copy of Marlan Davis' *Affordable Aluminium V8s* article on D+D Fabrications and Baker's Auto Repair's respective work, experience and specialities. The contact details for both these experts can be found in the appendix.

8-4-5-1 Closing the bonnet with an oil filler protruding upwards may prove a problem. You can reverse the rocker covers so that this filler moves to a right rear location or, …

8-4-5-2 … unscrew the tube. Ensure the filler cap has an o-ring and does not foul the rockers and/or rocker shaft.

Chapter 9
Fitting out a V8 engine bay

As my research for this book progressed, I deduced that each supplier has strengths and weaknesses in their one-stop complete kit. Therefore, while I still favour using proven parts for a conversion, I think it better you 'cherry-pick' – buying a brake kit from here, an engine installation kit from there and a suspension upgrade kit from somewhere else! It may result in a slightly more expensive conversion, but overall a better car.

With each purchase you need to establish that the kit in question is sound, and I think it important to seek reference contacts from customers who have fitted the kit and can assure you that it both fits and works well.

Consequently, I have elected not to try to evaluate each supplier's one-stop conversion kit, but to look at the much more numerous upgrade kits individually and within the appropriate chapter. This chapter is focused on getting the heart of the TR7 – the V8 engine and gearbox – into the car.

THE PRE-ASSEMBLY PREPARATION
The cross-member/ K-frame

The engine mounting brackets on a TR8 and TR7-V8 are NOT affixed to the chassis frame, but welded atop the cross-member/K-frame as shown in 9-1-1. I would like to have offered you a drawing of a mounting bracket or a supplier of the same – however, the trade feels you are best to either buy a new TR8 frame, or a refurbished TR7 one with mounting brackets pre-welded in place, taking poor home welding out of the equation.

So, given that you are going to have to buy a pre-welded assembly, the question is, do you buy:

1) a genuine TR8 frame (they are still available)
2) a refurbished TR7 frame modified to form a TR8 replica
3) or a frame with lowered non-standard mounting brackets such as

9-1-1 The V8 engine mounts were welded to the sub-frame to reduce noise and vibration, but also allow for some latitude when it comes to squeezing the engine in under the bonnet/hood.

you will see at photo 9-1-2 (overleaf)?

Option 1 is the most expensive of the choices, but perhaps is the route to follow if your TR7 frame is rusty, bent or not worth refurbishing.

If my TR7 frame was in good condition, ever mindful of the cost issue, and if I was planning sooner or later to fit a power-steering rack, I would choose option 2. It is cheaper

SPEEDPRO SERIES

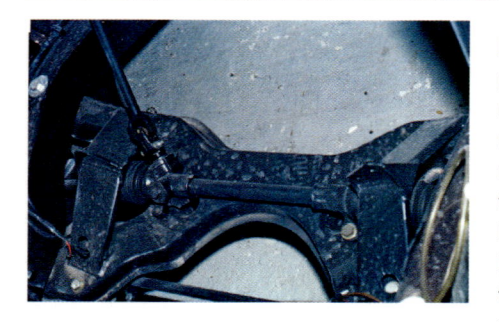

9-1-2 This is a manual rack affixed to a lowered pair of V8 engine brackets but, in my opinion, the more powerful an engine you are planning, the more prudent it is to keep open your power-steering option.

than a new genuine TR8 frame, and it is my opinion that the more powerful the engine, the greater the need to fit wider section tyres, thus the heavier the steering is likely to be at slow speeds. You could certainly start by fitting your TR7's original manual rack, particularly if it is in good order, but this route keeps the PAS option open.

Relatively low-powered, low-cost TR7-V8 conversions with, say, 185-section tyres should find manual steering perfectly in order for most circumstances. This is advantageous because it enables you to use option 3, which reduces the height of the V8 engine in the engine bay. These frames still have the engine mounting brackets fabricated, but they are made about 1in (25mm) lower than the TR8 brackets. The difference is difficult to spot in a photograph, but such a frame should lower the carburettor dashpots by, I estimate, ½in or about 12mm which could, when aided by V8 spacers between frame and chassis, allow the continued use of an early single-bulge bonnet.

The bodyshell
This is a unique opportunity to correct any imperfections within the engine bay. Strip out any dubious or unsightly pipework or electrical looms. Correct any minor areas of corrosion, and possibly cut out PART of the battery/wiper-motor mounting 'tray' – if, that is, you intend to relocate the battery to the boot/trunk. If appropriate, re-paint the bay, replace brake, clutch and fuel-lines and generally take this opportunity to rejuvenate the engine bay.

To make provision for the V8's gearbox cross-member you will first need to remove both seats, the carpeting and trim from the area where the original gearbox mounting went, and push the pair of original gearbox cross-member stud-plates up into the cockpit from below the car. They will be re-used later, once the new gearbox cross-member location has been established.

The gearbox
The vast majority of readers will be fitting fast road and ultra-fast road V8 engines with a Rover 5-speed gearbox behind, and thus this chapter is focused on helping them make the engine-fitting go as smoothly as possible. Readers with competitive cars and/or different gearboxes should find the following generally helpful, but in need of minor changes.

If your original TR7 (5-speed) clutch is fairly new and in excellent condition, fast-road cars may reduce their initial conversion costs by re-using the TR7 clutch parts – but bearing in mind the work involved in a clutch change, I would recommend a new 3-piece SD1 set.

The engine
An SD1 engine has a slightly extended front end compared to a Rover P5B and P6 engine. If you are fitting an engine with a P5B/P6 front end, it should go in fully assembled. In the case of an SD1 engine you are rebuilding, you may find it easier to fit the front-end components (front crank pulley, water-pump pulley, alternator and cradle) after you've got the engine and gearbox in the car. If you are fitting an assembled engine, you will need to remove the crank pulley and, I suggest, the water pump pulley. You should be able to get the engine in with the water-pump body and alternator in place.

This is a unique opportunity to prepare the 'new' engine before dropping it into the car. If spraying the outside with a degreaser and power-washing it off, do remove the rocker shafts beforehand, thus closing all the valves. Obviously you should check the rocker shafts and rockers before re-fitting them. The camshaft is vulnerable on Rover engines, and if the engine has done 50000 miles or more then a look at it may surprise you. If a new one is necessary, do be sure to fit new (hydraulic) cam-followers. The timing chains on the Rover engine stretch and the (plastic) camshaft sprocket wears, so this could be the opportunity to replace/upgrade both with a duplex chain and hardened steel cam sprocket.

Check the flywheel ring gear, and if you are considering lightening the flywheel, this is the moment. When fitting the clutch to the flywheel, I strongly recommend centralising the clutch-plate on the flywheel with an alignment tool.

Whichever front frame you use, you need to fit the steering rack to the frame and the lower steering column to the rack. I would suggest you then pre-assemble (off the car) your engine, sump, gearbox and flexible engine mounts. We went into more detail in chapter 5 for steering racks and in chapter 8 for the sump – if you've got it right, you should find minimal but sufficient clearances between sump and

FITTING OUT A V8 ENGINE BAY

9-1-3 This backward-facing view shows that the flexible engine mount is located to the rear/far side of the K-frame.

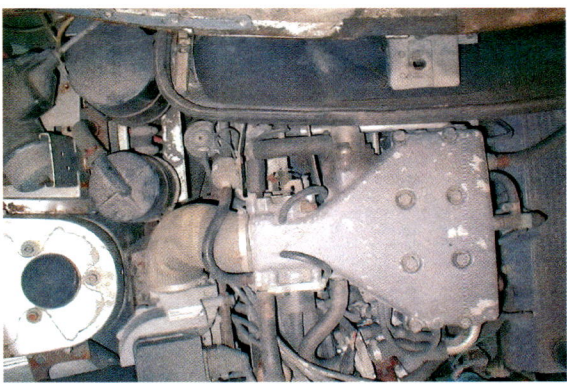

9-1-4-2 ... the problem does not arise with the earlier Federal SD1 or TR8 plenum, although ...

9-1-4-1 The Hot Wire plenum comes very close to the bonnet latch, and may necessitate moving the whole engine forward, although ...

9-1-4-3 ... you will alleviate the situation if you put a slight swerve into the air intake.

9-1-5 This is a Rover V8 about to be dropped into an MGB. The picture is relevant in that the very thin front pulley is from a Rover P6, and would allow the TR7's engine to move forward, increasing plenum chamber clearance and helping align the gearlever in the prop-tunnel.

frame, but this is the time to find and correct any problems!

If you are fitting an engine with an SD1 front pulley arrangement, there is one crucial detail you need to get right during the next step. The flange on the engine's flexible mounting normally drops down to the rear of the K-frame cross-member, as seen in picture 9-1-3. There are two exceptions to this rule ...

If you are fitting a 'Hot Wire' Range Rover EFI intake (plenum), seen at 9-1-4-1 to 9-1-4-2, you will likely have to fit the flexible mountings in front of the cross-member to create clearance between the plenum and bonnet latch and/or modify the air intake as shown in 9-1-4-3..

If you have Rover P5B or P6 pulleys at the front of your engine as per photograph 9-1-5, you may think space behind the radiator would be less critical and that using the front of the cross-member will be OK. This is true, and it would help align the gearlever in the prop-tunnel. However, you may find the space between radiator and front pulley useful for electric fans so I suggest you follow the 'behind the cross-member' rule anyway!

FITTING THE V8

There are two ways to get the V8 into a TR7's engine bay. The professionals will mostly elect to drop it in from the top, some with, some without the gearbox

SPEEDPRO SERIES

9-2-1 If you are dropping the pre-assembled engine and gearbox in from the top with the K-frame already in situ, you are best to raise the rear wheels (safely – perhaps on a pair of ramps) before starting.

9-2-2. With the gearbox attached, the engine goes in at quite a steep angle. This route would be appropriate only if the front suspension was still fitted to the car.

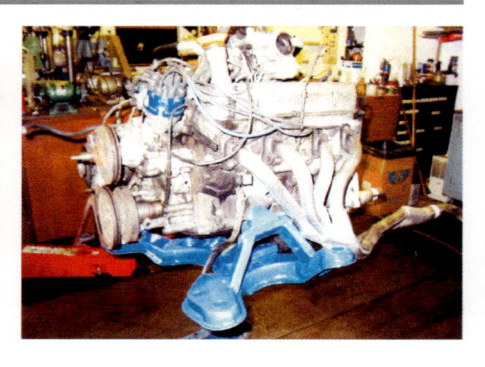

9-2-3 The exhaust manifolds will need to come off and the clutch and gearbox fitted, but nevertheless this shot will give you the general picture of what a pre-assembled, up-from-below sub-assembly looks like. I think, however, it is a good idea to trial-fit the manifold to the heads.

9-2-4-1 Lift up the tail of the gearbox to the floor. Ensure the cross-member is centralised, using the old holes to retain correct alignment. The original holes will be between 25 to 50mm in front of where the new holes are needed for the four stud-plates, so ...

attached, but all with the K-frame in place as per photo 9-2-1. We see a top-down engine assembly in progress at 9-2-2.

However, I think most amateurs carrying out a full V8 conversion (which requires a change of K-frame), particularly those without a great deal of headroom, will find the job easiest if they pre-assemble frame, rack, engine, gearbox and gearbox cross-member. This sub-assembly (picture 9-2-3) can then be offered up from below the engine bay. More detail shortly, but naturally the front suspension is assembled later, once the frame, engine and gearbox are fully secure in the car.

You can pre-assemble the front suspension on the frame, but I think this only adds to the complexity of marrying the frame/engine/gearbox assembly to the shell. Furthermore, when fixing the engine to the sub-frame and subsequently fixing the frame to the chassis, I would not tighten the fastenings up fully ... leave each a couple of revolutions on the slack side in order to give yourself a little manoeuvrability. When the engine and gearbox are home you may want to take up some of this slack, but you might find it advantageous to only fully tighten the engine, K-frame and gearbox mounting fastenings once the exhaust system is in place.

The 'up-and-under' method is best accomplished with the frame sitting on a 1 metre-long wheeled trolley, which positions the frame about 15cm off the ground. You would be wise to spend a little time buying, borrowing or making a suitable one before sitting the frame at what will be the front end. In my experience, your nearest waste-ground or river bank will almost certainly yield a damaged ex-supermarket trolley to serve as a metal-framed starting-point.

Raise the front of the bodyshell and carefully secure it with at least two axle stands, positioned under the shell just forward of the middle. Wheel the frame, engine and gearbox sub-assembly under the shell. I use two trolley jacks under the front, but a block and tackle above the shell will be equally effective. Remove the axle stands once you are clear of the underside, and slowly lower the shell onto the frame/engine/gearbox/trolley, feeding the steering column link onto the top column as soon as possible.

You will need to fit four spacers and bushes between the frame and the chassis. It seems universally agreed that polyurethane bushes are best. However, opinion varies as to the correct length of the metal spacers and fastenings, but I would use standard/stock length spacers and bolts until much later in the conversion when, perhaps, you become convinced that you have no alternative but to lengthen them. Whatever the length of the spacers, note that the domed washers go on the rear

FITTING OUT A V8 ENGINE BAY

9-2-4-2. ... re-drill from under the car using the cross-member as a template. Push the original two pairs of studs through their new holes from inside the cockpit, and secure the gearbox cross-member from under the car.

9-2-5 Clive Wheatley's twinned Rover gaskets, which considerably quicken gasket orientation.

9-2-6-1 Both types of TR8 exhaust arrangements use the same manifolds as far back as the bell-housing ...

9-2-6-2 ... thereafter, the twin-pipe system continues, with two parallel exhaust systems along the length of the car, using a silencer/muffler in the centre and towards the rear of each over-axle pipe.

9-2-6-3 The single pipe system extends both manifolds for a few feet, before joining them into a single exhaust (and silencer/muffler) about halfway down the length of the car.

mountings. More detail appears shortly under the heading 'Closing the bonnet'.

You will need to lift the rear of the gearbox up until the gearbox/transmission rear cross-member is hard up against the bodyshell, as seen in 9-2-4-1 and 9-2-4-2. As a matter of interest, the TR8 has a staggered cross-member allowing the holes in the bodyshell to be identical with those in a TR7. However, you cannot buy the TR8 gearbox cross-member, and while you could cut and carve your TR7 one it's far easier to simply re-position the TR7 cross-member with four additional holes. Use rubber blanking grommets to close the four original holes.

The gearlever/shift could now appear a shade too tall. If this is indeed a problem for you, either shorten the gearlever itself (my recommendation) or fit a pair of spacers (about 20mm long) between the cross-member and the bodyshell.

The gearlever will have moved back by approximately 25-50mm, into the same position as the TR8's, but it should still be accommodated within the original hole. However, if you have difficulties engaging second and fourth gear, you might need to consider shortening the gearbox top extension. This is rarely necessary, but in any event I wonder if you noted my MG RV8 trick in chapter 7?

THE MANIFOLDS
The exhaust manifold and system

The ease or otherwise of fitting the exhaust manifold/headers depends upon their quality. Fit new ones of the best quality you can afford, and lay the flanges along a flat face before handing over your cash. Do not be tempted by a pair of used ones – it is highly likely that the flanges will have distorted and they will be the very devil to fit.

Buy a set of the 'twin' gaskets pictured at 9-2-5 and a tube of smooth exhaust paste that, when the time comes, is best applied on BOTH sides of the gaskets. Even with these twin gaskets it needs a great deal of care to ensure you have the gaskets the correct way round. It is very easy to part-close an exhaust port. It is easier if socket/Allen-headed fastenings are used along the bottom row of holes.

Most TR7-V8 conversions will want to use a proven TR8 system. On the TR8, you can choose between two types of exhaust system (explained in 9-2-6-1 to 9-2-6-3). The systems

SPEEDPRO SERIES

come in mild steel and stainless steel, but since exhausts rust from the inside – fuelled by the water vapour produced during the combustion process – the stainless option is really the only long-term practical route to follow. It is more expensive in the short-term but will repay itself several times over, particularly if you are laying the car up for much of the winter months each year.

Our Stateside cousins will want to know that there were three different types of catalytic converters used on TR8s. The late 'Federal' spec converter for EFI systems has a longer and larger diameter casing with slightly shorter piping attached to it than the early Federal converter. The 'California' converter has the larger diameter casing with integral intermediate pipe. The early and late Federal spec converters also appear to have slightly different lengths, and are not interchangeable unless you also replace the intermediate pipe. The dividing point between the early and late Federal systems appears to be about VIN 201308. The parts catalogues may say California, but true California systems will have cats with attached intermediate pipes and mounting bosses for the fuel-injection oxygen sensors. The TR8 has a balance pipe between the two systems, seen at 9-2-7.

The K-frame can present major fitting problems for the manifolds, and non-standard/stock lowered sub-frames exacerbate this. Typical changes you might be required to make are heating and bending the front manifold pipes to get them on the car, and then flattening (slightly) the curve at the bottom of the manifold/header to clear the sub-frame. Probably some, but by no means all of this aggravation is the fault of the exhaust system manufacturer.

Having resolved any K-frame related problems, you need to fit

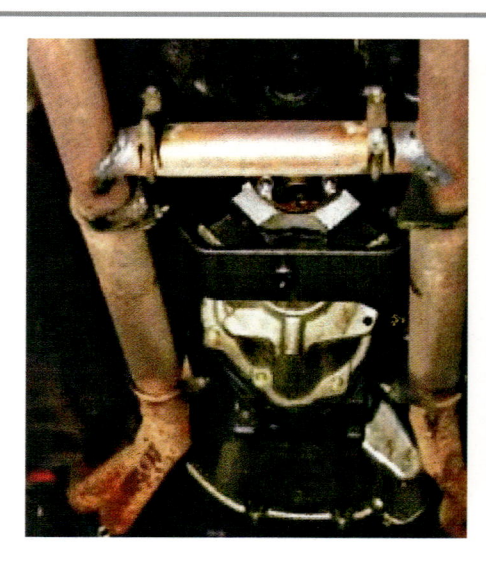

9-2-7. The balance pipe acts as an expansion box and also reduces noise emissions.

the exhaust pipe(s) themselves. It is tempting initially to set the exhaust tight up to the underside of the shell, in order to maximise ground clearance. The problem is that heat radiated into the cockpit is then considerable, necessitating some reflective insulation under the floor areas of the shell and under the carpet, too! It is best to fit the underside reflective material before starting on the exhaust system itself. The obvious secondary remedy is to drop the exhaust down slightly away from the floor, which might be practical if you have bought a twin-pipe kit with rear boxes only. A twin system without the centre boxes gives a fabulous V8 sound (might be a bit marginal noise-wise in some places) and allows for more ground clearance.

The exhaust manifold/header comes uncomfortably close to the steering shaft. The larger the diameter of the pipe the manifold/header is made from, the more likely this will be a problem. If you have trouble with the exhaust manifold fouling the back edge

9-2-8 Fitting difficulties over the rear axle's trailing links may necessitate cutting and re-welding some tail pipes.

of the sub-frame, you should first ensure you have assembled the flexible engine mountings BEHIND the frame's engine brackets. Another 'trick' that may help improve manifold/header clearance is to fit (if you have not got one already) a metal spacer kit between sub-frame and shell. This increases the exhaust to shell distance.

Surprisingly, the best V8 exhaust arrangement from a performance point of view is the single rear-pipe system, partially on view at 9-2-8. However, there may be some fitting difficulties.

The engine's efficiency is also determined by the diameter of the manifold/headers and the exhaust system, hence all the advertisements about 'free-flowing' systems. Much of what the ads say is true, but you need to keep a few points in mind when buying an exhaust system; firstly the use that you expect of the car, and secondly that big is not necessarily beautiful. The use you expect to put the car to will determine the rpm range where you want the most torque most of the time. This dictates the diameter of the

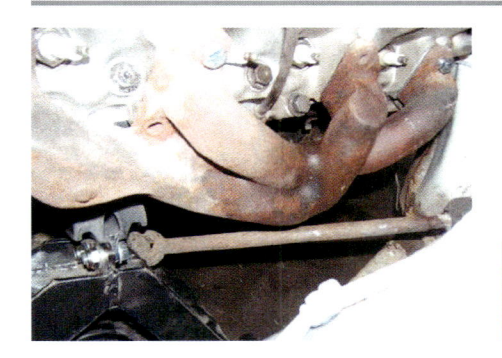

FITTING OUT A V8 ENGINE BAY

9-2-9-1 A view of a standard, cast iron, Range Rover exhaust manifold on the all-important driver's side of this TR7-V8 conversion. All looks well from here ...

9-2-9-2 ... and here, too. Clearly, the Rover flange and twin outlets will need to be matched using a Range Rover down pipe as the next section of the exhaust system.

9-2-9-3 The other side of this LHD car has the starter motor. Unsurprisingly – as this was a Range Rover engine, starter and exhaust – there were no problems here either, and the manifold cleared the car's chassis frame, too.

9-2-10-1 The larger of these clamps is from Walker while the small one comes from Dave Bean. SuperTrapp's version is more or less identical to Dave Bean's offering.

9-2-10-2 These work like exhaust clamps, but are stronger and made so that you can butt together the pipes.

manifold tubing, and for your engine displacement and expected rpm there will be an optimum tube diameter. Too large a bore, and the speed of the exhaust gases are slowed, the scavenging of the cylinders is impaired, and the efficiency of the engine is not optimised. It is true that a smaller set of manifold pipes has a lower maximum capacity of exhaust gases than larger ones, but the exhaust in the smaller pipe moves faster and scavenges better. So, provided the capacity of the manifold is adequate for the gases generated by your expected rpm, a smaller diameter may be better than a large one.

There is no finite formulae I can give to determine the optimum manifold pipe bore – you will have to rely mainly on the experience of friends or the advice of an exhaust specialist. As a rough rule, a road-going and powerful V8 will mainly operate between 2000 and 4000rpm, and consequently will need 1.5in, possibly 1.6in primary tubes. Much larger and you'll lose the bottom-end torque.

Whatever your engine, the more gentle and smooth the bends away from the cylinder heads, the more effective the exhaust system. In this context, when looking at exhaust manifolds/headers, be sure there is no evidence of the 'necking' restrictions that occur when the tube is bent while empty or filled with sand. You need an exhaust manifold and pipework that has been bent using a mandrel – which reduces the necking to negligible proportions.

Range Rover exhausts

If you are fitting a Range Rover engine, you will likely find the engine comes with its cast exhaust manifolds (pictured at 9-2-9-1) in situ. This suggestion may not sound as sexy as fitting a TR8 exhaust system, but I think you will find it a lot cheaper to buy a pair of Range Rover down-pipes to marry with the exhaust flanges at 9-2-9-2 and 9-2-9-3 – which may influence many readers!

Acquiring a system

Pre-fabricated and well proven exhaust systems are available on both sides of the Atlantic from all the usual TR-V8 conversion specialists.

A tip when fitting and removing any exhaust system – it is easier if you use the special smooth clamps seen in pictures 9-2-10-1 and 9-2-10-2. They do not crush the pipes when fitted, and are available from Dave Bean Engineering. SuperTrapp or Walker's Mega Clamp will

111

SPEEDPRO SERIES

9-2-11 This wrapping is difficult to fit to block-hugging manifolds in situ, and may best be applied before the manifolds are fitted to the car. Do not, in any event, take the wrapping beyond the part of the engine bay where the car offers protection from water splashes. The various Speed Shops sell the product, but if in difficulty contact Agriemach.

be found in Summit Racing's catalogue. Other sizes are available, but for TR7-V8 conversions Summit's part numbers are:
 WLK33228 – 2in diameter
 WLK33229 – 2¼in diameter
Remember when fitting the manifolds to the cylinder heads that the torque limit is quite low, and that you risk stripping the threads in the heads if you over-tighten the bolts.

Start the engine for the first time and run it for just a few minutes, before allowing it to cool completely. Re-torque the fastenings. The key to a reliable head/header seal is to now get the engine tuned correctly as quickly as you can. Do not run the engine and certainly do not drive the car until you are sure the engine is running as well as it can. Get a mobile tuning specialist with gas-analysing equipment in as soon as possible because an out-of-tune engine can run hot and warp your fabricated manifolds/headers before you know it.

Once you are sure the tune is correct, drive the car gently (initially for no more than 15 minutes) and again allow the engine to completely cool before you re-torque the fastenings. Now you can try the car a little more vigorously, and for a whole 30 minutes! Again, re-torque the fastenings once the engine is cold.

Final stage is to use the car normally but, once cold, to check the manifold/header fastening torque after every run, and to keep doing this until there is no movement of the fastening each check.

If leaks subsequently occur between the head and a manifold flange, it is heat that – directly or indirectly – is the primary cause, and you need to search for and remedy any local or general overheating. A bespoke/custom copper gasket will help, but involves a lot of work, and in the vast majority of cases should not be necessary.

Exhaust wraps

I touched on wrapping the exhaust manifold/header in the last chapter. This practice not only protects the starter-motor, but reduces the under-bonnet/hood temperatures. Furthermore, it increases the exhaust gas temperatures, which increases the speed of the gases and thus their scavenging of the cylinders. Nevertheless, in spite of these advantages I would advise against using them on mild-steel manifolds/headers, because there is a danger they will increase the temperature of the steel so much that permanent damage could result. Even half-wrapping (i.e. leaving a gap between wraps) can increase the temperature of a mild steel manifold to the extent that distortion and/or gasket damage is probable.

Fabricated manifolds made from stainless steel are less likely to be affected by running them at the elevated temperatures brought about by wrapping. Even so, I would only half-wrap even stainless manifolds/headers to err on the side of caution. You can view a fully wrapped stainless steel example at 9-2-11.

9-2-12 The valley gasket forms an (open) 'U' that goes under both faces of the inlet manifold, and is arrowed here.

Inlet manifolds

We touched on this subject in chapter 8 and will discuss the various options, or at least some of them, in chapters 12 and 13. However, here I wanted to mention a couple of fitting tips.

It may well be that the inlet manifolds for your late engines (ex-Range Rover 4.0 and 4.6 for example) are machined to accept the later thicker gasket, in which case you will have to use the composite gaskets. Nevertheless, if you experience problems when fitting composite gaskets to an early engine, try a genuine Unipart version. If you are still in bother, use the shim gasket on view at 9-2-12 from RPI.

The second aspect to be aware of when fitting a valley gasket is the end seals seen at 9-2-13. These (should) prevent oil from escaping from the front and rear of the cylinder block. I would wager that these are the most frequent places a Rover V8 leaks oil, so

112

FITTING OUT A V8 ENGINE BAY

9-2-13 It really is worthwhile cleaning the threads in the top of the block that will eventually take these clamp-bolts. Check, too, that the bolts you intend to use will screw in far enough to fully clamp the whole length of the valley gasket, but fully tighten these bolts until the inlet manifold has been installed and tightened.

they need to be assembled with care. Properly positioning the rubber seal on the metal clamps is obviously important, and after a few tries I found it best to stick the seal in place the night before fitting the valley gasket.

ALTERNATOR AND RADIATOR

With the engine in you need to attend to the front of it, and if not already in place you need to fit a suitable water pump, pulley, alternator and cradle, and, if applicable, the a/c compressor bracket. The TR8 arrangement can be viewed at 9-3-1. When fitting a Range Rover 3.5 or 3.9 to a TR7, the only major clearance issue will likely be the alternator height – which will have to be lowered to clear the bonnet/hood. It is likely that you will also have to remove the belt guard too. One solution is seen in picture 9-3-2, but you can also lower the Range Rover alternator by mounting it deeper in the main bracket with the result shown in picture 9-3-3-1. You will need to drill new holes and grind/cut off the excess

9-3-1 This alternator location is standard SD1/TR8 and therefore presents no problems, although SD1 style engines are few and far between for US converters.

9-3-3-1 Range Rover 3.9 with lowered alternator, using the following modified mountings.

material surrounding the old ones, and this can be seen at 9-3-3-2. It will also be necessary to shorten the support rod as depicted in 9-3-3-3.

Also, if you are going for a power steering rack, a late Range Rover remote reservoir needs to be fixed on – I recommend – the left-hand headlamp mounting panel. On TR7s with air-con the old relay/drier mounting bracket makes a good base for the steering

9-3-2 This is a Range Rover front cover and water pump with the alternator mounted on the right via an SD1 bracket, which offers plenty of bonnet clearance and is therefore an option, provided you are not planning to fit an air-con compressor.

9-3-3-2 These comparisons show where material must be removed from the alternator bracket, and the lower mounting holes re-drilled (in line with each other).

9-3-3-3 The stiffening brace will also need to be shortened at the timing cover end and re-drilled.

reservoir – although you would need to move the relays to the right side, and the drier too if the compressor is fitted on the right.

SPEEDPRO SERIES

9-3-4 A modified TR7 radiator for a V8 conversion. You will note that, in this case, the respective in and out tanks are clearly too small for the enlarged pipework.

The cooling components are first up and the radiator is the obvious next step. The V8 radiator and original TR7 radiator are basically the same size, but a good V8 one has a core with greater cooling capacity and larger inlet/outlet pipes/necks to match the engine's enlarged hoses. Some V8 radiators in cool climates may get away with merely soldering larger necks to an existing TR7 radiator, and can be seen at picture 9-3-4. Another approach is to solder original TR7 tanks to a new higher capacity core. This leaves the user with the wrong size inlet and outlet pipes for the V8 engine. So there are things to be cautious of, and we will look at the different features, quality and materials used in good V8 radiators in chapter 10.

Whichever radiator you purchase, it will need to be moved forward. The standard TR7 radiator mounting brackets allow you to see the top of the radiator, while a V8 installation requires the radiator be moved forward such that the front nose panel hides the top of it from sight. There are, in fact, two mounting positions for a V8-engined car. The more frequent installation repositions the radiator vertically in Triumph's non air-con pose, while owners with air-con may wish to adopt

9-3-5 This shot shows the forward angle radiator that Triumph adopted for TR8s fitted with air-con.

the top-forward Triumph air-con angled position, seen in photograph 9-3-5. It is probably worth pointing out these respective radiator positions are not carved in stone, and provided you move the radiator forward to make space for the engine, fans etc., there is no reason why a converted car with a vertical radiator could not also accommodate air-con!

Nevertheless, let us first focus on how to install a V8 vertical radiator forward of the usual TR7 location. You can purchase the three V8 mounting brackets (two upper brackets and one lower support), but currently the rubber grommets do not fit at all well and you are therefore better off modifying your originals. The TR7 top brackets are shown in photographs 9-3-6-1 – these need to be straightened roughly as per 9-3-6-2, then cut along the bend and a U-section added to lengthen it. 9-3-6-3 shows the right-side modification to provide the coil mounting. Wedgeparts will modify your brackets using its welding jig, but it is in your interests

9-3-6-1 This is a top bracket at the initial modification stage, but you really need a less corroded example.

9-3-6-2 An original TR8 top rad bracket in black, while in primer is the right-side modified version.

9-3-6-3 At the left of this picture is a genuine left-hand TR8, showing space to mount the coil. Current reproductions omit this detail, which some may feel is a further reason to modify your own brackets – as seen in primer here.

to ensure the used brackets you send for modification are rust-free and the studs are not stripped. You then fit the modified top bracket facing forwards instead of backwards, solving half your radiator re-location problem.

The TR7 lower radiator support

FITTING OUT A V8 ENGINE BAY

9-3-7-1 It is also necessary to make up a pair of adapter brackets, seen here, to reposition the original TR7 lower support channel. Prepare the captive nuts in the chassis carefully, by slowly winding a tap (or a bolt with a couple of vertical hacksaw cuts down it) using lots of lubricant ...

9-3-7-2 ... this removes all the debris from the threads before you fix the new intermediate brackets in place, re-fastening the support channel in its new home and connecting up the bottom hose.

channel is re-used unchanged but in a forward location (dictated by the captive nuts positioned by the factory), and lowered via a pair of additional intermediate brackets. You can see this operation in photographs 9-3-7-1 and 9-3-7-2 and buy the brackets from Wedgeparts.

For an angled radiator installation that replicates a genuine air-con TR8, there are only two components – the big fan frame seen in picture 9-3-8, which also serves as the upper mount, and a one piece lower mount already seen in picture 9-3-5. However, since these frames are no longer available, you either need to go for a vertical radiator or to fabricate a similar support from, I suggest, an aluminium angle (pic 9-3-9).

Coolant expansion tanks, electric fans and wiring details follow in later chapters, but in summary, twin electric fans for non air-con cars are best mounted behind the radiator in 'puller' configuration. You must wire the electric fans via a relay – this can be located anywhere convenient, but the nearer the battery the better. The live feed for

9-3-8 This is the rear view of a TR8 rad/fan mounting frame with, in this case, Wedgeparts improved fans in place.

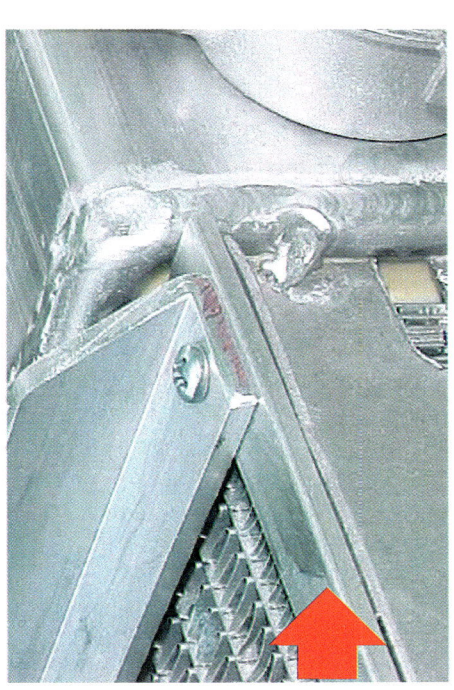

the fan-relay can come from a spare connector on the terminal block, fitted as standard/stock in the battery's live cable.

The thermostat housing for V8 engines could cause a little frustration when trying to run your top hose to the radiator. Genuine TR8 housings had the outlet pipe angled at about 3 o'clock, but are no longer available. There are some 12 o'clock housings on the market but your best solution is to use a Buick GM part number 1194041 which sends

9-3-9 A flat section of aluminium (arrowed), was required to space the angles out from the radiator for added clearance for the fan fixings.

SPEEDPRO SERIES

9-4-1 If you are finding the bonnet will not close because it is hitting the carburettor dashpots (the usual problem), your first check is whether you have this later/double-bulged bonnet fitted to the car.

its outlet off at 2 o'clock. They are available from Glen Towery.

CLOSING THE BONNET/HOOD

The next step in your conversion is to fit the bonnet/hood, but not the catch. Firstly you need to lower the bonnet/hood very slowly to avoid potentially denting it. If it fully closes you have done well, but you are not quite home and dry yet because you need to check for clearance.

You need to position a small lump of Plasticine, Blu-tac or some alternative pliable material atop the highest point in the engine bay. In the case of SU and/or Stromberg carburettor cars the location is easy to spot, but with AFB and EFI cars you may have to think a bit. Close the bonnet again and this time push down until it is fully closed. Upon opening you will find out if the engine/bonnet clearance is adequate from the thickness of the plasticine. It is difficult to say what is adequate, but personally I would want ½in (12mm) to allow for engine flex under load.

If you have not managed to close the bonnet in the first place, or found you have inadequate clearance, read on – there are lots of solutions!

9-4-2 To lower the engine onto the K-frame, cut the brackets here, remove their excess height and re-weld them back to the sub-frame – however, you will never be able to fit a power steering rack.

Basically, the genuine TR8 engine assembly was squeezed into the original TR7, and to do so Triumph had to resort to a second bulge in the bonnet/hood (picture 9-4-1), even when using the lower-profile Stromberg carburettors. Naturally, if yours is a single-bulge bonnet the first remedial step is obvious – you need to find a double-bulged bonnet/hood. Give some thought to a fibreglass one. I am not a fibreglass panel enthusiast, but they are much lighter than the original steel panels, and can be modified very easily for minimal cost. Therefore a local air scoop or extra bulge can be incorporated into the fibreglass panel, perhaps as a short-term expedient.

If the bonnet/hood still won't shut, the next common and well-publicised solution is to retain the (hopefully polyurethane) bushes between the frame and chassis, but add four steel spacers above them. This was how Triumph fitted the V8 into the TR8. You can turn them up yourself or buy the ready to fit versions, which come in varying thicknesses from about 10mm to 20mm. You will need correspondingly longer bolts, too. Interestingly, this practice should not raise the centre of gravity or the front of the car. If anything, it lowers the front roll-centre a fraction.

If desperate ... the engine mounting brackets on the TR8 are about 1in higher than is absolutely necessary with a manual steering rack. Look under the front of the V8's sump/oil pan and see how much clearance you have with the K-frame and steering rack. If you judge there is more clearance than absolutely necessary, you can shorten the mounting brackets from the K-frame at the point shown in photo 9-4-2.

At this point we need to partly

116

FITTING OUT A V8 ENGINE BAY

9-4-3 Most carburettors can have their dashpots (arrowed) shortened to increase bonnet clearance, but for the cost involved it may be better to think AFB carburation.

9-4-4. This is actually a 3in deep air filter, but the beauty of the AFB carburettor and a Low Rider 2in deep air filter is that they will give you a 20bhp increase.

separate fuel-injected cars from carburettor induction. The height of the electronic fuel-injection plenum chamber can be lowered – we will look at reducing the height of both the early Federal and the later Hot Wire systems in chapter 13. If your car employs carburettors, read on.

Shortening the carburettor dashpots is your next option. I would suggest you take an objective look at the carburettors you are using. Ensure that the ones fitted are ideal for your purpose, and before you rush off to get the dashpots on your existing carbs shortened, consider whether HS6 SU carburettors might not be easier to set up and tune over Stromberg and/or SU HIF6s. Find a pair of the much simpler HS6s, try them on the car and then get their dashpots shortened where picture 9-4-3 shows.

Alternatively, the angular Rover inlet-manifold arrangement can be modified or replaced, and AFB carburation employed. You'll also need a low flat air filter, similar to that shown in picture 9-4-4. The beauty of this solution is that it will give you a 20bhp increase, albeit at extra expense.

CONCLUDING POINTS

You can fit the bonnet/hood catch mechanisms now, and check out the bonnet support location. Normally this is fitted to the left of the engine compartment, but with certain induction methods it may be prudent to relocate it to the right side to avoid fouling the air cleaner. The strut tower is drilled to accept the telescoping support on either side, but you may need to drill the bonnet/hood and fit the appropriate captive nuts.

There will be a number of electrical changes to complete, and these are detailed in chapter 14.

TR8 carbon canister set-ups are scarce – where required by local regulations to absorb fuel tank vapours, the TR7's small one should be used. The larger one is a Jaguar part from the Series II/III XJ, and if the battery is to be relocated then the canister can be mounted on the old battery tray. Rimmer Bros stock (at the time of writing) the TR8 dual carbon canister bracket.

Once you have made all your engine modifications, a rolling road session is a wise investment. One session can get all those trick parts working together properly. In comparison to the amount of money that can be spent on the overall conversion, a rolling road session is a drop in the ocean.

Equally, a four-wheel alignment check will ensure the car handles as you hoped it would, while a corner weight check will set up your adjustable suspension properly.

117

Chapter 10
Cooling – all engines

About 30 per cent of the heat generated by combustion will be transferred to the coolant, and subsequently to the atmosphere. One of the major concerns when upgrading the engine in any car is the difficulty of keeping the coolant under control, particularly in two operational circumstances. Cooling the engine can become problematic when traffic slows our progress to a crawl and/or when you are driving the car flat-out. The solution to both of these is to anticipate and plan what to fit where in the first place.

We will need to consider oil cooling too, but the prime focus of this chapter is on keeping the engine coolant at an acceptable level. Needless to say, the problems vary from engine to engine so we will initially look at the facilities that should be built into the 4-cylinder engines before moving on to the more difficult 8-cylinder engines.

SUMMARY
The 4-cylinder

The 4 cylinder engine cooling system operates in a slightly different way to many engine cooling systems. When the engine is cold, the water bypasses the radiator. When the thermostat heats up, it closes the bypass path and forces the water through the radiator. Therefore the original equipment-style thermostat MUST be used, and the thermostat should never be removed as the system will quickly boil.

For standard and mildly tuned 8-valve, 2-litre engines the original radiator is perfectly adequate, provided it is in good condition and not blocked by corrosion or sludging. However, a single 12in (300mm) puller electric fan is recommended in preference to the original viscous/mechanical fan.

In the UK, for 'stage 2' uprated 8-valve engines and any 16-valve engine it is prudent, but perhaps unnecessary, to fit a bigger radiator. However, this

10-1-1 Expansion bottles were fitted to TR7s until 1978, and should be replaced on all cars regardless of engine capacity.

becomes essential in warmer climates such as much of the USA enjoys. Usually a three-core brass unit will be adequate.

There are three types of coolant tanks used on TR7s and they are worth discussing, as the correct tank can help the cooling of your engine a great deal.

COOLING – ALL ENGINES

10-1-2-1 A post-1978 metal header tank in the ideal 2000cc front-right location helps cooling, although this also requires changing the thermostat housing and upper hoses.

10-1-2-2 This is a left side header tank mounted on the right of the engine bay, in order to save buying a new right tank – although you will need to buy new TR8-style mounting brackets.

The simple plastic expansion/overflow tanks seen at 10-1-1 were fitted to TR7s until 1978, and must be replaced with a post-1978 metal header tank (photo 10-1-2-1) regardless of the engine in your car. If you acquire a left side tank, you ideally need the radiator designed to work with it, although the left tank can be mounted on the right of the engine bay, as you can see in picture 10-1-2-2. Do not simply swap the outlets on the existing radiator, because the later radiator is an entirely different cross-flow design – although it is an upgrade well worth considering.

As a safety precaution, you may care to drill and tap a small hole in the top of the 2000cc thermostat housing to act as a bleed valve, but this should not really be necessary.

V8 engines

The V8 engines present a greater cooling challenge, particularly as the capacity and tune of the engine along with the local ambient temperatures increase. The standard/stock 8-valve and the TR8 radiator are actually the same size, although the original TR8 version has one additional row. It is possible to modify a TR7 radiator (right hand header tank models seen at 10-1-3) by having a radiator shop install larger upper and lower hose outlets, but this is only satisfactory with modest V8 engines in temperate climates. Owners would be much wiser to regard the TR8 spec core with larger and repositioned TR8 inlet/outlet pipes as their car's minimum specification radiator, and then only suited for the most basic of 3500cc V8 conversions.

Furthermore, V8 conversions require the radiator be moved forward, as discussed in chapter 9 and seen in photos 10-1-4 and 10-1-5. In fact, the factory TR8s used two different cooling system arrangements depending on whether the car was equipped with air-conditioning or not. The non-air-conditioned TR8 has the radiator mounted vertically – albeit further forward and lower than a TR7 – and, originally, a mechanical fan driven from the crankshaft. The air-conditioned models have the radiator mounted both at an angle and further still under the front nose panel. The lower radiator mounting is different between the models.

The air-conditioned cars used twin electric puller fans, whilst the heater only cars used just the viscous coupled fan to cool the engine at slow forward speeds. The blades of

10-1-3 This is the radiator that is normally fitted to right-hand header tank cars.

10-1-4 The radiator on a 2000cc TR7 is both vertically installed and in view, whereas ...

10-1-5 ... a V8 conversion requires the radiator be moved forward, and in fact becomes out of sight. Note that the header tank orientation and location has also changed when compared to photo 10-1-2.

the mechanically-driven fan protrude through to the chassis rails, and are prone to damage from below. For this and several other reasons, a pair of diagonally-mounted 10in electric puller

SPEEDPRO SERIES

fans are recommended, whether the car is equipped with air-conditioning or not.

BUILDING COOLING INTO THE CAR

The detail with which you build your car in the first place can have a major effect on how hot it runs.

Engine build quality

High quality engine building is one initial factor affecting temperature, and those with engine building experience will usually start out with a cooler running one. The difference may well level out as the internal friction in an amateur's engine eases with use. However, initial build quality can extend to other temperature increasing factors – a restricted or poorly routed exhaust system, lean mixture, retarded timing and/or obstructions blocking air flow through the radiator.

Flush the waterways

An important detail concerns the heat transfer within the engine, starting with the exchange of heat from cylinder to coolant. Obviously, engines need to have a good flow of water around them and the waterways on most engines can silt up. Always have the block pressure-washed before it is assembled. If you are fitting a used/assembled engine, take the trouble to flush the block thoroughly with one of the numerous de-scalers available. The two-part ones illustrated at 10-2-1 usually work best, but must be thoroughly rinsed afterwards.

Watching the temperature

Initially, you MUST fit a reliable and accurate means of monitoring the coolant temperature. This basically means deciding between electric and mechanical temperature gauges. Being of relatively modern construction, TR7/8

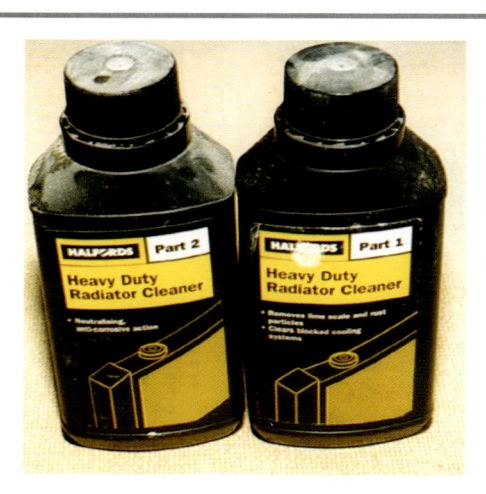

10-2-1 There are many brands of two-part radiator cleaner, but these tend to be more aggressive than mild single-flush chemicals, and are recommended when alternative flushing routines have failed. Note that 'Part 2' is a neutralising agent; important if you don't want to end up with a leaking radiator.

temperature gauges are reasonably sensitive and reliable, although the gauge in V8 cars will tend to read high with the headlights on. A remedy for this is described in the electrical chapter. There are lots of high quality, accurately calibrated electrical temperature gauges on the market, but I have found nothing more accurate than the original MGB mechanical expanding-alcohol temperature gauge, and use it on all my cars regardless of their marque. They can be purchased with different dial calibrations if you are prepared to search outside what the MGB spares stockists offer. These gauges do, however, need careful installation, and a coiled tube shown in 10-2-2 is one essential. If poorly installed, the capillary tube will be broken by engine vibration, the contents spilt and the gauge will stop working.

There is an almost unlimited variety of inlet manifolds for Buick, Rover, Chevy, and Ford engines.

10-2-2 This photo illustrates the correct way to install the capillary tube for a dual mechanical gauge. As the pipe seems too long for the car (the excess length is intended to act as a flexible joint between a vibrating engine and static body), it sometimes gets routed round the side of the engine bay and then straight to the front of the engine. The correct way is to clip it to the side of the rocker cover, coil as much as possible into the 2-3in diameter loops you see here, before fastening it to the top of the footwell. It adds a touch of class – as well as providing a little added support – if one of the heater water pipes is threaded through the coil. With the capillary installed this way, the engine can jump about as much as it likes since the coil takes up the vibration.

Naturally, the original engines will have a selection of inlet manifolds but aftermarket ones, including Edelbrock and Offenhauser, are available too. Most come with provisions for temperature senders/fittings. If the manifold fitting doesn't match the sender you want to use, there are adapters available that will adapt anything to anything!

You can verify the accuracy of your gauge in the workshop, by using one of the many infrared thermometers now available at reasonable prices. These also have the advantage of making it possible to check many different locations on the engine, thus identifying relative hot spots.

COOLING – ALL ENGINES

Modern fuel
Some over-heating problems are difficult to handle in that they are partly out of your control and relate to modern day fuels. If your engine already has a highish compression ratio, or you elect to increase the compression ratio too much you run the risk of generating lots of heat using low octane fuel, but not much additional power. The ideal CR will very much depend on the fuel available to you and the intended use of the car. I would expect the majority of UK fast road engines to be running with a compression ratio of between 9 and 9.75 to 1, but the CR is something that needs resolving locally, for different countries use different methods to calculate their octane rating!

Battery/charging capacity
Stopping and starting the engine in traffic may not do the battery's charge much good – although prolonged use of the electric fan does nothing for the battery-charge either. I suggest initially fitting the largest capacity battery you can in the space available. You also need to increase the alternator's capacity, as electric fans and/or electric water pumps can singularly or collectively discharge even a high capacity battery. Both the battery and alternator capacities contribute to cooling the car, and I discuss increasing the alternator's charging capacity in chapter 14.

The radiator
The standard/stock TR8 radiator is available 'new', in the context that you must supply a TR7 unit in part exchange. However, the standard TR8 radiator will have limited applications beyond a very modestly powered V8 conversion used in a fairly temperate climate. Fortunately, there are numerous improvements that can be made over the standard/stock units. There are four ways to assess/compare the effectiveness of a radiator.

- The greater the tubes surface area, the better the dissipating heat to the fins. Thus, a single long oval tube is best because the cooling fins only make contact with the flat sides of the vertical tubes, not the rounded ends. For example – a single 1in wide tube is better than two ½in wide tubes, because the 1in tube only loses fin-contact at two ends, compared to the losses incurred by the four ends of the ½in tubes. The lighter weight of aluminium allows 1in (25mm) wide tubes to be fitted with wall thicknesses that can withstand the coolant pressures.
- The higher the fin-count, the better a radiator's ability to transfer heat to passing air. The conductivity of a standard/stock TR8 radiator can be increased by 15 per cent by fitting a high-pack core, or by 30 per cent by fitting an 'S' pack core. You can achieve the same effect by installing the radiator at a slightly angled fit, thus reducing the speed of air through fins and improving the transfer of heat.
- The (front to back) depth of the radiator. However, the benefit of, say, an extra row of tubes is often over-stated. The air flow through these radiators can be slower, while the extra tubes (at the back of the core) do not proportionally add to the cooling capacity of the radiator, since they are 'running' in hot air.
- The material the radiator is made from affects its construction. Copper is the better conductor, but if 1in wide tubes were fitted the wall thicknesses necessary to prevent 'ballooning' (and the weight and cost) would be completely unacceptable. Therefore, aluminium radiators are more effective than copper (and brass) units, for they have wider tubes and consequently more heat transfer area.

10-2-3. An excellent example of an upgraded V8 radiator made, in this case, from 0.080in thick 5052 grade marine aluminium. This Wedgeparts quality product uses 0.065in thick take-off tubes and is satin finished for longevity.

While core design has more bearing on heat transference than material the core is made from, the core's material makes an important contribution to the effectiveness of a radiator. Brass is the material used in the vast majority of radiators (including the standard TR7 and TR8) because it is easy to work and relatively cheap. However, both copper and aluminium have superior heat transfer properties. Copper is heavy and much more expensive than brass, and consequently you find few radiators made from it. Furthermore, copper radiators have smaller tubes and soldered joints that reduce their effectiveness, despite the metal's superior conductivity. Aluminium is cheaper than copper and much lighter than brass, but usually necessitates a thicker core. Nevertheless, it is the material of choice for performance cars because the weight of a radiator is outside the wheelbase, where weight reduction is doubly important. A typical aluminium V8 radiator is seen at 10-2-3.

So although expensive, an alloy radiator offers both weight reduction and, by way of its construction, improved heat-transfer. In the USA, Afco, Allstar, Griffen, Howe and Modine

SPEEDPRO SERIES

3 and 4 core aluminium radiators are very well thought of, and cool some pretty hot cars! However, I think you would be prudent to purchase through a specialist with 'hot' TR8 experience. In the USA, Towery Foreign Cars, TSI and Wedgeparts all have that experience and are recommended.

The grade of aluminium is very important too, and you are best seeking radiators made from marine grade aluminium, particularly as internal corrosion is a major issue with alloy radiators. In that context, read the coolant additives section below particularly carefully, and seek advice about sacrificial anodes when considering an alloy radiator. They sell for $6 and are made from zinc or magnesium (the latter is possibly better) in order to reduce internal salts and corrosion.

MAXIMISING FLOWS
Air flow

You can improve high-speed cooling by maximising the flow of air through the radiator. The following are some ways to achieve this objective:
- Fit a front rally-type spoiler or valance. These not only look good, but reduce the air flow under the car (helping front road-holding) and direct that air through the radiator, thus reducing the coolant temperature, too. We see one at 10-3-1.

Make sure the air flow cannot get around the sides or over the top of the radiator. Since the baffles for V8 air-con cars have been unavailable for some time, they might be a good candidate for a re-manufacturing project if anyone has the inclination. Meanwhile, it may take some time to hand-make a set of alloy deflector panels, but they can reduce running temperatures by 10 per cent so it will be time very well spent.

Obviously, the primary contributor

10-3-1 This rally spoiler will be of particular benefit to V8 converted cars because the new radiator will be moved forward and down by the mounting brackets that come as a fitting kit.

to good air flow is getting lots of air into the radiator – what is not so obvious is ensuring the air can escape easily from the rear of the radiator without building up pressure. Most hot air from the radiator/engine bay escapes down the propshaft tunnel, but the Wedges bonnet vents are helpful. Additional bonnet vents are really only effective when the car's speed is above 30mph, and then only when they are positioned in an area of (relatively) low air pressure. A short area behind the leading edge of the bonnet is at low pressure, and may be helpful. At the trailing end of the bonnet the windscreen generates a high-pressure area, and this is where most motor manufacturers place the heater intake for that reason. Consequently, the vents positioned towards the rear of the bonnet may help air exit the engine bay at slow speed but could actually allow air to enter the engine bay at high speed!

MGB V8s use gauze-covered holes cut in the low-pressure rear of the wheelarches to good effect, and this may be something to consider for your TR7-V8. A partially finished example is shown at 10-3-2.

Ensure that there are no

10-3-2 This is the inner wing/fender aperture fitted by Rover to its MG RV8 models. Note the strengthening lip welded around the periphery of the hole.

10-3-3 The works rally cars had front bumper mounting brackets slotted to allow for the vertical movement of the bumper, in order to maximize air flow to the radiator. They also had the oil cooler mounted to the right side of the radiator with an air-duct that we also see in this shot. Note, too, the adhesive registration numerals that don't obstruct the radiator.

unnecessary obstructions (such as badges, auxiliary lights, horns or an accumulation of dirt/bugs) preventing the absolute maximum of air flow to the front of the radiator. Make sure the front number plate neither obstructs the air nor deflects it from entering air intakes. If in doubt fit an adhesive number to the bonnet or body (taking care not to contravene the law in your location!) and/or adjust the height of the front bumper to maximise air flow (picture 10-3-3).

At slow speed, assist air flow

COOLING – ALL ENGINES

through the radiator via fan(s). Mechanical and electric fans are explored later in the chapter.

To direct more air into the cockpit, fit a scoop over the heater's inlet – although in non air-con vehicles the water flows through the heater matrix all the time, and hot and cool functions are achieved by diverting the air flow around the matrix. For the coolest air, the water flow should be stopped and/or the heater matrix bypassed.

Coolant

Coolant temperature is a balancing act, and you can over-cool an engine. When you first start an engine, particularly on a cold day, it is often necessary to inject extra fuel by 'choking' the mixture in order to get the engine to run reasonably well. The thermostat provides an essential restriction in the coolant flow to speed the 'warm-up', allowing the engine to operate without additional fuel and the subsequent emissions that result from a low coolant temperature. So, too low an operating temperature is not good for either the engine or the environment, and the thermostat is there to keep the temperature at the optimum.

In fact, engines generally operate with improving efficiency as the coolant temperature increases. Most engines will not run efficiently below 82°C/192°F, and many only minimise their emissions if they are operating at 88°C/200°F degrees. In fact, almost all fuel injected engines need 88°C/200°F degrees to operate effectively. So you need a thermostat that is hot enough to ensure your engine runs well, but cool enough to keep the coolant temperature acceptable when driving/traffic conditions slow you down. Three 'start to open' thermostats are usual in Europe. You will find the temperature at which yours starts to open stamped on the top or base of the piston. In

10-3-4 The air-bleed on the periphery of the thermostat (arrowed) MUST be upright if it is to allow all of the air trapped in the manifold to escape.

Europe, 82°C is 'normal', with 76 and 88°C alternatives available, depending on whether you want to run your engine hotter or cooler than normal. In the US there are, I believe, 170, 180, 190 and 200°F choices.

Your first task is to fit the most suitable thermostat for your engine and conditions. However, the volume of coolant flowing through the system also clearly has a major impact on the effectiveness of it, and the following details need exploring:

The one way bleed valve (that allows trapped air in the manifold to escape) must be installed in the 12 o'clock position to be effective (picture 10-3-4).

Initially, you can drill three (going up to six if necessary) ³⁄₁₆in (4mm) diameter holes around the base of your thermostat to increase the continuous flow of water around the system.

Unless you are fitting an electric water pump, do NOT remove the thermostat completely – it provides some back pressure which keeps the water in better contact with the block and consequently aids heat transfer. As an alternative to drilling holes to increase the coolant circulation, you can remove the thermostat's central piston – but expect warm-up times and pollution to increase.

The anti-corrosive properties of coolants deteriorate with age and the system needs to be drained, flushed and re-filled with new coolant/antifreeze every year, every two years maximum. This is particularly important when aluminium components come in contact with the coolant, as would be the case with most V8 conversions and moves towards imperative if you also have an aluminium radiator.

The core of the radiator is vital

SPEEDPRO SERIES

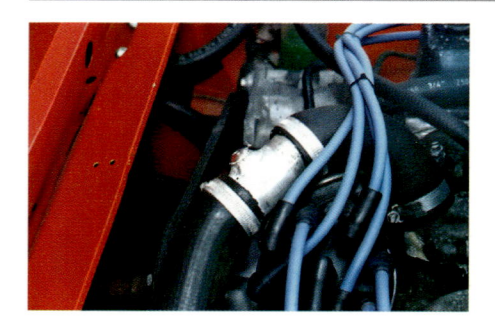

10-3-5 This simple bleed screw is a very good idea for any car with a looped top hose.

in that it must not be obstructed by corrosion or silt, which obviously not only degrade the core's ability to act as a heat exchanger, but also restrict the volume of water passing through the radiator. Thorough flushing is the obvious first step, but if you have the slightest doubt as to the cleanliness of your radiator's core, either replace the whole radiator or have the existing one re-cored.

A loose but slipping fan/drive belt can cause engines to overheat and alternators to undercharge. A worn fan belt can appear adequately taut, but still slip because it is driving on the bottom flat of the pulleys, not the sides of the 'vee'. Don't go to the other extreme and over-tighten the belt.

Radiator hoses deteriorate over time due to heat, and the effect of the additives and the decomposed rubber tends to clog the radiator tubes. If overheating only occurs at high speed, check the bottom hose is rigid enough to prevent it collapsing at high engine revs. Bottom hoses collapse when the water pump moves coolant faster than the radiator can supply it, and the problem is very hard to detect. Today reinforced silicone hoses are available, and worth fitting for their longevity and strength.

The diameter of the crankshaft drive and/or water pump pulleys obviously affects the rotational speed of the water pump. You will increase your water pump's speed if you increase the diameter of the crankshaft pulley, but it may be more practical to reduce the size of the water pump pulley. You do need to be careful when considering this solution. If the pump is running too slowly then increasing its rpm will help. However, if the pump is already operating at an effective speed, increasing its rpm will likely do more harm than good as you could provoke 'cavitation' around the impeller, reducing the water flow!

The top hose from engine to radiator has a hump in the middle of its run, which makes bleeding the air out of the V8 Wedge very difficult. Try to ensure the top hose lies as flat as possible between the engine thermostat housing and the top of the radiator. Some conversions have a big 'loop' of water hose that encourages air locks. In fact, the airlock problem is more common than you may imagine, but avoidable by fitting a bleed nipple. An example is at picture 10-3-5.

Conventional water pumps

The effectiveness of the water pump is crucial. Upgraded mechanical pumps are available but so too are electric pumps. Replacement water pumps vary in quality and efficiency. If the temperature increases when driving, it's a good idea to consider an Edelbrock or a Weiand high flow mechanical water pump. A Weiand Team G water pump was tested and shown to be 100 per cent more effective than the standard/stock Rover V8 pump it replaced.

FlowKooler claims that its water pumps produce 20 per cent more flow at 2000rpm and 100 per cent more flow at 900rpm than any other pump on the market today. Not only will this result in better water circulation, it will also generate more water pressure inside the block, helping to suppress engine hot spots and steam pockets. Furthermore, it claim its pumps are very mechanically efficient, resulting in less power loss.

As a general rule, engines with 'V' belt drives have a clockwise rotation and serpentine belts run anti/counter clockwise. It is essential that any aftermarket water pump you purchase has the correct rotation for your drive system.

Space rarely poses difficulties in front of the engine in most TR7-V8 conversions, thus the standard/stock SD1 water pump usually presents no problems. Nevertheless, you might like to know that there are shorter Rover pumps available. For Buick and early Rover engines, the standard Rover P6/MGB GT V8 water pump is 4.5in between the engine face and the front of the nose where your mechanical fan (if used) would be mounted. Alternatively, you could use a short water pump from an air-conditioned Buick Special or Olds F-85. Simco's 1353A measures 3.8in from the gasket surface to the front of the pulley, and a '64-'67 Buick 300 water pump – which also measures 3.8in – fits Buick, Olds or Rover SD1 V8 blocks.

FANS
Mechanical puller

As mentioned earlier, the TR7 and non air-con TR8s used a mechanical fan. The standard/stock TR8 had seven blades, was assigned part number 614739, and mounted on viscous coupling part number ERC94. In some very hot climates, it may be necessary to retain a mechanical fan on road-going cars to provide additional air flow through the radiator. In this event, it is best to fit a more effective aftermarket

COOLING – ALL ENGINES

fan and dispense with the potentially troublesome and expensive viscous coupling. If you need the fan operating most of the time you do not need a viscous coupling, and a straight engine driven fan without one will suffice.

A mechanical fan works best at high revs – just when it is not required! It also consumes power – estimates vary from a couple to 5bhp, but it definitely causes a reduction, which most readers will agree is rather undesirable! Thus if your coolant stays at an acceptable level most of the time without a mechanical fan, I suggest you remove the fan and the viscous mount and fit or upgrade electric fan(s).

If you feel a mechanical fan essential, you need to attend to its efficiency. A shrouded mechanical fan running about 1in (25mm) from the closest part of the fan to the radiator will pull air through the core, while the clearance allows for movement in your engine mounts and some flexing of the fan. Generally speaking, all fans are most effective when fitted about halfway within a peripheral shroud. Lightweight and relatively thin mechanical 'puller' fans (photograph 10-4-1) are available from most mail order equipment dealers, such as Summit Racing Equipment, and a fan diameter of 14in (350mm) should clear the radiator hoses. Avoid flimsy plastic or fibreglass fan blades, though, since these have a tendency to flex under heavy load and chew a hole in the back of the radiator.

If you doubt the wisdom of omitting the viscous coupling, consider the following coupling problems. Fan noise is sometimes evident during the first few minutes after start-up, until the coupling can redistribute the silicone fluid back to its normal disengaged condition. Noise can also occur continuously from 2500rpm if the clutch assembly is locked-up due to an internal failure. You

10-4-1 An excellent example of a fixed fan, but effectiveness would have been increased had a shroud/cowl been fitted around its periphery.

can check for clutch failure by trying to rotate a static cold fan by hand. If it's locked-up or if there is a rough grating feel as the fan is turned, the clutch needs replacing!

Then there is the opposite problem – looseness. If you can spin the fan over by hand (engine stopped, of course) without drag (say it spins through four or five revolutions) the clutch needs replacing. If you can feel slight lateral movement at the end of the fan blade (say ³⁄₁₆in or 5mm) this can be a normal condition due to the type of bearing, so long as the radiator is not in danger.

These clutches are normally filled with silicone fluid and small leaks are probably of little consequence in the short-term. If however the leakage increases, you can expect the unit to fail in the near future.

Electric fans

Electric fans these days provide the slow-speed cooling for the vast majority of modern cars because they are only in use when needed. Where fitted, the standard/stock Triumph yellow fans draw large quantities of current for the air they move, and are best replaced by modern units. In any event, they are no longer readily available new and are not easily serviced. TR8 electric fans in air-con vehicles were triggered cleverly, and any rewiring you do needs to take into account that they were electrically connected in series for low speed and in parallel for high speed using relays. Low speed triggering was controlled by the thermoswitch at the radiator, while high speed was initiated at a higher temperature by a thermoswitch on the engine.

There are plenty of modern electric fans available for Sprint or V8 conversions, but first let us address how an original TR8 might be more or less invisibly upgraded. Brad Wilson of Wedgeparts discovered that the fans from a 1997 through 2004 Porsche Boxster have exactly the same mounting pattern, and now uses and sells them for TR8s. It is necessary to drill out the mounting tabs to accept a 6mm fastener or use a thicker wall sleeve, since the Porsche uses a 5mm fixing. Wedgeparts points out that the Boxster fan is a two-speed unit, and consequently it is also necessary to construct a new wiring harness.

For the majority of readers, the effectiveness and numerous suppliers of today's electric fans make them the way to go. The fan units are enhanced by their blade design, by being close coupled to the radiator (they are usually held in place by thin plastic 'ties' to the radiator itself) and by the use of a peripheral shroud. You will see a typical example at 10-4-2 (overleaf).

The specialist electric fan companies have a rule of thumb that may interest you. They recommend 70 per cent of the radiator core be covered by an electric fan(s), which in the case of a V8 conversion means you need to fit two 10in (250mm) units diagonally across the radiator. Various TR specialists prefer different makes of fan, and you have a wide choice. Base your selection on the fans that will fit in

SPEEDPRO SERIES

10-4-2 An excellent example of a modern electric fan awaiting close-coupling to its radiator. These blades are straight but some of the very latest fans have curved blades which, the maker claims, further increase the effectiveness of the fan. Note the bottom hose with its integral thermostatic fan switch (which I would couple to the fan via a relay).

the space available, move the highest volume of air (measured in cfm), and are close-coupled and shrouded. It is an added advantage if the blade of the fan(s) can be easily reversed but this detail reminds me to mention that the orientation of the blade is important, and must be such that air is moved through the core of the radiator and not pushed away from it.

While we will look at some aspects of the electrical circuits in chapter 14, there are a couple of details that need emphasising here. A relay is essential to control the fan(s). Most of the fans we are thinking about will take 15 to 20 amps current – without a relay, you will grossly overload not only the thermostatic switch that automatically controls the fan, but the manual over-ride switch, too.

I think you are best fitting an adjustable thermostatic controller/switch, as seen at 10-4-3. They are available from Kenlowe and usually fitted into the top neck of the radiator. However, there are two alternatives to think about. First off, a two-speed

10-4-3 The adjustable thermostatic control of an aftermarket fan.

switch fitted into the pre-prepared position in many Rover V8 inlet manifolds, an example of which can be seen at 10-4-4. Then there are non-adjustable thermostatic switches with (about 5) different trigger-temperatures available, and these fit any car. We see an example in picture 10-4-5, which is a stainless steel bottom water-pipe with the thermoswitch mounting welded in situ. This raises the question as to the best place to trigger your electric fan. The top hose has been the traditional point, but it has to be pointed out that modern cars tend to trigger the electric fan from the cooler bottom hose.

Whichever thermostatic switch you use, a 20 or 30 amp relay is also required. Part number 2193956 is available from Lucas, although any reliable four or five pin relay will be fine. If using an adjustable switch, I think you should initially set the Kenlowe controller to trip about halfway between 'normal' and 'hot', or about 90°C (190°F). You do not want the fan(s) to cut in too early or too frequently. Many make the mistake of having the fan come on at 'normal'. That is too early.

10-4-4 The arrow points to a sensor for the electric fans. On some V8 manifolds there may just be a triangular pad here which needs to be drilled and tapped. On others an 'Otter' sensor may be present (secured with three small bolts), but beneath the sensor the usual M22 x 1.5 thread may be present, meaning that virtually any switched sensor from Volvo, Saab etc. will fit. Furthermore, some of those sensors are two-speed units which is even more versatile and desirable.

10-4-5 The modern approach is to fit the control switch for electric fans into the bottom hose, thereby controlling the temperature of the water as it goes into the engine.

COOLING – ALL ENGINES

Pusher fans
Electric pusher fans are mounted in front of the radiator and are notorious for their vulnerability to the elements. Failure due to water and debris ingress over the years brought the car manufacturers to increasingly mount electric cooling fans on the engine side of the radiator and there should be sufficient space for puller fan(s) in most TR7-V8 conversions. However if you do need to resort to front-mounted pusher fan(s) remember some will get very little exercise and that you would be prudent to operate the manual over-ride switch for a few minutes each time you take the car out.

Puller fans
Provided you have planned for their installation and left sufficient space, there is much to be said for puller fans. You can usually fit a much larger diameter fan behind the radiator, and a 14in puller will provide for about twice the area that the best combination of pushers generates. Furthermore, in this location the fan motor is in a warm air flow from the radiator, which quickly dries out any moisture that has managed to penetrate it. Nevertheless the usual combination is a pair of 10in electric fans mounted diagonally and you'll get the flavour from picture 10-4-6.

Perma-cool's 16in fan generates 2950cfm air flow, is the highest volume fan I've seen, and would solve all sorts of cooling problems – if you can fit it onto the radiator and into the space between the engine and radiator. It was 3.75in (95mm) front to back – which might be too long for some conversions. If space is a problem, consider a MG RV8 electric puller fan, with its thin profile shown in pictures 10-4-7 and 10-4-8. Summit, in the USA, offers what looks like a suitable range of fans in its catalogue, and MRG 1987 looks a good bet. In the UK you could consider the range of Pacet engine fans in Demon Tweeks' catalogue such as models CF88, CF99 or PF1606, although these units can extend backward by 3 or 4in (75 to 100mm).

Electric water pumps
12-volt Davies-Craig electric water pumps are available from MAW Solutions in two sizes. The larger pump not only circulates water very effectively, but also allows you to eliminate the original thermostat, water pump (housing and impeller) and of course the associated pulley. The smaller electric booster pump is hermetically sealed and features a robust magnetic (i.e. brushless) motor. The makers claim it is ideal for use as a booster for car cooling systems where it improves water circulation right throughout the engine block. It is intended to supplement the existing mechanical water pump, but nevertheless has a flow-rate of 800 litres (175 gallons) per hour and will operate over a range of -40 to +130°C. The unit is roughly 2in x 2in x 4in (50 x 50 x 100mm), has ¾in (20mm) hose connections and weighs slightly over ½lb

10-4-6 This twin fan assembly, including the frame, was used on US TR8 models with air-con. The left curved-blade model is a Porsche Boxter spare, used as a replacement for the original Fiat Marelli (yellow) fans. Today's electric fans can be close-coupled to the radiator, obviating the need for a frame.

10-4-7 A vertical view of a 'close-coupled' fan with the radiator on the left. The fan blade housing and the electric drive motor are on the right of the photograph.

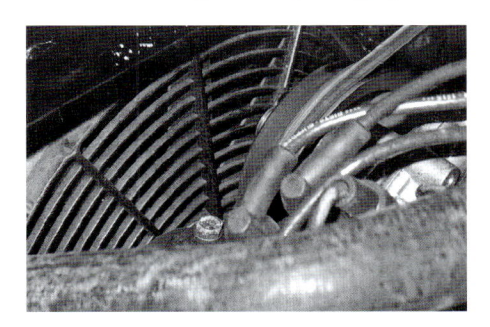

10-4-8 This is an RV8 electric fan positioned behind the radiator, 'pulling' cooling air through the matrix. The fan is particularly valuable because it doesn't have a motor protruding backwards into the engine bay to interfere with the fan belt, water pump or the various pulleys.

(225g). The centrifugal pump's motor has an impressive 15000-hour life, and draws 1.3 amps at 12 volts.

SPEEDPRO SERIES

The larger (5.1 x 5.1 x 3.1in, or 128 x 131 x 77mm) pump seen in 10-5-1 is more powerful, in that Davies-Craig claims flow rates of 1200 litres to 4800 litres (300 to 1300 gallons) per hour. They say that it increases cooling capacity while giving you more engine power – in fact, they say up to 20bhp (15kW) more power! Certainly the hose fittings are larger, accommodating 1¼ to 2in (30 to 50mm) hoses, while current requirements are up to a maximum of 7.5 amps and motor life expectancy reduced to 2000 hours.

The unit can be utilised in two ways:
- It can be installed as a complete replacement for the existing, mechanically-driven pump, in which case an electronic sensor/controller (available separately) must be fitted too. The existing pump is deactivated or in many cases may be removed, and a shorter drive belt fitted. The controller electronically senses engine heat and adjusts the rate of flow from the pump, maintaining the coolant temperature you set even after engine shutdown, if you wish. Converters with space problems between timing cover and radiator may care to think about removing their mechanical water pump completely, fitting a flat cover with water take-off over the aperture, and putting one of these units in its place. This installation will cost about £300.
- Alternatively, the pump may be fitted to provide a very significant boost to the existing mechanical water pump, in which case it can be controlled either by a manual or an automatic on/off thermal switch. The thermal switch seen at picture 10-5-2, and recommended for this purpose, is part number 0401 from Davies-Craig. This installation saves about £100 but adds nothing by way of mechanical efficiency or pulleys, belt etc. If you are going to follow this route, you are

10-5-1 Davies-Craig's electric pump kit which does for coolant circulation what an electric fan does for air circulation! The pipework will be approximately 2in (50mm) in diameter, which should help you 'scale' the size of the pump. The pump can be purchased with or without ...

better off buying its smaller pump and fitting that as a manually controlled auxiliary unit.

Incidentally, whenever the electronic controller is fitted, it should be done well away from the harsh conditions often prevalent in the engine bay. The cockpit is favourite. If you replace your conventional water pump with an electric pump you automatically remove any possibility of fitting a mechanical fan unless the fan is crankshaft driven as with the original TR8.

I do not know any details but understand the Weiand division of Holley also offers electric water pumps.

COOLANT ADDITIVES/ ALTERNATIVES/TIPS
Antifreeze

There is more to the use of antifreeze than perhaps some readers thought!

The greater the percentage of antifreeze you run, the higher the boiling point of your coolant – at least up to 70 per cent antifreeze.

Always run on the road with at least 50 per cent antifreeze, but race with 70/80 per cent antifreeze.

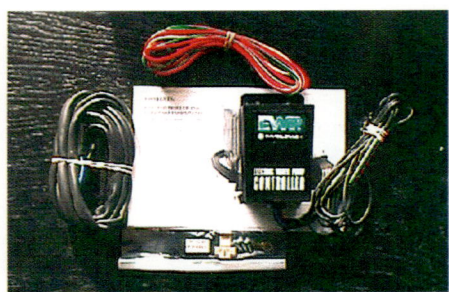

10-5-2 ... its electronic control unit/kit shown here.

Most cheap antifreeze contains phosphates and these are harmful to aluminium. Therefore buy the best antifreeze you can and certainly one with a reputable name specifically recommended for "mixed-metal" or aluminium engines. Volvo green coolant specifically states on the container that it is phosphate free.

Check that your choice claims to be harmless to rubber.

Religiously change your V8's coolant annually so that the corrosion inhibitors are kept up to strength. It is equally important to replace the antifreeze annually, if you have an aluminium radiator.

Tests show that aluminium corrosion can be extremely low even in the presence of phosphate, as long as the silicate inhibitors are not depleted. Once the silicate is depleted, aluminium corrosion rapidly accelerates. Note, the TR7 has an iron block but still has an aluminium cylinder head!

Distilled water is preferable to tap-water

An alternative formula is 50 per cent safe-for-aluminium antifreeze, 50 per cent distilled water and Water Wetter (more shortly) in powder form.

Additives

I have come across two coolant additives that are reputed to improve the

COOLING – ALL ENGINES

speed at which the coolant collects and gives up heat, and are an alternative you may care to explore.

Water Wetter is added to the coolant after the system, including any antifreeze, has been drained. In operation in very high ambient temperatures it seemed to work well for me, and to reduce the engine's operating heat – although that is very subjective. The instructions said it worked best if the system was drained of antifreeze, and I was slightly concerned that without its antifreeze and corrosion inhibitors the water passages in my Rover aluminium engine could be corroding. Consequently, I drained the Water Wetter as soon as possible and refilled with new antifreeze. Water Wetter works by breaking down surface tension in the coolant to improve heat transfer. The resulting improved thermal conductivity reduces hot spots and vapour bubbles as well as lubricating water pump seals. I note the latest publicity says the product can be used with antifreeze.

Agriemach claims its product Radiator Relief to be the best coolant system additive on the market today, and that it can be used with or without antifreeze. It is designed to function in two ways – first and foremost by reducing operating temperatures by as much as 30°F. As an additional bonus, it speeds warm-up times by about 50 per cent. 32fl oz (880cc) is sufficient for 15 litres of coolant.

Alternative coolant ('For-Life')

Developed during the Second World War for cooling radar installations, this ethylene glycol-based coolant stays liquid down to –40°C (thus antifreeze is unnecessary) and only boils at about 180°C. Furthermore, in its For-Life form, it is mixed with an excellent detergent that keeps water passages clean and rust-free. Available from Demon Tweeks in the UK, it must NOT be mixed with water but used undiluted after first ensuring the coolant system is flushed clean. An additional bonus is that it warns of head gasket failure by changing colour from red to yellow. For topping-up, keep a small container of For-Life in the boot/trunk, and avoid adding any water and/or antifreeze. To fill your system the cost will be about £30 in the UK – but For-Life is effective for ten years.

Radiator cap

Modern radiator caps increase and simultaneously regulate the pressure in the cooling system. Each cap will have a pressure rating in lb/in^2. For every additional pound of pressure, the coolant's boiling point increases by 3°F.

Air-conditioning notes

The most important issue when working with refrigerant under pressure is to observe the safety precautions that need to be taken.

The original TR7's compressor is a York piston pump that requires 12bhp. If you are fitting a V8 into a TR7 with air-con, upgrading to a radial pump is advantageous. The later pumps are quieter and should only take about 3bhp. Similarly, the heart of the original TR8 system is the compressor. The TR8 used the widely available General Motors/Delco R4 model, but if an actual R4 is unavailable, the majority of aftermarket stores will have a direct replacement with minimal differences. The most common difference will be the low-charge protection method and it may be necessary for you to fit an alternative low-pressure switch to your new unit.

The other crucial component is the condenser, which is located in front of the radiator making it vulnerable to mechanical damage. A few bent fins are not a major concern as long as there are not too many, but damage to the tubes certainly is and will necessitate repair by a specialist or finding a used replacement.

A replacement compressor may involve drive belt complications, made a little more confusing by the fact that Unipart lists the current replacement belt number as GCB20770, which is an 11mm wide belt, when in fact a 13mm width is required. Furthermore, the length of your drive belt will be dictated by whether the new clutch pulley diameter has changed.

A genuine TR8 compressor is driven via an intermediate jockey pulley from the crankshaft, but the adjustment is awkward and not made any easier by the antiquated tensioner design located beneath the compressor. The solution is to replace the original adjuster with a threaded rod, as shown in photo 10-5-3.

You will almost certainly need to replace the receiver and capillary connection for the Ranco valve. A Visteon part-number 540027 or Four Seasons part-number 33258 will do nicely, and either will bring an integral switch connection. The switch on the replacement drier will likely possess

10-5-3. Some machining of the alloy mounting bracket and modification of the compressor brace will be required.

SPEEDPRO SERIES

the wrong characteristics. However, the sole purpose of the original Ranco valve was to turn on the electric fans when high side pressures rise, thus increasing the flow of air across the condenser and restoring the efficiency of the a/c system. Be sure you leave the drier capped until ready for use – if exposed to the air for more than a few minutes it will be ruined.

Very few of the original TR8 hoses are available, so you will need to visit your local hydraulic hose shop for replacements or repair of an original set if you can find one. Once connected the system (except drier and compressor) should be power flushed in order to remove debris, before you evacuate it. To evacuate you will need some form of vacuum pump. It is not necessary to buy an electric pump if you have an air compressor, as Harbour Freight sells a device that generates a vacuum from compressed air.

For those fitting a Range Rover engine (where the compressor is on the right-hand side), adding air-con to the car will provide some additional challenges, in particular finding space to route the high and low side hoses back to the bulkhead/firewall for connection to the evaporator. There will already be a myriad of pipes and hoses in that area, and you need to allow for the space needed by the fresh air intake.

It appears possible to reuse the TR7 condenser and turn it horizontally 180 degrees, so the inlet/outlet is now on the right. You will need to re-drill both the mounting brackets and the condenser to make use of the TR8 mounting holes in the chassis rails. As with the radiator, the V8 condenser is tilted further forward than the TR7. The drier will also need to be moved across to the right side and a set of custom air-con hoses made. Most hydraulic hose specialists should be able to do this using the fittings from the old hoses.

10-5-4 This is an auto gearbox cooler, but you can use the same location and mounting arrangement for an engine oil cooler.

Cooling the oil

An oil cooler also contributes to lowering the engine-temperature. We looked at the engine end of an oil-cooler's circuit in chapter 8, but here the actual cooler and where to put it warrant a few lines. They come in a variety of sizes and configurations, and your Wedge specialist will doubtless have a kit to suit your climate and intended use.

A ten-row oil cooler, connected by flexible pipes to the engine and remote oil filter, is suited to most road-going V8's in the UK. You may feel an enlarged oil cooler is important if you live in the warmer areas of the US, in which case a higher capacity cooler from Summit Racing Equipment could be used. Its 'Perma-Cool' units come in four sizes, the smallest of which is designated PRM 201 and copes with 450bhp engines. It

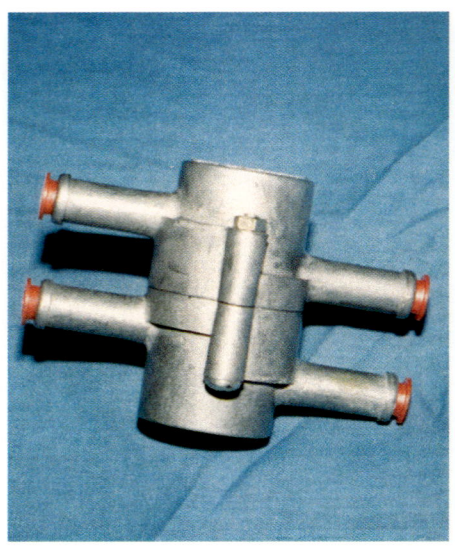

10-5-5 This thermostatically-controlled oil valve recycles the engine oil until it reaches its operating temperature, whereupon the valve allows it to pass through the oil cooler.

is 1.5in deep, 6.5in wide and 18in long (38x160x450mm).

You will need to fit an engine oil cooler in front of the radiator, roughly in the location normally occupied by an automatic gearbox cooler (picture 10-5-4).

If you fit an oil cooler and live in a moderate/cool climate, there could be occasions when your engine oil does not need cooling, and you are doing it no good at all by over-cooling the oil. In these climates the thermostatically controlled oil valve seen in photograph 10-5-5 (fitted in line with the oil cooler) is a very good idea. The valve will not pass oil to the cooler during start-up, or indeed whenever the oil is below a good operating temperature, but will allow it passage to the cooler when necessary.

---

www.velocebooks.com/www.veloce.co.uk
All books in print • New books • Special offers • Gift Vouchers

Chapter 11
Improving the sparks

All the best induction equipment in the world is useless if you cannot ignite the charge. In any car an effective ignition system is very important, and you need to consider carefully what to expect from it. The upgrades available are endless. There are some absolute basics that every owner needs to attend to first – in the case of TR8s, relocating the ignition electronics away from the confines of a hot distributor housing! No, you cannot get more basic than that – nevertheless, inside the distributor is not the ideal place for your ignition module.

THE IGNITION SYSTEM
The original contact breaker ignition system is one of the major causes of breakdown and under-performance. It is required to produce a nice fat spark (the bigger the better) consistently in hot or cold, rich or lean conditions. The basic design is now long in the tooth and not surprisingly, today's engines are fired quite differently – the most modern run without a distributor and use numerous (not one) ignition coils.

Most readers will understand the basic workings of a contact breaker ignition system but not everyone will have thought that at 3000rpm, the make/break of the points has to occur 100 times per second in a 4-cylinder engine and 200 times per second in an 8-cylinder engine. Each opening and closing of the points generates an additional small low tension spark, which in isolation is of no consequence. However, over say 100 hours (6000 miles at 60mph) and at just 100 times per second, it is understandable that these sparks will eat at our contact breaker points and wear will take place.

However, as one gets into further detail there is more to concern those who seek reliable high-performance because the coil, also working at least 100 times per second, needs about 15 milliseconds to reach its peak magnetic saturation. Consequently, it has insufficient time to reach full saturation above 2000rpm in a 4-cylinder engine and 1000rpm in an 8-cylinder, which explains the multi-coil ignition systems in modern high-performance cars.

CONTACT BREAKER IMPROVEMENTS
In addition to the 'burning' issue, another disadvantage of contact breaker points is that they bounce at high revs – or at least the 'heel' that follows the distributor's cam does – causing misfiring and lost performance. Most of us fit 'Sports' coils – the Lucas version can be seen at 11-1 overleaf – to improve our sparks and help starting and road-going performance, but more secondary voltage from the coil necessitates more primary current through the coil and across the points. The higher the current across the points, the shorter their life. Therefore, there is a lot to be said for replacing the points and condenser with a retro-fitted breakerless

SPEEDPRO SERIES

11-1 From this shot it's not easy to appreciate that this is indeed a Lucas 'Sports/Gold' coil. It pushes out a fatter spark, but at the expense of the life expectancy of the contact breaker points.

system. If you have a standard or fast road car then this is a step you should seriously consider, if only to improve the reliability of the ignition and reduce the service required by the original contact breaker system. There are numerous options to choose from ...

Retro-fitted breakerless systems

The reliability and fatter spark generated by breakerless systems makes them very attractive for all engines. However, for early 8-cylinder engines the argument for electronic ignition is particularly strong. The more lobes (bumps) on the distributor cam, the more difficult it is to control the points and, in particular, stop them from bouncing at medium to high revs. The modern electronic ignition systems offer advantages in that bounce is eliminated and maintenance reduced. Furthermore, after at least 25

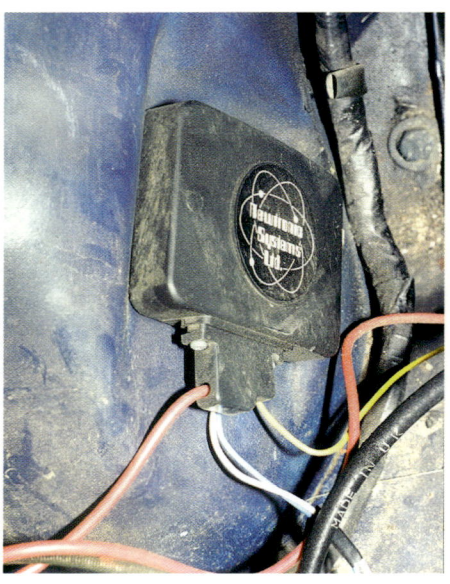

11-2 A typical external amplifier module, in this case a Newtronic one, which marries to the ...

11-3 ... Newtronic chopper disc fitted to the cam that once opened and closed the contact breaker points.

years' use most bearings in the body of the distributor are worn, resulting in some side-play in the shaft and further inaccuracies in timing. The systems we are exploring all render shaft-play inconsequential, and thus rejuvenate all but the most worn distributors.

In outline there are two types of system – magnetic or optical. Both systems use an amplifier (a typical one is at 11-2) to turn a minuscule

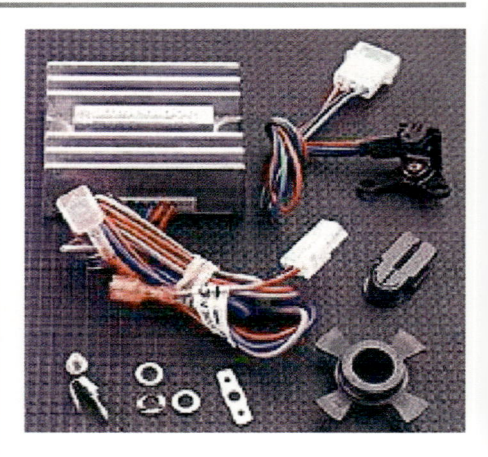

11-4 The Lumenition system as you might receive it. An outline as to the ease of fitting is included in the main text.

initial pulse into something sufficiently powerful to switch the coil on and off, in the same way as the contact breaker has done for years! However, it is the way that initial pulse is generated that separates the two systems. The magnetically activated systems have four or eight equally-spaced tubular magnets fitted inside a circular disc. The disc is fitted over the cam that once opened the points. A sensing module fitted to the distributor's base-plate produces a tiny electrical pulse every time a magnet passes. The optical systems use a chopper disc mounted over the same cam, but these discs have four or eight slots to 'chop' an infrared beam passing between a light emitting diode and a silicon phototransistor – you can see a shot of my Newtronic disc in picture 11-3. In this system it is the transistor mounted on the base-plate that generates the initial electrical pulse.

The latest breakerless types of aftermarket system available are also changing with amazing rapidity. Breakerless systems from Lumenition can be seen at pictures 11-4 and 11-5, while Petronix/Alden's 'Igniter'

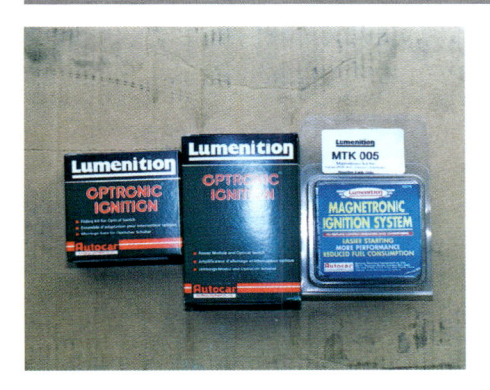

IMPROVING THE SPARKS

11-5 Lumenition makes the optically and magnetically triggered breakerless systems we see here.

11-6 Currently the most compact of the breakerless ignition systems available is the Alden 'Igniter' we see here. Alden systems are known as 'Pertronix' in the USA.

11-7 The arrow draws your attention to an important detail – it is essential that the distributor drive (in this case a late female) tang and the oil pump drive in your engine marry.

system is commendably compact (see picture 11-6), and fits within the distributor body/cap without the need for external amplifiers. I am sure that before this book is in print it will have real competition, but the Igniter system looks a little like a mini-cassette and, like all these systems, is very easy to fit indeed. It is magnetically activated (my preference too) and completely replaces the points and condenser arrangement.

Distributor replacements

In some cases it will be helpful to replace the distributor and the ignition trigger. Non-US TR7s were fitted with a Delco (Europe) points distributor, incorporating mechanical/vacuum advance. This certainly was a fairly reliable unit, but nevertheless will still benefit from a breakerless upgrade using one of the kits already described. However, pre-1980 US TR7s were fitted with a Lucas 'Opus' electronic distributor which proved highly unreliable, as the electronics were contained within the body of the distributor. In the interests of reliability, this ignition system – although breakerless in concept – is best replaced with one of the modern breakerless systems we have explored.

Post-1980 US TR7s used essentially the same Delco distributor body as any other car, but with factory fitted electronic ignition. The module was located externally (under the coil) and was a Delco France part, and consequently is also found on Peugeots of the era. The amplifier module is situated on the inner wing adjacent to the brake master cylinder, is a standard GM part and is still widely available. Unfortunately, the pickup coil and vacuum retard unit are now almost impossible to source as spares.

It is possible to retrofit a Lumenition system to the US version of the Delco distributor. This requires changing the base-plate to the European type, which is not a problem, but it is also necessary to machine the distributor shaft, too. Therefore, you may wish to fit a standard European Delco distributor even though the advance/retard curves will be different. All my cars run with Piranha/Newtronic breakerless systems which I favour because of their reliability, and because you can replace the whole distributor base-plate during the upgrade and retain the original and components as spares.

V8 engines offer an even wider choice of distributors. Buick 'points' distributors can be fitted to almost any Buick/Rover engine – indeed, early Rover 35D8 distributors from Rover P5B/P6 engines similarly will work well, although for the reasons already outlined the bodies are best equipped with a modern breakerless ignition trigger. There is one complication to look out for – the once-male tongue on the bottom of the distributor drive changed to a female tongue. The location of this vital detail is clear from picture 11-7.

Factory TR8s were fitted with Lucas electronic ignition as standard, but for the same reasons as with the US TR7s, it proved unreliable. The solution is to fit one of the latest Rover/Lucas distributors from a Land or Range Rover or choose a system such as Lumenition or Crane, both of which supply their equipment as a kit and recommend you locate the electronics as far from the engine as is practical (photo 11-8).

SPEEDPRO SERIES

11-8 This TR8 has been fitted with a Lumenition breakerless system. The amplifier module (arrowed) has been put in the coolest place Jim TenCate could think of – on the inner wing.

The development work that Rover/Lucas carried out over many years of V8 engine production paid off, and the latest distributors were very effective and reliable. Up to about 1982 the amplifier was inside the distributor, and a loose, black 'flash cover' was used. These were the vulnerable 35DE8 'Opus' units. After that date a clear, fixed flash cover was employed, and 'constant energy' improvements made to the distributor. One such example can be viewed at photo 11-9, but two later models were issued. The first modification took the amplifier onto the inner wing along with the coil and ballast resistor – this distributor (coded 35DLM8) can be viewed at 11-10. The very latest V8s (and best, using distributor 35DM8) had the amplifier – used without a ballast resistor and necessitating a special coil – back with the distributor, but now on the outside.

For converters with an eye for adding the GM engine-management discussed in chapter 13, the later units (mostly from Land and Range Rover) had the added advantage of being fitted with a magnetic pickup compatible with the GM ignition module.

11-9 The latest Constant Energy ignition system mounts the amplifier on the side of the Rover distributor (arrowed here). However, there is also nothing to stop you replacing the Opus system with a modern electronic ignition trigger.

Ballast resistors

A ballast resistor and a 7-volt coil are fitted to help the car start. The coil is normally fed from the ignition circuit via the ballast resistor, but when cranking the engine an additional lead connects to the coil, carrying as near 12 volts as the car can manage. It will probably provide about 9, possibly 10 volts, and thus generates a healthy spark from a 7-volt coil. For those transplanting an SD1 engine, ignition circuits included, you need to be aware that many SD1 electronic distributors require this 12-volt feed from the smallest spade terminal on the starter motor to the aluminium cased ballast resistor. By this method, the resistor wire built into the TR's wiring harnesses is obsolete.

Drawing D11-1 shows the SD1

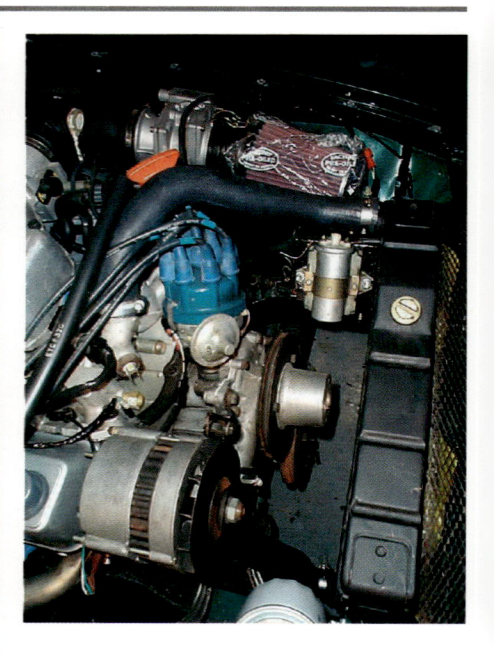

11-10 This is a late Lucas Constant Energy system with the separate AB17 amplifier acting as a saddle for the coil. Both amp and coil are mounted away from the engine heat with the mounting plate also acting as a heat sink. In contrast to the earliest Lucas electronic systems, this is an effective and very reliable system with operating principles that are exactly the same as those used on modern engine management systems.

electronic wiring arrangements for the ballast resistor and the related SD1 Opus ignition circuit. Other distributors or systems demand different wiring arrangements, particularly aftermarket ignition systems such as Crane, Mallory, MSD, Accel, etc. Follow the manufacturer's recommendations as to whether or not a ballast resistor is needed.

Whether a ballast resistor is needed or not is usually determined by the ignition coil. There are two ways of deciding this. If your coil is marked as a 6- or 7-volt unit, you will need a ballast resistor in the 'ignition-run' circuit. If the

IMPROVING THE SPARKS

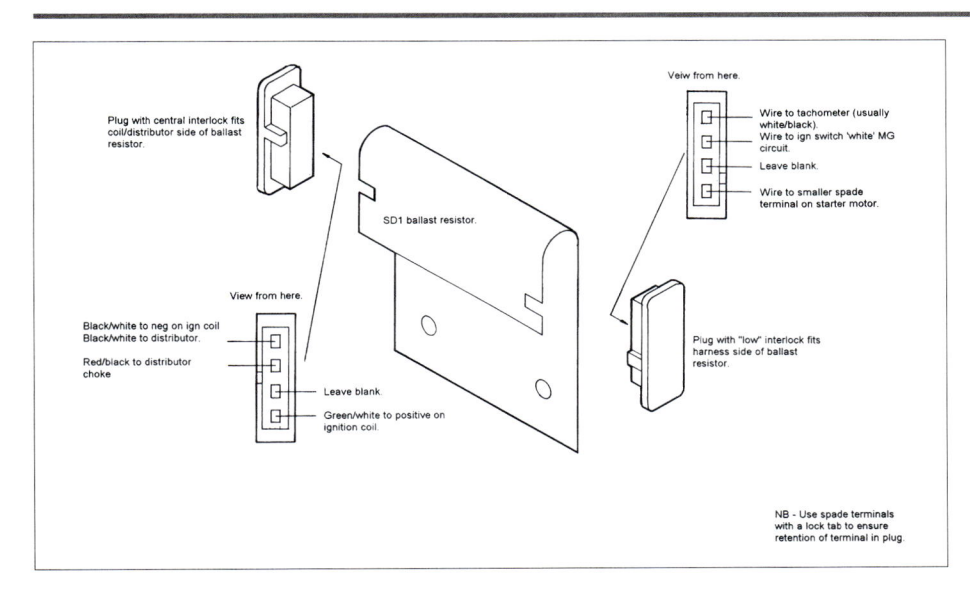

D11-1 The early SD1 ballast resistor wiring arrangement using a Lucas 35DE8 distributor.

coil has no external markings but an internal resistance of 1.5 ohms or less, a ballast resistor is needed. On the other hand, a coil with external markings of '12 volts', or an internal resistance of 3 ohms or more, does not need a ballast resistor.

If the coil you buy comes with a resistor and you are about to fit it to a TR7 with its pink wire resistor built into the front harness, do NOT incorporate the supplied ballast into the car's ignition circuit. You will have two ballast resistors in the circuit and performance will suffer. Preferably use the existing (pink wire) resistor, or bypass it as described above before installing the new ballast resistor.

HIGH-TENSION IGNITION COMPONENTS

If you want the best performance from your car, improved or standard, it is very important to use top grade, high-tension ignition components. The distributor cap, plugs, high-tension leads and coil are all equally and vitally important to both the short-term performance of the car and its ongoing reliability.

Distributor caps

Reactions and experiences are mixed as far as distributor caps are concerned. Most have had no problems with any make of cap while others are convinced there is trouble around the corner if you use anything other than a genuine Lucas cap. I always pay the extra and use genuine Lucas, and have never had a problem.

Sparkplugs

The sparkplugs and ignition leads can also have a deceptively good or debilitating effect on the car's performance, and both warrant our close attention, starting with the humble sparkplug. We mostly take these for granted, but the standard design can affect performance via its 'temperature', and many people may not appreciate that the concept has been improved with multi-earth electrodes. Let's brush-up on one or two of the subtleties of the traditional single electrode sparkplug, since quite large sections of this book address engine modifications and there is little point in improving the engine and then fitting the wrong plugs! In fact, such a step may not only nullify your best efforts but also result in expensive damage.

There are numerous modifications that will not affect the choice of sparkplug. If you plan no more than a change of air filter, inlet manifold, exhaust manifold/header silencer/muffler or distributor, then it is unlikely you will need to consider a change of sparkplug from the specified original. However, if you increase your engine's compression ratio, change the cylinder head configuration, introduce a gas-flowed head or change the pistons, then a change of sparkplug may be helpful. Modifications that increase the compression ratio are likely to generate more power. With more power comes more heat, which may necessitate the sparkplug removing more heat than was the case in the engine's original configuration. Thus it is usual to fit a 'colder' plug as an engine's level of tune is increased. We will need to check symptoms, but in these circumstances you might be well advised not only to fit colder plugs, but also to adjust the plug gaps to take account of the denser mixture that results from increasing the compression ratio.

So, what are the symptoms that might signal a change to a colder plug is needed? Pre-ignition is the simple answer, for this MIGHT be the consequence of the sparkplug tip getting too hot. Assuming that you have raised your compression, that there are no other causes of your pre-ignition, and that you are not experiencing plug fouling, then a plug that conducts more heat away from the tip is worth trying – the next, 'colder' plug should reduce tip temperatures by 75/80°C. In any event, it is better to run with too cold a plug than too hot a one. The worst that can happen with an overly cold plug selection is that your plugs will foul up. On the other hand, too hot a plug will result in pre-ignition which can cause serious engine damage, so study your plugs closely for signs of silver or black specs, melting or breakage at the tip, any of which signals pre-ignition problems.

If you are experiencing plug fouling problems following engine modifications, do check the plugs closely and don't be too quick to fit a hotter plug. True, it will conduct less heat away from the tip, will therefore run at a higher temperature and thus burn off more of these deposits – but first you need to assure yourself there are no other problems requiring your attention before hotter plugs are fitted, particularly if you have already raised the combustion temperatures by increasing your compression ratio. Naturally, the type of deposit/fouling can vary and needs to be reviewed. Heavy dry black deposits can suggest an overly rich mixture and potential carburation problems, retarded timing, or simply too wide a plug gap. Wet black oily deposits can indicate a leaking head gasket or piston ring/valve-stem problems. The latter may not necessarily be serious if you have just rebuilt the engine, as some gentle running/breaking in (with the correct oil) may improve the situation. There are lots of alternatives to consider before you resort to a hotter plug. Incidentally, it is very difficult to thoroughly clean the insulator within a fouled sparkplug, and so the plug is unlikely to be fully recoverable and is best replaced.

The sparkplug gap just mentioned warrants further discussion in the context of engine upgrades. First, let us bear in mind that a sparkplug is made for many applications, and that the gap set at the factory during manufacture may be a very popular gap, but may in fact not be correct for even your standard engine, never mind your uprated one. So start with the OE recommended gap, remembering that an insufficient gap can cause pre-ignition, while too wide a gap can generate misfires, loss of power, and poor economy, as well as the problems mentioned in the previous paragraph. If you have raised the compression from OE spec, you could reduce the gap by about 0.002/0.003in, or if you have fitted a high powered ignition system you can open the gap by about the same amount. In other words, if you have both raised your compression and fitted a high-powered ignition system you should stick to the recommended OE gap setting! If in doubt, always use a slightly wider gap in preference to a slightly smaller one, thereby reducing the risk of pre-ignition.

A final detail for those switching to EFI or engine management systems (i.e. systems controlled by an on-board computer), particularly if you experience erratic idling, misfiring at high rpm, engine run-on or abnormal combustion: stray voltages from your ignition system may confuse your electronics, and the fitting of 'Resistor' sparkplugs can improve that situation. As their name suggests, these have a resistor built into the core that is also used to reduce radio interference and will make little or no difference to your engine's performance.

And you took your sparkplug for granted! Now all you will be worrying about is how to select hotter or colder plugs. I wish I could report a standard system for plug grading, but since there is no uniformity from manufacturer to manufacturer I will have to note two contrasting examples and let you establish the specifics for your preferred brand. The concept is simple – one group of manufacturers uses a higher number to denote a colder plug. The justifiably popular NGK brand uses this system, so its BP6 plug is the next colder plug to its BP5. On the other hand, Bosch uses a lower number to denote a colder plug!

Finally, we must look at the newest design of sparkplug available – the multiple-earth electrode plug – and its benefits. The design is not that new, as VW was using a triple electrode plug on production cars from the early 1980s, but the multi-earth plugs are now widely available and benefit the user of standard ignition systems in two ways. We will explore these in a moment, but first what is a multiple earth electrode sparkplug? Photograph 11-11 compares the traditional single electrode plug with a 4-electrode replacement.

The first benefit offered by such plugs is performance. The traditional design slightly shrouds each plug's spark from the incoming air/fuel mixture, but the multi-earth design does not. In truth, I have not noticed a major leap in engine performance. I have only used the new plugs for a short period, and suspect that the performance benefit may be in comparison to the latter part of a traditional plug's life. The multi-electrodes are supposed to

11-11 The improvement made to even the common sparkplug is evident here, with the newer four earth version on the right.

IMPROVING THE SPARKS

remove more heat from the plug, to keep the electrodes cooler and to fire more effectively in difficult combustion conditions.

The second benefit is longer life for the newer sparkplugs, possibly with less drop-off in performance. The multi-electrodes allow the electrical spark to choose its route to earth. It will always select the nearest earth electrode until that electrode wears, whereupon the spark will select an alternative route to earth. This clearly extends the life of the plug. Most major manufacturers make this design now. Depending on the company, they are available with 2, 3 or 4 earth electrodes.

I have a caveat – they may not be suited to capacitive discharge (i.e. very high voltage) ignition systems, and you should check with the respective manufacturers of both your intended ignition system and sparkplug before marrying the two together.

I mentioned that multi-electrodes may offer longer life between service intervals. Bear in mind that development of sparkplugs also continues apace, and that 'platinum' plugs are now available with a service life of 60000 miles, while Ford has introduced platinum plugs to its modern modular V8s with a service interval of 90000 miles.

Any chain is only as strong as its weakest link, so with that in mind we now need to look at the ignition leads.

The plug leads

Like the sparkplug, the plug lead has changed dramatically in the last few years. The silicone-based lead has completely taken over from the now obsolete copper and carbon-cored leads, but for any form of ultra-fast or competitive use an induction-wound core is recommended. There are several grades and, for that matter, several manufacturers. For conventional coil ignition systems, 7mm high-tension leads are probably satisfactory, although the 8mm size is better. For those with some of the more sophisticated ignition systems you are advised to use 8mm leads, while 8.5mm leads are probably best for ultra-fast road and competitive applications. You will appreciate that the larger the lead, the greater its insulation, which will reduce the chances of cross-firing between leads.

Magnecor is one of several manufacturers which makes ignition cables suited to any upgraded ignition system. In fact, TRs with the standard ignition systems may benefit from their superior grade 7mm and 8mm cables/leads. These leads are specifically designed to conduct the maximum output generated by the ignition system to the sparkplugs, and to provide suppression of radio frequency and electro-magnetic interference. The 7 and 8mm cables incorporate a ferri-magnetic core for radio suppression, and a 2mm chrome-nickel, 120-turns-per-inch winding designed both to provide magnetic suppression and a capacitive reserve to help ignition coils regenerate at high revs. Insulation is via an EPDM insulator with fibreglass reinforcement, all covered by a high strength, heat-resistant silicone rubber jacket. The 7mm cable jacket is designed to withstand 400°F (190°C) and the 8mm cable jacket some 450°F (210°C). Magnecor claims that when used on older, worn engines or engines operating in extreme ambient temperatures, easier starting and improved running under load will be noted. Also, the 8mm leads will resolve many of the problems usually exacerbated by the installation of many high-energy aftermarket ignition systems. It suggests that some engine modifications subject the standard ignition leads to extra heat, which can destroy non-silicone insulated cables. Like the sparkplugs, there is much more to many auto components that are so easily given little or no thought.

However, we are not finished yet – at least we are not finished with the very top-end of ignition-lead technology for there are 8.5 and even 10mm leads available for the competitors. Magnecor's KV85 Competition (8.5mm) and R-100 Racing (10mm) ignition cables are designed for racing applications and/or where ignition cables are required with a heat resistance in excess 450°F (210°C).

All Magnecor components, including the cable, speciality terminals, boots and crimping tools are available separately should you want to make your own ignition leads.

CHARGING THE IGNITION COIL

The standard ignition coil is quite suitable for standard cars enjoying no more than spirited road use, although you would be wise to at least upgrade to a Lucas 'Gold', Bosch 'Red', Bosch 'Blue' or Aldon 'Flame Thrower' coil for fast road use. Of these the Bosch Blue is probably the most potent, generating some 47000 volts and necessitating a breakerless ignition trigger. However, the coil's recharge constraints explored earlier remain a weakness at least for the ultra-fast road and competitive cars, even with all the above high-tension improvements in place. You will recall that even with a 4-cylinder engine, the coil had insufficient time to fully re-energise itself once the engine exceeded 2000rpm – or barely above tick-over/idle for some 'hot' engines! Today, we have improvement opportunities – if not for the ignition coil itself, at least for the way its magnetic field is regenerated for each spark. Called a capacitive discharge system, this achieves its objective by

SPEEDPRO SERIES

incorporating capacitors within a (new) ignition module. These capacitors are charged up to about 350 volts, which is, of course, much higher than the cars 12 volts. The high voltage is then discharged across the coil's primary circuit, thereby dramatically shortening the coil's regeneration time.

Before we outline what systems are on offer, some of you may be interested in how that swifter coil charge is utilised to best effect in advanced ignition systems. Increasing the sparkplug gap and getting a nice fat spark across is, of course, the simple answer to getting the most out of all high-performance ignition systems. Surprisingly, the amount of energy needed to sustain a spark across a wide gap is not significantly different to that for a small gap. However, it is what happens before the spark 'strikes' that is different and increases with the size of the gap. Preceding the spark, the ignition system, even a conventional one, creates a plasma between the electrodes to provide a path for the spark to follow. A swirling, dense air/fuel mixture makes it hard enough, but the higher the compression the more difficult it is for the pre-spark plasma to form. It therefore makes sense that the higher the voltage, the better the chances are of bridging the gap and doing so quickly (we are looking for instantly!).

A conventional ignition system, particularly one used with a high-compression engine turning high rpm, can and does 'miss'. This is not (usually) the fault of the ignition system failing to present some sort of spark to the plug, but more likely that the spark was insufficiently strong or sustained to ignite the cylinder charge. A higher voltage would certainly have helped, but a very much higher voltage sparking across a bigger gap would have helped enormously! Obviously the surface area of spark presented to the mixture increases proportionally with the gap, and thus we can be talking about 25 to 50 per cent increases. However, a much higher voltage sparking across a bigger gap several times is likely to ignite the charge, every bit of it, every time! Hence the value of capacitive and multiple discharge systems and why we are examining them now.

Jacobs makes such a system (called Energy Pak Computer Ignition) and can provide the essential compatible coil. It is a combination of capacitive discharge and multi-spark ignition. This automatically fires multiple sparks per cylinder, spanning 20 degrees of the crankshaft rotation up to about 3000rpm. With the naked eye there appears a series of four discharges to the plugs at each firing. Obviously you only need one to fire the cylinder's charge in most circumstances, but this stream of sparks virtually guarantees that the plug will fire under the most adverse conditions, including very high compression ratios. Above 3000rpm there is insufficient time to fire each plug more than once. You get a glimpse of the primary Jacobs components in photos 11-12 and 11-13.

Alternatively, you can consider an even more sophisticated capacitive discharge system. The Automatic Controls Corporation in the USA makes a Multiple Spark Discharge (MSD) unit. The primary capacitive discharge voltage of the MSD system is 470 volts – nearly 40 times the TR's original 12 volts! The MSD6A is the most popular kit for the TR6 engine, unless you also want the rev limiter feature, in which case ask for the MSD6T. You may find one refinement interesting, fun and indeed useful; the MSD system allows you to adjust the ignition timing either

11-12 Phil Vella took this great shot of a Jacobs 'Ultra-Coil' for me. It forms part of an MSD kit and can only be used in conjunction with its ...

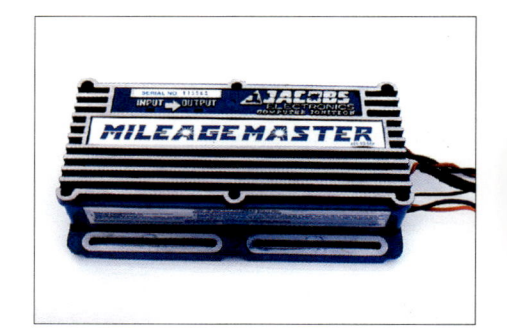

11-13 ... multi-spark discharge 'black box'.

11-14 Dick Taylor kindly contrived this shot to illustrate not only the model 60BTM MSD unit, but also, just to the left, the (normally) remote ignition adjustment control.

IMPROVING THE SPARKS

way by up to 7 degrees ... from the drivers seat! The MSD unit is available from Summit in the USA and Real Steel in the UK, and can be seen in picture 11-14.

Crane Performance offers its Fireball HI-6 multiple spark capacitive discharge electronic ignition. This has a built-in, programmable rev limiter, and can be run with either Crane's PS91 coil for road or its PS92 for competitive applications.

These products can be fitted to 4- or 8-cylinder engines, of course. Earlier in this chapter I stressed the wisdom of a breakerless trigger for the ignition system; you may therefore be surprised to hear that these products can be used, if required, with standard contact breaker points or one of the breakerless systems. One of the main reasons for eliminating the points was to bypass the associated maintenance. If used in conjunction with original contact breaker points, the small low-tension current required by this kit all but eliminates maintenance of ignition points and sparkplugs. Nevertheless, I stil suggest you fit one of the breakerless systems to trigger your capacitive/multi-discharge sparks!

Users of capacitive discharge ignition systems assure me that sparkplugs do not foul with this unit, even if you run a colder plug – which reduces the likelihood of pre-ignition in high compression engines – and/or increase the plug-gaps. One member of the TR Register tells me he runs a sparkplug that is two grades colder than standard with a 0.050in (1.25mm) gap! Furthermore, hot and cold starting was always difficult with Weber carburettors (they tend to run rich at lower engine revs) but the problem went away with a big fat capacitive discharge spark. Apparently, you can occasionally detect that the large-gapped plugs are fouling under slow running, but they clear within seconds of putting your foot down.

Furthermore, he assures me that high-speed misfires are no longer a problem – probably due to the magnetic trigger used in this last example. If you stay with contact breaker points they apparently last about ten times longer than normal, as the usual arcing between the points is practically non-existent. The only maintenance required is an occasional check to be sure SOME gap is present, since the 'heel' of the points eventually wears, even with a well-lubricated cam. Remember that some cam bounce is inevitable at high rpm, and I would strongly recommend a breakerless trigger in spite of the point-retention option (apparently) returning when you use capacitive discharge!

Finally, current prices for capacitive discharge systems in the USA make the option very attractive indeed, so shop around! Don't forget to cost the new matched coil and the breakerless trigger – not to mention a really good set of plug leads.

A final thought-provoking point – as the induction system increases in capability and the effectiveness of the coil, plugs and plug leads improve, the limitations of the rotor arm and distributor cap become more exposed, and indeed form the weakest links in the high-tension distribution system. You could generate faults within your arm and cap – which have otherwise given years of excellent service – purely because the rest of your system is stressing them more than ever. As a consequence of this, modern high-output ignition systems do not distribute the spark via a distributor, but have the direct coil-to-plug connections seen in many engine management systems.

ENGINE MANAGEMENT IMPROVEMENTS

We have spent some time examining how to get a bigger, more consistent spark fired across an ever-widening sparkplug gap. All good stuff, but we have not improved upon the point at which that spark ignites the mixture. The systems have all retained the original concept of an ignition advance curve that is controlled, to put it in basic terms, by mechanical weights and springs. In other words, we now have the ability to generate a bigger bang but not, as yet, the refinement to control the delivery of that bang! The problem is that engine development has shown that the optimum point at which the spark needs to be delivered varies, and certainly does not follow the sort of simple curve that centrifugal force generates, with or without vacuum control. At some points in the rpm range the ignition needs to be slightly retarded, while an increase in rpm of only 500rpm necessitates an amazing amount of ignition advance. These are jobs routinely carried out by electronics in today's motors – this is now the case for all TRs via the engine management systems outlined in chapter 13.

www.velocebooks.com/www.veloce.co.uk
All books in print • New books • Special offers • Gift Vouchers

Chapter 12
Carburettor induction

CARBURETTOR DESIGN PRINCIPLES

As you plough through this chapter, bear in mind that we will be discussing three types of carburettor:
- The variable choke design used by SU and Stromberg that is seen on original TR7 and TR8 engines, and to some extent on the lower performance TR7-V8 engines.
- The horizontal fixed choke design used by Weber and Dellorto, which is largely reserved for use on very high-performance engines.
- The four-barrel down-draught performance carburettors (called AFBs) fitted to mid- and high-performance V8 engines.

Also, as you read this chapter, remember that better performance is not just a matter of improving the carburation. The compression ratio, inlet and exhaust manifolds and tracts, timing, camshaft, ignition systems and air filters all contribute to overall performance – as does the emulsification of the fuel.

ATOMISATION

Electronic fuel-injection (EFI) offers an alternative to a carburettor for inducing fuel into your engine. EFI enjoys two very important benefits over carburettors. Firstly, you do not need to compromise with the size of the inlet tract as you do with a carburettor. In a carburettor, the fuel is drawn into the air flow by a venturi – which consequently needs to be small enough to create the essential 'suck' at low revs (say, when cranking), yet large enough to minimise air flow restrictions at very high revs. Secondly, EFI fuel is pressure-sprayed from the injectors, aiding emulsification of the fuel. Millions of small droplets are uniformly – ideally conically – distributed within the air stream and make for better combustion.

These are two (of several) reasons why injected fuel is usually more effective than most carburettor induction systems. While EFI is the focus of another chapter, I make the point here because, with an EFI system, you can do something to improve the spray and/or emulsification by testing each injector and cleaning/changing the setup until the spray pattern is satisfactory. However, outside of changing jets or needles, there is little you can do to improve the fuel emulsification of any carburettor – it's all down to the design of the carburettor and that is beyond your control. Needless to say, emulsification is one of the vital details that carburettor designers pay a great deal of attention to, and in order to explain the differences and benefits of the various carburettor designs, we need to spend a moment on the subject.

There are several places where fuel can be injected into a carburettor's incoming air stream. Like me, you probably never gave any thought to whether fuel injected at the edge of

CARBURETTOR INDUCTION

12-1-1-1 The auxiliary venturi in this 40mm choke Weber injects the fuel as centrally as possible for maximum engine efficiency.

12-1-1-2 While the design is slightly different for the 45mm version (which surprised me), the principle of central injection of fuel is retained.

12-1-2-2 It's less obvious with the piston right up (picture 12-1-2-1), that the bridge inevitably acts as a restriction, but you can see the constriction as the piston descends. Did you spot the anti-run on valve in the throttle disc at the back of this and the preceding picture?

the air steam was the same, better or less effective than a centrally-injected fuel spray. However, the more centrally the fuel is injected, the better the emulsification is likely to be. Consequently SU, and probably Stromberg, will have spent hours trying to get the same superb emulsion as Weber and Dellorto but won't have succeeded – which is why a DCOE Weber usually provides that little bit more top-end performance than an SU or a Stromberg. There are several contributory reasons, but the primary one is that Weber and Dellorto carburettors spray fuel into the centre of the air stream, making for greater uniformity of fuel/air emulsification. You can see the principle in photograph 12-1-1-1 and 12-1-1-2. The design of SU/Stromberg carburettors requires the fuel to enter on the edge of the air stream – which does not permit the same degree of uniformity of emulsification. Furthermore the SU/Stromberg 'bridge' also causes an irretrievable loss in top-end performance. You can check out my point by studying photographs 12-1-2-1 and 12-1-2-2.

That said, the SU and the Stromberg are very good carburettors for what they are – and more particularly for what they cost – and served well the cars we are focused on, as confirmed by photos 12-1-3-1 to 12-1-4-2. Both

12-1-2-1 The fuel enters the incoming air stream at the point arrowed, right on the (bottom) edge of the air flow. The design of the carburettor makes a change impossible.

can in fact be made to run very well indeed, and twin SUs/Strombergs are generally quite underrated. Further,

12-1-3-1 This twin HS6 SU carburettor setup will be familiar to most UK owners ...

141

SPEEDPRO SERIES

12-1-3-2 ... while the very similar Sprint carburettor arrangement was not lacking in performance.

12-1-4-1 The carburettor-equipped TR8 used Stromberg carburettors mounted on a pent-roof manifold ...

12-1-4-2 ... just like the SD1 V8 engine. Note the conical, directly mounted K+N air filters.

SUs are FAR easier to adjust than any other carburettor. Consequently, many enthusiasts should look at getting what they have correct before moving on to exotica. Few would believe that the mid-range acceleration from both SU and Weber DCOE carburettors can be identical – which bears thinking about considering the respective costs of each and that most of us are more interested in acceleration than top speed. However, the uniformity of the Weber's spray pattern will always give the 'Doppio Corpo Orizzontale' model E the superior top-end performance. The Italian nomenclature means, by the way, double body horizontal type E.

Whatever the carburettor, it is important that cool air is delivered to them. Not only must it be as cool as possible and filtered, but also it should not be forced into the carb. This is usually achieved by fitting a couple of 2in (or maybe one 3in) diameter flexible tubes from the front of the car, but on a TR7 you can remove one of the plastic covers at the top-front of the inner wing/fender and pick up the air stream from there. This was how cold air was supplied to the TR8. Allow the cool air to discharge adjacent to the carburettors' air filters but do not try and 'close-couple' the ducts to the carburettors. Carburettors need to suck tranquil air in, not have it forced in supercharging style!

If maximum bhp is what you are after, side-draught Webers (or Dellortos) are what the TR7 4-cylinder engines need, while most V8s will use an AFB (aluminium four-barrel) down-draught. The last few per cent of V8 power may still require (several!) DCOE, but only a very few cars will be going there. So, why are we wasting our time exploring the SUs? There are several very good reasons, starting with the fact that the majority of TR owners do not need the last few per cent of power from the top-end of their engine. Secondly, most would prefer not to spend sizeable sums of money unnecessarily. Far from being outclassed, the SU still causes the majority of engines to go extremely well. Tuning and jetting DCOE side-draught and AFB carburettors needs to be done on a rolling road, which is fine for the competitors, but I guess the majority of readers would like to set up their carburettors themselves. This is quite practical with SUs. Finally, economy; the original equipment twin SUs give a good balance of efficiency, as well as delivering good miles to the gallon – something Webers, Dellortos and AFBs are not noted for.

So the faithful SU does have a lot to offer many enthusiasts, and if we could give it a sportier image, it might even become the carburettor of choice for the majority of readers. I purely plan to explore the SU, although my comments are just as applicable to Strombergs. However, if I were about to tweak carburettor(s), I would first switch to SUs if my car was fitted with Strombergs!

THE SU CARBURETTOR

Many engines are fitted with Stromberg carbs that are very effective, and generate as much power as the SU with fewer emissions. They are, however, much more difficult to adjust than the SU, and while they will perform perfectly well you might eventually want to change.

SUs come in two forms – the earlier, to my mind preferable, HS range and the later, more complex (for little benefit) HIF range. When buying SU carbs, go for the HS version with the float chamber to one side of the carburettor body. HIF versions have an integral float chamber below the main body, and can flow a shade more air

CARBURETTOR INDUCTION

than the HS versions. That said, you are best avoiding SUs with waxstats on the bottom, since the heat on the waxstat can incorrectly adjust the SU! Also avoid SUs with the anti-run-on valves incorporated in the throttle butterflies (picture 12-1-2-2). The valve restricts the smooth flow of mixture past the butterfly.

The vast majority of Rover engines you buy with carburettors in situ will have carbs with conventional dashpot heights. Of course, this worked well in the original application, but in a TR7-V8 conversion you may need to acquire or have modified a pair of 'short-dashpot' SUs. If you need to go down that route (discussed in more detail in chapter 9), do think about the version of SU carburettor you are about to buy/modify. I think HS versions are simpler and thus preferable.

The standard SU setup (needles, springs and damper oil) will be correct for the standard/stock Triumph engines, balanced between reasonable power and acceleration with fuel economy. Before embarking on any carburettor tuning, ensure that the carburettors are indeed set up to factory standards and in good condition (i.e. there are no air-leaks). So with your car running as the factory intended, how do we improve the acceleration? By reading on!

Road tuning stage 1

The SU/Stromberg carburettors work on the principle that the greater the engine vacuum, the higher the carburettor piston lifts, which in turn withdraws the tapered fuel-control needle from its 'jet' thus allowing more fuel to be drawn into the incoming air-stream. So, the shape or profile of the needle(s) is very influential to the performance (and economy) of the car. Rarely are cars fitted with SU carburettors and 'rich' needles, as the manufacturer will have spend a great deal of time establishing what are the most fuel-efficient (thus leanest) needles they can fit. Consequently, you can improve the road-going performance of your car simply by changing your existing SU needles to a 'richer' profile.

A richer profile means a thinner needle – but thinner only from the neck down. Carburettor specialists will be able to tell you what the next richer profile is for your car/engine tune, or you can get much information about SU needle profiles from the internet. If the profile you seek is not available you may find the same length needle is used for a different size of carburettor (i.e. some needles are common across 1½in, 1¾in and 2in carburettors). Alternatively, from the hundreds of needle types listed it may be that the profile you seek is available in a longer style. However, needle diameters vary from 0.090in through 0.100in to 0.125in, so when comparing needle profiles take care to only consider those with the correct base shaft diameter for your carburettor(s).

All SU carburettors run more efficiently with radiused air intakes, so any first level tuning should include radiused plates or 'stub-stacks' at the entry to the carburettor. Furthermore, a non-pressured supply of the coldest air possible is vital.

Road tuning stage 2

The second part of SU performance improvement is to increase the speed that the piston, and therefore the needle, rises when the throttle is depressed. If the speed of piston-lift is slow, the injection of extra fuel will be slow and the car's acceleration unexciting. Conversely, if the piston responds relatively quickly, the injection of extra fuel will be increased and the car's acceleration proportionally improved – over and above whatever you achieved with richer needles. You control the speed at which the piston raises by two factors – the thickness of the oil in the damper and the strength of the piston or return spring. Thinner oil and a weaker spring both contribute to increasing the speed of damper rise while, conversely, thicker oil and stronger springs decrease the speed at which the damper rises

At least four different strength springs were used in SU carburettors. The weakest are colour coded blue, red are a grade stronger, then yellow, and the strongest (or most resistant to the rise of the piston) is coloured green. The red springs are the most common and are almost the lightest in weight, offering less resistance to piston lift than say, yellow springs, therefore providing slightly better engine acceleration. You can try blue springs too, of course, and can also try putting thinner oil in the dashpot dampers. Make changes one at a time and in small increments. Do not, for example, change the springs and the damper oil simultaneously and expect to measure the changes in acceleration objectively.

If possible, it is best to carry out your experiments using a second set of pistons, needles and, of course, springs. By keeping your standard piston/needle/spring combination unaltered, you will always have a reference to fall back on if you try something inappropriate or find the consequences of your experiment unacceptable. For each change, in the absence of a rolling road in your garage, run a series of acceleration tests over 0 to 30mph, 0 to 50mph, 0 to 70mph and 40 to 70mph for each change. Faithfully record not only the times, but also the specific parameters of each test. It is so easy a week or two later, or even after a few tests during the same day, to find yourself wondering whether test 5 was with thick, thin or even no oil in the dampers!

SPEEDPRO SERIES

12-1-5-1 These are K+N KN56-1400 pancake air filters in front of the SUs with a heat shield behind the carburettors. This heat shield would be even more effective were it to have self-adhesive, heat-reflective foil on the rear face.

12-1-5-2 You certainly get a large filter area in place via this route – although these, possibly original Rover paper elements, make fitting an air intake almost impossible and are best replaced by equally large but more free-flowing modern versions.

12-1-6 While there will no doubt be many satisfied users, I must say that I doubt the cost benefits of buying the manifold and four decent modified SU carburettors. I think an AFB carb will be more cost-effective. Not sure of the vehicle shown in this shot but it's a Rover engine!

A fast road car's state of tune and the setup you choose for your SUs needs to be a compromise between the needle profile and the speed of piston movement. The beauty of the SU carburettor is that you can choose, and if you need more detail as to how to bring about the transformation I strongly recommend Des Hammill's *How to build and power tune SU carburettors* (also a Veloce publication).

Improved air cleaners

As we just touched upon, the needles need to be the correct ones for the engine, its tune and the carburettor's return/damper springs. Different companies have different opinions as to what spring/needle combination works best, and if you were to call three different suppliers seeking their recommendation I would be surprised if they agreed as to what needles/springs you should be using! However, all would agree that any standard engine with standard air cleaners should have the standard needles fitted to it initially, as they have been selected by SU to give best possible power with economy for that engine. They would also offer the same advice about richer needles being essential to complement the greater air stream permitted by free-flow air filters of the K+N type (picture 12-1-5-1) – although picture 12-1-5-2 offers an interesting and practical alternative.

Track day/competition tuning

One absolutely unique advantage of the SU carburettor is that you can drive to a track day on a standard pair of SUs, and change the piston/needle/damper assemblies in the paddock to your pre-set, 'competition' top-end assemblies. After enjoying your spirited track event you can revert to your 'road' pistons/needles in a few minutes and drive home quite normally.

The uniformity of atomisation from SU carburettors can probably be improved in V8 engines by fitting four 1¾in SUs – something those who race on particularly tight budgets may wish to experiment with. This approach should bring about some improvement in air/fuel distribution and performance. There are induction systems that use four SU carburettors mounted on a fabricated manifold, but I would not bother trying it unless you can easily lay hands on such a manifold, an example of which is pictured at 12-1-6.

Your prepared and tested SU 'race' top-ends will be fitted with thin profile needles, probably no oil in the dampers and with the return-damper spring weakened, and sometimes omitted altogether. This will increase the acceleration and mid-range performance to that of a Weber, knock a complete hole in your mpg economy and put you to within a few percent points of a Webers' top-end performance – perhaps only 5 or 8 per cent less. All that for about £10 and some rolling road setup times. However, for absolute maximum performance Webers are the route to take – some examples will be found at 12-1-7-1 and 12-1-7-2.

Other SU tips

Whatever your SU, readers upgrading 4-cylinder engines may care to fit a heat shield between the carburettors and the heat generated by the engine and its exhaust manifold. You may have noted an example in photo 12-1-5-1. They are particularly helpful when unleaded fuel is in use, since this boils at a much lower temperature than leaded fuel.

For those living in hilly, even mountainous regions, SUs have one

CARBURETTOR INDUCTION

12-1-7-1 A pair of DCOE 40s on this Speke-built car might have been a waste of money.

12-1-7-2 Neil Sawyer's V8 rally car mimics the early works cars, and uses a pair of Weber DCOE 45s mounted via Repco adapters to a Buick inlet manifold. The water pump is a Rover P6 unit, and you might just spot the Lumenition ignition amplifier mounted top right in the picture.

generate sufficient vacuum within the carb to draw fuel into the carburettor's venturi in road conditions. If you over-provide choke size, your engine may not generate enough air speed to draw fuel evenly, at least at low rpm. So in general, standard or fast road 2-litre engines should stick to (twin) 1¾in (45mm) chokes. The one exception to this might be the Sprint 2-litre engines, tuned examples of which could be the entry point for HS8s, as photograph 12-1-8 confirms.

However, let's explore some alternative carburettor options for Rover V8s.

V8 AFB INDUCTION

The vast majority of V8 converters will instinctively think of fitting an aluminium four-barrel carburettor atop their V8 engine – and provided you choose the correct size of carburettor for your engine capacity, one of these products will serve you very well indeed, regardless of your engine manufacturer. There are other makes of AFB carburettor available – Demon, seen at 12-2-1 and 12-2-2, being one example – but since Holley and Weber (the latter also marketed as Carter and Edelbrock) have largely made this a two-horse race, space dictates I focus on these leading brands. I will explore the differences and advantages in a moment, but first a few details need to be cleared up:
• The original Buick/Olds/Pontiac 215/3500 engines mostly came fitted with a Rochester AFB carburettor, an example of which is seen at 12-2-3 (overleaf).
• The Weber AFB carburettor is entirely different to the DCOE range of carburettors.
• Weber, Carter and Edelbrock four-barrel carburettors are all manufactured using the same Weber base casting. An example can be seen at 12-2-4 (overleaf).
• Holley carburettors are, however, quite

further advantage – they automatically correct the mixture level when the air thins over changing elevation.

It is important not to over-provide choke or carburettor bore size. It is tempting to think your standard 2000cc TR7 will go better with 2in instead of 1¾in SU carbs. This is, in fact, unlikely to be the case for road-going cars, because it is absolutely essential to

12-1-8 Gary Fuqua (Classic Sports Cars) has warmed up his Sprint and, amongst other changes, beautifully adopted a pair of ex-Jaguar SU HS8 2in carburettors and some low-resistance air filters to provide the induction.

12-2-1 A Road Demon carburettor about which I have heard several good reports.

12-2-2 I like the fuel level sight-glasses in the float chamber but would much prefer a manual choke to the electric one seen in the previous shot.

different and also very highly regarded. They are shown in 12-2-5 (overleaf).

The Holley
Originally developed in the USA for the '215' GM Buick and Oldsmobile

145

SPEEDPRO SERIES

12-2-3 A Rochester AFB carburettor from about 1963. Unfortunately, these do not suit a TR7-V8 conversion due to their unfavourable height requirements, although the manifold they sit upon is both cheap and effective.

12-2-4 One of the Weber trio of AFB carburettors – an Edelbrock. Most parts for these carburettors are interchangeable.

12-2-5 This is Holley's model 4150, with its 390cfm capacity and twin metering plates/float chambers, fitted pannier-style in front of and behind the carburettor body.

12-2-6 Before unboxing your Holley carburettor, make sure it has 'List 8007' stamped on it: Holley makes other identical-looking carbs. This one is for 8-cylinder, 390cfm engines like your Rover unit.

12-2-7 It is important to feed and blank off the Holley apertures as appropriate. From left to right of this photo are: outlet under accelerator pump – blank off; outlet to left of choke – blank off; angled outlet above choke – connect to rocker box; angled outlet under front float chamber – blank off; mid-height outlet from front plate – connect to distributor.

V8 engines, this USA carburettor is a frequent and favourite method of improving the performance of most V8 engines. Holley makes a range of carburettors – so you must get the right model or 'flow-rate' for your particular engine capacity. All the expert speed shops and aftermarket suppliers will be able to advise you on the options most suited to your particular engine, tune and capacity. There are 'double-pumpers' available. These are fitted with two accelerator pumps and, to my mind, are not the best option for road-going cars. The version you need has a secondary vacuum facility and, pre-fitted, a secondary metering plate and jets.

For the 215in^3/3500cc engines at the modest end of our power bands, the 8007 390cfm series shown in photo 12-2-6 works well – after being set up on a rolling road. Check that 'list 8007' is stamped on the top where the air filter mounts before unboxing the unit.

As supplied, the Holley has an electric automatic choke and, if you retain this method of choke actuation, will need only a 12v supply wired from the 'on' side of the ignition switch. Therefore, with the ignition switch 'off', so too will be the power to your carburettor. Take great care to ensure it is a 12v line you take to the carb and not, say, a 7v supply from your coil. A small earth lead is also required – all this can be seen in photo 12-2-7. Check that the choke flap does not foul the air filter, particularly if you find the idle speed is elevated.

The initial Holley 4160 setup needs some explanation, for in my experience it rarely runs straight from the box. Most will at least need 'jetting' for your particular application. Depending upon which of the numerous Holley models you purchase, you may find it essential to fit a secondary metering plate and jets, thus bringing into use the relevant pair of secondary barrels shown on the right of photo 12-2-8 (and the spec to Holley model 4150).

Modify the choke flap on the primary barrels (to prevent over-choking) by machining three holes in the flap (shown in photo 12-2-9). Fit much smaller main (primary barrel) fuel jets to obviate flooding and cylinder washing.

This work necessitated a whole series of adjustments and minor alterations on a rolling road and doubled the initial cost of the carburettor, making it an expensive choice. Consequently, there are some rules I suggest you adopt if you are thinking of a Holley. Be sure to

CARBURETTOR INDUCTION

12-2-8 The Holley as delivered has only the front (left) metering plate in place. The right side float chamber was supplied but was useless until a longer fuel transfer tube and rear barrel metering plate were fitted. (The new plate is situated by the throttle cable mounting screw.)

12-2-9 With the choke flap fully shut, the three additional hole modification carried out by Oselli when upgrading the Holley carburettor can be clearly seen. The car starts first 'twist', summer or winter.

12-2-10 A Carter 500cfm carburettor viewed from the front of the car. Note the electrically controlled choke on the left side of the picture (also an excellent view of the heat shield).

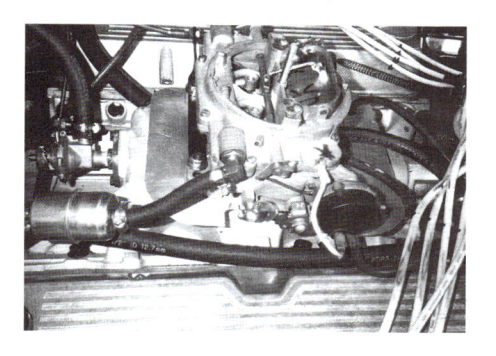

12-2-11 Here is another, rather clearer, view of a heat shield intended to reduce fuel percolation. It can clearly be seen front and rear of the Carter 500 carb with another cut-away area, this time for the choke mechanism.

buy your inlet manifold and carburettor from one expert source, and do the deal based upon an all-inclusive package that includes setting up/jetting the carb so that the engine will run initially, and subsequent tuning on a rolling road. Holley carburettors are notorious for blowing power valves, and modification kits ($10-$15) are available to prevent this which should be included in your package deal. If your intended supplier of Holley and inlet manifold cannot offer this service, find another source!

The Weber range

In 1957, Carter (now Weber) came out with a new generation of four-barrel carburettors called AFB (aluminium four-barrel). The compact design, light weight, simplicity of operation and flow capacities quickly made the AFB popular, and it is currently offered as Carter's 9000 series incorporating electric chokes, simple linkage connections, and positive crankcase ventilation (PCV) valve activation. All have dual pattern drilling on the base-plate, to marry to both 5.125 x 5.625in and 4.25 x 5.625in intake manifold bolt patterns.

The best Weber carburettors for the 215in^3/3500cc and 3900cc V8s are either the 400 (9400) or 500 (9500) cfm models. The 300in^3/4900cc engines will need the 9500 model shown in photographs 12-2-10 to 12-2-12. The 400cfm model has the ideal capacity for the 215in^3 or 3500cc engine, but unfortunately it is no longer available new, and any second-hand ones you can find tend to be expensive. While the 500cfm unit is theoretically a little too large for these displacements, it nonetheless works well on 215/3500 engines (something that I can confirm). Perhaps this is a tribute to their flexibility.

Weber 500cfm carburettors are readily available from speed equipment stores and mail order outlets in the USA, such as Summit, at around $200. They have the added attraction of reputedly working straight from the box, and any tuning that is required is easily accomplished (picture 12-2-13, overleaf). The same ranges of carburettors are available in the UK from RPI Engineering.

Edelbrock models are virtually the same as Weber/Carter, although each uses a different part number. The Edelbrock 1404 (shown in photograph 12-2-14, overleaf) is very similar to a Weber 500cfm (model number 9500) with a manual choke!

Holley/Weber comparisons

Performance is bound to be the first comparison, and drawing D12-1 (overleaf) shows the detail. These graphs of power and torque are the results of tests carried out on my own standard SD1 3500cc engine, with the original Holley 4150 carburettor replaced by a Weber 9500/Edelbrock 1404. The timing was advanced from the Holley's three degrees BTDC to six BTDC for the Weber, but that was the only alteration made. Fuel was 95 RON unleaded.

SPEEDPRO SERIES

12-2-12 When is a Weber an Edelbrock? Answer, when it's got an Edelbrock nameplate affixed to its front. This photograph gives us the opportunity to double-check the vacuum connections required for the Weber range of carburettors. You will note the large vacuum pipe that exits the body centrally (between the two mixture adjusting screws). This needs blanking off, as does the smaller pipe that can be seen just to the right and slightly lower. Connect the other small outlet (to the left of centre) to your distributor. The constant vac connection to the brake servo goes to the rear of the carburettor.

Up to 4000rpm the performance of the carburettors is in fact inseparable! The Holley started to run out of fuel above 4000rpm, when it becomes possible to see some difference between their respective performances. However, remember that most of us use 4000rpm+ infrequently, so in truth, the difference in performance is negligible!

You may be interested in the differing methods of construction and adjustment. The Holley is assembled from three main components: a main body and two (pannier-style) float chambers bolted fore and aft. This construction means there are assembly joints below the level of the fuel and, although there are gaskets incorporated into the design, I found it essential to frequently tighten the eight float chamber retaining bolts to avoid the smell of fuel in the car. The Weber, on

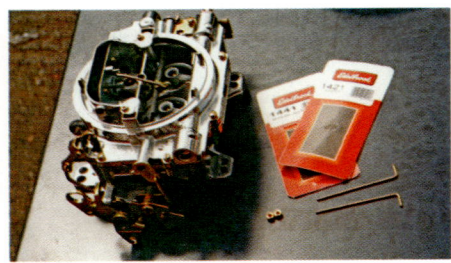

12-2-13 The Edelbrock control rods are rather like SU needles. I was putting these into my new carburettor to go atop my 3500cc Rover engine. RPI can definitely pre-jet this range of carbs for your engine for a small additional fee, or advise on, and supply, the most appropriate jets for your engine, leaving you to carry out the simple fitting task.

the other hand, is built from two main sub-assemblies split horizontally above the fuel level. Both carburettors use two primary and two secondary venturi, fed via twin float chambers.

The fuel/air ratio of Holley carburettors is adjusted by selecting and fitting primary and secondary fuel transfer jets. A range of jet sizes is available to weaken or enrich both of

12-2-14 This picture also shows the front of the carburettor (note the pipe connections) but is included to show the Edelbrock foam air cleaner. This particular example had to be lowered by a couple of inches to allow this TR7 bonnet/hood to close.

them. The fuel metering of a Weber is very similar to that of an SU carburettor, in that the fuel is fed from low down in the float bowls and drawn up through the fuel channel in the carburettor's body. As it passes into the carburettor it also has to pass through a jet, although two vacuum-operated metering needles (rods, in Weber's terminology) further govern its flow. Therefore, the combination of jets and needles in the Weber makes jet selection less critical than with the Holley.

Furthermore, it may take an

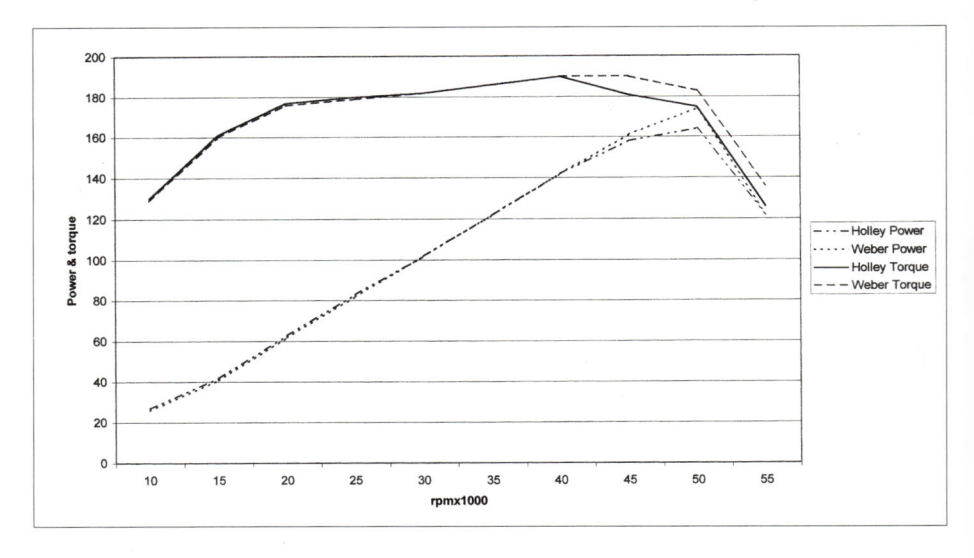

D12-1 Holley and Weber comparisons.

CARBURETTOR INDUCTION

inexperienced mechanic some time to change either of the Holley's primary or secondary jets. The task involves a major strip down of the carburettor. This can take a couple of hours if one includes removing all the old gaskets (a good re-assembly tip is to smear the new gaskets with grease or Vaseline) and float chamber cross-tube. The Weber's needles and jets take 10-15 minutes to change.

Both carburettors have a cold start enrichment facility. The Weber's is manually operated by a conventional Bowden cable (although an electric auto-choke is also available), whereas the Holley employs an automatic electric choke as a standard/stock fitting. However, as a matter of interest, I rarely use the choke. If the weather is cold enough to require a richer mixture first thing in the morning, I give the accelerator/gas pedal a couple of presses while cranking the engine to encourage the carburettor's pump to enrich the mixture.

Both makes employ an accelerator pump to inject extra fuel on opening the throttles. Both work well, although the Weber has the additional advantage of allowing the stroke to be easily adjusted, whereas the Holley requires the substitution of a new/different pump.

The respective methods of operation are interesting, particularly the transition from primary to secondary chokes. The Holley pulls open the primary throttle plates fully as you start to accelerate and the engine starts to move up the rev range. When sufficient load is achieved, the resulting vacuum will start to pull open the secondary throttles against a control spring. Naturally, the secondary throttle's opening point is critical. If it's too early, it will cause mid range over-fuelling, but if it's too late, you will notice a mid-range flat spot due to a weak mixture. The selection of the Holley's secondary jets and the vacuum control spring is both tricky and important.

The Holley's sole reliance on vacuum-actuated secondary chokes can result in some fuel inefficiency. For example, when you are pulling hard up-hill, the extra load/vacuum will try to open the Holley's secondary chokes when they are not actually required.

The Weber's primary to secondary transition has two important additional controls which are not present in the Holley range: a throttle linkage to the secondary chokes, and a further pair of plates that need engine vacuum to open them. Consequently, the Weber's secondary choke will only open when the throttle is at least 70 per cent open and the engine is pulling sufficient vacuum to open the additional plates. This arrangement allows for good fuel economy, bearing in mind the capacity of the engine.

AFB inlet manifolds

Both makes of carburettor will fit on any of the wide range of inlet manifold options open to you. Obviously, you have to be governed first by the engine that you are selecting your inlet manifold for, but differing styles of inlet manifold can alter the room taken up above the engine – perhaps not dramatically, and in many other installations the difference is immaterial. However in a V8 conversion, ½in (10mm) can be the difference between closing or not closing your bonnet/hood! So height is an important consideration when selecting an inlet manifold, quite apart from its significant effect on the performance of your engine.

For US-based Buick/Rover 215 engine enthusiasts, particularly those on tight budgets and moderate performance targets, do not pass over the original Buick/Oldsmobile/Pontiac inlet manifold too swiftly. They make the fitting of hoses much easier, the resulting performance can be very satisfactory and costs can be kept to about $50-$75! In the UK, those seeking modest expenditure and performance can have the 'roof' of the original Rover inlet manifold machined flat, and a plate glued/screwed or better still welded to it, as seen in photo 12-3-1.

For those anxious to maximize their engine's potential, the list of inlet manifolds is amazing – but personally I would short-list and explore the relevant Offenhauser or Edelbrock manifolds for your engine. Offenhauser is the US company that developed inlet manifolds for, amongst others, the GM (now Rover) V8 engine. Initially, it made the single port model that is still preferred by some experts. This is still available and mounts the carburettor a shade higher (remember, height is critical in your TR7 conversion) than the alternative, 'dual-port' design. Edelbrock manifolds are also available and two models are mentioned with some frequency – part number 2198 and its 'Performer' part number 2121.

Installations

Possibly less important in the UK, but whatever manifold/carburettor you use,

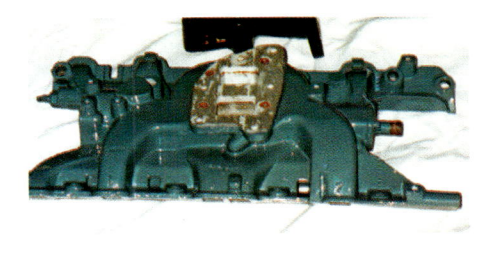

12-3-1 A modified Rover V8 inlet manifold. Some light secondary machining is usually advisable to ensure the plate is dead flat, ready for the AFB carb of your choice. Take care when removing the roof to ensure the resulting cross-sectional opening is as large as your AFB carburettor requires at full throttle.

SPEEDPRO SERIES

two problems can occur. The first is 'heat soak' from the inlet manifold and its contents. In fact, when I switched from a Holley to an Edelbrock carburettor (on the same manifold), I had to fit an Edelbrock thermal barrier between carb and manifold, even in the colder UK climate, in order to reduce hot restarting difficulties caused by heat soak. Edelbrock retailers can supply a thermal barrier in several thicknesses – mine was 0.375in (10mm) thick, but thicker and therefore more effective ones are available, and can be used if you have the under-bonnet space available.

In hotter climates, heat percolation of the fuel in the float bowls and/or vapour lock in the fuel-lines adjacent to the carburettor can occur. Obviously, hot starting difficulties will result and in these circumstances a heat shield and/or a thermal plate between the carburettor and the intake manifold may be required. However, most proprietary heat shields available are made from aluminium, and it is my belief that you would get superior performance using a thin sheet of non-heat conducting material, such as paxalin, fibreglass, Kevlar or another (preferably fire retarding) laminate. You will certainly improve the effectiveness of the aluminium shields if you apply a self-adhesive reflective insulator called 'Thermo-Shield' – available from Summit in the USA, and via Agriemach Ltd and Demon Tweeks in the UK. However, this will do nothing to stop carb/manifold direct heat transfer through the aluminium, and while you can also fit the thermal barrier I mentioned earlier, you resolve both problems at once with the non-metallic shield solution.

The aluminium shields are no doubt available from several sources. We saw examples of heat shields in photographs 12-2-10 and 12-2-11. To the best of my knowledge, no one in the UK supplies ready-made heat shields, although they are easily made from a piece of 10in^2 (250mm) material of about 0.125in (3mm) thickness. In the UK's climate, however, the necessity for a heat shield should be minimal.

RELATED INDUCTION DETAILS
AFB air filters

Rather like the inlet manifold issue discussed above, the actual air filter you fit will very much depend upon the capacity of your engine and the headroom available. The options are numerous but I would guess that the most frequently used air filter, particularly amongst moderately powered conversions, is the 'Low-Rider' 14in (350mm) diameter x 2in (50mm) high assembly. A K+N replacement element will reduce air stream restrictions, and their element is re-usable, too.

Watch that the height of a deeper air filter does not foul the bonnet. If the front proves a problem, it is possible to have the manifold's carburettor mounting face re-machined such that 0.200in (5mm) is removed from the front edge and nothing from the back. However, TR7-V8 converters may find that the back of a large diameter, 3in (75mm) deep filter fouls on the front lip of the fresh air intake. To resolve this, you may find it necessary to dish the front lip of the air intake – an example can be seen at photo 12-3-2-1.

Your choice of automatic or manual choke might also have an impact on the air cleaner you can use, since low-profile air cleaners will be competing for space around the carburettor air inlet where the auto-choke is located. Even seemingly innocuous bulges on the carburettor housing in the area of the intake flange can have a make-or-break impact on low-profile air cleaner selection! Consequently, you would

12-3-2-1 This is a 3in deep air filter atop a Holley carburettor – not that you see much of the carburettor! However, note the dished front to the air inlet to provide clearance for the filter's 14in diameter.

be prudent to take advice and buy the inlet manifold, carburettor and air filter simultaneously from an experienced TR7-V8 specialist.

K+N's filters are very popular and deserve your consideration. Its assembly part number 60-1280 is suitable for any engine up to 400bhp, and comes from its Xtreme range. The part has a 14in (350mm) diameter – the same as the Low-Rider – but its NET height above the carb flange is 2.75in (70mm). The gross height is 3.8in (95mm), and it sits atop the 5in diameter of a Holley or Weber AFB with a single top stud mounting.

Pipercross has recently introduced its PX800 specialist design for Holley carburettor air filtration. This has a recessed base-plate that extends almost to the base of the carburettor, therefore allowing for much greater filter depth and a high-capacity foam filter element, while retaining minimum overall height. They are all available from Demon Tweeks in the UK and most speed shops in the US. Incidentally, the Weber/Carter/Edelbrock 400 and 500 carburettors use the same Low Rider/Mr Gasket 14in diameter air filter as the Holley. Consequently, I presume the Pipercross alternative will also fit the Weber four-barrel carburettor.

CARBURETTOR INDUCTION

12-3-2-2 There are two Holley air cleaners, sitting on two AFB carburettors; you will likely require only one. They appear ideal from a bonnet headroom aspect, but you still need to check the front edge carefully. It is available from JEGs under part number 510-64280.

Holley also recently offered a dual element air cleaner that gives the appearance of twin side-draught carburettors, as you'll see from photo 12-3-2-2, yet sits atop a standard AFB carburettor air-intake flange. At over $200 it is a little pricey, but really looked ideal for cars with under bonnet/hood clearance issues.

Fuel pumps

Regardless of your carburettor, a solid state electric fuel pump is advisable. If you like the SU fuel pump, at least get one of the electronic versions now available (picture 12-3-3). Facet Silver Top pumps should be sufficient for smaller engines in non-competitive use, but a Red Top (picture 12-3-4) may be prudent in competition. However, I would suggest a Facet Red Top for 8-cylinder cars up to ultra-fast road, but you may need to take advice and run two pumps for competitive use. They are available from Demon Tweeks, and are an essential contributor to this performance package, particularly if you are expecting to 'press on' occasionally.

The pump is best mounted just below the bottom of the fuel tank. I have used a Red Top with a Weber AFB carb

12-3-3 If you are thinking of using an SU fuel pump, I strongly recommend one with the relatively new electronic triggering mechanism seen here.

for many years without any problems. If you experience carburettor flooding as a result of higher fuel-line pressures (this is possible with SU carburettors that cannot cope with more than 4psi), I suggest you try fitting an adjustable fuel pressure regulator in the engine bay to overcome this problem. Picture 12-3-5 shows a fuel pressure regulator in this context. They not only lower the pressure in the fuel-line, but also smooth out the pulses that cause some pumps to have difficulty achieving an even and constant fuel-level in the float chambers, even when the carburettors are not flooding.

FURTHER READING

How to Build & Power Tune Holley Carburetors, by Des Hammill (Veloce Publishing). How to choose and specify for road or track. Component identification, including metering blocks. *Holley Carburetor Handbook* and also *Holley Carburetors and Manifolds*, by

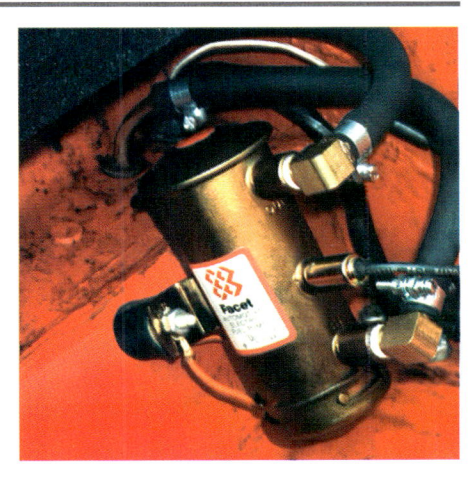

12-3-4 A Facet Red Top fuel pump can also be used, although it generates a shade more pressure than is ideal for SU carburettors.

12-3-5 We saw a fuel pressure regulator (not to be confused with an EFI component of the same name) a few pictures back. This is the beast in close-up.

Mike Urich (published by HP Books) gives flow-rate calculations and advice on how to select the best Holley for your application. They are available from Summit in the US or John Woolfe Racing in the UK.
Holley Carburetors, Manifolds and Fuel-injection, by Bill Fisher and Mike Urich, covers selection, installation and tuning information for a wide range of Holley carburettors. 224 pages.
Holley Carburetors Manual, by Dave Emanuel, is a guide to selecting, modifying and rebuilding Holley 2- and 4-barrel Holley carbs. Illustrated, 128 pages.

Chapter 13
Electronic fuel-injection & engine management

Electronic fuel-injection is, to my mind, the best induction system you can have. At the beginning of the previous chapter on carburettor induction I outlined the compromises in the inlet tract that are essential if a carburettor is going to work at both cranking and high revolutions. EFI has no such limitations. Today's EFI systems are far more sophisticated than the original Lucas/Bosch 'L-Jetronic' systems that were used on our TR7 (picture 13-1-1) and TR8s (picture 13-1-2) in the 1970s and 80s. However, I hope to have closed the technology gap by the time you finish reading this chapter.

Most of the Wedge EFI systems went to California, but it would seem that many TR8 owners do not agree with my view of the excellence of EFI induction, and removed the fuel-injection from their cars in favour of carburettors. They found the setup of carburettors easier, and the resultant induction arrangement vastly more tuneable than the EFI systems installed

13-1-1 The TR7 4-cylinder engine Lucas 'L-Jetronic' electronic fuel-injection (EFI) system.

by the factory. However, today we have the benefits of re-programmable ECUs (engine control unit), which can be substituted for the original ECU and allow much greater flexibility and tuneability.

A complete swap/conversion of either a 4- or 8-cylinder system will not gain you much additional fuel mileage, but might give up to 10 per cent more power. Traits such as hesitation and

13-1-2 A standard TR8 8-cylinder engine EFI system with one variation – a low-resistance air filter.

poor throttle response from the 4-cylinder cars should be eliminated, making the car smoother, livelier and more responsive. This makes town-

ELECTRONIC FUEL-INJECTION & ENGINE MANAGEMENT

driving a pleasure, requiring less gear changing, and gives a smooth and progressive engine response. I also find my EFI car starts instantly; thus a retro-fitted EFI system, particularly when incorporating a re-programmable ECU, will be an ideal induction method for the 2000cc engine and advantageous for the 8-cylinder engines, too.

EFI controls the injection of fuel. Full engine management not only controls the fuel supply, but interacts with and controls the ignition timing, further enhancing the tractability and smooth-running of the engine. Modern engine management systems also allow you to access and adjust the fuel and ignition system 'mapping', and thus the tuning of the engine. This is usually achieved with a laptop computer, as we will see later in the chapter.

I have already made several references to electronic controls of one kind or another. If you have a blind-spot when it comes to matters electrical, then electronic control of fuel and/or ignition systems might be something for you to think twice about – unless you have a mate who knows his positives from his negatives!

4-CYLINDER BOSCH EFI

If you are keen to give your 4-cylinder TR7 engine EFI induction, your most cost effective route is to find a complete ex-TR7 system. However, suitable full systems may not be as plentiful as you would wish, and you may have to supplement any shortfalls from other cars. The problem with transposing part or all of another car's system is that the TR7 has several unique features, which we will explore shortly. The Fiat Spider is the one car I've heard of with many EFI parts that can be used in a TR7, although the K+N aftermarket filter for a BMW 320i and/or Fiat Spider will bolt right up to the TR7 air flow meter.

13-1-3 Here we see several of the TR7's unique features in situ. The arrowed component may puzzle some readers – it is the fuel pressure regulator (FPR), with the vacuum hose that controls the fuel pressure running down the picture to the plenum.

You will see the major part of the TR7 EFI setup in photograph 13-1-3, but we need to explore the components that are particular to the TR7 in case they prove elusive.

The inlet manifold seen at 13-1-4 is, to the best of my knowledge, unique to TR7s. The plenum-chamber (13-1-5) is a tubular air-box that connects the air flow meter to the inlet manifold, and is also unique to the Wedge. Your worst scenario is that you will need to have the standard inlet manifold welded and machined to accept the four injectors, and possibly to fabricate a plenum from an ex-TR6 one (shortened with the diameter increased).

You will need an EFI TR7 fuel tank. As we explore in section 13-4, it is possible for experts to add a second sender to an existing tank, but those same experts can also fit a standard/stock TR7 tank with a return pipe and swirl pot, as per photo 13-1-6. In the UK this is an option offered by S+S Preparations. It is also possible to fit a separate swirl pot into the feed pipe to the fuel-pump. You will still need a fuel return facility adding to the tank, but a separate swirl pot avoids major surgery on your fuel tank. Talk to some of the

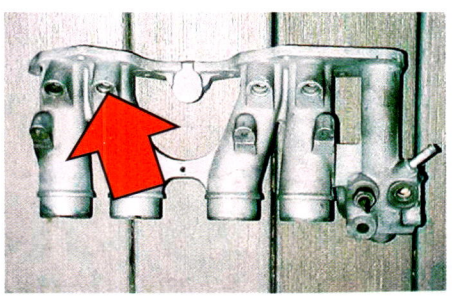

13-1-4 The inlet manifold has four (one arrowed) injector mounting plinths cast into it. I understand that there are a few new ones still tucked away on (very dusty) dealer shelves.

13-1-5 The plenum, probably unique to the TR7. These, too, are occasionally available.

13-1-6 This is not, of course, a Wedge fuel tank; nevertheless, the incision for a swirl pot (an ex-Ford Granada in this case) is clear to see.

153

SPEEDPRO SERIES

13-1-7 A TR7/8 EFI fuel-pump (blue) and filter (silver). Almost any external Bosch EFI pump assembly will suffice, and you will note how similar the TR7 and TR8 pump/filter arrangements are later in this chapter.

13-1-8-1 The car's ECU is visible in situ beneath the glove-box, now the cover has been removed. The spare one gives you a better idea of what to look for.

13-1-8-2 The electronics within a US ECU. They are more reliable than often thought, most EFI problems emanating from the components that require moving parts (throttle potentiometer and air flow meter, for example). The soldered joints to the PCB' connections are known to crack, and need checking and remaking where necessary.

13-1-9 The original air filter box is seen here and best discarded in favour of the K+N style low resistance unit seen in place. This is a TR8 size filter – smaller conical filters will suit TR7 EFI.

speed or racing shops – most will offer fuel swirl pots. Furthermore, you need to protect all fuel lines and components from exhaust pipe heat.

All EFI systems require a high-pressure fuel pump and filter. An original TR7 pump and filter can be seen at 13-1-7, and will need to be copied. The breaker yards will offer plenty of alternatives if an original TR7 arrangement is not forthcoming.

Your TR7 EFI parts should include an original ECU photographed at 13-1-8-1 and 13-1-8-2, but you may find it best to replace this with a re-programmable controller right from the start. This makes the initial installation more expensive and perhaps slightly more complex, but you jump a couple of generations as far as EFI technology is concerned. We will explore programmable ECUs later in the chapter. You do, however, need to be mindful of the compatibility of the injector's impedance with the programmable ECU you plan. Check, but I think you will find the four original TR7 injectors have impedance of 2 ohms – in most instances, you will need to change them to 16 ohm injectors.

There is an alternative. Although the original ECUs were not designed to be re-programmable, specialists can these days play tunes on them. Superchips bases its business on fitting new chips and re-mapping original ECUs. There are fitting centers all over the world, so a visit to Superchips' website (contact details in the appendix) might also be helpful preparation. Your choice largely depends on your own expertise and/or that of your local expert.

Regarding the engine bay, there are some easily resolved differences between a carburettor and EFI car. The oil level dipstick is different, and the bonnet latch is best re-located. A blanking plate is required to cover the unused fuel-pump aperture on the engine, a couple of new/different brackets are needed for the air-intake system, the heater-feed pipework needs re-routing, and an inertia cut-out switch should be coupled to the fuel-pump. The original air filter seen at 13-1-9 is definitely not required – there are plenty of low-resistance filters that would be better employed.

If a genuine ex-TR7 EFI system is not available, or there are parts missing or unserviceable, then it might be practical to get the basic L-Jet system from an appropriate non-TR7 donor. It is likely that you will still need the parts mentioned that are particular to the TR7, but an alternative L-Jet donor should provide you with most of your needs. The inlet manifold off a non-TR7 donor is unlikely to fit your TR7, but the locations of (and even the actual mounting bosses for) the respective sensors may be very helpful.

There may be a temptation to strip the first EFI-inducted car you find but, while your donor parts may well be made to work on your TR7, I think you are best ensuring that the donor car is fitted with one of the L-Jet systems. There were two sister analogue systems, the LE and LU, the LU being the US system used by the TR7 with a Lambda (oxygen) sensor and start control system. By this route, the parts

ELECTRONIC FUEL-INJECTION & ENGINE MANAGEMENT

13-1-10-1 This is the air flow meter, with its ...

13-1-10-2 ... 'flapper' method of measuring air flow volume in plain view here.

will be interchangeable. The injector synchronization on an L (or derivative) system is triggered by the low-tension pulse from the coil to the distributor's normal ignition points – thus the L, LE and LU systems can be coupled easily to a standard/stock TR7 distributor.

The slight complexity of a Lambda (oxygen) sensor will only require a small boss to be welded to the exhaust system; but in fact, these systems will run without the oxygen sensor connected too, in what is called 'open loop' mode. The TR7 EFI cars were fitted with a Lambda sensor.

If in doubt, the L-jet Bosch EFI system employs a flapper type of air flow meter seen in pictures 13-1-10-1 and 13-1-10-2. The system was mainly used between about 1977 and 1990 (there are a few earlier and later examples) on a wide variety of high volume European, Far Eastern and US cars.

If you elect to search for a complete system, you may be as well finding a vehicle employing Bosch's next development – the LH system. This also uses a standard distributor to both fire the ignition system and trigger the injector pulses. The LH system improved upon the L-Jet AFM because of its less obstructive air mass (or 'Hot Wire') meter, seen in photograph 13-1-11. A Lambda sensor in the LH system improves emissions of course, but also improves fuel mileage – so they have advantages, although the LH system was not so widely used (only Volvo, Saab and, wait for it, Porsche). This system employs digital electronics, so none of the electrical components should be mixed with the analogue components we explored earlier. There are large numbers of Volvo 240s in breakers' yards these days and the 2000cc capacity is identical to the TR7 displacement. I would acquire the Volvo's ECU even if you have in mind replacing it with a modern, re-programmable one.

As an aside, the 'L' in these Bosch systems stands for 'luft', the German for 'air'. 'LH' stands for 'luft heis' (hot air).

8-CYLINDER BOSCH EFI

Turning now to the 8-cylinder EFI system and donors, I think the first thing to make clear is that you can retro-fit an EFI system to a previously carburettor-inducted Rover V8. There is one slight difference – the inlet ports on an EFI engine require a small injector-clearance recess be filed in the lip. This is, of course, best carried out with the heads off the block, but can still be done if your heads are already secured (with a little extra care to retain/trap the swarf). In either case, you need to buy an EFI valley gasket – which you will find already has the requisite injector clearance notches in place. Pack the

13-1-11 The long-term reliability of the LH air mass meter seen on the left is better than the L-Jet's flapper meter, since there are no moving parts to wear.

13-2-1 An original TR8 EFI arrangement. Note the wide triangular 'Federal' plenum, the right side air intake and the proximity of the cockpit air intake to the rear of the plenum.

ports and the surrounding area with greased cloth (to catch the swarf) and use a ¼in (6mm) diameter circular file to form each clearance in the head's inlet ports. Blend the notch backward into the mouth of the port by about ¼in.

As for V8 donor cars/systems, the obvious one is best – an ex-Rover SD1 3.5/3500cc 'Federal' flapper system will bolt straight to a Rover engine. It will be similar to that originally fitted to a TR8, except that the plenum will take air from the other side of the engine bay, and consequently the AFM will be on the opposite side to the original TR8 seen in photo 13-2-1.

This, and indeed the Hot Wire systems, will run better and require

155

SPEEDPRO SERIES

13-2-2 My transposed SD1 EFI system, with the air intake through a conical K+N filter from the left side of the engine bay.

13-2-3-1 The ideal cold air intake for the engine is provided by Triumph just behind the headlights. All you have to do is ...

13-2-3-2 ... duct the cold air to your engine. Original EFI TR8s were feed air through a fibre-board duct next to the radiator.

13-2-4-1 Whatever the state of tune of your engine, it is important to align the exhaust ports and gasket with the manifold/header, and to smooth the interfaces between head and manifold.

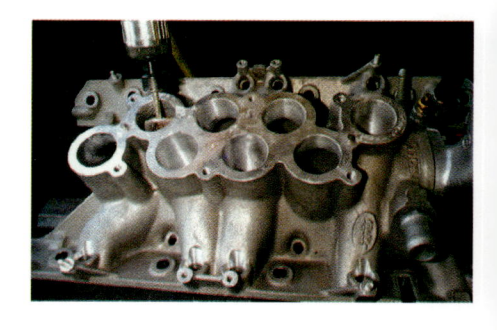

13-2-4-2 This is an EFI inlet manifold/track, but regardless of whether it is EFI or carburettor induction you are using, the internal gas passages need to be free of casting marks ... though it is unnecessary to polish them.

less maintenance with a free-flowing air filter replacing the original 'box' and slightly restrictive arrangement. I use the conical K+N filter seen in photograph 13-2-2. However, it is always best to feed an engine with the coldest air available – a duct from the original carburettor intake holes from behind the headlights (picture 13-2-3-1 and 13-2-3-2) is a conversion option.

For increased performance, you can carry out 'gas flowing' with a rat tail file, taking particular care to match the inlet and exhaust ports with their respective manifolds. Work can be seen in progress at 13-2-4-1 and 13-2-4-2. It should be possible to gain the area of about one half of an inlet! Alternatively, you can replace the SD1 plenum with a Rover Vitesse plenum. It has a larger bore, better matching to the inlets and should improve performance, but may bring bonnet clearance difficulties (more in a moment).

Like the 4-cylinder engines, it is practical to replace the original V8 Rover unit with a suitable re-programmable ECU if you seek to tune your engine or have a mismatch between the capacities of engine and EFI system.

The standard L-Jetronic fuel system generally, and injectors in particular, run out of puff at about 200bhp, when the injector opening time is at its maximum. For more power the fuel flow rate must be increased by, in the first instance, fitting a variable fuel pressure regulator. These increase the fuel pressure by up to 1.7 times the norm, when called for. As a second step, new injectors with a higher flow rate are required. The standard Rover SD1/TR8 injector is Lucas part number 52808001. It is used on many EFI-inducted cars too, and has a dynamic flow of 4.62mg of fuel per pulse and static flow of 137.2g per minute. The higher flow rate injector is part number 5208005, with dynamic flow of 6.1mg and static flow of 173.3g.

Naturally, later Range Rover Hot Wire systems can also be fitted, ideally as an engine/EFI single package, but the EFI can be retrofitted – although when transposing a non-TR Rover EFI system there could be bonnet closing difficulties. You will need to resolve them either by fitting spacers between the K-frame, reducing the height of the EFI system, or through a combination of these adjustments.

The early Federal (often called the Flapper or Air Flow) system used on the TR8, and seen earlier in picture 13-2-1 and many SD1 models, should cause minimal bonnet clearance difficulties if the correct sub-frame spacers have been used. It should not be necessary to resort to machining the plenum on a TR7-V8 for bonnet clearance reasons,

ELECTRONIC FUEL-INJECTION & ENGINE MANAGEMENT

13-2-5 The Plenum from Rover Hot Wire EFI systems was, of course, never intended to be accommodated within the TR7 and TR8 engine bay, so you might find it necessary to 'lose' a little height and/or dish the front of the air intake when fitting these later systems.

13-2-6-1 Making a Hot Wire EFI fit! An excellent before (on the right) and after comparison of the lower plenum chamber, or central casting, that required machining top and bottom to aid a reduction in overall system height sufficient to close a standard TR7 bonnet. The eight 'trumpets', or rams, will also receive machine-shop attention at a later date, but their top face should first be measured (from the top lip of the casting), and only then removed from the centre casting.

The trumpets are an interference fit, aided by some sealer, and will be stubborn, but any badly damaged ones are replaceable. Ram removal may be aided by drilling a pair of 5mm holes right at the root of each ram to enable you to get some leverage.

From the bottom face of this central casting have 15mm (about 0.6 inches) machined off. On assembly, this will drop the fuel rail down to the point where it may touch the lower casting extensions in one or two spots. Should this prove the case, just ease a couple of mm off each of the affected protrusions. Another consequence of this machining will be complete removal of the shoulder onto which the two front and rear rams sit, and a reduction in height of the four central shoulders.

Turning our attention to the top lip of this central casting, have re-drilled the two locating dowel holes in the top face (it might save some hassle if their depth was increased at this point, before you lose their position!) We need to take 3mm off the top lip and then proceed with caution (ensuring prior to each cut that you retain, undamaged, the threaded holes for the vacuum (servo) and two adjacent 'take-offs'). The most you can expect to remove from the top lip is 4mm but, with luck, you will reduce the overall height of this casting by perhaps 18.5-19.0mm.

assuming a later double bulge bonnet is in use. However, you may need to consider reductions to allow fitting of the car's fresh air intake.

The regular SD1 plenum, and certainly later mass-meter (known colloquially as Hot Wire) plenums are more problematical, as you will see in photo 13-2-5. Systems transposed from Discovery and/or Range Rovers are not only taller, but extend back by a further 1in (25mm) and might cause some concern, although I have heard of trouble-free transplants.

Before you start machining lumps off either EFI system, remember two things: 1) Even Triumph found it necessary to fit a second bulge in the bonnet line. 2) It is less fraught to alter a fibreglass bonnet moulding at home than irreversibly alter your EFI plenum. If you do elect to raise the line of any bonnet, do ensure the additional bulge is in the same material as the original, be that steel or fibreglass, otherwise unsightly cracking round the joint will result after a period of heating and cooling.

The height reduction of a Hot Wire system is explained photographically at 13-2-6-1 to 13-2-6-3, but if you are going to maximize the reduction, the work involves some very special machining of the eight inlet trumpets, the plenum chamber cover and the lower plenum chamber. Naturally, there is little point in machining more off the assembly than you have to, so I suggest you take the machining one step at a time starting with the lower plenum chamber, only moving on from there if you are still experiencing difficulties closing the bonnet.

With the earlier Federal system, it is actually easier to lower the plenum because it is both simpler in the first place and there is only one face from which you can remove metal. Drawing D13-1 (overleaf) may help to clarify where the metal could be removed from, but the object is to drop the throttle

SPEEDPRO SERIES

13-2-6-2 Stage two of the lowering exercise. Here, the un-machined unit is on the left and it is clear to see that we need to remove metal from the bottom of this top plenum chamber. How much? Start with 7mm and then proceed with caution for it is important not to remove so much metal that you break away the sealing edge it 'makes' with the central casting. You will possibly manage 9mm if you are prepared to run several lines of weld (alloy, of course) along the revised seal line and subsequently machine flat the seal face. However, we will presume a height reduction of 8mm in this component making an overall reduction of 26.5mm (18.5 + 8mm). From the photograph it will be noted that this machining process 'breaks into' the lower of the three tapped holes in this casting. The holes provide mountings for the idle speed stepper-valve and, in view of the light weight involved, most EFI conversions dispense with the lowest bolt and achieve a satisfactory seal with the remaining two. It will become obvious, but you will also need to unbolt and discard the water heating adapter from beneath the throttle housing.

13-2-6-3 The third comparison photo in this series shows the original on the left and the 26.5-28mm lower assembly on the right. It will come as no surprise to read that the numerous fixing bolts are too long and will need to be reduced/replaced to effect this sub-assembly. The eight central casting to manifold bolts will be 15mm over length and the six top plenum bolts will prove 13mm too long.

body, if necessary, virtually onto the rocker cover top, with the water-heated throttle attachment discarded from the underside of the throttle housing. You do not want to remove more metal than is absolutely essential, and in fact you should not find it necessary to take more than a few mm from the plenum for a TR7-V8 conversion. However, as you can see it is possible to lower the top by up to 28mm in some cases, although 25mm (1in) is more prudent. The technique is to assemble the rocker covers and Federal throttle body, accurately measure the distance between them with a vernier, and have your friendly local machinist remove as much metal as you require. In any event, you do need to leave a small clearance – say 0.5mm. As we have already discussed, this machining is best done in stages, but there is another reason to proceed cautiously. The lowered throttle body must not crush numbers 3 and 5 injectors or the fuel rail. Once you have settled on your new plenum height, it is likely that you will need to shorten the fuel-feed hoses to each injector.

PROGRAMMABLE SYSTEMS

If you have an engine but no induction system, or have fitted a system from a donor car and wish to fit your own programmable ECU, there are now some aftermarket alternatives to consider. The big advantage of the aftermarket systems is that you have some technical back-up if you strike installation or operational difficulties.

There are numerous suppliers of programmable systems, and you will need to decide between full EFI kits; full engine management kits; programmable ECUs that fit piggy-back on your current one; and what I guess will be the most interesting to TR7/TR8 readers, programmable ECUs that replace your current ECU. A few examples should give you the flavour of the many available.

Superchips' fully-mapped ignition conversions using the Lumenition optronic distributor trigger are well proven. The conversion requires the distributor base-plate be tack-welded so no movement is possible, after which the Lumenition trigger is simply connected to a solid extension of the camshaft and therefore engine rotation. A remote ECU is re-programmed by Superchips, but is easily altered by use of a dedicated hand-help programmer that can be hired or bought separately. These systems are 'only' 2-dimensional, but the mapping is still far better than any mechanical system can ever achieve. Consequently more torque,

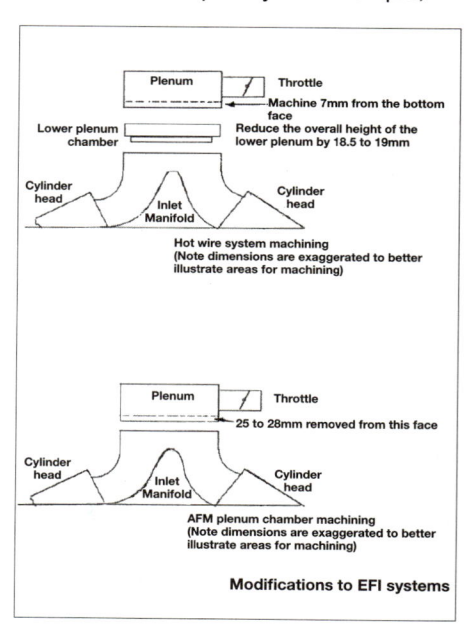

D13-1 Lowering a Rover EFI plenum.

ELECTRONIC FUEL-INJECTION & ENGINE MANAGEMENT

An Edelbrock Throttle body (TBI) injection sitting atop a Ford 302. Full TBI kits are available from Edelbrock and several other manufacturers.

a smoother engine, more power and better fuel efficiency are quite normal improvements.

Edelbrock

There are numerous alternative makes of programmable/tuneable EFI systems, one of which (an Edelbrock) can be viewed at picture 13-3-1. Space prevents me exploring each comprehensively; nevertheless, I hope my choice and comment will give you an idea of what is available. I think the first point to emphasize is that each supplier should be able to provide a choice of proven fuel maps, which gets you off to a great start. However, since we are focused on old-timer cars, I would advise you to start by short-listing only those systems that specifically offer fuel maps for your engine and its tune. This may exclude several suppliers who have focused their marketing and technical resources on more recent engines, or solely on V8s.

In most cases you will need a laptop computer in order to carry out DIY tuning. In these situations, you also need to ensure that your computer's ports (i.e. Serial, USB, etc.) are compatible with your short-listed suppliers' hardware, and that your operating software will talk to theirs (Windows 95 or better is a frequent stipulation). However, the Edelbrock system is tunable but comes with its own stand-alone programming unit, so you do not need a laptop for it – a detail that some may find preferable.

Haltech

The E6X is the latest Haltech programmable ECU offering 'real-time' programming of fuel-injection and ignition on 4, 6 or 8 cylinders. Its E8 ECU is capable of controlling sequential injection on 4, 5, 6, 8 and 10 cylinder applications. With 8 channels able to control injection and ignition duties, the E8 can support most modern engines with multi-coil ignition systems, as well as conventional distributor ignition systems and various auxiliary engine functions.

MoTeC

The M48 is MoTeC's engine management system ECU, providing sequential injection and individual cylinder fuel/ignition trims for up to 8-cylinder engines. It uses 3-dimensional fuel and ignition mapping and ignition control, giving you the ability to drive your ignition modules and set your spark timing to its absolute best.

MoTeC claims that all M48 models have the accurate control necessary to meet legislated emissions requirements, including closed-loop narrow band lambda control. It can utilise nearly all original equipment and aftermarket ignition triggers, modules and coils, and be triggered by either a hall effect switch, a logic drive or a magnetic sensor. The M48 reads its sensors 2400 times per second, and the entire control program is recalculated 200 times per second, which demonstrates its power. Furthermore, there is a comprehensive group of computer software tools available for the M48, including:
- Engine setup, tuning diagnostics and utilities.
- Monitoring, data logging and analysis.
- Utilities for loading new program code and enabling special features.

Holley

Holley is best known for its performance carburettors, but also offers the Commander 950 injection system. These multi-point EFI systems are available in kit form and intended to provide all the components and hardware needed, including intake manifold, billet throttle body, billet fuel rails, injectors and related miscellaneous parts that have been partially pre-assembled and tested prior to packaging. The heart of any EFI system is the programmable ECU and Holley claim theirs is easily be programmed and provides the user with a high level of tuning flexibility. The Holley system allows for real-time tuning of all parameters via Windows based software. I think they are mainly aiming for the Ford and Chevy V8 market.

MegaSquirt

MegaSquirt markets a programmable ECU in kit form, suitable for engines with up to 16 cylinders. It is attractive for several reasons – not least the cost, the established forum, factory on-line support and technical repair facilities that are available. MegaSquirt has set out to offer EFI without the user requiring:
- Programming skills – the necessary codes are already loaded, and tuning is done via a straightforward Windows application.
- PROM burning experience – a serial port connection facilitates fuel tuning parameters as well as software updates.
- Advanced electronic skills – if you can solder and follow directions, you should be able to assemble MegaSquirt's kit. (However, do note that you are required to assemble the ECU, which requires soldering the numerous electronic components onto the ECU's PCB

SPEEDPRO SERIES

13-3-2 This shows Webcon's EFI equipment mostly on the far side of this 6-cylinder engine, with the ignition control module (note, no distributor) this side of the engine.

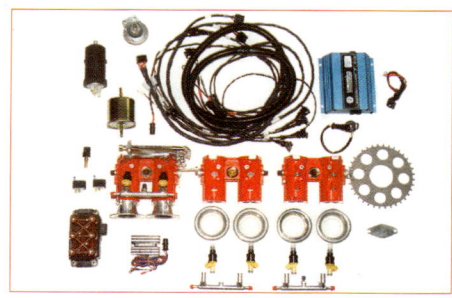

13-3-3-1 The Lumenition equipment comes in a kit. This is for a 6-cylinder car, but a 4-cylinder kit will be very similar and also include a Bosch fuel pump and filter, a rising-rate fuel pressure regulator, the wiring loom, the programmable ECU, the crankshaft pulley timing wheel, the inlet manifolds, mini-trumpets, injectors, fuel-rail sections, timing sensor and amplifier.

13-3-3-2 A 4-cylinder Lumenition EFI application.

– perhaps not everyone's ideal basis for an EFI system.)
- The latest in laptops – MegaSquirt stipulates a serial ported laptop running Windows is all that is required.

There are four elements to the MegaSquirt control system, and drawing D13-2 may help identify them. There are two processors to choose from and three PCB options. The faster chip in the V3 (latest) PCB will give you the best and most easily installed system. The software consists of an embedded code (also known as firmware to the experts) stored in the ECU, and the tuning software which is stored in and operated from your laptop. The tuning software also allows you to monitor the system's satisfactory operation.

The MegaSquirt system would be ideal if used as the ECU in conjunction with an existing (if now ageing) Bosch L or LH-Jetronic set of hardware from a TR7, TR8 or Volvo. MegaSquirt mentions, but I felt with only limited enthusiasm, simultaneous ignition control, albeit at extra cost. The benefits are considerable – if perhaps costly – so it is good to know that you could initially install its EFI system and then, at a later date, explore the other half of full engine management. However, let us move on to some 21st century full kit engine management options.

Webcon Alpha

In addition to high-performance carburettors, Webcon also produces engine management systems for racing and rally cars, and some notable very high-performance sports cars. It offers the motoring enthusiast a series of components that can be assembled into a kit of parts for either EFI or full engine management, for any 4-, 6- or 8-cylinder engines. One such application can be seen at 13-3-2. The kits include programmable ECUs, along with the requisite parts for throttle body injection, pumps, computers, amplifiers (to upgrade the initial signal to a level that will open your injectors) and sensors for a DIY engine management installation.

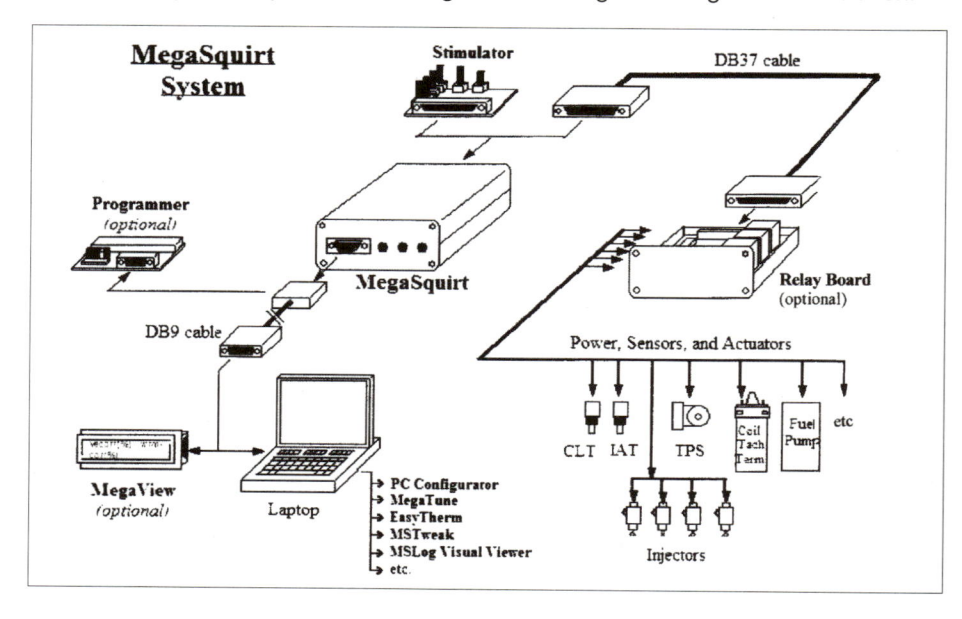

D13-2 The four elements of the MegaSquirt control system.

ELECTRONIC FUEL-INJECTION & ENGINE MANAGEMENT

The drawback is that only a Webcon specialist with the necessary diagnostic equipment can adjust Webcon systems. However, its components are of the highest quality, and the product is sophisticated, providing a very tractable performance system.

Lumenition

The background to this potential supplier is a successful range of electronic ignition products, some of which are reviewed in chapter 11. Its kits are available for 4-, 6- or 8-cylinder engines, and you will see a couple at 13-3-3-1 and 13-3-3-2. Within each kit you get sensors to provide your ECU with environmental information on ambient air temperature and pressure, coolant temperatures, and throttle and crank positions. Thus, your system will understand every situation and supply the appropriate fuel volumes and optimum ignition timing for all circumstances.

This system's advantage lies with your ability to plug your own laptop into the system and alter the mapping to suit your own circumstances ... and if you don't like what you've done, you can change the mapping back, or do something different again. A real 21st century toy with practical applications for the motoring enthusiast! EFI can be fitted and supplemented by any of the ignition enhancement systems outlined in chapter 11 or upgraded with the appropriate Lumenition 'sparks' package at a later date.

ROVER V8 ENGINE MANAGEMENT

John Wilson of Custom EFIs devised a method to enjoy up to the minute engine technology on a Rover V8 by way of retrofitting a modern GM fuel and ignition control system. He has written the DIY guide detailed later and I am indebted not only to John but also to Brad Wilson at Wedgeparts, who has built these systems and gives us a précis of them here.

The problem with most Rover/Bosch V8 donor systems is fourfold. First, they use proprietary computer chips in their ECUs, and those chips must be re-programmed if you are to optimize the retrofitted system; second, the components for those systems tend to be rather costly; third, they are mass air flow (MAF) based, which makes them unnecessarily complex; and fourth, few are complete engine management systems.

These disadvantages are overcome by retrofitting a modern engine management system with integrated ignition control, in addition to the EFI and diagnostic information codes as an added bonus. This is achieved thanks to modern GM systems retaining their data on a removable, re-programmable 'chip', thus making re-tuning these systems much simpler than was the case with earlier engine management systems.

There are two major classifications of the fuel-injection side of the GM system – throttle body injection (TBI) and port fuel-injection (PFI). Both are suited to the Rover V8. TBI seen at 13-4-1 functions much like an electronic carburettor, with two large injectors mounted in the venturi above the throttle butterflies. PFI/multipoint systems have an injector for each cylinder mounted near the intake valve, and are thus a more complex installation but provide more precise fuel metering.

Both options are relatively simple in their use of manifold absolute pressure (MAP) sensing to determine engine load, instead of the more complicated Bosch air flow methods. MAP systems are also known as speed density systems, which can perhaps best be described as the

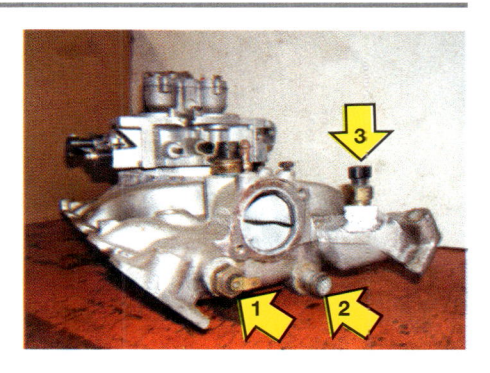

13-4-1 TB injection is easier to install than PFI but is not so efficient, since the fuel is not metered quite as evenly to each cylinder as with a mulitpoint system. Some of the sensors I have picked out may be interesting. Arrow 1 is the usually existing sender for the temperature gauge; arrow 2 is the existing manifold to water pump connection; arrow 3 is the water temp sensor fed to the ECU, and requires a new platform welding to the manifold.

opposite of engine vacuum. A h gh MAP reading equals low vacuum, thus high engine load. Light load produces low MAP readings, or high vacuum. The MAP sensor in picture 13-4-2 (overleaf) requires only a vacuum hose to the intake plenum or throttle body.

Throttle body injection (TBI) and port fuel-injection (PFI) have a number of common features and requirements, and we will start by exploring them.

COMMON FEATURES
Fuel supply

As mentioned earlier, EFI systems circulate high-pressure fuel to the engine and return the excess to the tank. Factory injected TR7s and TR8s used a tank with two holes. These tanks are now rare, but a standard single hole tank can be modified by specialists. One route is to form a second aperture, weld a locking ring (as in photo 13-4-3-1) and fit an old sending unit (with pipe), seen at 13-4-3-2.

SPEEDPRO SERIES

13-4-2 A close-up of the MAP sensor as mounted on the side of the plenum. MAP systems are much less sensitive to vacuum leaks, which are the scourge of MAF-controlled EFI, but merely generate increased idle in a MAP system.

Owners of carburetted TR8s will already have a two-hole tank, but fitted with a low-pressure in-tank electric fuel pump on the left side, and a fuel level sending unit on the right. In this situation, the latter is replaced with a TR7 sending unit, part number TKC3408. The in-tank pump is discarded, but its mounting re-installed to form the fuel-return. New fuel-return lines are still available under part number PKC381. These are installed on the left-hand side of the transmission tunnel, using plastic pipe clips in existing holes in the handbrake reinforcement panel.

A high-pressure EFI fuel pump is required, mounted on the right-side rear bulkhead. The three-piece bracket assembly (off the car) is shown in 13-4-4-1, and on the car in 13-4-4-2. The studded and centre brackets are still available under part numbers TKC5819 and RKC4714, but the left bracket – which also incorporates the exhaust hanger and rear brake hose-mount – will need to be fabricated using an aftermarket YKC2119 exhaust hanger and the original brake hose-bracket, as in photo 13-4-4-3.

PFI systems require 35psi, and

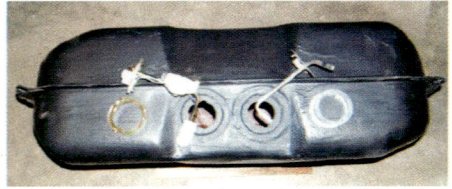

13-4-3-1 A single-hole fuel tank modified by forming a second locking ring followed by professional cleaning and coated by Moyers of Pennsylvania.

13-4-3-2 An old sending unit has been re-fitted to the right side hole to provide a fuel return inlet. It's as well to remove the level sensor first.

some alternatives are mentioned in the companion book *How to restore TR7 and 8*. TBI systems only need about 12psi. Ideally, the pump needs to accept a 7.5mm ID fuel hose at both ends, and Airtex makes a generic replacement pump for both TBI and PFI systems with that size fitting. Part numbers are E8094 and E8228 respectively.

The fuel pump and fuel filter also need to be attached to the centre bracket, with the pump using Jaguar part number CAC2481 (plus some layers of electrical tape). Bosch fuel filter number 71028 (the same as on factory injected cars) is fitted in the loop with the rubber strip, but opinions differ about whether is it preferable to locate the fuel filter before or after the pump. Factory practice was after the pump, but the danger with that approach is that should a blockage occur the filter could rupture, and it leaves the pump vulnerable to dirt. Later Rover cars, such

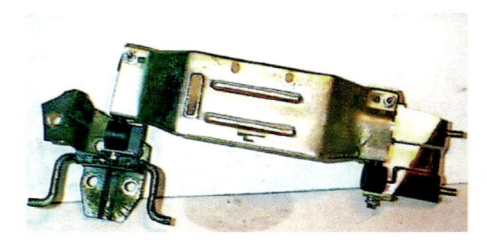

13-4-4-1 The three-piece fuel pump/filter mounting as used on factory TR7/8 EFI cars. It is mounted on the right rear bulkhead. Not essential for carb to EFI conversion, but simplifies mounting of the fuel pump and filter.

13-4-4-2 The fuel pump and filter assembly as installed in the car on the right rear bulkhead.

13-4-4-3 The left-hand bracket made up from existing TR7 brake hose brackets ZKC2245 and YKC2119, and a piece of steel bent to shape.

ELECTRONIC FUEL-INJECTION & ENGINE MANAGEMENT

as the MG RV8, use two filters – a small pre-filter before the pump and the main EFI canister filter after the pump, making this look like the preferred method.

Wiring harness

Whilst the specifics of the wiring harnesses obviously differ between TBI and PFI systems, a number of features are common to both. Painless Performance offer harnesses for both systems, but one can also be built from scratch with the added advantage that it can be made to the exact length required. Space and copyright issues prevent the inclusion of circuit diagrams, but they are readily available in GM factory service manuals and on the internet.

A TBI system uses a 1227747 ECM, commonly found in GM full size pickup trucks as well as some older Astro/Safari minivans. PFI systems use the 1227730 ECM found on 1990-1992 Chevrolet Camaro Z28 and Pontiac Firebird models with the 350in^3 tuned port injection (TPI) engine. The PFI ECM can also be found in 6-cylinder Chevy Berettas, but you will need a Z28 Memcal!

For readers outside the USA, these ECUs, the GM manuals, sensors and even wiring connectors can be found on eBay. Components for TBI systems are also usually quite plentiful in breakers' yards in the USA, but less so for PFI parts. Colour and tracer colour wires for looms can be readily obtained from Vehicle Wiring Products in England or British Wiring in the USA. Kimball Midwest offers a large range of pigtail connectors for specific sensors. The terminals used in the ECM connectors are GM part number 12146447 for 22/20 gauge wire, and 12146448 for 18/16 gauge. The former is needed for modern 'thin wall' 32 strand cable.

The interface between the fuel-injection harness and the main vehicle harness is not difficult, provided the three categories of connection are adhered to:
1) Hot at all times – a fused, direct battery, thus a constantly live feed.
2) Hot in run – GM terminology for 12-volt ignition switched current. Since the amps required by EFI systems are considerable, this feed should be via a relay to relieve the ignition switch and original wiring.
3) Earth.

The ECU is best located under the glove compartment, mimicking factory practice, but the GM unit requires a special 5mm mounting stud (part number 12337892) that clips to the casing.

Sensors

As with wiring harnesses, the sensors used in both systems are similar in function but different in detail. One should purchase sensors based on the vehicle applications, as discussed in the Ignition section below.

Idle air control (IAC)

The IAC sensor (stepper motor) controls the flow of bypass air around the throttle plates for a smooth idle. On a TBI system it is on the throttle body. PFI location depends on what type of plenum is used. Range Rover Hot Wire plenums place the IAC at the rear of the plenum, in a housing (part number ETC6214) that the GM IAC will screw into. When using an earlier Federal air flow plenum, it is necessary to mount that housing where the over-run valve is located.

Throttle position sensor (TPS)

The TBI system's TPS mounts on the throttle body, but to ease subsequent air cleaner fitting and bonnet clearance, it is necessary to buy one with a horizontal connector as opposed to the more common vertical style.

For the Hot Wire PFI system, the throttle position sensor needs to be

13-4-5 The GM TPS mounting plate and drive dog kit that are required to mount on a Rover plenum.

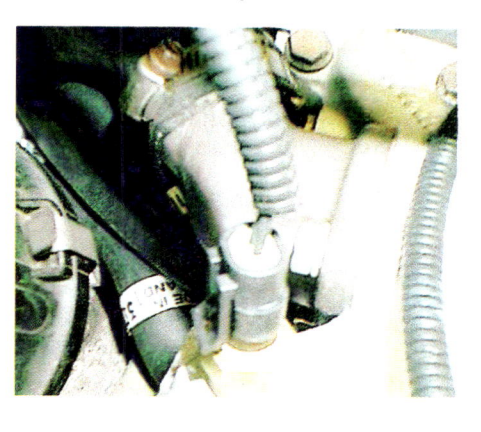

13-4-6 This is a GM coolant temperature sensor fitted via a small aluminium plate welded to the left front coolant passage. However, all Rover EFI manifolds incorporate a sensor that can be re-used, although some ECU re-mapping may be required.

located on the plenum at one end of the throttle shaft, so it is necessary to use a GM TPS that in turn requires the mounting hardware shown in 13-4-5.

Coolant temperature sensor (CTS)

For the TBI system a GM sensor needs to be located in the left front water channel in the intake manifold. This requires a small aluminium boss welded to the manifold, and then drilled and tapped as shown in 13-4-6).

Manifold absolute pressure (MAP)

The MAP sensor for both systems is an external sensor requiring a vacuum

SPEEDPRO SERIES

hose connection to the plenum or throttle body. Be sure to select a vacuum source that is full manifold vacuum, not 'ported' vacuum. Both systems use the same one-bar GM sensor for normally aspirated engines.

Oxygen (O_2)

The oxygen sensor for both systems is a single-wire, non-heated type. Bosch part number 12014 works well. It needs to be located in one of the down pipes (before the catalytic converter, if fitted) and reasonably close to the exhaust manifold. JEG's offers a steel bung, part number 555-30740, for this purpose.

Diagnostic link (ALDL)

Not a sensor, but nonetheless the link seen at 13-4-7 forms a vital part of the system! They are the same on virtually all GM cars so are extremely common in American breakers' yards.

Check engine light

One terminal on the ECU is for a check engine light, also known as an SES light or MIL. Unfortunately, it is difficult to use one of the spare lamps in the TR7/8 instrument cluster unless one modifies the PCB because the ECU gives the light a ground whereas the bulbs in the cluster require a feed!

Ignition timing and control

GM TBI and PFI systems also control ignition timing. Fortunately, the pickup in Rover distributors 13-4-8-1 and 13-4-8-2 is compatible with the GM ignition modules. The timing is controlled by the ECU, so the distributor's weight mechanisms need to be disabled by welding (picture 13-4-8-3), the vacuum advance left disconnected and the line sealed.

TBI uses a 1989 Chevrolet full-size truck module and PFI a 1991 Chevrolet Camaro Z28 module.

13-4-7 An ALDL diagnostic connector can be salvaged from almost any late model GM vehicle and refitted with new GM part number 12034046 terminals.

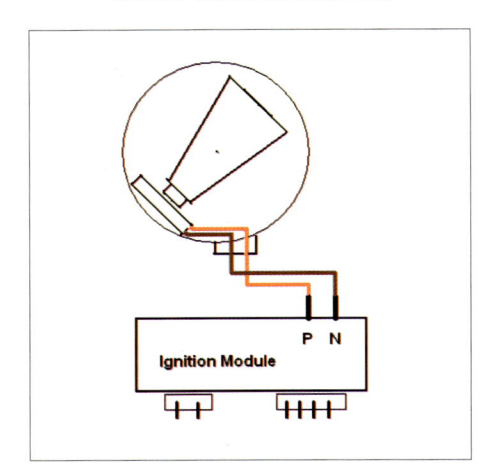

D13-3 Wiring the distributor pickup to the GM ignition module. Note that the wires inside the Rover distributor are orange and brown. The terminals on the module are marked P and N. Orange must be connected to P and brown to N.

The module should be mounted as close as possible to the distributor, as shown in 13-4-8-4. The two terminals opposite the sealed connectors must be connected to the distributor pickup as per drawing D13-3. If they are reversed the engine will run very poorly. The mounting method also must provide efficient heat transfer and earthing for the module.

That concludes the common features, so let's look now at components specific to each system:

13-4-8-1 A 35DLM8 Rover distributor. Rover distributors are easily identified by their code numbers. 35 is the prefix for all V8 distributors (originally meaning 3500cc), D is always the next letter and 8 (for 8 cylinders) always the last digit. However, it is the letters that follow the D that provide the detailed identification. E signifies an early and undesirable Lucas Opus system. M signifies early constant energy systems with a separate remote amplifier, hopefully located in the coolest place you can find. LM signifies the later constant energy system with the module on the distributor body.

13-4-8-2 A 35DLM Constant Energy distributor with a two-wire distributor-mounted module. There is an even better three-wire distributor, or you can buy a Land-Rover remote conversion kit that mounts the module away from the heat and vibration of the distributor body.

THROTTLE BODY-INJECTION
Mounting the throttle body

The biggest change required by TBI involves the intake manifold. An original

ELECTRONIC FUEL-INJECTION & ENGINE MANAGEMENT

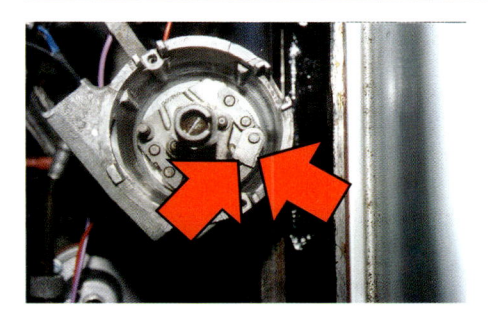

13-4-8-3 Hopefully, you will be able to see two weld spots (arrowed), that basically lock the mechanical advance mechanism to allow the electronic advance curve to have full control of this car.

13-4-8-4 The GM ignition module for both TBI and PFI systems needs to be mounted near the distributor. A substantial piece of aluminium angle ensures good heat transfer and earth connection.

13-4-9 This is the underside of many BL and Rover inlet manifolds, showing the heater pipe connections. One plate connection is fixed to the arrowed end, while the full-length return pipe speaks for itself.

Rover V8 manifold (photo 13-4-9) is the preferred basis of the change because it has provision for a heater return pipe. One pipe is pressed into the casting and circulates water through to the back of the manifold, but not all aftermarket manifolds offer this facility. Thus the recommended route is to modify the factory manifold to accept a throttle body. The work is similar to that described in the previous chapter when fitting an AFB carburettor to a Rover manifold. Machine the carburettor 'roof' from the manifold mount and weld an aluminium plate which, in this case, can be drilled and tapped for the EFI throttle body. This solution has the additional benefit of maximizing bonnet clearance.

Accelerator cable
Accelerator cables designed for Holley carburettor conversions can be used for TBI conversions. Cables intended for RHD use may be a shade too long for LHD applications, but automotive cable specialists can make the necessary adjustment, as seen at 13-4-10.

Air intake
TR8 owners with the original Stromberg carburettors can make up an adapter enabling their stock air cleaner boxes to be reused as shown in 13-4-11-1. To secure the centre portion, two of the throttle body bolts are replaced with the threaded rod as in 13-4-11-2.

PORT FUEL-INJECTION
A PFI system requires you start with a Rover EFI manifold and plenum assembly. Either the earlier air flow meter type (picture 13-4-12-1, overleaf) or the later Hot Wire (13-4-12-2, overleaf) style will be satisfactory, although the latter is preferable because it will require less modification. The Hot Wire assembly requires the TPS change already discussed, but note from picture

13-4-10 Using the original inlet manifold boss and bracket mounting can make fitting a throttle cable easier.

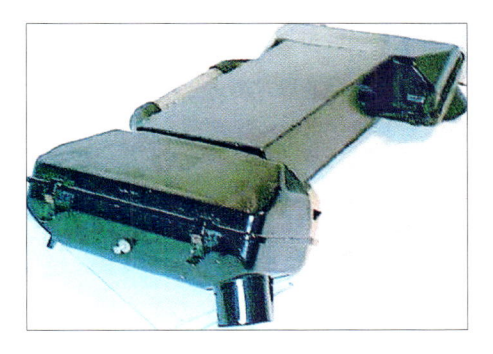

13-4-11-1 If you cannot find an aftermarket air cleaner, this home-made adapter enables original TR8 air cleaner boxes to be re-used with throttle body injection but ...

13-4-11-2 ... you will also need to extend the twin mounting studs as seen here. Note the throttle body unit and twin EFI injectors.

165

SPEEDPRO SERIES

13-4-12 –1 An ex-SD1 Federal air flow meter (sometimes called a 'flapper') system with the cold start injector (arrow 1), the extra air valve (arrow 2) and the over-run valve (arrow 3) shown. The over-run valve (sometimes called the decel valve) was originally fitted to relieve high manifold vacuum on deceleration in order to minimise emissions. All three positions require removal when you fit a GM EFI system. Two will require blanking plates, but the decel valve location is ideal for the idle air valve or stepper motor.

13-4-13 the proximity of the idle air housing to the bonnet latch.

The earlier air flow meter plenums shown in 13-4-14-1 require rather more adaptation. The cold start injector and thermo-time switch will need to be removed and blanked off. The overrun valve will need to be replaced with a spacer and IAC sensor housing as shown in 13-4-14-2. It is also necessary to mount a GM TPS in place of the Rover part and, as photo 13-4-14-3 shows, the approach is similar.

Fuel injectors

The older air flow meter systems used 2 ohm impedance injectors. These are unsuitable for use with GM electronics and will damage the GM ECU. Thus Rover's later Hot Wire 16 ohm impedance injectors are required, regardless of the style of plenum intended. However the older style injectors use square cut O-rings at the

13-4-12 –2 The later and preferred counterpart, the 'Hot Wire' system, in this case from a 3.9-litre Range Rover.

13-4-13 The close proximity of the idle air housing (on the back of the plenum) to the bonnet latch prevents the air intake from being re-fitted, unless you modify the intake.

manifold end and a barbed hose fitting at the rail end. Interchangeable high impedance injectors may prove difficult to find, but you can modify the manifold seats for them. If you are tempted to retain the original low impedance injectors, you must either modify the existing GM ECU to accommodate the change or add an (expensive) 'injector driver' via www.acceleronics.com.

Accelerator cable

The choice of throttle cable for a PFI system will depend on what vehicle the plenum came from. The best strategy is to obtain a cable from the donor vehicle and have the pedal end fitted with a TR7 bulkhead fitting by an automotive cable

13-4-14-1 The early Federal Rover SD1 intake and plenum as used on USA specification cars, incorporating two essential modifications ...

13-4-14-2 ... an IAC housing (ETC6214) replaces the original over-run valve and ...

13-4-14-3 ... a GM TPS mounted where the original throttle potentiometer went. The drive dog and mounting plate are similar to those used with a Hot Wire plenum.

specialist. In most cases, later Range Rover throttle linkages can be fitted to earlier SD1 intakes if necessary.

ELECTRONIC FUEL-INJECTION & ENGINE MANAGEMENT

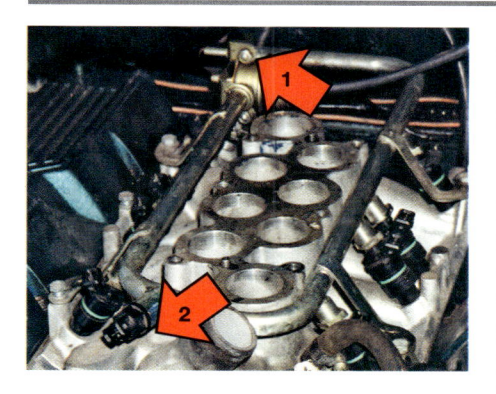

13-4-15 This mass air flow (MAF) part-assembled plenum shows the fuel pressure regulator (FPR, arrow 1) and fuel rail perfectly. The fuel temperature sensor (arrow 2) at the front of the rail is not used with the GM system, and can remain disconnected or be replaced with a fitting to allow connection of a fuel pressure diagnostic gauge or injector cleaner.

Air intake

Rover's duct (part number ESR1611) was used, and can be seen in 13-4-16 with its metal sleeve drilled and tapped to accept the IAT sensor.

Diagnostics and programming

For tuning you will need:
- Scan tool. For detailed troubleshooting and tuning a laptop computer (Win 95 or higher) running WinALDL software for TBI or Datamaster for PFI gives the ability to log data as the vehicle is driven, in addition to providing more detailed diagnostics. Both software companies can also provide details of constructing or purchasing the cable to connect the laptop to the ECM.
- Tuning software. This creates the data file that is stored on the EPROM chip. For both TBI and PFI, Tunercat has a user-friendly interface for modifying the engine mapping tables and constant values.
- EPROM programmer. The programmer 'burns' the data file that was created by the tuning software on to the EPROM. A good choice is the Pocket Programmer 2 (photo 13-4-17). An additional HDR1 Memcal adapter is needed for PFI.

EPROM chips are reusable, but repeated UV takes its toll. TBI chips are part number 2732A. They are extremely difficult to extract from the plastic holder without breaking pins. PFI chips are 27C256. Some Memcals may have a removable 27SF512 electrically erasable flash chip.
- EPROM Eraser: Uses ultra violet light to erase the data from the chip. BK Precision 850 is a good choice.

CONCLUSION

Aside from meeting the criteria listed at the beginning of this section, the effectiveness of any induction method can be gauged by two results – how the car runs and the emissions. Brad Wilson's GM PFI 3.9-litre automatic achieves 18-19mpg on the highway, compared with a friends stock, carburetted TR8 automatic that only manages 13mpg. Furthermore, the GM injected car starts and runs smoothly on mornings at least as cold as –10°C. The exhaust emissions complete a very satisfactory picture. Without the need for exhaust gas re-circulation or catalytic converters, the emissions for both injection methods are comfortably below local limits (HC 300ppm and 3 per cent CO). The TBI provides HC 187ppm and CO 0.84 per cent, while the PFI system is capable of HC 64ppm and a CO reading of 0.54 per cent.

The multi-point injection is thus the most effective and, while there are variables such as secondhand parts and the costs of machining, you can fit a Hot Wire-based PFI system to your car for about $1500. The TBI system is even cheaper at about $1000, but this assumes you already have a laptop. You will also need to budget $250 for the tuning hardware and software.

13-4-16 An adapter sleeve and housing for the IAT sensor is vital to the EFI system, and doubles to connect a K+N air filter to the intake hose. K+N and similar air filters are widely available at auto-parts stores. Nuts were welded to the sleeve at three and six o'clock relative to the sensor, to facilitate securing the sleeve to the inner wing.

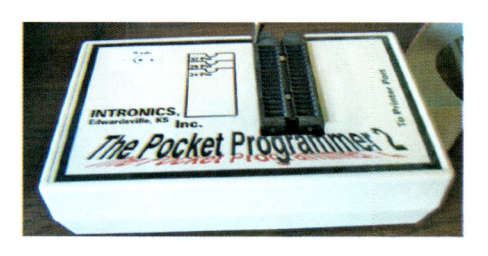

13-4-17 The desktop EPROM burner connects to your PC via a parallel port.

Where an alternative source is not stated, the remaining specialised parts referred to in this chapter are available from Wedgeparts (see appendix for contact details)

FURTHER READING

Bosch Fuel-injection and Engine Management, by Charles Probst. Published by Robert Bentley Publishers, ISBN 0-8376-0300-5. Lists Bosch EFI system and applications to the early 1990s.

Super Tuning, by Alex Walordy. Provides tuning information on Holley fuel-injection systems.

DIY Guide to Custom EFI by John Wilson, Custom EFI, Georgia. Details of GM EFI installation to Rover engines.

Chapter 14
Electrical and instrument improvements

The Wedge cars all suffered from one common and fairly frequent problem – poor electrical reliability. This is due partly to the following:
- The car is more electrically complex than any previous TR (take the headlights as one example).
- It used poor quality unsealed switches in the dashboard and exposed loom connectors in the engine bay.
- We expect our TR7s and 8s to provide reliable service long beyond the car's design life (the youngest cars are over twice as old as Triumph anticipated as I write these words)
- We rarely take the necessary preventative measures to ensure longevity of the electrical circuits.

I devoted much of the electrical chapter in *How to restore Triumph TR7 and TR8* to the number of earth/ground connections, the necessity of keeping each in good order, and how to improve their longevity. I also listed a number of areas where I felt it helpful to upgrade the electrical circuits generally, to incorporate relays and to fit extra fuses. I am not going to duplicate that information here, but if your car is a constant electrical nightmare, acting bizarrely or you seek to improve its reliability, remember that the car has a number of electrical weaknesses for which there are proven solutions. The earth routes via the chassis provide half the electrical circuitry within the vehicle, thus all feed and earth connections need to be scrupulously clean.

ALTERNATOR UPGRADES

TR7s used three types of alternator – the standard 17ACR (36 amps) model, an uprated option (the 20ACR), and the 25ACR (65 amps) for heavy-duty applications. While generally the original TR7 and TR8 alternator output is rarely a problem in the UK for unmodified cars, as soon as you start fitting electric cooling fan(s), you can put the alternator under strain. This is particularly likely if you live in an area of high traffic density.

Higher intensity headlamps will pull a few more amps, an electric fuel pump, particularly a high-pressure EFI pump, will need more amps, and an EFI or engine management system will need a lot more energy to keep your car running smoothly. Then there is the power necessary for air-conditioning fans, although these are mostly applicable to US cars.

Wherever you are, or whatever the capacity or tune of your engine, it is essential to properly supply the electrical system and recharge the car's battery. A 55 amp rated alternator is the minimum recommended these days. When EFI is in use we certainly must add another 10 amps capacity, and a further five when a heated rear screen is in use on FHC variants. In the UK, therefore, we could be looking at a 55-65 amp alternator shown in picture 14-1-1. For US cars a 65-amp alternator

ELECTRICAL AND INSTRUMENT IMPROVEMENTS

14-1-1 This is a new 65 amp alternator. It is about 5in (125mm) in diameter and may be difficult to squeeze into some engine bays.

14-1-2-1 Cheap, but not small. This 55 amp unit was salvaged from an EFI Austin Montego, and is around 5in in diameter.

14-1-2-2 The three fastenings arrowed can be undone and the front plate rotated through 120 degrees to align the pivots correctly for the engine mounting arrangement.

is required, but with air-conditioning 80 amps may be prudent, particularly when hot ambient conditions dictate the frequent use of two electric fans. In fact since just the standard/stock TR8 radiator fans draw some 32 amps when running at high speed (80 amps on start-up), a 100 amp unit probably would not be over-kill for an A/C equipped car in hot climates. Needless to say, all these requirements exceed even the largest alternator fitted to a TR7 or 8, thus an upgrade is mandatory.

A used alternator is perfectly acceptable when carrying out a V8 conversion - provided its capacity is adequate. Donors can include the larger heavy-duty TR7/8 units, Range Rover alternators and of course the ever-present SD1 alternator. The SD1's alternator is either 23ACR or 25ACR and consequently has a higher output than the vast majority of TR7 alternators. As these alternators and similar models were fitted to a wide range of BL cars, a trip to your local breakers yard may reveal something like that seen in pictures 14-1-2-1 and 14-1-2-2 and will usually be a direct bolt on installation. The alternator's alloy identity label should say not only the alternator series (which is not so important) but also its output in amps – and you'll be looking for something in the 55 to 65 amp range. Do take an hour before bolting any used larger unit to the car to change the brushes at the back of the alternator and take the opportunity to fit a new fan/drive belt.

Fortunately new modern alternators are getting much more efficient, so the output capability for any given size of alternator is increasing. Picture 14-1-3 endorses this point. This is aided by the trend of incorporating the cooling fan inside the alternator, and this can be seen in photograph 14-1-4. Size for size, therefore, with the output of the alternator about double what it was

14-1-3 Consider this much smaller, lightweight unit with its internal fan.

14-1-4 A modern high amperage alternator, in this example a Mitsubishi unit, with internal fan. Because of the increased torque required to rotate such units, they are today often driven by an entirely different drive belt that supersedes the single-vee belts we are more used to seeing.

five to ten years ago, the necessity for a larger amperage alternator need not create a space problem, even inside the most crowded engine compartment.

In the UK, Robsport has those seen at 14-1-5 (overleaf) and other options available. However, you may care to visit your local breakers yard and look for small alternators. They are common on modern Japanese cars and

SPEEDPRO SERIES

14-1-5 A neat, lightweight and very small 45 amp capacity alternator. This particular model may give too low an output for road-going use but, using the large diameter pulley in shot, may suit racing applications.

14-1-6-1 This nice Grinnall conversion has the alternator in a lower than standard SD1 location. If you fit the alternator above this alloy cradle in front of the rocker cover (as on an MGB V8, Rover P5B or Rover P6), it is likely that the terminations will be a problem. This location avoids the front of the rocker cover ...

14-1-6-2 ... as does this alternator location, which looks the size of an SD1 but has clearly been mounted using a fabricated and extended bracket.

14-1-7 This is the Range Rover alternator location and mounting arrangement.

thus, I'm sure, you will find one that is small enough. You also need to ensure that the direction of rotation, wiring/mounting arrangements as well as the output potential are suitable for your intended application.

In the US, converters need hardly go further than their nearest speed shop where General Motors' (Delco) internally regulated alternators, called type SI, are the units of choice for most V8 conversions. The GM alternators come in a couple of sizes/amperage ratings – 10SI and 12SI – and are relatively inexpensive. These are probably one of the most common alternators in the US and are available everywhere. However, a look at www.madelectrical.com/electricaltech/delcoremy.shtml will give more information. The exact model chosen will depend on the amperage required and the clearance available in the alternator's proposed mounting position. D+D Fabrications have Delco 80 amp three-wire units available.

Incidentally, I think you are best avoiding single-wire alternators. They cost more than the equivalent three-wire, have no advantage in a TR7 or TR8, and don't work until the engine revolutions become elevated. A standard three-wire will generate usable amounts of current at idle. The idea of a one-wire alternator is to simplify installation, and while this may work on many cars the vast majority of TR7 and TR8 have three wires (some later years have two-wire alternators) connected to the Lucas alternator, so the substitution of a single-wire unit has little merit.

We touched upon V8 alternator location for the Rover engines in chapter 9, but to recap – the most usual place is in front of the right-side rocker cover as we see in photo 14-1-6-1 and 14-1-6-2, with an alternative shown in picture 14-1-7. There is no room for the conventional plug between the rear of the alternator and the front of the rocker box cover, but inside a Lucas alternator's plug you will find two or three 'flag' (right-angled) terminals. You can buy proper moulded 'boots' to use as insulators in place of the plug, but do not use tape as a substitute for the plug/cover – it gets hot and oily and comes undone sooner or later with disastrous results. If you can find some PTFE adhesive tape, stick this to the rocker box as an insurance against vibration bringing your booted terminals into contact with the rocker cover.

On a GM SI alternator, the location of the two smaller wire terminals can be located at 3, 6, 9 or 12 o'clock by slightly opening the case, rotating it to one of these four positions and closing. This might be something to look for when buying a new, uprated alternator.

Do not overlook the need to upgrade the power carrying cable from the alternator to the starter solenoid. The solenoid terminal acts as a primary distribution point, being connected directly to the battery by a much larger cable. The cable size to carry 55 to 80 amps is quite thick, and frankly I find it difficult to terminate and route – thus you may find fitting two parallel cables easier, especially if your alternator uses

ELECTRICAL AND INSTRUMENT IMPROVEMENTS

studs and ring terminals as opposed to the one piece spade-type connector just described.

The size of the extra cable will depend upon the original cable's carrying capacity and that required by your enlarged alternator. If you are upgrading to say a 60 amp alternator, bearing in mind all TRs had at least a 36 amp alternator and cable, it will be advisable to fit a second cable that is capable of carrying the extra output (24 amps in this example).

In the UK, a 44/03 sized cable carries 25 amps. However, if you are moving up to an 80 amp alternator I think you are best throwing out the original cable and fitting a pair of new cables each capable of 40 amps – namely 84/03. In US gauges, a 10ga wire will safely carry 40-60 amps, an 8ga will carry 60-80, and 80-100 amps can be carried by a 6ga. There is a table of European and US wire sizes and their respective current carrying capacities on page 175.

If you need a TR7 service-exchange alternator, note that Robsport's replacement alternators are all 18ACR units – which provide a few extra amps output compared to the UK's standard TR7 alternator.

BATTERY RELATED MATTERS
Location

In a right-hand drive TR7 the battery is positioned over the exhaust, while all V8 conversions that retain the battery in the engine bay will also position it over an exhaust manifold. Inevitably, these batteries run at a warmer temperature than is ideal. Relocating a TR7's battery to the boot may be a bit extreme but V8-converted cars might find copying the TR8 battery position to be particularly advantageous. Although the TR has bonnet louvres, V8 under-bonnet

14-2-1-1 This Wedgeparts battery relocation kit presumes you will place the battery to the right side of the boot, allowing the cables to run INSIDE the cockpit through the front bulkhead/firewall, straight to the V8 starter motor.

temperatures are much higher than is ideal for a battery.

There are two views on the boot battery issue. Certainly the battery is not cooked, nor does it dry-out and its life is consequently extended. Further, there is more space available in the boot so you can fit a higher amp-hour capacity battery, too. Kits are available from Robsport and S+S Preparations in the UK, while pictures 14-2-1-1 and 14-2-1-2 show a boot kit from US supplier JEG. Robsport can also supply a TR8 shaped boot carpet that goes across the floor and over the battery, both protecting it and ensuring it is not an eyesore.

If you are using a simple lead acid battery in the boot it is desirable to vent any fumes. In the original TR8, a polyethylene tube was fixed to the top of the battery hold-down and passed through a hole in the floor. The low pressure underneath draws out any corrosive fumes. A similar arrangement should be fashioned for a retrofit installation.

There is a minor downside, in that you also need to modify the engine bay loom to take account of this cable re-routing. However, I am not convinced

14-2-1-2 The kits vary in some details but include the necessary cables and instructions to achieve this. Be sure to at least protect the positive terminal with a plastic cover.

the boot location is entirely a good idea. If you relocate the battery to the boot you take two retrograde steps – you reduce the available luggage space, and take the considerable weight of the battery from inside the wheelbase to a much less desirable location outside the wheelbase. Now, if we could find a battery location INSIDE the wheelbase, particularly one that is low-down, I might be more enthusiastic. Might a small battery be squeezed behind one of the seats?

Naturally a lead/acid battery located within the cockpit/cabin is unthinkable – but what about an 'Optima' gel battery? There are other makes and sizes available, but Optima gel batteries feature two thin lead plates wound into a tight spiral cell, with an absorbent glass mat in-between to hold the gel electrolyte. They cost more than a conventional lead acid battery but have innumerable benefits. They are non-spillable and thus can be mounted in almost any position. They do not vent, so can be mounted in the cockpit if required and, because there is no venting, the terminals will not corrode. They have high power density, rapid recharge capability, are maintenance

SPEEDPRO SERIES

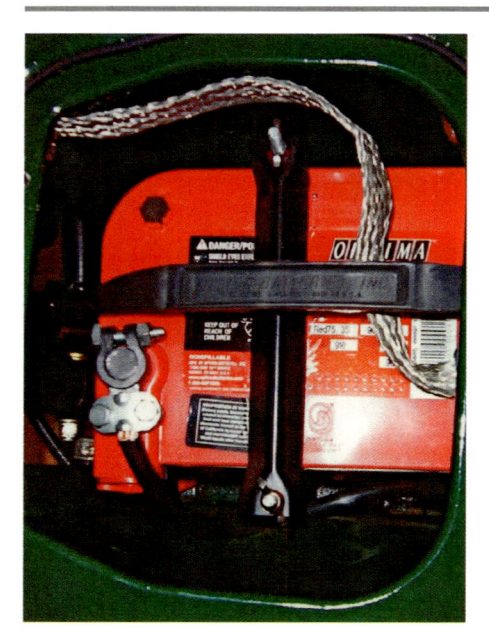

14-2-2 An Optima gel battery with traditional TR7 posts is also available with US GM-style side terminals. It is truly maintenance-free and has an amp rating of 720 at 0°F, and 910 at 32°F.

free, and deliver higher, more consistent voltage under load. Gel batteries are ideal for infrequently used cars as they do not lose their charge while unused.

You may be able to find a used one at a breakers' yard to try, but check out the following new batteries too:

OPT8022-091 Dual terminal top and side post battery (red top)

OPT8004-003 Dual terminal top and side post battery (red top)

OPT8002-002 Top post battery (red top)

Furthermore, the passenger seat location will roughly halve the length of cable run to the starter as compared to a boot location – which can be an advantage. As you can see, they are available with various terminal arrangements. Smaller sizes are available but typical dimensions where space is not restricted would be 9.4in (240mm) long, 6.8in (170mm) wide with a height of 7.6in (190mm). This model has standard top terminals (the same as any standard battery as we see from picture 14-2-2).

Battery drain

If you don't drive your Wedge every day, you could find that it is reluctant to start when the time comes. Lead acid batteries do slowly discharge, which is why products like 'battery conditioners' are so popular. However, if you feel that your battery seems to lose its charge particularly quickly there could be several additional reasons:

The first is a fairly common Wedge problem – the boot light may be operating with the lid closed. The light only draws about 0.25 amps, but after a week the vast majority of batteries will be quite flat. Check that the light goes out with the lid about 6in (15cm) away from fully closed. If not, adjust the right angle bracket that sits in front of and operates the push switch.

The second drain concerns the station-memory that is a feature of most car radios. Modern radios usually require two feed wires – an ignition-on feed and an always-live one, the latter being required to retain the station settings. The current drain is only tiny – perhaps 0.025 amps – but sufficient to drain most of your battery's charge over the course of 4 to 6 weeks when added to the internal losses suffered by most lead-acid batteries. The answer is to buy a radio without station-memory (not actually that easy these days) or be prepared to lose your presets when you isolate the car's electrics.

Thirdly, the ECU/ECM in almost all electronic fuel-injection systems also requires a constant supply to power the computer memory. Therefore, when power is removed from the ECM, it is not uncommon for the car to run

14-2-3 This isolator switch makes/breaks the main cable leading from the battery to the rest of the car, and provides both a safety feature and, with the key removed, some added security from casual theft.

somewhat roughly at first until the computer has re-learnt the operating parameters.

Lastly, there is the clock and on some cars the alarm – all contributing to battery drain.

Battery/electrical isolators

A rear battery position, be it in the cockpit or in the boot, lends itself to your fitting an isolator switch of the type seen in photo 14-2-3. This completely eliminates external battery drain. If located on a bracket mounted on the heel board behind the drivers seat, you would have an easily accessible method of isolating the electrics in an emergency.

Alternator voltage control

The 1980 and 1981 Triumph cars are fitted with a Lucas battery sensed alternator, which is vulnerable to problems and best replaced with an alternator without battery sensing if/when you are replacing the alternator.

In fact, one problem with the TR8s was so frequent that Lucas recommended that the engine bay loom be modified to prevent overcharging the boot-located battery. When positioning the TR8's battery in the boot, Triumph saw the opportunity to locate the

ELECTRICAL AND INSTRUMENT IMPROVEMENTS

14-2-4 This is a shot of the hand-built loom in a works rally car. It makes the point about the value of fitting an individual relay to each circuit, to put no more than a small control current through the respective switches.

TR7 and TR8 switches

Sadly, these were regarded generally as being of poor quality, and are a source of electrical unreliability. The alternatives are to replace the switches with improved modern units, which will alter the appearance of the cockpit, or to fit relays to each switch circuit to reduce the current each original switch is required to handle. The TR7 and TR8 had more relays and electrical complexity than any previous TR model – nevertheless, the added complexity of a relay to implement the mini-current control of the switch is, in my view, invaluable. An example is shown at 14-2-4.

TR7-V8 engine bay wiring modifications

Unfortunately, the 4-cylinder and V8 engines have their various ignition, ancillary and instrument electrical feeds in quite different places within the engine bay. In fact, they could hardly be more different if the designers had planned it that way, so we had best compare the locations of the electrical feeds:
- Starter –
TR7: left rear side of engine.
Rover V8: right rear side of engine.
- Alternator –
TR7: front right.
Rover V8: SD1 and TR8 engines use front right adjacent to the rocker cover. Range Rover engines place it front left.
- Ignition coil –
TR7: 1979 or earlier, lower right bulkhead/firewall. 1980 and later, rear of right inner wing/fender.
Rover V8: mount the coil plus any ballast resistor (if applicable) plus any amplifier (if applicable) towards the left front of the engine bay opposite the distributor. The inner wing/fender is ideal as it provides a cool 'heat sink'.
- Distributor –
TR7: rear centre of engine.

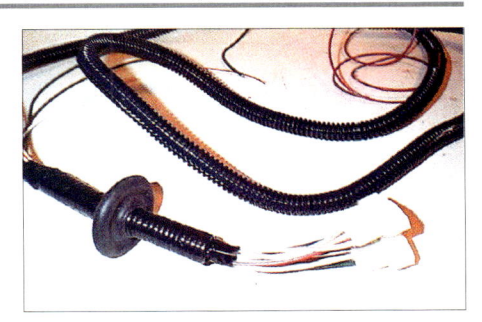

14-2-5 This is a Wedgeparts engine bay loom for an air-con conversion. It is a little more complex than most conversion looms, but will give you the flavour of what is required. Note the re-used multi-pin connectors in the foreground and the long, un-terminated tails on each wire.

Rover V8: left front – feed from the left side of engine bay.
- Oil pressure sender –
TR7: right, lower rear of engine.
Rover V8: right, lower front of engine.
- Coolant sensor –
TR7: front underside of intake manifold (right hand side of engine bay).
Rover V8: right front of intake manifold.

A number of the TR7's wires will no longer be required (anti run-on valve, choke heater and air-conditioner cut out) and can be safely omitted if you are making a new harness, or safely capped if you are modifying your old one. These are identified in the accompanying drawings that will be explained very shortly.

There is a wide range of electrical connectors in use within an SD1, and if you are transferring an SD1 engine to your TR7 you are as well to keep every connector you can on the engine – at least until the TR7's engine bay harness is complete and working. It will look something like photograph 14-2-5.

If you are already worried, note that the S+S Preparations wiring loom supplied with its V8 conversion kit enables you to couple the repositioned

power tap inside the cockpit in a more benevolent environment, but this necessitated the voltage control sensing wire passing through the bulkhead via a multi-pin connector in the engine loom. In spite of its supposedly protected location, any corrosion in this connection results in high resistance, which caused the alternator's voltage regulator to 'see' a low battery voltage even when the voltage on the other side of the connector was correct. This over-charging brought about overheating, and in due course destroyed the battery. To follow the Lucas directive, you should take advantage of your new engine bay harness and cut the thin brown wire in it, then reconnect the wire to the battery cable terminal at the starter solenoid.

There is a less prevalent but second possible source of problems with single-wire alternators – a broken sensor wire will also make the regulator detect low battery charge. The TR7/8 regulator has a zener diode that is supposed to handle this eventuality, but if you are replacing the alternator anyway I suggest you opt for a two-terminal voltage regulator without remote sensing to end both these potential problems.

SPEEDPRO SERIES

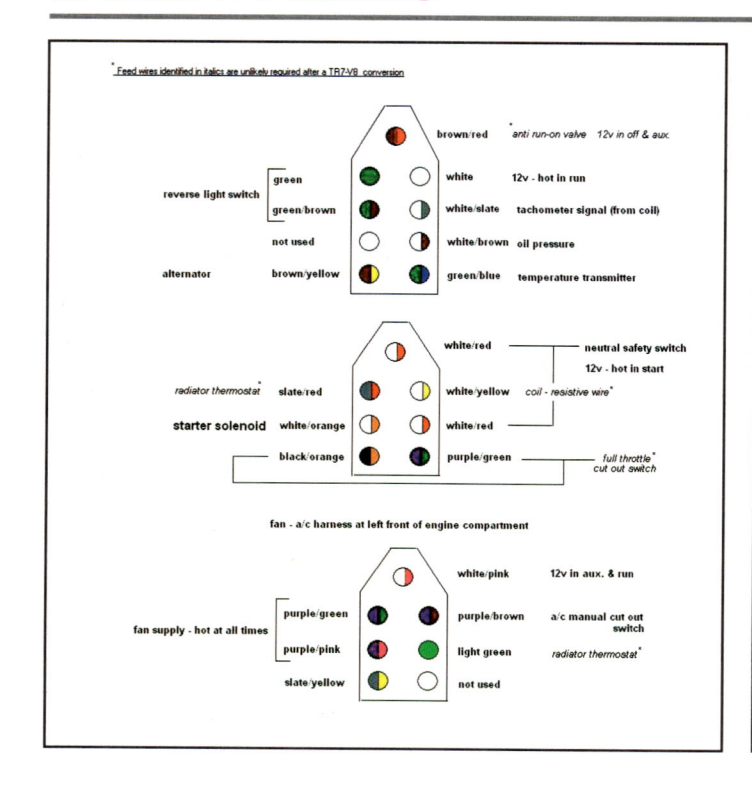

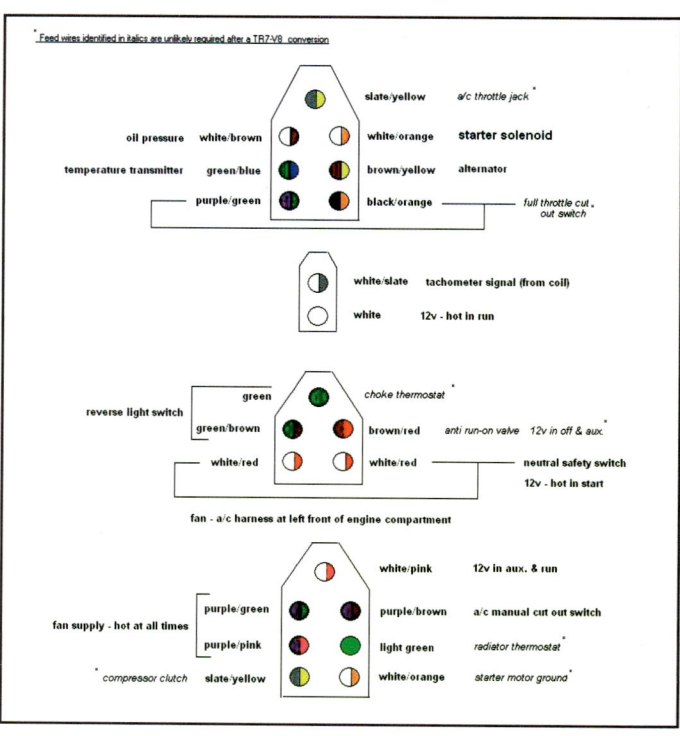

D14-1 Multi-pin connectors on US cars until late 1979.

D14-2 Multi-pin connection detail for 1980 and later cars.

starter motor, temperature sender, alternator and oil-pressure switch to the car's existing circuits with minimum difficulty. The wiring diagram supplied with the kit explains the connections and shows how to incorporate the SD1's Lucas (Opus) electronic ignition into the TR7's original ignition circuits. The S+S diagram does not cater for wiring the electric fan nor, should you choose to upgrade the ignition system, for the electrical wiring of this unit, because such kits include an individual diagram designed to meet the specific needs of each product.

Preparing your own harness

The changes needed are best accomplished with the engine bay harness out of the TR7. You will find the collection of multi-pin plugs and mating sockets under the dashboard, and will hopefully find drawings D14-1 and D14-2 help you locate the (several) multi-pin connectors for the engine harness/loom. You may be wondering why there are two drawings. The first covers most of the cars produced for North America until late 1979. During this time the ignition coil was fastened to the RH bulkhead/fire wall, and one 9-pin and one 7-pin connector – located under the right end of the under-dash – were used to marry the engine to the main loom.

In 1980, the coil was moved to the right side necessitating a different wiring arrangement, hence drawing D14-2. The white and white/slate wires that were formerly in the 9-pin connector under the right side now moved to the left side of the under-dash and were fitted within their own 2-pin connector. The engine harness connectors then went to 7 and 5 pins and the remaining wires were rearranged! A couple of other clues might help identify which harness your car has. The location of the header tank (left-hand tank cars are 1980 models with the revised loom connectors) and the brighter warning lights in the instrument cluster are also a feature of 1980 models.

After you have identified and disconnected all the multi-pin plugs and sockets for your car, you can remove the engine bay loom and take the black wrap-around tape off the whole harness. To carry out the changes required, you could lay the loom on the floor and judge the length of the wires using a tape measure. I personally found it better to get the engine and the respective electrical ancillaries in place and to cover the wings/fenders

174

ELECTRICAL AND INSTRUMENT IMPROVEMENTS

with a heavy cloth. You can then lay the harness actually on the car to judge the lengths required for each individual wire, and to cut them very generously over-length.

My first priority would then be to establish which of the existing wires is both of sufficient capacity and long enough to reach its new destination via the new route you will need to plan. When adding to or replacing a section of harness I always use numerous loose (i.e. loops of) twist-ties at about 12in (300mm) intervals, roughly holding the original loom to any additional or replacement cables I add.

The best approach to any wiring alterations your car needs is to tackle one circuit at a time. This probably means you will have a growing number of electrical wires lying around as you add each extra wire. This is absolutely no problem, provided you follow a few basically obvious rules.

Get yourself a good-sized drawing of what you are trying to achieve. Currently, about 6 TR7 and TR8 diagrams are available from Wedgeparts, or you can use a workshop manual and progressively enlarge and stick together the engine bay wiring diagram until it forms a working size guide – say A3. Draw in any wires/colours/relays etc. you intend to add to the loom for additional auxiliaries, electric fans being the most obvious example.

Allow a very generous termination allowance at both ends of each new/repaired wire. Once all the new wires have been added, you need to make the loose cable ties redundant by applying bands of self-adhesive PVC tape at every 'tail' or end, every junction, and at about 12in intervals along the straighter lengths. When the repair/additional wires are in place you will need to bind the whole bundle back together, after you have heat-shrunk a sleeve over any splices or terminations that have been necessary. Slip the sleeve over the joint and then use a heat gun or cigarette lighter to make the sleeve shrink down to the size of the original cable.

It is in your interests as well as those of subsequent owners to use the same colour coded identification/insulation covering as the original TR7. To do this job properly you need to buy not only the correct colour, but also the correct current-carrying replacement wire. We will get to capacities shortly, but if extending/altering a harness, buy new wiring colours that are identical to the original TR7 colour codes. For example, if the TR7 wire from the ignition switch to the coil is white with black tracer, stay with white/black even if the length, routing or the donor engine's wire to the coil is a different colour. I think you run the risk of confusion if you try to switch to the donor car's colour codes halfway across the engine bay. I guess there will be occasions when my suggestion causes a completely satisfactory wire to be replaced 'unnecessarily', but in the long run I think this policy will resolve more problems than it creates. A used loom from another Wedge or SD1 is a useful source of the correct coloured wires. There is an additional factor to consider when seeking to maintain wire colour consistency. Nowadays, modern vehicle wiring uses 'thin-wall' cable which for a given cable size offers greater current carrying capacity. For example, standard 28/0.3mm is rated at 17.5 amps, whereas thin-wall 28/0.3mm is rated at 25 amps! Furthermore, the range of colours offered in thin-wall is now greater than for standard cable.

The (current carrying) capacity of electrical wires is determined by the number of 0.3mm individual strands woven into the insulation sleeve. Consequently you will need to count the strands within the wire (9, 14 and 28 are the most common, but there is higher capacity wiring available too) and order the appropriate length of replacement wire in the correct colour and capacity. If in doubt, ALWAYS fit the next higher capacity cable. For example, if you have removed a 14 strand wire (capacity is 8 amps) but cannot get a 14 strand replacement, and/or you are expecting to put extra load on that wire by fitting, say an electric fan, then ALWAYS go up in capacity to perhaps a 28 strand wire (in fact, you will need to increase the capacity further if you really are going to add an electric fan). In this example you will then be ordering a length of 28/03 wire – which has, incidentally, a capacity of 17 amps – or, to handle each fan's 15 amps, order a length of 44/03 cable with its capacity of 25amps. The following table may help:

Amps	European cable size	Amps	USA cable size/gauge
5	9/0.3	5	18
8	14/0.3	10	16
17	28/0.3	15	14
25	44/0.3	20	12
35	65/0.3	30	10
42	84/0.3	60	8

Watch for and replace individual wires with surface corrosion. I was caught-out early in my car restoration 'career' by a wire that seemed quite sound, although I could see it had surface green/corrosion all over each strand and, I subsequently discovered, this corrosion ran quite some distance under the insulation. Corrosion on the exterior of the wires will still allow them to carry current, but makes it almost impossible to make a satisfactory and/or lasting end termination. Consequently such wires need replacing.

The insulation round wires situated near heat, say those servicing the distributor, tends to become brittle and can break. Such wires are best replaced as a matter of course.

The terminations at the end of each wire are absolutely crucial to the reliability of any electrical harness. If the terminals are still securely attached to their wires then they could provide many years of further service – provided they are not corroded. Our friends Stateside can buy a product called D5 De-Oxit, which I understand cleans and de-oxidizes old electrical terminations. To protect new terminals, DW Electrochemicals offers a product known as Stabilant 22A, which is available through Volkswagen/Audi dealers. In the UK you may have to spend a little time cleaning-up corroded terminals with very fine emery paper – not forgetting to check those terminals buried inside any push-in multi-block connections. The individual spade terminations can usually be released from the block by finding the securing tang on the spade terminal and 'unlocking' it with a needle or similarly thin probe. If you have the moulded multi-pin connections, then a tedious but worthwhile clean-up of any corroded pins is required.

When it is necessary to replace any terminals, do buy the correct replacement spade, pin or whatever (there are many differing types). The care with which the end terminations are fitted to the loom is crucial to its longevity and reliability. The majority of terminations are best only affixed to the loom once the loom and respective electrical component are re-installed in the car, to ensure wire lengths are cut correctly. All should be crimped twice – one 'flap' to the stripped wire and one to the plastic insulation in order to give every termination some mechanical strength. Then the first flap needs to be soldered to the bare stripped part of the termination. NEVER be satisfied with a pure crimped termination and do not forget to slip any insulation sleeve that is required over the wire before you crimp the terminal in place.

Ripaults 7- or 9-pin white connectors are no longer available, but the housings are fairly indestructible and the male and female pins can still be bought from electrical specialists on both sides of the Atlantic. To re-use the original housing(s), flatten the locking tangs/barbs (there are two) on each pin and withdraw pin and wire from the rear of the housing.

NEVER twist bare wires together and wrap a bit of insulating tape round the joint – that WILL let you down sooner rather later and could be the cause of a fire.

It really is far better to replace the whole of any cables that are too short, broken or corroded, but there will be circumstances where it is impractical to remove the whole loom in order to 'splice' an extension to a spur in the loom. In this event there are some important practices to follow for the best results. Firstly, where there are several wires to join, stagger each individual joint at about 1in (25mm) intervals. Bare about ½in (10mm) of each wire to be spliced and slip a 1in length of shrink-sleeve over the end of one of the two wires to be spliced. Push the two-halves of the splice together so that the individual strands intermesh but do not splay out, and then carefully solder the two wires together. Ease the shrink sleeve over the splice and use an electric paint-stripping gun to shrink the sleeve tight over the splice. Repeat the process for each wire in the splice, and then hide and strengthen the join by wrapping non-adhesive PVC tape generously over the join and as much of the original loom covering as is practical.

Just before you are ready to put the refurbished loom back in the car, hang one end of it from a door knob and bind it tightly (use about a 50 per cent overlap) with the non-adhesive PVC binding tape. This is especially made for the job and is available from the auto electrical specialists listed in the appendix.

A very light smear of silicone grease (failing which, copper slip or petroleum jelly) should be applied to each connection as you subsequently push your electrical connections together. This will aid conductivity and ensure corrosion is kept in check. This is particularly valuable for any connections within the engine bay.

Shrink sleeve can be bought in various sizes from many electronics outlets such as Maplins, Tandys or Radio Shack. Addresses for electrical cable and termination suppliers appear in the appendix.

You need to run a live feed from under the dash to the new electric fuel pump underneath the rear bulkhead. This necessitates lifting seats and carpet, plus removing bulkhead trim panel. After removing bulkhead trim from inside, position the pump then drill two holes for the mounting bracket and one for live feed (pushed through a grommet, of course).

The existing battery to starter motor cable will be too short in any event and needs replacing (discussed shortly).

ELECTRICAL AND INSTRUMENT IMPROVEMENTS

14-3-1 The dual gearing arrangement provides these relatively small aftermarket high-torque starters with a huge increase in torque over a conventional starter. These units are also much lighter than a conventional starter and draw less currrent. The starter solenoids are positioned above the starter body and are angled slightly away from the engine, assisting clearance with the frame rail.

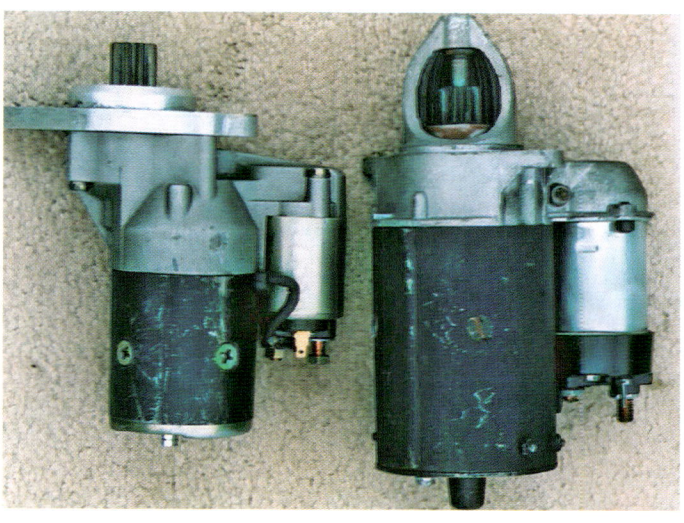

14-3-2 Weber gear reduction starter motor on the left compared to the standard Buick/Oldsmobile aluminium-nosed starter. Buick/Olds also used a cast iron-nosed starter motor which can be identified by its 0.5in (12.5mm) larger diameter.

STARTER MOTORS AND WIRING

High-performance starter motors

In general, the original starter motor for your engine will be the most cost-effective route to actually turning your engine over. However, there could be occasions when the expansion capacity of the engine and/or a high level of engine tune overtaxes the standard starter. You may wish to reduce the weight of the front end of your car and/or reduce the current drawn from the battery by the starter motor.

Whatever your engine, there is almost certainly an aftermarket gear-reduction, small starter-motor upgrade that will solve several of these problems in one go. The design features a small 'gearbox' in the nose of the unit (seen in picture 14-3-1), so that the starter motor drives a small gear encased in the starter housing. In the UK, Cambridge Motorsport will be able to supply you, while in the US a gear reduction starter for the all the engines we are focused on will be available at about £200 ($350) from Tilton Engineering Inc (part number 54-100022). For Buick/Rover engines, the cheaper alternative seen at photograph 14-3-2 is available from Weber via D+D Fabrications. TSI also supplies high-performance starters for Triumph/Rover V8 engines. A standard Range Rover starter from the late 1980s to early 1990s is also a lightweight permanent magnet design that works well.

Battery to starter cable

A bench vice, solder and a small gas torch may work for you, but a first class termination is essential so crimping the starter-motor end termination to any new, necessarily extended cable is perhaps best left to an auto-electrical specialist. You will be able to fit the battery terminal without much difficulty but, in some circumstances, you may find a professional distribution arrangement such as that shown in picture 14-3-5 (overleaf) advantageous. A cost-effective source for the new cable is arc-welding cable. It is very pliable but you need to ensure it is not adversely affected by heat from the exhaust manifold.

Whenever the battery is relocated to the rear of the car, the positive (red) battery cable is best routed inside the car. The junction of the right hand inner sill panel and the floor is ideal, because on almost all later cars there will be a pre-drilled hole on the right side of the bulkhead just below where the main harness exits to the engine compartment. This hole was common to all Wedges but was primarily there for the factory's TR8 battery to starter cable! Thus, you need to find a suitable rubber grommet and run the extended cable through this hole to the starter.

Starter earth

Remember over the next few lines that

SPEEDPRO SERIES

14-3-5 A distribution or connection arrangement such as is shown here may simplify some starter, alternator or general wiring connections. This example incorporates some fuel-injection wiring and the two relays – one is for the fuel pump, the other is the relay for ECM ignition-switched power feeds.

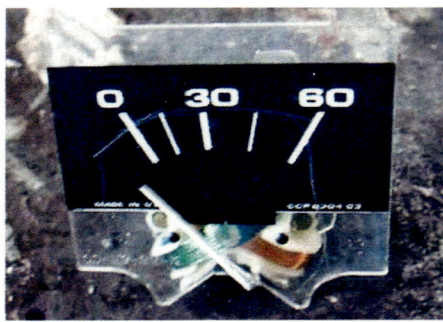

14-4-1-1 This Rover SD1 oil pressure gauge has an upward orientation – you may want to find a downward dial, but either way will likely need to trim a small amount from the face.

14-4-1-2 You can make a completely new mounting bracket in alloy if you prefer, but adjusting the original clock fixing is probably quicker.

you cannot over-earth a car's electrical system. When moving the battery rearwards, you need to ensure there are no subsequent earth problems. The obvious first step is to use a very hefty cable from the earth terminal on the battery to the chassis of the car, and a second one from the engine to the chassis. In both cases a substantial insulated cable may be used but it is probably easier to use a pair of (still substantial) open braided earth-straps.

If you have adopted a boot battery location, you may find a convenient tapped hole in the frame on the right side. It needs to have its face cleaned of all paint, a substantial ring terminal attached to the cable/braid from the battery, and a light smear of petroleum jelly over the mating surfaces to ensure longevity.

The SD1 engine uses the alternator mounting bracket for the engine earth strap, but I think it better to supplement this slightly weak method. Leave the original strap in place by all means, but add a second substantial braided strap from a convenient bell-housing bolt to a cleaned spot-face on the shell or an old coil mounting stud.

INSTRUMENT UPGRADES
General upgrades

Be careful when stripping the instrument cluster for any upgrading work. The plastic becomes brittle with age, and you need to ensure that you have undone all the securing screws before trying to lift the cover. Then undo three more screws and slide out the clear plastic panel. Take off the black plastic cover to reach the speedo and tachometer securing screws (three each), taking particular care not to touch instrument faces with your fingers. If you are intending to fit an integrated oil-pressure gauge, you will need to measure the front/back depth of the clock and its fixing bracket. Remove the clock and its fixing bracket, but retain the bracket.

Oil pressure gauge

Most of the UK specialists will be happy to supply you with a kit to allow you to view the engine oil pressure. Some offer a separate and self-contained instrument, others a short cut to the following 'integrated' solution whereby you replace the Wedge's (usually by now fairly useless) clock with an oil-pressure gauge mounted within the instrument cluster.

To implement the latter and to my mind preferable solution, you will of course need to acquire and fit a suitable gauge – bearing in mind that the wrong shape/size gauge could look quite incongruous. Again, the specialists can help, but a used V8 Rover SD1 oil-pressure gauge shown in picture 14-4-1-1 is cheap, readily available and fits. You will need to reduce the depth of the clock fixing bracket seen in 14-4-1-2 and remake the fixings, so that the oil gauge will eventually 'sit' at the same depth as the clock. You will also need to drill a small hole in the white plastic back of the instrument cluster to allow the instrument's additional wires out of the dash without them showing, as per photograph 14-4-1-3. You may need to open out one of the mounting holes, so that the oil-pressure gauge cannot short to the bracket.

Probably the trickiest part will be fitting a small additional half-blanking plate over half of the hole where the clock came from, without it being obvious. It might be best to epoxy-glue

ELECTRICAL AND INSTRUMENT IMPROVEMENTS

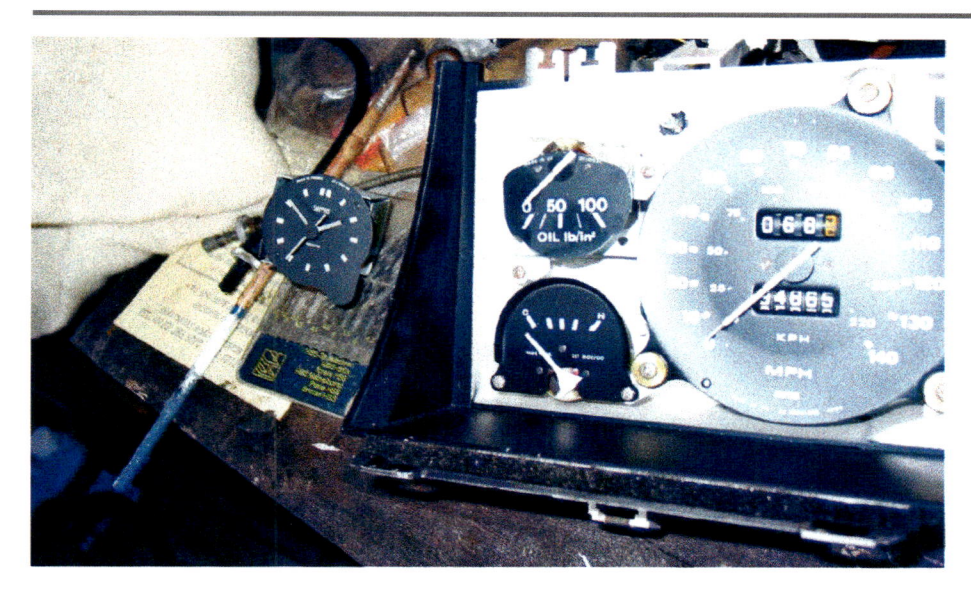

14-4-1-3. You may need to open out one of the mounting holes so that the oil pressure gauge cannot short to the bracket.

this plate (after painting it matt black) to the black instrument finisher. At least you don't need to apply any writing to it!

The gauge has three terminals that, when viewed from the back, need to be connected as follows:

Right terminal to the feed from the sender unit.

Middle or bottom terminal goes to a convenient earth.

Left terminal requires connecting to the white circuit that becomes live when the ignition is on.

You will probably find a white feed under the speaker grill, but there is nothing to stop you taking a new white wire to the fuse box or any other convenient power feed point. However, avoid all white/tracer (e.g. white/black) wires.

The sender unit fitted to the SD1 V8 engines needs to be connected to the system, and the wiring incorporated into your engine bay harness. The SD1 pressure switch comprises three wires connected to the fuel pump by way of a safety interlock, such that when the engine stops the oil-pressure falls, which stops the fuel pump. To incorporate the safety interlock circuit into a TR7 conversion you will need to remove the anti run-on wiring from the sender. The V8 sender has the same appearance as that used on the TR7, but is activated at lower pressures, so the V8 sender is the one to use.

The TR8 arrangement can be seen at D14-3, but if looking at the sender from the terminal end you will notice a space. Moving clockwise from the space, terminal 1 is the common terminal that is connected to the fuel pump. This enables the fuel pump to be powered from one of two sources depending on the state of the oil pressure switch. So, terminal 1 is connected in series with an impact switch, which disables the pump in the event of a frontal impact. Power is supplied as follows:

Via the next clockwise terminal 2, which is only connected to terminal 1 when there is no oil pressure. This terminal is also connected to the red/white wire that energises the starter solenoid, thus providing power to the fuel pump whilst cranking the engine.

Via terminal 3, which is the normal 'run' feed from the white ignition circuit. This connected to terminal 1 only when oil pressure is present.

On the TR8, the oil pressure light is connected between the ignition (white) circuit and the fuel pump feed. If the oil pressure switch is not detecting oil pressure, it will not be supplying power to the pump and the voltage at the pump will be near zero. The 12 volts on one side of the bulb and the near zero on the other will cause the bulb to light. The current needed to illuminate the bulb is not enough to run the pump, so it will remain inactive.

Some early fuel-injected cars have this fuel pump cut-off safety feature incorporated into the AFM via a relay, and thus will likely have only two wires attached to this oil pressure switch

V8 temperature gauges

The temperature gauge in V8 cars is very susceptible to earth restrictions, typically when the headlights are switched on. If

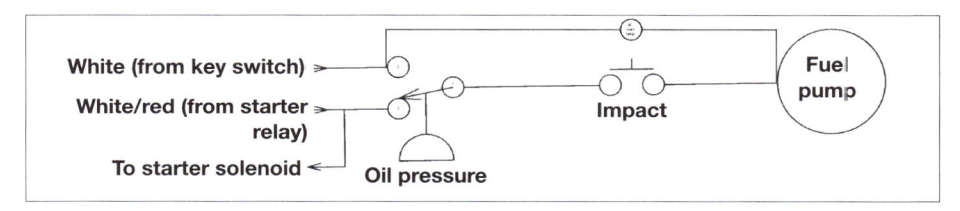

D14-3 Wiring the oil pressure safety switch.

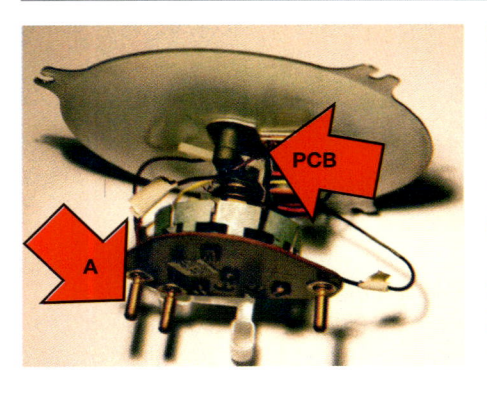

SPEEDPRO SERIES

14-4-2-1 With the needle protected, place the rev counter upside down on your bench and locate the red wire that goes from the pin (arrow A) to the 0.001-microfarad capacitor on the PCB (arrow PCB). The capacitor is ...

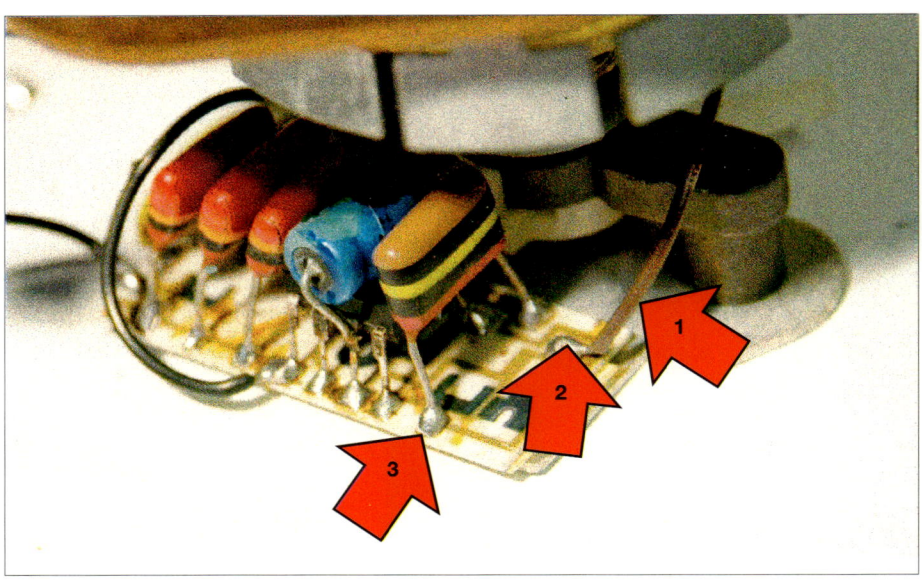

14-4-2-2 ... the first component on the PCB next to the red wire (arrow 1) that comes from pin A. Solder the 47kohm resistor between the point where the red wire is soldered to the PCB (arrow 2) and the outside leg of the 0.001-microfarad capacitor pointed out by arrow 3.

your (V8) car's temperature gauge climbs by two needle widths you will usually resolve the problem by installing an additional earth wire from the gauge to the chassis.

Speedo re-calibration

If you have altered the rear axle ratio or significantly changed the rear tyre size you will need to have the speedometer re-calibrated, either by changing the drive pinion in the gearbox (discussed in chapter 3) or through an instrument repair specialist.

V8 tachometer (RPM counter)

The existing 2-litre TR7 tachometer must be changed or modified to suit the V8 engine, which gives twice as many pulses per revolution as the 4-cylinder unit. There are three solutions:

1) There are some stocks of brand new TR8 tachometers if you can find them. This is a direct replacement and can be quickly identified by the 'red' sector on the dial face covering 5500rpm to the end of the scale at 7000rpm.

2) Purchase an already modified TR7 unit from your supplier on an exchange basis.

3) The cheapest option is to convert your own existing rev counter using a 47kohm, 5 per cent ¼-watt resistor. It will cost you a few pence from Maplin or similar electrical suppliers, and so long as you can use a soldering iron, the alteration is easy. Start by removing the dashboard. Remove the three screws and withdraw the instrument from the spring-loaded terminals where it plugs into the main printed circuit board (PCB). The next two steps are best illustrated, so look to pictures 14-4-2-1 and 14-4-2-2 and follow the captions.

Check your soldered joints carefully and in particular that the new resistor is not shorting to any of the tracks on the PCB. Consult someone with electronics knowledge if you are unsure. It is optional, but you can also glue a piece of red paper to fit between 6500 and 7000rpm on the dial face (as illustrated by 14-4-3) if you wish.

Instrument panel lighting

The illumination of the panel is poor, although four 2.2 watt bulbs are used. However, each sits beneath a green cover intended to spread and 'soften' the illumination. Start by ensuring the green diffusers are clean, but you can gain a slight increase in illumination by removing the green bulb covers completely. They have a bayonet fitting. A further (slight) increase might be possible by adding silver reflective foil to the back of the black mask panel or alternatively 'painting' the back with chrome paint used for finishing plastic model kits. In the USA, the Eastwood Company supplies a special paint (part number 10005Z) for restoring the reflective surface to light housings, etc.

Before reassembling the instrument panel, remove the two large

ELECTRICAL AND INSTRUMENT IMPROVEMENTS

14-4-3 The official 'red line' marking on a V8 tachometer goes here.

connectors from the rear of the panel and carefully retain the fingers in each plug using a small hockey stick metal probe.

ELECTRIC WINDOWS

S+S can provide kits to upgrade both the TR7 and TR8. Both kits fit inside the doors, and thus there are no external boxes to spoil the car's appearance. If you complete this modification before you carry out any re-trimming to the doors, you can fit your new door trims without holes for the window winder, enhancing the internal appearance of the car's trim, too.

The TR7 (and 8) window-winder mechanisms are vulnerable to breakage, and it may be prudent to invest in two new window-winder mechanisms as part of this upgrade. Fitting the kit requires you cut off the end of the mechanism (the piece that pokes through the door trim) and saw a slot in the now stub-end of the drive. Onto this you couple the new electric drive, but since the winder-mechanism is a crucial part of ongoing reliability it is worth starting with the best you can, i.e. new mechanisms.

IMPROVED LIGHTING
Courtesy lights

The TR7 original courtesy light was of French origin and similar to those used by Citroën and Renault in the 1970s. Wedgeparts now stocks a door courtesy lamp that closely matches the appearance of the original (black surround) type, but requires some minor modification of the door trim panel and wiring to fit. There is a slight variation in operation. Original lamps operate as follows – with the lens flush with the door the lamp is off, with the lens tilted up the lamp is switched on, and with the lens tilted down the lamps operate when a door is opened.

Instead of being off in the neutral (flush) position, the new style lamp will light with the lens flush and a door opened. When the doors are closed, the map light function is activated by tilting the lens either up or down. Thus, it is a matter of owner preference as to whether the lamp lights in the up or down (but not both) directions depending upon installation.

To fit the new lamp it will be necessary to widen the aperture in the original trim panel by approximately 1mm on either side. This is easily accomplished with a sharp knife. Electrically it will be necessary to replace the locking black spade connectors on the door harness with insulated spade connectors.

A visit to a Citroën breakers yard may yield an AX's light(s). The edges of the Citroën lens are sharper than a TR7 or TR8 lens making the Citroën's appear larger, but otherwise the fitting and working arrangements will be very similar to Wedgeparts' solution. On the other hand, the Renault interior lamp is reported as fitting exactly. The colour is dark grey and the electrical connections slightly different, being 3 spade terminals. If neither of these are available, try (in the UK) Marina/Ital lights.

Direction light audible warning

The flasher unit is usually hard to hear in a roadster. Most auto parts stores can provide a 'loud' flasher unit, but I solved the problem using a couple of cheap (computer) buzzers wired into the flashing/direction light circuit. The units cost £1.50 each from Radio Spares, but Maplins or any similar store will have suitable 3-18 volt units. RS part numbers were 231-2793 or 295-9386 although any similar specification alternatives will get your attention. You need two, one each for the left and right signals, and they need to be connected after the direction switch on the steering column. They will operate simultaneously with warning lights on the dashboard.

The original equipment flasher unit has been found to be unreliable, having a varying flash rate, and a replacement two-wire electronic unit from an auto parts store should be considered.

Extra direction flashers

On US cars, amber sidelights were fitted to the ends of the front bumper. These operate when park and headlights are in use but do not flash with the direction signals. These sidelights may be retrofitted to UK cars in place of the current black blanking piece, and although they are probably too low to meet current safety standards, they can be made to flash by virtue of a direct connection to the direction flasher wiring.

For US vehicles, the parking light function can be retained and the flashing function added by disconnecting the black ground wire on the amber sidelight, and connecting the now empty terminal to the direction lead circuit on each side of the car.

Chapter 15
Engine transplant projects

I felt that exposure to the difficulties experienced and solutions employed by various Wedge enthusiasts during their V8 conversions would be helpful to those contemplating a similar project. Since you can choose what level of complexity you are prepared to undertake within your V8 conversion, I also felt it would helpful if I took this opportunity to explore both ends of the spectrum. I am very grateful indeed for the time, information and photographs generously provided by Steve Redway on his simple, easy UK-based project, and Jay Foster on his complex mechanical and electrical transformation carried out in the USA.

STEVE REDWAY'S ROVER V8 CONVERSION

The conversion of my sound but performance-lacking late TR7 FHC was quite complex, somewhat more expensive and certainly more time consuming than expected. However, shoehorning a Rover V8 lump into the car proved to be the conclusive 'mod' to get a real TR under your right foot. Some may decry the non-originality of the car, some think other engines are better but for sheer ease, value for money, popularity and spine-tingling sounds, the Rover 3.5-litre V8 is the unit to go for.

I carried out my modification in two phases, starting with upgrading the brakes and suspension using proprietary kits. The work was worthwhile in both respects and I'm pleased to report little by way of excitement or difficulty.

If you are keen to keep the conversion a low-cost project you will first need a donor car. Either a 3500cc Rover P6 or the SD1 pictured at 15-1-1 is ideal, and the cheapest way of getting the motor, the bell-housing (if it's one of the rarer manual versions), 3.08 ratio back axle, brakes, plus other goodies you may need. Don't forget that if you want to save money in the long run, wait

15-1-1 The Rover SD1 donor. You could use a Range Rover or V8 Land Rover (but both donate low compression V8 engines with some other oddities as well), or any of the other cars fitted with this popular engine.

for a manual version to become available because this will bring the flywheel, clutch mechanism and, of course, the manual gearbox that the majority of TR enthusiasts prefer. Engines are available from other sources, such as breakers' yards, Rover, Land Rover and TR spares companies, but these options rarely allow you to see and hear the motor running. Furthermore, purchased

ENGINE TRANSPLANT PROJECTS

individually the parts will be more expensive, although you will not have the problem of disposing of an empty and unwanted SD1 shell.

The engine on my donor SD1 was reasonably quiet. The oil pressure was about 35psi at 3000rpm when hot, and there didn't seem to be any excess smoke from the exhaust. A compression check revealed 145 to 180psi per cylinder, which is satisfactory. The next step was to get the engine and gearbox to part company from the car, and although the task is fairly straightforward, it does require a substantial hoist. To speed things up I decided not to bother about the niceties of stripping the SD1, and using the angle grinder I hacked into all the engine, gearbox and exhaust connections that weren't required. This allowed me to get the engine and gearbox out in about five hours and into the dry of the garage (pictured at 15-1-2) to examine and clean it.

My intention basically was to drop the engine and gearbox straight into the TR7 as is – no engine rebuilds for me. However, I separated engine and gearbox and decided it was necessary to fit a new SD1 clutch, a replacement ring gear to the flywheel and new dog assembly to the starter. Incidentally, the ring gear was quite an expensive item and not all that easy to fit, because it has to be chiselled off and the new one heated to around 170°C before dropping back onto the flywheel. It is the contraction of the cooling ring gear that fixes it permanently to the flywheel. The starter rebuild necessitated a call to the local friendly Lucas agent to get a repair manual, which saved the day at no charge either, and I was able to reassemble the repaired starter. I elected not to re-marry the gearbox to its engine, so finished off this stage of the conversion with liberal use of Smoothrite paint, which made the V8 unit look much more presentable.

The back axle needed to come out of the Rover SD1 in order to donate its 3.08 gear ratio. If you fail to effect this change you'll end up with a useless first gear, high revving cruising speed and the quickest 0-60 time on the block! The job proved more difficult than I originally thought and really needed some specialist tools. Firstly (under the very well supported Rover shell) the propshaft, rear axle extension housing and brake drums have to be removed. Not too difficult, were it not for the petrol tank getting in the way. With the help of a large persuader, the half shafts were released from the internals of the back axle by belting them out!

I drained the axle of oil, removed the backplate from the rear casing, and un-bolted and carefully removed the crown wheel assembly. There was talk in the manuals of needing a special Churchill tool for spreading the casing. Luckily I didn't, but removing the pinion was very difficult, as I just did not have a spanner big enough to undo the pinion nut (1.25in x 20 UNF). Rover recommends another, no doubt expensive, special Churchill tool that locks the pinion at the same time as allowing you to undo the pinion nut. I must have phoned around every Rover agent in the south west of England in an attempt to scrounge one, to be told that they either didn't have one, had mislaid it or never touched SD1 back axles. Ultimately and fortunately a friend of a friend came to my rescue with a tool specially made for the job – a very stout elongated box spanner to which we attached a set of Stilsons and a 4 foot length of scaffold tube. With a chisel rammed down under the pinion to lock it – shock horror – we just managed to shift the pinion nut, allowing us to drive the pinion out through the rear axle casing with another large persuader.

So the rear 3.08 ratio axle parts pictured at 15-1-3-1 and 15-1-3-2 were

15-1-2 The 3500cc Rover engine, home and dry.

15-1-3-1 The Rover pinion half of the essential 3.08 crown wheel and pinion was ...

15-1-3-2 ... ready to be transferred into the TR7 axle casing, but although the job is probably best entrusted to a specialist to get the pinion-bearing pre-load correct, the cheapest quote was £100.

183

SPEEDPRO SERIES

15-1-4 Removing the TR7 engine and gearbox in one piece requires you first remove the fan and ...

15-1-5 ... bring the assembly out at a very steep angle.

15-1-6 This is my SD1-based ventilated disc upgrade fitted several months before the engine transplant was started.

15-1-7 To counteract torsional V8 engine movement, I initially tried not fitting any spacers, thinking that the TR8 sub-frame dimensions would locate the engine correctly. I reverted to these ½in spacers quite quickly!

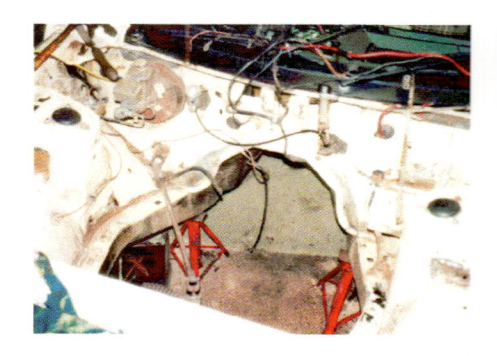

15-1-8 The ideal repair panels were (then) hard to find, so I used stiff card to reproduce the shape of the holes left after the rusty metal had been cut away. I transferred these shapes onto metal and chopped them out with small tin snips.

ready to be transferred into the TR7 axle casing, but I decided to leave the axle ratio change until I had got the car running with its V8 engine. With all the parts out of the SD1, the forlorn shell was towed away to the breakers and it was time to separate the original 4-cylinder engine from the TR7.

The engine and gearbox combination require the fan assembly be first removed. You can see this in progress in photo 15-1-4. The steep exit angle (about 45-degrees as seen in picture 15-1-5) necessitated lots of headroom even with the back of the car jacked up, but the job was completed without much drama worth recording here!

Now came the time to select the supplier for all the parts on my long shopping list. I knew I needed a V8 radiator, engine sub-frame, propshaft, exhaust etc., and had been looking around for quite some time. I chose the company that was able to supply the most parts off the shelf and offered the best value. I had previously used it for brake (picture 15-1-6) and suspension parts and found its service good and their prices 'negotiable' as well. Accordingly the parts were ordered and swiftly appeared in my garage. However, there was a vast range of options and the actual ordering put me in the middle of a minefield of choices! I decided on a single pipe large bore exhaust system fed from a pair of four branch manifolds, which features the delight of a colossal 3in exit pipe. An original TR8 engine sub-frame and propshaft should guarantee a sound foundation for the project with, I thought, the bare minimum of spacers to get the engine to clear the bonnet.

I had been looking at a number of TR7-V8s and had yet to find two fitted with identical thickness spacers. My belief was that the original TR8s fitted with Stromberg carbs needed no spacers at all with the engine sub-frame mounting directly onto the chassis rails. Thus using a proper TR8 sub-frame should only require the ½in spacers you see in photo 15-1-7 to give the necessary clearance for the slightly taller SU carbs. I had seen cars with 1in spacers fitted, which I thought must be due to the odd dimensions on some modified TR7 sub-frames.

Whilst the TR7's engine bay was empty I spent time cleaning and inspecting it. No one familiar with a TR7 will be surprised that there was some rust I needed to repair, on view in photo 15-1-8. Welding the new metal in the engine compartment presented no unforeseen difficulties, with it soon becoming clear that the time spent

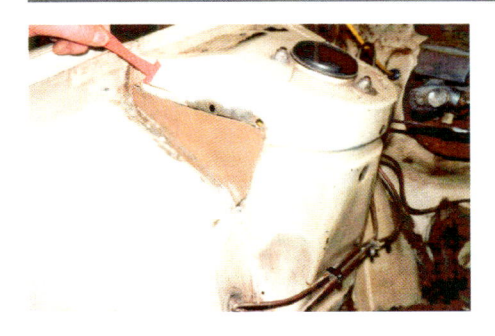

ENGINE TRANSPLANT PROJECTS

15-1-9 A little angle grinding and filler followed and the repair ...

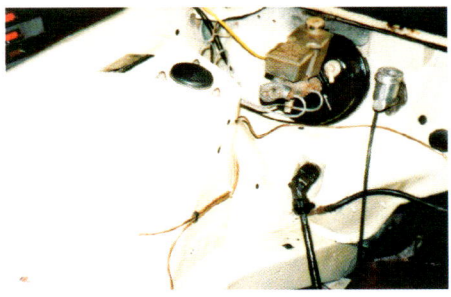

15-1-10 ... was almost invisible.

15-1-11 The manual TR7 rack was re-used and fitted at the second attempt.

15-1-12-1 With the entire engine, gearbox, exhaust system, propshaft and hoses as one assembly, I had to pull the whole lot forward by about an inch, remounting the engine on the forward face of the sub-frame mounts to achieve this manifold fit.

cutting out and flush fitting the patches (seen in 15-1-9) for the suspension turrets was time well spent. After a rub down the whole engine compartment was primed and painted (pic 15-1-10). I filled the seams at the rear of the inner wings with expandable foam (messy business) and covered the result with silicone seam sealant.

I started re-assembly with the new sub-frame. It soon became clear that I should have dismantled the steering rack to enable it to pass through the engine mountings. This was duly done (15-1-11) by just unbolting the steering arms from the stub axles.

Dropping the V8 lump in took a friend and I about 6 hours. The garage was very cramped, which made the job more difficult and extended the time somewhat. First I lowered the gearbox roughly into position and held it up with ropes. The V8 was then lifted as high as our hoist would go and the TR pushed forward under the suspended engine. It soon became apparent that to get under the front apron the engine would have to be lowered into the engine bay at an angle, not level as we thought initially. We raised the lump back to maximum height of hoist, pushed the TR back out of the way, lowered the lump to ground, repositioned the lifting ropes, lifted the engine, pushed the (now grubby) TR back into position and lowered the lump

a second time. Wrong angle – think again!

We tried lifting the rear of the TR to an amazing angle but that was no good, as the engine would still not clear the TR's front apron.

We repeated the whole process a fourth time – this time with the back of engine higher than the front. Success – the lump started to slip into the engine bay, albeit with the sound of rendering metal. I straightened the wiper mounting bracket, but you now have a very good idea why we took so long! Eventually we mated the engine onto the rear of the engine sub-frame mounts as per the TR8, fitted the rear gearbox support after drilling new holes in the floor pan, and bolted the new propshaft in place. Pretty straight forward eh?

The Kenlow electric fan went in ahead of the new radiator and new radiator supports. It's worth mentioning here that the captive nuts are already in the chassis legs for the bottom mount. My top hose came from the SD1 donor car, but the lower one was too short. The TR8 bottom hose supplied with my conversion kit was long enough but seemed far too large for the radiator's 1 3/8in diameter bottom hose outlet. The supplier had said to clamp it up real tight but this did not seem to work too well, so I reverted to lengthening the old SD1 hose with an internal sleeve.

The exhaust system was the single most expensive item in the kit, and proved to be the most difficult part to fit. I found it necessary to hack bits off it to get it to line up. I have since heard that this was the norm for a TR8 exhaust system, though whether they are better now I am unsure. The main problem was that with the manifolds fitted, they fouled both the chassis rail and the steering shaft on the driver's side. It was clear that no amount of gentle persuasion would get them to clear so I supported the engine on a trolley jack and moved the whole engine and gearbox assembly forwards. The result can me seen in pictures 15-1-12-1 and 15-1-12-2.

I fitted the high output Facet (pic

185

SPEEDPRO SERIES

15-1-12-2 The forward location now gave sufficient exhaust manifold/header clearance, but necessitated re-drilling the floor pan to accommodate the latest position for the gearbox cross-member!

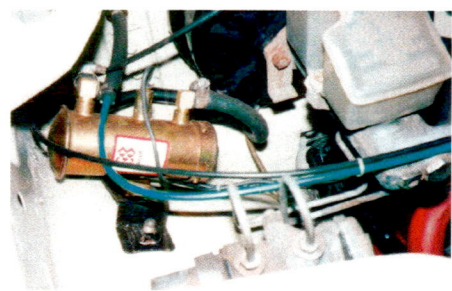

15-1-13 Usually fitted vertically, this is the Facet 'Silver Top' fuel pump.

15-1-14 The SD1 ballast resistor is mounted behind the coil. Note the adjustable thermostat control for the electric fan.

15-1-13) fuel pump and plumbed it in, added a new shortened gearstick, bodged the SD1's accelerator cable and installed a new longer choke cable. The major outstanding task was making up the new engine-bay wiring loom. Basically, what I had to do was extend the original coil wiring over to the SD1 ballast resistor and coil seen in photo 15-1-14, on the opposite side of the engine bay. I needed to provide a 12-volt supply for the fuel pump and fan, extend the main battery feed to the alternator and starter (they are now on the opposite side on the engine bay too), plus link in the various engine sensors (temperature, oil, low water).

Using the original SD1 engine loom and socket, I manufactured a new loom covered in oil-resistant heat shrink sleeving. It goes across the TR7 engine bay via the front apron and is held in place with plastic P-clips that make it look quite a neat job. Potentially, this loom can look like a rat's nest and to my mind spoils many a conversion, so time spent here is well worth the good end result. The starter solenoid power and fuel pump power comes via the oil pressure switch for safety, and a new battery lead was manufactured from 16mm multi-strand ultra flexible arc welding cable, then duly installed by securing it across the sub-frame to the alternator connections.

Modification of the rev counter was next up and required the dash be taken apart. I removed the instrument cluster and separated the rev counter/tacho to reveal the printed circuit board on the back of the tacho, to which I added a 47kohm resistor to halve the ignition pulses read by the instrument.

With power on, everything seemed to test satisfactorily, so I connected the coil, pulled the choke out fully, open the garage door and turned the key. The engine cranked enthusiastically but other than that ... absolutely nothing.

I checked that all the leads were on the correct spark plugs and pulled a couple of plugs out for inspection. Bit odd – one side of the V had dry plugs and the other wet ones. I checked the fuel feed to the two SUs which seemed to be OK, so I started to look at the timing. The distributor had been off the engine for checking (and its safety) when re-installing the engine, but I had been ultra careful to set her back on top, dead centre – hadn't I?

With the cap off the distributor and the engine cranking, it dawned on me that the crank goes round twice for one turn on the rotor, so there is a false TDC. Sure enough, by removing the oil filler cap I was able to see via the two rockers when piston 1 reached TDC, that the crank pulley showed TDC ... but that the rotor arm was 180 degrees out! Five minutes later the fan belt screamed, burning paint smells wafted in the air and water oozed from all the hoses as pressures built up – but the engine was running, the rev counter worked and the clutch operated too. A result!

The car was dropped off her axle stands for the first time in a couple of months and the bonnet offered up. I had to change to longer sub-frame spacers and bolts to create some more bonnet/SU clearance, whereupon the bonnet closed OK. The car performed faultlessly, even though with the standard TR7 back axle still in place, first gear was useless and cruising at 4000 revs in 5th gear only gave 90mph – but she made the most spine chilling

ENGINE TRANSPLANT PROJECTS

noises, even while travelling relatively slowly in traffic!

I changed the needles in the SUs to BAFs, which produced a remarkable increase in power with acceleration now limited by the speed at which I could change gear and the traction of the tyres. The rev counter really became a bit of a blur. Changing the engine oil increased the oil pressure dramatically, especially after flushing the engine with diesel/oil 50/50. However, the funny thing was that the exhaust note became more muted – she became a bit like a big cat purring on a full belly.

Resisting the temptation to play further with my new toy, a couple of days later I reversed her into the garage and lifted the back end to change the back axle ratio. Removing the TR7's axle is a straightforward job, but is made much easier with the help of a mate as the complete assembly is quite heavy. It also helps to spray all the exposed threads with WD40 the night before. After draining the axle we removed the crown wheel and pinion oil seal and exposed the dreaded 1.25in 20UNF pinion nut. However, using the custom pinion box spanner, the Stilsons and scaffold pole did their work and this time we had the pinion nut off in a flash! A couple of taps with a soft faced hammer and the original TR7 pinion was out too.

I had read and re-read the Rover manual, which had not shied away from describing an axle rebuild. It bases its instructions on mathematical calculations of shimming needed for the pinion and crown wheel, after measurements made with the aid of a dummy pinion, part number something or other – which needless to say wasn't the nearest tool to hand in my little toolbox! Not only that but I seemed to have only a very small selection of shims. I'd had to leave the (collapsible) pinion spacer on the 3.08 Rover pinion in place, because I couldn't drift the bearing off to get to it. Thus Rover's precision method became impractical before I even started! I was forced to improvise, basing the rebuild on three parameters:

- Backlash of the crown wheel measured with a dial gauge.
- Meshing of the pinion/crown wheel teeth as observed with engineers-blue.
- Pre-load, which is the turning torque of the pinion measured by turning the large pinion nut with our invaluable box spanner.

I calculated that the torque to tighten the pinion nut and to collapse the new 'once only' spacer would necessitate a hefty chisel to keep the pinion from turning. Yes, I know it sounds agricultural but I could not find a better way of doing the job without the correct factory tool. I practised re-assembly using the old collapsible spacer to get the feel for it collapsing and to see the teeth profile on the crown wheel (in engineers blue,) before putting a new spacer in and doing it for real. The outcome was about 15in/lb of pre-load, 0.006in of backlash (both within the upper limits) but a somewhat ill-defined blue tooth profile. So I re-assembled the axle back into the car, whacked some SAE90 into her and bled the brakes.

In fact it was not quite that simple because, judging from what I saw, it is well worth inspecting the brake lines, unions and flexibles very closely at this point. The lines were very difficult to remove from the wheel cylinders and impossible without the correct metric spanner for the brake unions. I also found it worthwhile checking and freeing the hand brake linkages and operating levers (common TR7 MOT failure points).

My fuel economy was transformed, no doubt assisted by the 26.5mph per 1000rpm, and cruising became much more refined. First gear found its purpose in life, and although acceleration is not as quick as with the 3.9 TR7 rear ratio, it is certainly more controllable. The back axle seems OK and there are no clonks. Perhaps just a little whine on over-run which I put down to the fact that I was unable to define the meshing pattern using engineers blue. Anyway, I didn't have any more different thickness spacers to use so couldn't get it any better even if I'd wanted to. For the time being, I'll live with it.

The exhaust noise with the single large bore system is not unduly excessive, but whilst talking about the exhaust system here's a couple of warnings. As I mentioned previously, I had to hack the system around a bit to get it to fit, but what I forgot to tell you was that it was difficult but important to find a fixing kit suited to a TR8. As a consequence, once the exhaust system was properly installed I had to swap (left to right) both fog light brackets in order to move the left-side light away from the silencer outlet.

For a long time I couldn't get the low water light to go out. It is interesting how this part of the electrical system works and worth explaining in a little more detail. A stainless steel probe is fitted into the side of the expansion tank that detects the presence of water as a resistance, electrically, to earth. It feeds this resistance signal to an electronics indicator unit, which in normal operation keeps the light out. When the water level falls in the expansion tank to clear the probe, the probe goes very high resistance and the electronic indicator unit detecting this turns the low water light on. What is interesting, however, is how the water path gets to earth to complete the initial part of the circuit. On my TR7 the header tank is brass but insulated from the bodywork on the

SPEEDPRO SERIES

vehicle by rubber, so no contact to earth there. The pipes connecting expansion tank to the radiator are the same, rubber and insulated so no contact to earth there either. The radiator is the same as well, mounted on rubber supports top and bottom. Therefore, the first earth point that the water meets is in the engine itself, which is fitted with a substantial earth strap to the chassis.

It was apparent that with a full complement of water and the low level light still on that there must be an airlock in the system, but try as I might I could not prove it or clear it. So taking the easy way out, I did what a number of earlier header tanks feature and fitted an earth wire to it and grounded it. Light out, everyone happy

A final but important summary of how many hours of toil were needed might be helpful – and yes, I realise at this speed I'd never get a job in a garage:

Rover engine out – 7 hours.
Rover rear axle internal out – 6 hours.
TR7 engine out – 6 hours.
Strip TR7 engine compartment and remove sub-frame – 10 hours.
Work to SD1 – 26 hours.
TR7 engine compartment repairs – 2 hours.
Fit sub-frame, install V8 engine, exhaust, rewire, cooling system fitted and run up – 68 hours.
Strip and rebuild TR7 back axle – 20 hours.
Total – 145 hours ... but worth every minute!

JAY FOSTER'S FORD 3800cc PROJECT

The vast majority of TR7-V8 conversions use a Buick or Rover engine, for good reason. I thought it would be interesting to explore at least one alternative of the many that are available, and the 3800cc Ford V6 looked like a good choice. The 3.8-litre Ford was an entirely new design, with a 90 degree V configuration providing 180bhp at 5000rpm and 215lb/ft torque at 2700rpm. The only similarity with the Ford 302 is that the distributor is on the front of the engine, although in 1995 Ford introduced a coil pack ignition system, which eliminated the distributor alltogether. The Thunderbird and Cougar both have low slopping bonnets, so Ford had to keep its engine design low making it ideal for a TR7 conversion. Jay Foster thought so too, and found a 1990 Ford 3.8 with SEFI and fitted with an EEC-IV engine control system that would be ideal to transform his TR7. He takes up the story of his project:

My initial TR7 conversion started with a 1978 Buick 3.8-litre V6, with a three speed automatic transmission and a 1984 Ford Mustang 7.5in axle, incorporating a limited slip differential and a 3.08:1 ratio. The Mustang differential was stripped of its mounting arrangement and the original TR7 arms and brackets were re-used. I took care to maintain the driveline angle and wheel camber correctly. There was no need to reduce the width of the Mustang axle, since it's only two inches wider than the TR7 and the difference could be corrected with offset wheel rims.

Initially, I retained Triumph's four link rear suspension system. However, I subsequently discovered that mounting the suspension links at TR7 height on the chassis provided very little leverage to hold down the back of the car under hard braking. The Triumph design causes severe brake dive, which is a consequence of the TR7's overall suspension design. In my view it required more than spacers under the front anti-roll bar to resolve the problem. Using some fairly inexpensive software from Performance Trends Inc. (www.performancetrends.com), I analysed

15-2-1 This rear suspension setup, including the base mounting plate, was removed from an Isuzu Impulse with a Lotus tuned suspension. The mounting plate is only bolted onto the Isuzu's trailing arm and is easily welded to the TR7.

the suspension geometry and came up with several advantageous changes, which necessitated a smaller fuel tank to make room for the new suspension components. Picture 15-2-1 shows the different rear spring that I used.

The suspension geometry investigation brought me to re-think my front suspension design, and indeed the power-plant. I now felt the 3.8-litre V6 from a rear-wheel drive Ford (15-2-2) a better bet. I found a 1990 unit already fitted with early 1990's Ford engine management electronics.

The Ford's low-profile intake manifold (later versions have variable rate port intake), cost, aluminium heads, header type, cast exhaust manifold and 298lb weight combine to make it a good choice. The engine is not only well built, but designed for performance. It has a double roller timing chain, roller

ENGINE TRANSPLANT PROJECTS

15-2-2 My Ford rear-wheel drive V6 seen on my garage floor. A mass air flow (MAF) system was my ideal, but one wasn't available. I considered retro-fitting carburettor induction to simplify the electrical installation and to avoid the need for an EFI fuel tank, but ultimately stayed with the Ford engine management system, and am very pleased with the end result.

15-2-3 The Wilwood clutch slave cylinder and my mounting bracket. The first two units had the push-rod fall out of the piston, resulting in a loss of clutch. On the third unit I stripped and reassembled it using epoxy resin glue that would stand up to hydraulic fluid.

15-2-4-1 The catalytic converters and exhaust crossover. The usual location for the converters is right after the exhaust manifold where the exhaust temperature is hottest. However, with my setup there was insufficient room here for converters and heat shields, so I needed to establish just how far back they could go without becoming ineffective.

15-2-4-2 The exhaust systems are the same configuration as used on the Mustang, so I used Mustang rubber mounts the rest of the way back.

rockers, high volume oil pump and domed 9.5 to 1 pistons as standard. The only weak points on these engines are the head gaskets. Ford used the cheapest ones it could find, which subsequently necessitated a recall programme. Consequently, if you plan to use a similar, used engine it would be wise to replace the head gaskets before installing it.

The transmission I used is a 1995 Borg Warner 5 speed manual with an 11.5in clutch. The gearstick comes up through the opening in the transmission tunnel towards the front of the hole, but is not a problem since there is a bend in the stick that places the gear knob in just the right place for most drivers.

Ford uses a cable system to operate the clutch that required I change the release mechanism to hydraulic components. I used a new Wilwood ¾in bore master cylinder in conjunction with the original pedal. The Wilwood slave cylinder required I fabricate the mounting bracket (seen in picture 15-2-3) that fastened to the front of the bell-housing. The slave cylinder was initially nothing but trouble, and can be seen leaking (again) in picture 15-2-3. I have cured the problem, but were I doing another conversion I would likely use a shaft mounted hydraulic throw-out bearing from Quartermaster or Mcleod Industries.

The original brake pedal was also retained, but the gas pedal had to be replaced. In any event the original TR7 carburettor was never completely open at full throttle due, in my view, to insufficient pedal travel. I also found the pedal too small and welcomed the need to weld in its place an accelerator pedal from a second generation Mazda RX7.

The exhaust as seen in picture 15-2-4-1 has a dual H-pipe crossover, twin catalytic converters and, shown in 15-2-4-2, free flow mufflers. Getting information from the manufacturers on the location of the converters so that they would get hot enough was difficult. I found some vehicles had the converter up to six feet from the exhaust manifold, and consequently mine ended up where the original mufflers sit. Picture 15-2-5 (overleaf) shows my exhaust support arrangements.

Replacement of the entire front suspension and sub-frame may be controversial but ranks amongst the best performance improvements I

SPEEDPRO SERIES

15-2-5 Two rods coming down from the transmission mount that support the exhaust.

15-2-6-1 Had Triumph designed a rear mounted anti-roll bar like this it would have reduced twisting and shaking of the body.

made. Triumph should have located the anti-roll bar to the rear of the front axle like that shown in picture 15-2-6-1, where the structure is more substantial. I did not specifically target Ford as a donor for the sub-frame and front suspension, but looked at all makes of rear-wheel drive cars for the best fit. The 1989 Ford Merkur XR4Ti proved not only to offer the best fit, but fast ratio power steering, 10in vented disc brakes and, as seen in 15-2-6-2, a rear mounted sway bar. The power steering system on some Ford models uses a speed sensitive system that gives a solid feel at cruising speeds. This is a stand-alone system that can be coupled to most of

Ford's power steering pumps (to limit the line pressure above 40mph), and the ECU module can be mounted under the dash and wired into the speed sensor circuit.

In Europe the Merkur is known as the Sierra and in the UK as the XR4i. The Ford Scorpio from the same years uses a common sub-frame but has 5 stud hubs with ABS speed sensors. It is also possible that the front track width might be wider than the Merkur. The XR4i's track width measured from the faces of the hubs is the same as the Mustang axle, which was ideal as it allowed me to use four identically offset wheels. The Merkur's sub-frame even allowed me to re-use the TR7 rear bolt holes, although I did have to form a pair of additional holes a few inches in front of them as seen in picture 15-2-7. Holes were also required in chassis rails to accommodate the front bolts.

The Ford sub-frame was made to mount to a flat length of chassis, but the TR7 frame is actually curved in just the wrong place! Consequently, I welded compensating spacers to the top of the Ford sub-frame. These can be seen in photo 15-2-8. Furthermore, the Merkur's sub-frame had no triangulation so I also welded a pair of braces to replicate the TR7's K-frame. Pictures 15-2-9-1 and 15-2-9-2 show the additional members that bolt to the original holes in the chassis.

I used a pair of front suspension struts from a 1989 Ford Escort instead of those from the Merkur, because they reduced the ride height and had a top anti-friction bearing to improve the steering. The springs still needed to be cut down about one turn in my case.

The Merkur hubs pictured at 15-2-10 required machining to allow them to marry with the Escort struts. This machining causes a slight steering axis inclination (SAI) error, also referred to

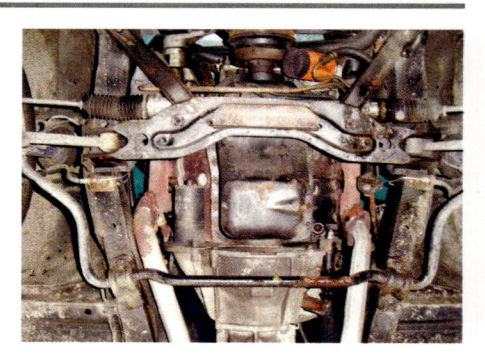

15-2-6-2 This provides an interesting view not only of the rear mounted anti-roll bar, but also the inboard end of the front suspension – not to mention the front end of the exhaust system.

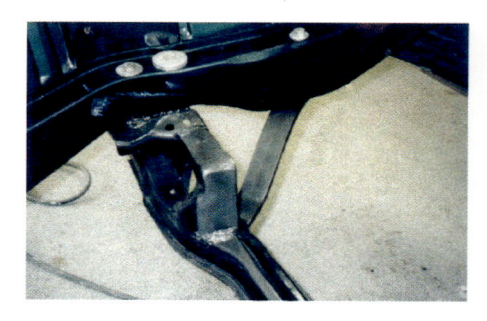

15-2-7 All four additional chassis holes for the Ford cross-member needed to be large enough to weld a spacer tube into the rails, in order to provide the bolt with something to tighten down onto without crushing that area of the chassis rail.

15-2-8 The arrow indicates one of the spacers I needed to weld to the Ford cross-member to allow it to bolt securely to the TR7's frame.

ENGINE TRANSPLANT PROJECTS

15-2-9-1 The angled braces to re-form the TR7's K-frame. Subsequently I realised that these would have been better welded to the underside of the frame in order to make the power steering rack easier to remove.

as king pin inclination on older cars with king pins instead of ball joints. The error is about ½in high and 1in to the outside. SAI is the measurement in degrees of the steering pivot line when viewed from the front of the vehicle, and is shown in drawing D15-1. This angle, when added to the camber to form an included angle shown in drawing D15-2, causes the vehicle to lift slightly when you turn the wheel away from a straight position and makes the steering wheel caster-return to the centre when released. My SAI was actually better than in some cars coming off the production line, so it was not essential I changed it, although in theory some loss of handling might occur.

The caster angle was improved over the standard TR7 front end by using the Ford sub-frame. Even so, I felt an adjustable camber facility might be a good idea, and cut and re-drilled the tops of my strut towers. The SAI errors cannot be fully corrected by an adjustable camber but I saw fine-tuning to be a big advantage.

I recognised that the chassis mountings for the anti-roll bar, seen in close up at 15-2-11, were critical. They clearly needed substantial reinforcement, but it was their location

15-2-9-2 For insurance, I also welded a skid plate to the bottom of the frame.

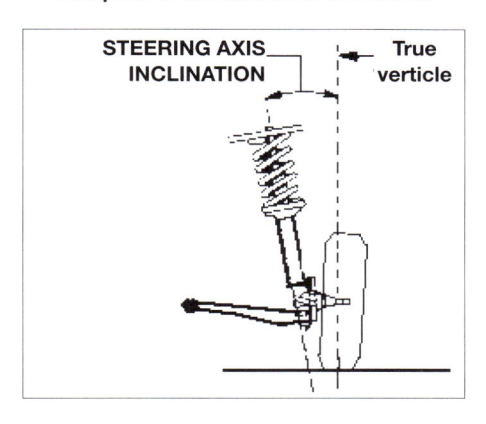

D15-1 Steering axis or, in earlier cars, king pin inclination angle.

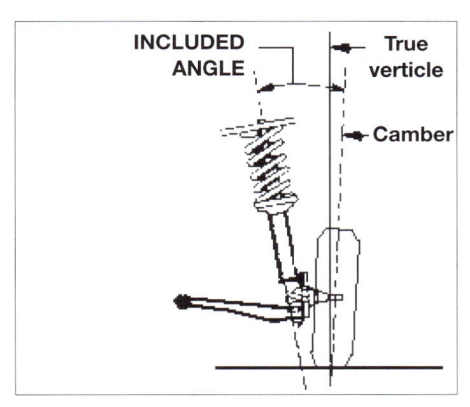

D15-2 SAI and camber included angle.

that caused me the most concern as an error of ⅛in forward or backwards could affect the steering and handling.

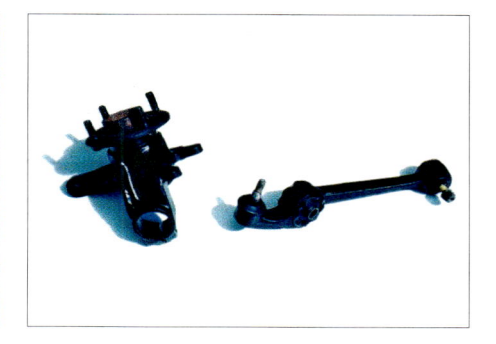

15-2-10 The Ford Merkur control arm and hub assembly. The hole in the hub required enlarging and the angle of the hole also had to be increased to correct the camber angle, since the tops of the struts were closer together than on the Merkur. These hubs are unique in that Ford modified them from front-wheel drive hubs. They are consequently stronger than most since they no longer have to carry the torsional loads of a drive shaft.

15-2-11 The anti-roll bar brackets from the Escort worked best, although it was the Merkur roll bar that I used which is seen here.

It is widely recognised that the TR7's brake system is in need of improvement. Not only were my front brakes too small for any type of driving, but Triumph's three-way system is dangerous in the event of a line failure. The Ford Escort brake booster, master cylinder, and pressure regulator pictured at 15-2-12 come in one nice package

SPEEDPRO SERIES

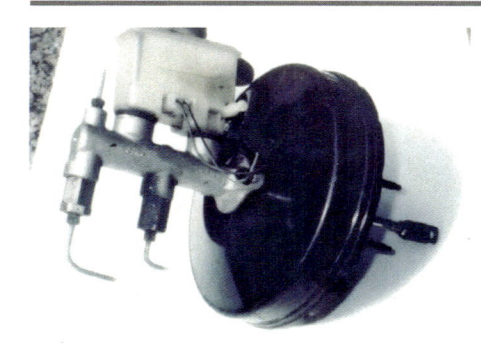

15-2-12 A quad diagonal (4-way) system was the minimal requirement for any car produced at the time, and I found this 1992 Ford Escort (Mazda) brake system that has subsequently worked very well indeed.

15-2-13 The fuel-line routing. Note three lines were required for the engine management system – fuel supply, fuel return and fuel vapour.

15-2-14 Here we see the bottom of the Ford Escort's fuel tank and the large metal canister fuel filter required by EFI systems. Note the handbrake cables in the bottom left of this shot.

and eliminate the need for the TR7's regulator. I also decided to run a line to each wheel in order to obviate a line running across the rear axle. With this system I was confident, in the event of a failure, there will be at least one front wheel and one diagonally opposite rear wheel still working. The Merkur's 10in (254mm) diameter vented front discs had a hefty single cylinder calliper and 9in (230mm) rear drums that I felt would stop the car in all conditions without brake fade, as indeed has been the case.

None of the TR7 and TR8 stock gas tanks were suited to modern fuel-injection. There was no baffling within the tanks to prevent fuel starvation to the pump, which could cause engine sputter and a dangerous loss of power. Consequently, I sought a modern tank, and found a 12-gallon one in a 1987 Ford Escort wagon. It only required its flanges bending down at the front and back of the tank to allow it to fit the TR7. I did need to cut an access hole in the rear deck to get to the internal fuel pump, over which I fitted a removable cover plate.

I fitted my TR7's battery in the boot, and took the opportunity to fit a stock Ford fuel inertia cut-off switch to the body, along with a relay and fuse. I removed all the fuel supply tubing and new fuel supply, return, and vapour lines were installed, as can be seen in picture 15-2-13. Since there was more room under the fuel tank than before, I installed the fuel filter (pictured at 15-2-14) there rather than under the bonnet. The fuel filler inlet required some modifications which can be seen at 15-2-15.

The radiator I used was a re-cored 1990 Chrysler product, chosen because the stock dimensions fit perfectly between the TR7 frame members, as you can confirm via

15-2-15 With the cover removed, the modifications necessary to marry the Ford tank inlet pipe (bottom) to the TR7 (top) are revealed.

15-2-16 A stronger lower radiator bracket was constructed to provide additional protection against curbs and road debris. Note the rubber mount isolating the radiator.

picture 15-2-16. Furthermore, it came with all the hose connections and mounts! The radiator expansion tank I used is from a 1992 GM Chevy Cavalier, and fits the contour of the inner fender perfectly. I fitted two offset cooling fans: a 16in puller mounted on the radiator and a 12in pusher on the condenser. The computer controls which fan will run depending on engine load, road speed and cooling needs.

The air-con uses R-134a with all new hoses that are compatible with the new freon. I found the standard TR7

ENGINE TRANSPLANT PROJECTS

air-con fairly easy to convert to 134a, since the hoses are plastic lined and do not leak the freon's smaller molecules like rubber hoses rated for R-12. I found the condenser plenty big enough for both types of freon and, since there is an expansion valve instead of a fixed orifice valve, there was no need to change anything there either. The system required flushing with one rated for 134a. I established that, unless the system can be power flushed, I needed to make sure I used oil compatible with both systems.

I used the stock Ford compressor. It has a radial pump and can hardly be heard running. The air-con clutch is controlled by the computer and cuts it out under heavy throttle loads. I kept the stock air distribution box, and added an electromechanical control unit for the temperature and vacuum servos for the air flow. A variable resistor in the temp control knob on the instrument panel signals the control unit's arm to move the original linkage. The vacuum diverter knob controls air flow to the servo units, mounted at the original arms on the air box. All of these components were removed from a Ford Taurus. The new system has proved quiet and smooth, and will also shut the outside air off when the engine is shut down.

I felt a stronger steering column with a more reliable ignition, wiper, and headlight dip-switch was needed. After some research, I decided the 1990 Mustang column seen in picture 15-2-17 was the best option. The entire framework that holds it to the firewall was removed from the Mustang and mounted to the TR7 bulkhead with only slight modification. Using the framework from the Mustang made the entire dash area much stronger, and I was able to tie everything in that area back to this frame. Using the Mustang column also made hooking up the electrical connections much easier, being Ford connectors. The steering column needed to be shortened by only 2in, but this proved more complex than I first thought as I did not want to compromise its ability to collapse in the event of a crash.

I elected to remove the prince of darkness from the car in the interests of uniformity and reliability. However the complexity of the electrical systems escalated dramatically. My donor was a 1990 Ford Thunderbird that required 12 full-size circuit diagrams from Helm Inc. (www.helminc.com) to understand and work on it. The complete harness and components were removed from the donor car. I kept the fuse panel in the back of the glove box, although the new panel used much-improved spade fuses. I also retained the original TR7 dash panel switches because I judged them reliable once the current passing through them was much reduced and only controlling the relays.

15-2-17 My new Ford steering column and wheel. I used an LCD instrument panel from a 1992 Mercury Cougar, which is the same as the Thunderbird. Modern instrument panels no longer use a cable to drive the speedometer – instead they are wired off a speed sender on the transmission. I found that a data link to the EEC was required to re-activate many of my initially disabled features and facilities.

The TR7 employed weights in each corner of the front bumper to damp out cowl shake. The new front suspension made it possible to remove these weights. Having now had a couple of years of driving, I had a good before-and-after comparison. The bumpers also look much better without the sagging ends and the car is, of course, that bit lighter.

Chapter 16
Weight watchers

I have already referred to the highly acclaimed performance of Lotus cars – achieved not so much by very powerful engines, but more through superb handling and very light weight. This generates a very high power to weight ratio, with the added benefit that the handling of the car is optimised by there being minimal weight, and therefore inertia, when changing direction or speed. The catch phrase "float like a butterfly, sting like bee" is apt, for every car on the road will enjoy improved acceleration, braking, cornering, responsiveness and the opportunity for greater fuel economy if you choose to minimise its weight.

So it does pay to get and keep your car's weight down to a minimum – no reduction is bad. Fibreglass body panels save a lot, and the doors, wings, boot lid and bonnet all need your thought if you are serious about reducing the weight of your car. You may also be interested to see picture 16-1. However, there are some particularly crucial areas where weight reductions on the chassis are doubly important:
- Unsprung weight – i.e. lightweight brake callipers and alloy wheels.
- Weight outside the wheel base – i.e. the radiator.
- Weight located high in the car – i.e. the cylinder head or battery.

There are also some within the engine that have the double benefit of not only reducing the weight of the engine, but its internal inertia, too.

We can be pedantic about reducing a vehicle's weight. In an aircraft you will rarely find, for example, a steel lever or pulley – they will all be made from aluminium for weight reduction reasons. Unfortunately, aluminium is significantly more expensive than iron or steel, which increases your material costs if you follow this practice in your car. Furthermore, most of the parts in question will have been made from iron and steel, and if you plan to have one made from aluminium it will be a custom job – inevitably further increasing your costs.

Nevertheless, it all depends upon how important improved performance is to you. If you are leading the TR Register championship with a couple of races to go and can see a 5lb weight reduction available, you may be prepared to pay for it. If you go on a couple of track days each year I doubt you will see that expense in the same

16-1 The inner door frame of a works rally car, peppered with holes to reduce weight.

WEIGHT WATCHERS

light (pun intended!). Therefore, I intend to leave the detail to each individual. You can decide on whether the benefits warrant the cost of replacing, say, your wings, starter motor, clutch slave mounting bracket or oil filler plug. All the specialists who have contributed to this book have invaluable experience and special products specifically intended to reduce the weight of your car. My focus will be on weight reductions that I think have a dual benefit.

UNSPRUNG WEIGHT

Items that are the road-side of the springs represent unsprung weight. If these are light then the car weighs less, but the extra benefit of minimising unsprung weight is that it dramatically affects the behaviour of the suspension generally. The work the shock absorber has to do, the extent to which the tyres stay in contact with the road and the car's road-holding all benefit. Thus the shock absorbers, hubs, brake callipers and discs, wheels and tyres and, at the back, the live rear axle all affect unsprung weight. The greater the combined weight of these components, the higher the inertia of every movement of the suspension. That is one reason why IRS cars are likely to have better road-holding than the live-axle cars we are focused on – the unsprung weight of a live axle is greater than the hubs and drive shafts of an IRS car. There are lighter, stronger live axles out there, but there is not much you can do to reduce the weight of any given axle. The original 4-speed axle is certainly lighter than the stronger 5-speed one, but would be a retrograde step. Thus, at the back-end, only the wheels offer a practical opportunity to reduce the unsprung weight of a live axle car, and only IRS offers the opportunity to reduce) your unsprung weight further.

The heaviest single unsprung component at the front is going to be the wheel/tyre, which is why you find small cars (like the Mini and most single-seater race cars) have minuscule ones. However, here too the debate is between a largish wheel with the capacity for powerful brakes, and a small, lighter wheel with possibly insufficient space for adequate brakes. I think it is clear already that I favour giving adequate braking the priority! There are some suspension components that can be made from aluminium, and you may get some ideas from photo 16-2. Then there is the compromise of tyre width. Obviously, the wider the tyre the heavier it is, but the more rubber it puts to the road and the better it grips. Generally speaking, from a road-holding point of view wide is good – so again, I think we need to forget the weight penalty! However, there is one wheel/tyre issue we can do something about – the material the wheel is made from. There has been a surge in the number of alloy wheels on the market in recent years and for very good reason, as this table illustrates.

Wheel	Approximate weight (lb)
15in diameter x 5J steel	16
15in x 5.5J alloy	14
15in x 6J Minilite	12.5
15in x 7J Minilite	17
15in x 7J magnesium	12.5

16-2 Bilstein front suspension leg, with extensive uses of aluminium for the spring seats and strut top mounting.

Staying with weight reduction opportunities at the front, if you have ever carried a pair of cast/original brake callipers home from the salvage yard, you will know straightaway that there has to be an opportunity for weight reduction here. A TR calliper weighs 15lb. It is not therefore surprising that there are numerous alloy callipers available, and one is on view at 16-3 (overleaf). They will save 50 to 60 per cent of the cast unit's weight and are to be very much encouraged, since they also improve heat dissipation.

The hubs to which your front wheels bolt are a weighty item, and again there is a 50 per cent weight-saving opportunity if you are really serious about unsprung weight reduction. "Where is the secondary benefit here?", I hear you ask "because all of that is countered by the heavier

SPEEDPRO SERIES

16-3 A Group 4 aluminium 4-pot calliper, designed to fit inside a 13in wheel, was used by the works TR7 and is the only aluminium 4-pot allowed in historic rallying. Note also the aluminium brake disc bell.

16-4 Bumpers hang outside the wheelbase, are usually heavy so therefore, from a performance point of view, are very undesirable. Sadly no longer available, this Viper rear valance/bumper panel one-piece light, fibreglass moulding offered an excellent solution.

disc/rotors you have advocated at every opportunity!". However, there is a secondary benefit – those with very powerful conversions will be able to order 5-stud wheel fixings.

WEIGHT OUTSIDE THE WHEEL BASE

The wheelbase is the distance between the centres of the front and rear wheels. Anything outside that distance is overhanging the wheelbase, and from a road-holding point of view is undesirable. The heavier any part or panel is outside the wheelbase the more undesirable it becomes. Technically, it is the polar moment of inertia you wish to minimise by keeping all the weight you can within the wheelbase. Not important? Well, lots of motor manufacturers think it is and go to great lengths to design cars with a "wheel at each corner". You cannot redesign your TR, although you will appreciate that a lightweight boot lid and/or bonnet will both fall into the double benefit category of weight saving.

Much of the weight in the bumper bars is in the steel frame. The UK plastic bumper covers are lighter than the US rubber covers. If you are serious about performance on the track then remove the front and rear bumpers (if race regulations permit), and fit a one-piece moulded valance and bumper (picture 16-4). For road-going vehicles, replace the heavy frame with a lighter version and/or use a fibreglass cover. DHC owners might note that removing the heavy metal from the front bumper will improve the handling but will increase body-shake.

The water radiator is way out there, and no lightweight. An aluminium radiator saves about 40 per cent and is outside the wheelbase. You can help a little by not placing the battery in the boot/trunk or carrying heavy items (say a heavy spare wheel or a large jack) in the boot. A light or 'space-saver' wheel is one solution, with the jack stored on the floor behind the front seats another suggestion. When on the floor they minimise body-roll by lowering the centre of gravity, which, in fact, leads me to ...

WEIGHT LOCATED HIGH IN THE CAR

The SD1 engine has its alternator high – in fact, it could hardly be higher – in the engine bay. Furthermore, alternators are no lightweight. A modern miniature lightweight alternator mounted in the same place will help, but some opportunities to fit the alternator low in the engine bay provide further benefits. No alternator wants to be mounted higher than is absolutely necessary. You can see one example of alternator relocation in picture 16-5. Do not overlook the savings you might achieve using alloy mounting components and/or pulleys, too.

The battery is relatively high in the car and certainly a weighty item at (depending upon the spec you use) maybe 40lb (18kg). There are various compact batteries available that will reduce this item by 10lb or so, for those not planning to relocate their battery. Weight distribution is an issue too, and the TRs are front-heavy – thus you

16-5 The low-mounted alternator on Neil Sawyer's works rally car is fitted to the left-hand side largely because, in his case, the dry sump pump occupies this space in the right-hand side of the engine. However, this is not a lightweight, but a 60 amp Lucas alternator to power the 600 watt lights needed for night rallying. In the summer Neil changes to a smaller and much lighter alternator, located in the same place.

WEIGHT WATCHERS

16-6 An aluminium water pump pulley and Rover P6 crankshaft pulley, which is still made from steel but is much smaller and lighter than the SD1/TR8 pulley.

16-7 A cast piston on the left compared to an Omega forged one on the right. At first glance the forged one looks shorter, but in fact it is only the skirt length that has been reduced.

achieve a double benefit if you relocate the smaller battery somewhere to the rear of the car, but within the wheelbase.

THE ENGINE

Within the engine there are two types of components relevant to weight reduction: rotating (e.g. flywheel, crankshaft, clutch and pulleys etc.) and reciprocating (e.g. con-rods, pistons, gudgeon pins, push-rods and rockers). Any weight-saving within the engine is welcome, but the savings from rotating parts have the triple benefits of reducing the weight of the engine, improving the front/rear balance and reducing the inertia of the engine, thereby improving its responsiveness. While reciprocating weight offers little by way of individual component savings (we are dealing in ounces saved), they are very important – but will reduce your bank balance more severely than the rotating reductions!

Rotating weight-losses are easiest to deal with first. We already covered some, but to emphasise the point, did you appreciate that the V8's front crank-pulley weighs about 5lb and offers a 50 per cent reduction opportunity? You will see an example at photo 16-6. On both the 4- and 8-cylinder engine, flywheels and clutches offer the greatest single weight reduction opportunity within the engine. However, it needs to be approached carefully, as too light a flywheel for your application can make driving the car a misery if it will not idle in traffic or take up on the clutch without stalling. Lightening the flywheel makes a huge difference to the responsiveness of the engine, because the extra weight has to be accelerated otherwise. You can lighten both flywheels by turning off the 'excess' metal. An experienced machinist should be able to get about 4lb off the 4-cylinder flywheels (to circa 16/18lb) and 8lb off a V8 one. I would suggest you try a car with those modifications in place first, but there is scope for milling out slots between the clutch bolt-holes to remove a further 3lb, which is valuable, since removing weight from the outer edge of the flywheel has the greatest benefit. Cost for all these operations is circa £125/150, and for the majority of fast road cars they offer good value for money. For the fastest cars, one of the numerous aluminium flywheels that are available can be fitted. They can weigh as little as 10lb including the ring gear but they are costly.

There are no material weight-reduction opportunities in changing the crankshafts on either the 4- or 8-cylinder engines. The steel replacements are certainly much stronger but offer no attraction from a weight point of view.

Time to consider reciprocating weight savings on con-rods and pistons. Gudgeon pins are part of the piston, and while push-rods and rockers do offer opportunities it has to be the major reciprocating parts on which we focus our attention. The con-rods are very important components in any engine but particularly in an engine likely to be used at high revolutions. Steel con-rods are the key and Carillo-forged steel rods, marketed under a variety of brand names, are about 0.5lb lighter per rod than original Triumph ones. However, you do need to think of a (very) positive benefit before you order a set, as they are about £150 per rod!

Pistons are equally (possibly more) important from a reciprocating weight point of view. The method of manufacture (cast or forged) has a major bearing on their strength, forging being a stronger manufacturing method than casting. Surprisingly perhaps, this also affects the weight of the piston, as too does the design – material thickness being obvious, but the skirt lengths seen at photo 16-7 also differ from piston to piston. Some pistons have cutouts in the base of the skirt, and any one of these variations can easily make a supplier's piston an ounce or two heavier or lighter than a competitive product. Sure, a couple of ounces is going to make no difference to the overall weight of an engine, but it makes an enormous difference to the inertia of that piston. So, in fact you cannot judge your success at weight reduction entirely by weight alone – strength counts too! Have fun planning what is right for you, your car and your bank balance.

Conclusion

With careful planning, you can spread improvements over a couple of years while still enjoying your Wedge. Tackle the safety related items first, starting with the wheels, tyres and brakes, followed by the suspension. Only then should you start on improving the engine. Reliability issues should be undertaken when working in each area of improvement. For example, check the wiring and connections whenever you service an item such as the lighting and charging components. Comfort improvements such as seating can be tackled whenever you feel like it if it makes you happy, but don't waste time and money on upgrading aesthetics rather than, say, improving the brakes.

It is better to buy a kit of parts from a TR specialist which is designed for one specific upgrade, such as the brakes, rather than buying the various components separately: e.g. a disc from here and a calliper from somewhere else. It may appear more expensive at the outset, but overall delays, disappointments and frustration will be reduced. A kit is more likely to be engineered as a whole. Thus, if you should have problems with its installation or performance then the one supplier is more likely to help you resolve the problem than if you were mixing and matching items sourced from various suppliers and possibly competitors.

Remember that you need to advise your insurance company of all modifications to the car before it is put back on the road. Furthermore, at least in the UK and I would presume in other countries too, you are obliged to advise the authorities of any change to the number of cylinders, the cubic capacity and the engine number of the car. If your authorities require more information than that, be sure to meet those obligations.

www.velocebooks.com/www.veloce.co.uk
All books in print • New books • Special offers • Gift Vouchers

Appendix

PRINCIPAL TR7 AND TR8 SPECIALIST CLUBS AND SUPPLIERS

Clubs

The TR Drivers Club, 12 Puxton drive, Kidderminster, Worcester DY11 5DR, England. Tel: 01562 825000.
www.trdrivers.com

TR Register, 1BHawksworth, Southmead Industrial Park, Didcot Oxon, OX11 7HR. England. Tel: 01235 818866.
www.tr-register.co.uk
Email tr.register@onyxnet.co.uk

TR8 Car Club of America, 266 Linen St, Rochester, NY 14620, USA. Tel: 585 244 9693.
www.team.net/TR8/crtr8cca
Email jworsley@yadtel.net

Triumph Sports Owners Association (Victoria), P.O. Box 5020, GPO Melbourne, Victoria 3001, Australia.
www.tsoavic.com

Vintage Triumph Register, P.O. Box 655, Howell, MI 48844, USA.
www.vtr.org
Email triumphtr2@aol.com

World Wide TR7 and TR8 Owners Club, P.O. Box 76, Tadcaster, North Yorkshire, LS25 9AG, England. Tel: 020 81235883.
www.tr7-tr8.com

UK performance specialists (in alphabetical order)

Agriemach Ltd, Wayfarers, Old Domewood, Copthorne, Crawley, West Sussex RH10 3HD, UK. Tel: 01342 713743.
www.agriemach.co.uk/products
(Exhaust tape wrapping and coolant additives)

AP Racing Ltd, Wheler Road, Seven Stars Industrial Estate, Coventry CV34LB, UK. Tel: 024 7663 9595.
www.apracing.com (Frictional racing products)

Auto Sparks, 80-83 Derby Road, Sandiacre, Nottingham, NG10 5HU, England. Tel: 0115 9497211.
www.autosparks.co.uk (Electrical cables, harnesses and components)

Brake Engineering, Redwither Road, Wrexham Industrial Estate, Wrexham, LL13 9RD, United Kingdom. Tel 01978 667800.
www.brake-eng.com (Specialists in re-manufacturing brake callipers)

Brian Kitley Triumphs, Somerset, England. Tel: 07704 457168.
www.briankitleytriumphs.co.uk (Remanufacture of Sprint engine and tuning parts)

BTU International Car Parts Group, Cherish View House, Strickens Lane, Garstang, PR3 1UD England. Te : 01995-605900.
www.btucarparts.co.uk (Electric window lifts)

SPEEDPRO SERIES

Burgess Automotive Performance Engineering, Unit 1, Amber Buildings, Meadow Lane, Alfreton, Derbyshire, DE5 7EZ, England. Tel: 01773 520021. Email peter@burgesstuning.free-online.co.uk

Cambridge Motorsport Ltd, Caxton Rd, Great Gransden, Nr Sandy, Beds SG19 3AH, England. Tel: 01797 677969. www.cambridgemotorsport.com

Clive Wheatley V8 Conversions, High Grosvenor, Worfield, Bridgnorth, Nr Wolverhampton, Shropshire, WV15 5PN, England. Tel: 01746 710810. www.mgv8homestead.com (V8 Engine Spares)

EBC, EBC Buildings, Countess Road, Northampton, NN5 7EA, England. Tel: 01604 583344. www.ebcbrakesuk.com/Automotive (Kevlar 'Green-Stuff' pad materials)

Frontline-Costello, 239 London Rd East, Batheaston, Bath, BA1 7RL, England. Tel: 01225 852777. www.mgcars.org.uk/frontline/ (MGB trailing link rear suspension)

GKN Driveline, Kingsbury Road, Minworth, Sutton Coldfield B76 9DL, UK. Tel: 0121 3131616. www.gknservice.com/gkn-ids/jsp/location/uk.jsp (Hi specification propshaft and u/j specialists)

Hi Spec Motorsport, Unit 5 Parker Ind Centre, Watling St, Dartford, Kent, DA2 6EP, England. Tel: 01322 286850. www.hispecmotorsport.co.uk (Brake upgrade kits)

Lumenition/Autocar Electrical Equipment, 49-51 Tiverton St. London SE1 6NZ England Tel: 0207 4034334. www.lumenition.com (Programmable ECU's and components for EFI and engine management systems)

Kenlowe Ltd, Burchetts Green, Maidenhead, Berkshire, SL6 6QU, UK. Tel: 01628 823303. www.kenlowe.com (Electric radiator fans)

MAW Solutions Ltd, P.O. box 177, Stamford, Lincs PE9 2WF, UK. Tel: 01780 765140. www.mawsolutions.com (Davies-Craig electric water pumps and thermostatic cooling fans)

Moss-Europe, Hampton Farm Industrial Estate, Hansworth, Middsex, TW13 6DB. England. Tel: 020 8867 2020. www.moss-europe.co.uk

Motor Sport Parts, Unit B Willowbrook, Bardfield Road, Bardfield Saling, Braintree, Essex, CM7 5EN, England. Tel: 01371 851375. www.motorsportparts.co.uk (Suspension components)

Newtronic Systems, Unit 3 BTMC, Challenge Way, Blackburn, Lancs, BB1 5QB, UK. www.newtronic.co.uk (Electronic ignition systems)

Racetorations, Caldicott Drive, Heapham Rd Industrial Estate, Gainsborough, Lincs, DN21 1FJ, England. Tel: 01427 616565. www.racetorations.co.uk (TR performance equipment)

Rally Design, Units 8-10, Upper Brents Ind estate, Faversham, Kent, ME13 7DZ, England. Tel: 01795 531871. www.raddes.co.uk (Brake and other performance equipment upgrades)

Rimmer Bros, Sleaford Rd, Bracebridge Heath, Lincoln, JN4 2NA, England. Tel: 01522 568000. Email sales@rimmerbros.co.uk (TR7, TR8 and Rover spares, engines and transmissions)

Robsport International, North House, Dunsbridge Turnpike, Shepreth, Nr Royston, Herts, SG8 6RA, England. Tel: 01763 848673. www.robsport.co.uk Email enquires@robsport.co.uk (TR7 and TR8 new and used spares, restorations and performance specialists)

RPI Engineering, Wayside Garage, Holt Rd, Horsford, Norwich, NR10 3EE, England. Tel: 01603 891209. www.v8engines.com (Specialists for standard and uprated V8 engines, transmissions and associated equipment)

Salisbury Transmissions, Wolverhampton. Tel: 01992 441195. www.salisburytransmissionseurope.com Email salisburyaxles@aol.com

Speedy Cables, c/o Caerbont Auto Instruments, Caerbont Enterprise Park, Abercrave, Swansea, SA9 1SH, UK. Tel: 01639 732213. www.speedycables.co.uk (Instrument suppliers and conversion specialists)

S+S Preparations, Glen Mill Classic Car Centre, Newchurch Road, Stacksteads, Bacup, Lancs, OL13 0NH, England. Tel: 01706 874874. www.ss-preparations.co.uk (TR7 and 8 spares and performance equipment)

Superchips Ltd, Buckingham Industrial Park, Buckingham, MK18 1XJ, England. Tel: 01280 816781. Email sales@superchips.co.uk or tech@superchips.co.uk (Performance improvements to ECUs)

SPEEDPRO SERIES

Superpro Europe Ltd, Home Farm, Middlezoy, Somerset, TA7 0PD, England. Tel: +44(0)1823 698437. Fax: +44(0)1823 698109.
Email: neil@superpro.eu.com (Polyurethane suspension bushes)

TR Enterprises, Dale Lane, Blidworth, Notts, NG21 0SA, England. Tel: 01623 793807.
Email info@trenterprises.com
www.trenterprises.com (Agent for safety devices roll-cages)

Webcon Alpha UK, Dolphin Rd, Sunbury, Middlesex, TW16 7HE, England. Tel: 01932 787100.
www.webcon.co.uk (Programmable ECUs and components for EFI and Engine Management systems)

Wolfit Racing. Tel: 01582 883885
www.btinternet.com/~jon.wolfe/wolfitt_products_1.htm
Email jon.wolfe@btinternet.com (TR7 and 8 performance equipment)

NON-UK PERFORMANCE SPECIALISTS

American Autowire Systems, 150 Cooper Road C-8, West Berlin, NJ 08091, USA. Tel: 1 800 482 WIRE.
www.americanautowire.com (Auto electrical wires and components)

Autoworks International, El Cajon, CA 92020. Tel: 619 4016900.
www.autoworksracing.com (Ford T5 clutch slave cylinder and bracket)

British Wiring Inc, 20449 Ithica Road, Olympia Fields, Il 60461, USA. Tel/fax: 708 4819050.
www.britishwiring.com (Electrical wire, connectors, terminals for UK cars)

Conversion Components, 16 Reservoir Street, Waihi 2981, New Zealand. Tel: +64 7 8638509.
www.conversioncomp.com (Conversion kits for 5 speed gearboxes)

Custom Engineered Fuel-injection Systems, Georgia, USA. Tel: 334 448-6158.
www.customefis.com (GM EFI and Engine Management adaptation specialists)

D+D Fabrications, 8005 Tiffany Drive, Almont, MI 48003, USA. Tel: 810 798 2491.
www.aluminumv8.com (Buick/Rover engine and gearbox specialist)

Dellow Automotive Pty Ltd, 37 Daisy St, Revesby, NSW 2212, Australia. Tel: (02) 9774-4419.
www.dellowauto.com.au (Gearbox adaptation kits)

EBC, 806 Buchanan Blvd, Unit 115-256, Boulder City, Las Vegas, NV89005, USA.
Email sales@ebcbrakesusa.com (Kevlar 'Green-Stuff' pad materials)

Haltech Engine Management Systems, 3 Centre Place, Wetherill Park, NSW, Australia, 2164. Tel: 612 97290999 www.haltech.com.au (Programmable ECUs for engine management).

Jacobs Electronics Technical Service, Mr. Gasket Performance Group, 550 Mallory Way, Carson City, NV 89701, USA.
www.jacobselectronics.com (High-performance ignition systems)

K-mac Suspensions, 366 Princess Highway, Rockdale NSW 2216, Australia. Tel: +61 2 95561799.
www.k-mac.com (TR7 top strut bearings and suspension components)

Lanocha Racing Systems, 3643 Jarrettsville Pike, Jarrettsville, MD 21084, USA. Tel: 410 5570003.
www.lanocharacing.com (TR7 body, brake and engine upgrades)

Magnecor, 24581 Crestview Court, Farmington Hills, MI 48335, USA. Tel: 248 4719505.
Email mag@magnecor.com (High-performance plug leads)

MegaSquirt
www.bgsoflex.com/megasquirt.html
Email megasquirt@msefi.com (Programmable ECU's for EFI and engine management systems)

Moss Motors, P.O. Box 847, 440 Rutherford Street, Goleta, CA 93116, USA. Tel: (800) 6677872.
www.mossmotors.com (TR spares)

Motec Systems USA, 5355 Industrial Dr, Huntington Beach, CA 92649, USA. Tel: (714) 8976804.
www.motec.com (Programmable ECU's for EFI and engine management systems)

Pertronix Performance Products, Tel: 800 8273758.
www.pertronix.com (Performance ignition specialists)

Pit stop - C and C Racing, Petaluma, California. Tel: 1 866 7223432.
www.pitstopusa.com (Online motorsports superstore)

Roadster Factory, P.O. Box 332, Killen Road, Armagh, PA 15920, USA. Tel: (800) 6788764.
www.the-roadster-factory.com (TR Spares)

Triumph Rover Spares Pty, 7 Magna Ct, Lonsdale, South Australia 5160, Australia. Tel: +61 8 83846933
www.triumphroverspares.com.au

SPEEDPRO SERIES

(Triumph and Rover spares, parts and upgrades)

TS Imported Automotive, 108 South Jefferson St, Pandora, OH 45877, USA. Tel: 419 3843022. www.tsimportedautomotive.com (TR7 and TR8 parts and upgrades).

Wedgeparts, Nashville, Tennessee, USA. Tel: 931 6455283/931 8010509. www.wedgeparts.com (TR7 and TR8 parts, upgrades and EFI specialists)

The Wedge Shop, 111 Dean St, Taunton, MA 02780, USA. Tel: 1 508 8805448 www.thewedgeshop.com

Victoria British Ltd, Box 14991, Lenexa, KS 66285-4991, USA. Tel: (800) 2550088 www.longmotor.com (TR Spares)

www.velocebooks.com/www.veloce.co.uk
All books in print • New books • Special offers • Gift Vouchers

Index

Air-conditioning 129, 130, 192, 193
Air filter – see K+N/air filter
Air flow meter (EFI) see EFI
Alternator 113, 120, 168-170, 172, 173, 196
Anti roll/sway bar 54, 61, 190, 191
    rear 66
Anti-dive kit 54

Balancing the conversion 11
Ballast resistor 134, 135, 186
Battery 171, 172, 196
Bellhousing – see Gearbox
Body – condition 11, 16, 18, 106
    fitting panels 46
    re-styling 43-46
    strengthening 43, 49-53
    turret 50
    welding 50, 51, 63
    wheel arches 44, 45
Bonnet/hood 12, 16, 104, 106, 116
    catch 107, 117
    closing solutions 116, 117, 186
Boot (trunk) 49
Brake – callipers 17, 20-26, 195, 196
    AP Racing 26, 28
    Capri 23
    Hi Spec 25, 26, 28
    Princess 24, 25
    radial mounting 25, 26
    SD1 24, 184
    Volvo 24
    Wilwood 27
    cooling 21, 38
    disc/rotor type 22, 27, 28
    drums 30, 32
    front/rear balance 30-32, 191
    handbrakes 33
    master-cylinders 28-30
    pad materials 21, 28
    rear 30-33, 57, 80
    safety 19, 20

    servo/boosters 28-30, 192
    size 17, 19, 20-28
Bushes – balanced kit 56
    polyurethane 54, 56, 57
    suspension 54
Buying see Purchasing

Cable (electrical) sizes 171, 175, 177, 178
Cam
    buckets 76
    shaft 76, 79, 102, 103
Carburettor – AFB 116, 117, 142, 145-149
    Anti-run-on valve 141
    Dashpots/dampers 117, 143, 144
    Design/atomisation 140, 142, 144
    Springs 143
    Stromberg 17, 116, 141, 142
    SU 17, 74, 116, 141-145
    Weber DCOE 13, 15, 68, 141, 142, 144, 145
Clutch 71, 84, 87, 88
    master cylinder 88, 189
    slave cylinder 88, 189
    thrust bearing 18, 89, 189
Coil – see Ignition
Contact breaker – see Ignition
Conversion kit 16, 17, 105
Cooling/coolant 113-115, 118, 123
    additives/antifreeze 128, 129
    bleeding 124
    electric pump 128
    tanks 118, 119, 187, 192
    water pump 113, 124
Cost of conversion 11, 182
Crankshaft 83, 197
Cylinder head 70, 72, 95-97
    compression 94, 95
    gas-flowing 97
    gaskets 95, 189
    shrouding 96
    studs 75
    torque sequence 77

Dampers – see Shock absorbers
Direction lights 181
Distributor – see Ignition
Door trim 47, 194
    lights 181
    safety bars 52, 53
EFI 16, 140
    Bosch 152-158
    GM (V8) 161-167
    programmable systems 158-161, 167
    TR7 153-155
Electrical – windows 48, 49, 181
    connections/terminations 175
    corrosion 175, 176
    harness prep 174, 175
    instruments 179-181, 186
    relays 173
    switches 173, 179
    V8 modifications 173-176
    vulnerable areas 168
Emissions 117, 167
Engine management 139, 161-167
Engine – 8-valve 12, 15, 68-70, 79
    16-valve 12, 13, 15, 68, 70-78, 87
    alternatives 13, 92
    Buick/Rover V8 12, 13, 15, 92-94, 106, 197
    capacities 13, 93, 94
    Chevy 13
    compression ratio 94
    fit/remove 71, 107, 108, 183, 184
    Ford 13,14, 188
    mountings 106, 107, 116
    pistons 197
    sources 94
    upgrading 98
Exhaust 15, 68, 70, 79, 109-112, 184, 185, 187, 189
    clamps 111
    wrapping 112
Expense – see Cost

SPEEDPRO SERIES

Fan – electric 16, 115, 119, 125-127, 175, 185
    mechanical 119, 124, 125, 184
Fibreglass panels 194, 196
Flywheel 81, 98, 106, 197
Fuel – pumps 151, 154, 161, 162, 186
    tank 153, 162

Gearbox/transmission
    4-speed 11, 80
    5-speed 11, 12, 18, 71, 80-82, 84, 106, 183
    automatic 86, 87, 130
    bell-housing 18, 80, 81, 87
    Borg-Warner 82-84, 86
    conversions 80, 81
    cross-member 90, 108, 109, 186
    extension housings 84, 90, 109
    flange 91
    LT77 – see 5-speed
    R380 84, 85
    SD1 – see 5-speed
    T5 18, 82, 83, 188
    Toyota Supra 18, 85
    Tremec 85, 86
Generator – see Alternator

Handbrake – see Brakes
Hawk – see Brakes – pads
Headlamps – fairing mods 47
Hub – 5-speed 63
    bearing 61
    front 190
    L-Jetronic – see EFI

Ignition 131
    breaker/breakerless 132-134
    capacitive discharge 138, 139
    coil 131, 132, 134, 137
    distributor 16, 69, 72, 132-134, 164, 165, 186
    Opus 133, 134, 174
    plug leads 137
    spark plugs 135-138
Inertia (increased) 14
Injectors – see EFI
Inlet manifold 112, 117, 120, 149, 150, 153, 156, 161, 165, 166

lowering 157, 158
Instrument upgrade 178

K&N/air filters 69, 71, 107, 117, 142, 144, 150, 151, 154, 165, 167
Kevlar – see Brakes - pads
K-frame – see Subframe

MacPherson – see Suspension
MSA Blue Book 50-53
MSD – see ignition

Oil – coolers 99, 130
    engine 79, 100, 101
    filters 69, 99, 100, 104
    gearbox 82, 83, 87
    pan – see Sump
    pressure 98, 100, 103, 178, 179, 187
    thermostat 130
Opus – see Ignition
Overheating 72, 79

Panhard rod 67
Planning 11-18
Polyurethane – see Bushes
Prop-shaft 91, 185
Purchasing 12

Radiator – brackets 114, 115, 192
    core 114, 120, 121
    flushing 120
    relocation 119
    water 113-115, 118, 119, 196
Rear axle 12, 16, 18, 62-65
    limited slip 65
    pinion 63, 64, 183, 187
    pre-load 65, 187
    ratios 63, 187, 188
    SD1 62, 63, 67, 183
    stronger 62, 63, 67
Relay – see Electrical
Roll-cages 49-53

Safety cages/bars 50-53
Seats – upgrades 48
    recovering 47
Sensors – see EFI
Shock absorbers 55, 56

Shore hardness – see Bushes
Speedometer – cable 89
    calibration 40, 180
Springs – lowered 55
    road 54, 55, 57
Sprint (TR7) 11, 16, 70-78
Starter motor 103, 104, 111, 177, 178
Steering – power 58, 60, 61
    rack 17, 58, 60, 106, 185
    top-strut 58-60, 190, 191
SU – see Carburettors
Subframe (front) 14, 15, 16, 61, 105, 108, 110, 116, 184, 190, 191
Sump 14, 15, 78, 100-102, 116
Suspension – front 55-57, 189, 190, 195
    rear 57, 65-67, 188
    rear arms 65-67
    trailing link 67
    upgrades 54-57

Tachometer 180, 186
Temperature gauge 120
Terminals – see Electrical
Thermostat coolant 123
Timing gear 72, 73, 77-79, 103
TR8 12
Tremec – see Gearbox
Trim – 5-speed gearbox 80
    dashboard 47
    hoods 47
Tyres – caring for 41, 42
    size 39, 40, 57, 106
    speed ratings 41

V8 wiring changes – see Electrical
Valance/spoiler 22, 43, 44, 122

Watts link 58, 67
Wheels – alloy 38, 195
    arch – see Body
    cooling effect 38
    diameter 35, 36
    importance 34
    MGF 35, 36, 38
    offsets 36, 37
    rim 36, 57
    stud pattern 34, 37, 39

Also from Veloce Publishing ...

How to restore Triumph TR7 & 8

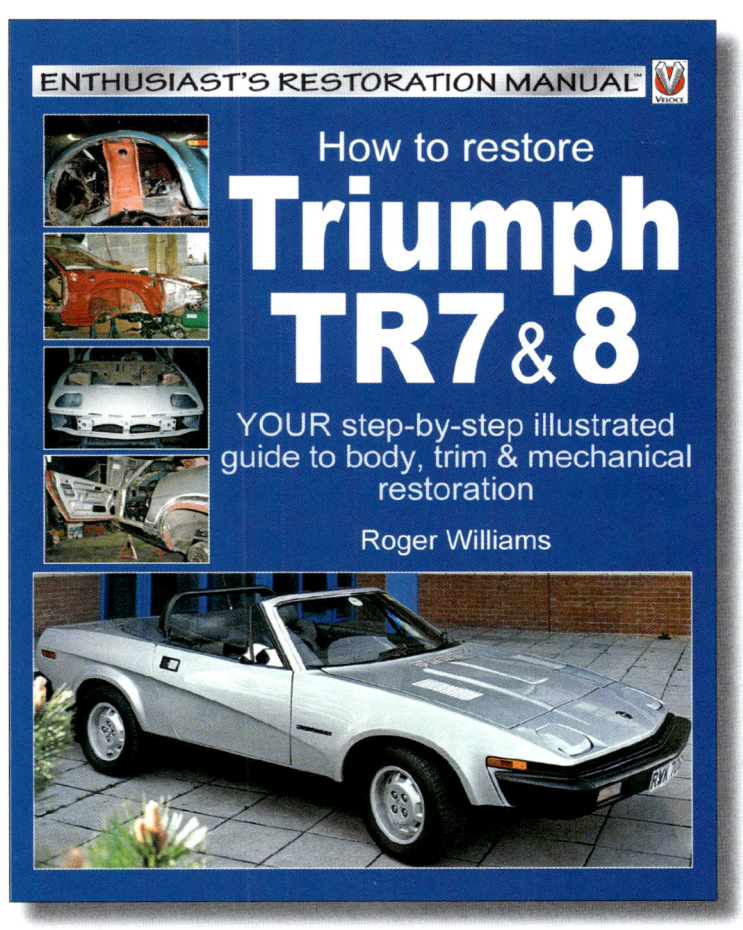

The step-by-step guide to planning and restoring your car in the most cost-effective way. Includes body, trim and mechanical restoration, left- to right-hand drive conversion, clubs, specialists and suppliers, welding and restoration techniques, and advice on what work to sub-contract.

ISBN: 978-1-904788-24-9

£24.99*

Complete guide to all aspects of restoration, including body, engine (4-cylinder & V8) and gearbox (transmission), suspension & steering, brakes, electrical equipment, interior & hood (soft top), painting & brightwork • How to choose and buy the right TR • Creating a restoration plan • Welding techniques • Left-hand drive to right-hand drive conversion • Clubs, specialists & suppliers • 176 pages and over 580 illustrations

*Prices subject to change, P&P extra • For more information telephone +44 (0)1305 260068, or email sales@veloce.co.uk • Visit us on the web at www.veloce.co.uk

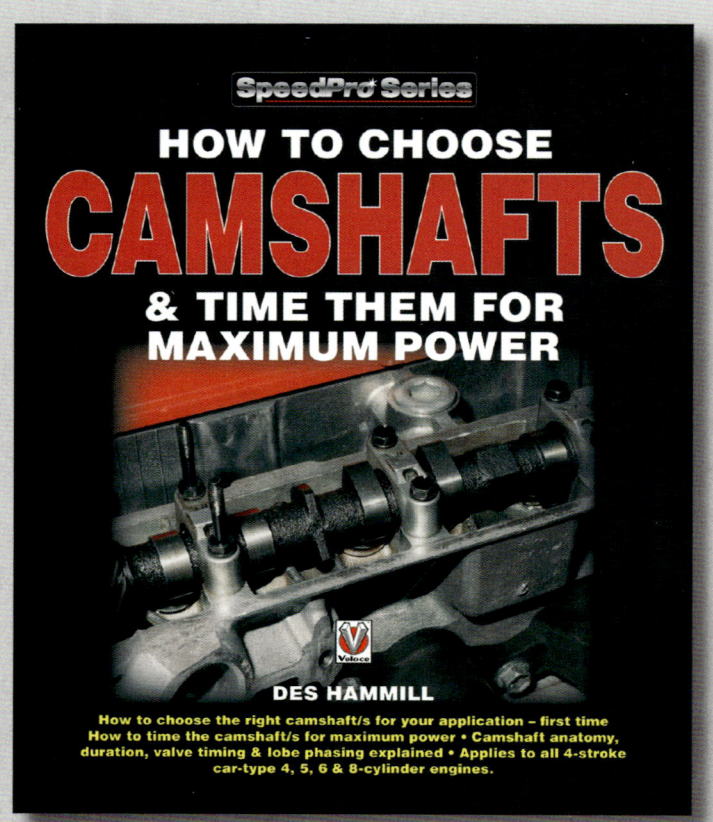

SpeedPro Series

HOW TO CHOOSE CAMSHAFTS & TIME THEM FOR MAXIMUM POWER
DES HAMMILL

How to choose the right camshaft/s for your application – first time • How to time the camshaft/s for maximum power • Camshaft anatomy, duration, valve timing & lobe phasing explained • Applies to all 4-stroke car-type 4, 5, 6 & 8-cylinder engines.

How to choose the right camshaft or camshafts for your individual application. Takes the mystery out of camshaft timing and tells you how to obtain optimum timing for maximum power. Applies to all four-stroke car-type engines.

ISBN: 978-1-903706-59-6

£14.99*

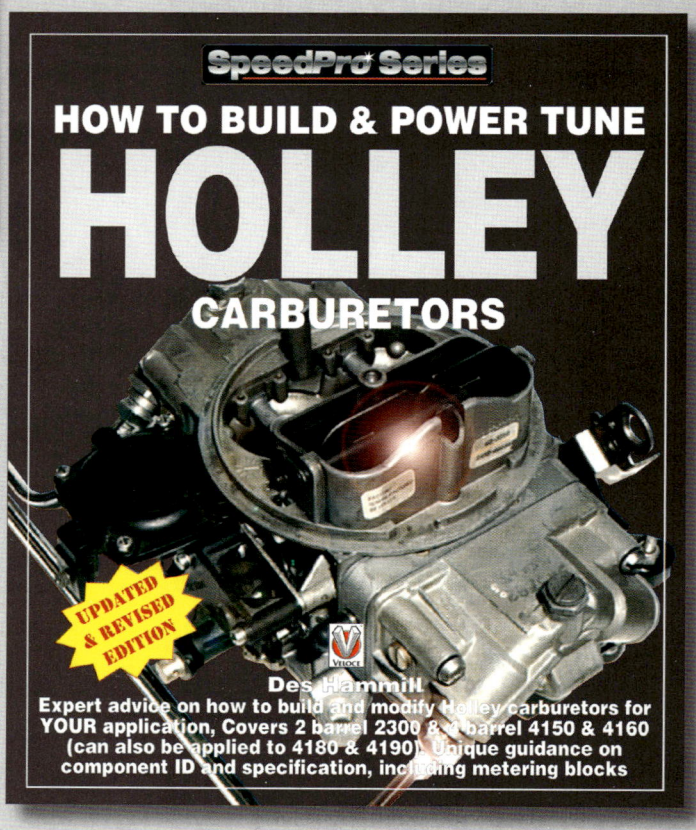

HOW TO BUILD & POWER TUNE HOLLEY CARBURETORS
UPDATED & REVISED EDITION
Des Hammill
Expert advice on how to build and modify Holley carburetors for YOUR application. Covers 2 barrel 2300 & 4 barrel 4150 & 4160 (can also be applied to 4180 & 4190). Unique guidance on component ID and specification, including metering blocks

Choose and specify Holley carbs for any suitable road or track engine. Uniquely, this book allows the identification of complete secondhand carbs and individual components, including all metering blocks; buy and build with confidence to ensure your Holley carb delivers maximum performance.

ISBN: 978-1-84584-006-8

£19.99*

*Prices subject to change, P&P extra • For more information telephone +44 (0)1305 260068 • Email sales@veloce.co.uk • Visit us on the web at www.veloce.co.uk

TR Trouble - No problem

The friendliest club for ALL TR's

- Quality Bi- monthly magazine
- Specialists in TR7/8 technical advice
- Local meetings and national rallies
- Run by enthusiasts for enthusiasts

Model Experts contactable by phone – **ADVICE** when you need it

Club Hotline call: 01562 825000

www.trdrivers.com

Real cars - real people - real help

Known as the friendliest Triumph club, the TR Drivers Club was formed in March 1981, six months before the cessation of the Triumph TR marque's production. Its mission primarily was to support the TR7 / 8, as these models were shunned as 'not real TR's' by the more traditionalist TR sports car clubs.

As a result of this, the TR Drivers Club now has over twenty five years experience supporting these particular models. The club is recognised as the leaders in supplying detailed technical support and information on modifying the last of the Triumph TR line.

The club has thrived since its early days and has a world wide membership of enthusiasts, owning all types of TR models embracing the entire range, ensuring the continued enjoyment of these British built sports cars.

FOR THE TR7/8 OWNER
WE STOCK IT ALL !!
COMPETITIVELY PRICED
PARTS AND ALWAYS THE
BEST QUALITY AVAILABLE.
DON'T FORGET -
WE ARE NOT LIKE MANY
SUPPLIERS,-
WE FIT ALL THESE PARTS
IN OUR OWN WORKSHOPS!!

Fully equipped mechanical workshop. No job too large or too small. Technical advice is always available - Call us with your troubles! Chances are we've had the problem many times before.

For "Cars for Sale" and
Secure Parts Ordering Service go to:

www.robsport.co.uk
enquiries@robsport.co.uk

Units 1-3 North End
Dunsbridge Turnpike, Shepreth,
Nr. Royston, Herts, UK SG8 6RA
Contact Simon or Rob
Phone: +44 (0)1763 262263
Fax: +44 (0)1763 262282

ROBSPORT INTERNATIONAL

We BUY
All TR's and Stags

FREE
Spare Parts Catalogue.
Call or email us
for your
copy!

Full
Expertise Backup

Keeping your TR7/8 on the road

TR7/8

Robsport International